DANIEL DEFOE

Contrarian

By the same author:

Daniel Defoe's Moral and Rhetorical Ideas

Presenting the Past: Philosophical Irony and the Rhetoric of Double Vision from Bishop Butler to T.S. Eliot

ROBERT JAMES MERRETT

Daniel Defoe

Contrarian

UNIVERSITY OF TORONTO PRESS
Toronto Buffalo London

Toronto Buffalo London
www.utppublishing.com

ISBN 978-1-4426-4610-0 (cloth)

Library and Archives Canada Cataloguing in Publication

Merrett, Robert James
Daniel Defoe : contrarian / Robert James Merrett.

Includes bibliographical references and index.
ISBN 978-1-4426-4610-0

1. Defoe, Daniel, 1661?–1731 – Criticism and interpretation. 2. Defoe, Daniel, 1661?–1731 – Psychology. I. Title.

PR3407.M55 2013 823′.5 C2012-908158-2

This book has been published with the help of a grant from the Canadian Federation for the Humanities and Social Sciences, through the Aid to Scholarly Publications Program, using funds provided by the Social Sciences and Humanities Research Council of Canada.

Canada Council for the Arts Conseil des Arts du Canada

University of Toronto Press acknowledges the financial assistance to its publishing program of the Canada Council for the Arts and the Ontario Arts Council.

University of Toronto Press acknowledges the financial support of the Government of Canada through the Canada Book Fund for its publishing activities.

Men do not know how what is at variance agrees with itself. It is an attunement of opposite tensions, like that of the bow and the lyre.

(Heraclitus)

I form the light, and create darkness: I make peace, and create evil: I the Lord do all these things.

(Isaiah 45:7)

Oh that one would hear me! behold, my desire is, that the Almighty would answer me, and that mine adversary had written a book. Surely I would take it upon my shoulder, and bind it as a crown to me.

(Job 31: 35–6)

Unto you it is given to know the mystery of the kingdom of God: but unto them that are without, all things are done in parables: That seeing they may see, and not perceive; and hearing they may hear, and not understand; lest at any time they should be converted, and their sins should be forgiven them.

(Mark 4: 11–12)

… nought so vile that on the earth doth live
But to the earth some special good doth give;
Nor aught so good but, strain'd from that fair use,
Revolts from true birth, stumbling on abuse:
Virtue itself turns vice, being misapplied,
And vice sometime's by action dignified.

(Shakespeare, *Romeo and Juliet*, II, iii, 17–22)

Without Contraries is no progression.

(Blake, *Marriage of Heaven and Hell*)

Contents

Acknowledgments

When Professor T.J.B. Spencer, my dissertation supervisor-to-be, told me in the summer of 1967 that the Shakespeare Institute had acquired the set of microfilms based on J.R. Moore's bibliography and that he wanted me to work on Defoe, I little thought this author would remain an informing presence in an academic career of over forty years. I had digested enough of Defoe's biography to realize that I had little in common with him except a decision not to enter the ministry. However, I accepted Professor Spencer's suggestion not only because I admired my mentor's scholarship on Shakespeare, Byron, and classical literature but also because the competing critical philosophies which I had gleaned from the course on the novel which I took from Malcolm Bradbury, Martin Green, Richard Hoggart, and David Lodge impressed me with their challenging, controversial, yet valid diversity. Subsequently, I have been applying various methods to the works of Defoe for the benefit of students and myself at the University of Alberta. Students' insights have contributed not a little to my argument. Of course, discussions with colleagues and friends have helped me make this book readable. Over many years I have become thankful for their encouragement to Douglas Barbour, Patricia Clements, David Gay, Isobel Grundy, John Lauber, Juliet McMaster, Rowland McMaster, Jim Mulvihill, Morton Ross, Fred Radford, and Garry Watson. My explorations of Defoe have also been encouraged by colleagues and friends at other universities: Paul Alkon, Michel Baridon, David Blewett, Robert Carnie, Brian Corman, Howard Erskine-Hill, Nicholas Hudson, William Kinsley, Samuel Macey, David Oakleaf, Ian Ross, Philip Pinkus, Peter Sabor, David Vieth, and Howard Weinbrot.

I want to thank Marcie Whitecotton-Carroll, formerly of the Department of English and Film Studies at the University of Alberta, for her help with word processing. I also wish to acknowledge a grant awarded by the Faculty of Arts for the production of the index.

As the notes to this volume attest, I have drawn on the work of many Defoe scholars. In particular, I wish to acknowledge my indebtedness to the Defoe scholarship of Paula Backscheider, Lincoln Faller, J. Paul Hunter, Maximillian Novak, G. A. Starr, and John Richetti as well as to the Herculean bibliographical labours of P. N. Furbank and W. R. Owens. For digests of recent sociological, cognitive, and philosophical movements I am much beholden to the works of Steven Pinker and Roger Scruton. The anonymous reviewers of my original manuscript have been extremely helpful in guiding me to strengthen my argumentation for the benefit of readers. Needless to say, however, I alone am responsible for the argument mounted in this volume. My research on Defoe has been materially advanced by the courteous staffs of the British Library, the Boston Public Library, and the Library of the University of Alberta. I also wish to thank Richard Ratzlaff, my editor at the University of Toronto Press, for his professional guidance and friendly encouragement. Thanks also to Judy Dunlop, who compiled the index.

To my wife, Kathryn Chase Merrett, who has responded with unceasing thoughtfulness to anxious disquisitions on the literary and intellectual problems arising from the works of Defoe during the long course of its making, I dedicate this book with love.

Preface

A lover of the "Science" of music who played the viol and lute, Daniel Defoe would have approved of Heraclitus's simile – in my first epigraph – about the "attunement of opposite tensions" that occurs when the taut bow moves on the lyre's tightened strings. For Heraclitus, the tensions both within and between bow and strings constitute an analogy for material and existential paradoxes that expose the limits of common sense. The dialectic by which Heraclitus insists that what is at variance agrees with itself defies inflexibly systematic attitudes towards creation, a challenge that pervades and enlivens biblical and literary texts in ways germane to Defoe's writings. In his multifarious nonfictional and fictional works, he respects conventional assumptions about the material and spiritual worlds by challenging them since he is most intent on inducing readers to meditate on the nature of being and on the workings of public and private discourse. Far from desiring to project a steady, consistent authorial image, he enriches readers' experience by deploying plural voices and dynamic stances that appeal equally to the intellect and imagination, a reciprocity best explicable by the critical methods of discourse analysis, reader-response theory, and *explication de textes*. Despite his passion for the English language, his colloquial energy, and his acute sense of stylistic decorum, he did not expect readers to rest content with superficial linguistic impressions: he discourages us from trusting that the verbal conduct of his personas is simply trustworthy, because he is eager to make accessible the deep structures of cognitive and spiritual awareness. Since the voices of his personas are, more often than not, repetitious, garrulous, and rambling, their verbal redundancies enable him to employ figures of irony, paradox, and anti-climax that invite readers to appreciate that expressive consistency and descriptive accuracy are delimited by semantic ambivalence and textual incompleteness. Typically he asks us to draw inferences from his texts rather than to rest single-mindedly on fallible narrative generalizations. He favours this discursive process partly because the one idea that he seems to have drawn unreservedly from John Locke is the distinction between person and selfhood, a distinction made manifest by the dynamic tensions in his first-person texts between narrated and narrating selves. A self-dramatizing yet self-effacing author who upheld the dialectical aspects of rational and spiritual identity, Defoe exploited the rhetorical scope afforded by impersonation. His purposeful deployment of masks and pseudonyms endured through a long career. Hence, he constantly wrote about how words work, how they are articulated and voiced, how humans perform as speakers, and especially about how we talk to ourselves.

That such discursive processes govern his non-fictional and fictional works suggests that to a degree he anticipated developments in semiotics and speech-act theory. In addition to being aware of contemporary philological debates, he recognized that the history of ideas since Plato and Aristotle had established that different discourses constitute different realities and that speech acts possess creative illocutionary functions. By imitating many voices and stances, Defoe realized that humans inevitably talk to themselves in plural and apparently inconsistent ways. This realization fortified his awareness of the inevitability of verbal and narrative illusion. While this awareness led him to depict self-delusion and self-seduction in his non-fictional as well as fictional works, it moved him to address concomitant ethical and epistemological problems by getting readers to look beyond literal meaning and direct signification. The ironies stemming from his double vision induce us to balance sympathetic imagination with moral judgment when we respond to his fallible personas. He appears to have refined his articulation of double vision upon suffering the judicial and social penalties that accrued to him after the publication in 1702 of *The Shortest-Way with the Dissenters* in which a ranting high-church clergyman pretends to be vulnerable to the victims of his vicious prejudices. A year later, defending this pamphlet in *A Brief Explanation,* he laments that "Thus a poor Author has ventur'd to have all Mankind call him Villain, and Traytour to his Country and Friends, for making other People's thoughts speak in his Words." If later impersonations failed to remedy his alienation from non-conformist readers, they led him to exert great efforts in engaging non-partisan audiences.

Acutely sensitive to political abuses of religion because his family belonged to a socially marginalized dissenting community, he thought hard about theology and spirituality from his early days when committing the Pentateuch to heart caused the Bible's words to flow with his blood. A keen opponent of those who decried religious orthodoxy, he was as intent on criticizing orthodox and non-conformist ecclesiastical practices from contrarian stances. Like John Bunyan before him and William Blake after him, he defied materialist and rationalist philosophies, deriding logically systematic habits of mind through "polarity thinking." It mattered greatly to him to be free to examine topics from contrary perspectives and to argue with himself so as to remain open to what cognitive science regards as the brain's "bicameral" structure. Despite his reputation for verisimilitude, he was not preoccupied with narrative realism. Far less influenced by Locke than literary history claims, Defoe, again like Blake, derived creative energy from turning figures such as that philosopher and John Milton into spectral opponents. Indeed, Defoe's lexical acuity, theological imagination, and contrarian mental habits speak to the call made in 2000 by J. Paul Hunter for "students of Defoe" to work out how he sought audiences and matched them up "with particular thematic and cultural concerns." His discursive habits and theological dialectic explicated in this study address Hunter's call for a fuller understanding of Defoe's "liberally complex Dissent." That this call reiterates what G.A. Starr says in his 1971 preface to *Defoe & Casuistry* shows how gradually criticism is coming to grips with Defoe. After claiming that "Defoe's attitudes were less exclusively Puritan than they are commonly taken to be," Starr states that his "Puritanism ... is a complex problem which calls for further exploration" since he refuses "steady allegiance to any single legal or moral code." In arguing that Defoe upheld the tenet that circumstances render cases of conscience contingent, Starr stresses the linear and paratactic nature of his narratives, setting episodic discreteness above rhetorical processes and theological dialectic. In following Starr with regard to Defoe's "powerful imaginative feeling for dilemmas," P.N. Furbank and W.R. Owens in *The Canonisation of Daniel Defoe* of 1988 refer to his "intellectual 'contrariness,'" their biographical focus lighting upon "a perverse and 'contrary'" mind operating in the paradoxes of *Conjugal Lewdness*.

In response to Hunter's call for fresh approaches to Defoe's "liberally complex Dissent," I argue that his non-fictional and fictional works open up equally to linguistic, semantic, rhetorical, theological, semiotic, and narratological analyses and that verbal, situational, and dramatic ironies dominate his writing because of his belief that figures of speech advance spiritual apprehension of the world. His metonymic and metaphorical extension of common terms is incrementally analysed in order to illustrate how he challenges political and social convention while inducing readers to develop moral inferences and spiritual insights. Applying the many aspects of discourse analysis to his texts reveals that Defoe asks readers to explore how words work for them rather than appealing to them on the basis of what since his days have increasingly become systematic generic distinctions between non-fiction and fiction. The most prolific of authors, Defoe adopted multiple and contrary stances on the most intricate of moral and theological issues. Hence, the main challenge he poses to critics is less to speculate on his personality and biography than to form conceptual frameworks that comprehend his diverse texts without unduly privileging latter-day generic assumptions. Of course, since his fictions remain accessible and popular, they necessarily receive maximal attention in my study. Still, given his protean authorial roles and contrarian outlook, I resist reading them wholly in terms of the literary categories of plot, characterization, and theme. Nor do I explicate them by means of singular interpretive modes. His texts are too rich for that; they do not aim at an organic unity but explicitly call out to be placed in plural and interdisciplinary contexts. Besides drawing on cognitive science and modern theology to amplify such contexts, I try to limit deductive generalizations, preferring to favour induction partly as a means of presenting textual examples that fuse idiom and abstraction, colloquialism and cerebral formality, and down-to-earth materialism and imaginative metaphors which constitute some of the wonderful polarities of his discursiveness. By thus focusing on narrative process rather than on narrative product, I make the case that Defoe was above all intent on making readers, as new historicism might say.

Chapter 1, "Contraries: Linguistic, Narrative, and Theological," demonstrates Defoe's exploitation of semantic vagueness and polysemy to show how he brings narrative recursiveness to the attention of readers. His discursive practices look beyond traditional philology in order to derive metaphysical and theological perspectives from polarity thinking. This chapter's major point is that, while he understood contraries as logical contradictions, in his creativity he subordinated logic to paradox even as he theorized about contraries and double vision. Chapter 2, "Just Reflections," discusses perhaps the most important key phrase in his fiction and non-fiction to show how he broadens its significance beyond the Lockean sense of reflection. The multiple uses to which Defoe puts the phrase exemplify his commitment to the incremental force of verbal repetition and lexical broadening. In illustrating and analysing the uses to which Defoe constantly puts the phrase 'just reflections,' this chapter evidences how and why he subordinates epistemology to theology and spiritual cognition. It also shows how he links consciousness to conscience in his desire to promote a dialectic of secular and spiritual values. That this dialectic governs his narrative theory is the topic of chapter 3, "*Serious Reflections*: An Apology for Faith and Fiction," which examines the third volume of *Robinson Crusoe* in the light of tensions between his prophetic and self-effacing, authoritarian and self-disparaging voices as he propounds how he wants readers to interpret his famous work. His conflation of the polar narrative motifs of the strange and the familiar, the domestic and the foreign, is instrumental to his exposition of the social and moral problems aggravated by storytelling which in turn underlie his contrary attitudes to visionary experience and spiritual insight. These attitudes are elaborated by an analysis of his contrary allusions to the Earl of Rochester and Milton as both positive and negative literary and religious archetypes. After setting Defoe's belief in typology in the context of his commitment to the Reformation, chapter 4, "Biblical Allusions as Narrative Resources," presents his intriguingly flexible references to the Scriptures, which he cites implicitly as well as explicitly, compounding and creatively adapting texts without always informing readers of their provenance. That biblical allusions, types, and parables are embedded into the dialogues and narrative of all his texts reflects a desire both to express his belief in the evolving nature of revelation and to encourage readers to develop spiritual acuity by searching for biblical words in their interior monologues. Chapter 5, "Political Impersonations and Cultural Implications," surveys his political and economic writings after George I's accession to argue that Defoe's commitment to the Whig party and religious Dissent was far from stolid. His writing from 1714 to 1720 afforded many opportunities to develop skills of impersonation and ventriloquism. Not only did he ironically adopt Quaker voices that allowed him to pose as a principled outsider, but also he spoke with satirical force in the guise of many political and religious stances. At the same time, he developed cross-cultural perspectives and contrary stances on Islam and Islamic culture which further exercised his taste for paradox and allowed him to invent ways of satirizing the secular degradation of the Revolution of 1688 with wry humour. The only chapter to treat his "novels" generically as a group, chapter 6, "Political Imaginings: Sacred and Profane," probes the tensions between idealism and anti-utopianism and analyses the dynamic relations between political fantasy and religious infidelity in his six major fictions. Detailing the contrariness of political vanity and abjection in most characters and narrators, this chapter views H.F., the saddler-narrator of *A Journal of the Plague Year*, as an exception. Still, H.F. treats public administration contrarily, speaking on behalf of the government and the populace by turns and blurring distinctions between historical description and political prescription in ways that directly exemplify Defoe's narrative theory.

Chapter 7, "Marriage and Matrimony: The Dialectic of Sex and Love," places Defoe's critique of gender relations in *Conjugal Lewdness* and *Religious Courtship* into the context of the competing jurisdictions that applied to marriage in the early eighteenth century. After touching on critical debates about the reciprocity of marriage and narrative as social structures, the chapter analyses sexual politics in *Moll Flanders, Colonel Jack,* and *Roxana*. A leitmotif is Defoe's semantic broadening of adultery, rape, and prostitution beyond their primary sexual denotations as these terms become metaphors that challenge conventional mores. Chapter 8, "Defoe's Imaginary: Narrative Inference, Figurative Expression, and Spiritual Cognition," collocates the linguistic, rhetorical, and theological methods of the previous chapters in order to refine the contrarian bases of his narrative practices that convey the conformity of intellect and imagination to readers. The chapter also details Defoe's skill at arguing in images that are contrarily allegorical. After elaborating his anti-rationalist theory of consciousness and cognition and proposing that, despite his disclaimers about preaching, he renewed pulpit oratory by his aesthetic conceptualization of the music of language and voice, the chapter analyses the narrative traps into which his personas fall. The inventive didacticism by which he engages readers is evidenced by the experimental modes that make the relations between characters and narrators contrary, rather than chronologically distinct, and that see narrative constantly recoiling on narrators. That the telling of stories becomes a major narrative action within the fictions and that embedded narratives often lay the foundation of ironical actions help explain the subtle reflexivity by which Defoe entertains readers by inducing them to confront characters' occasional loss of voice and consciousness and to acknowledge narrators' growing vulnerability to superstition and magic. Linguistic, narrative, and theological contraries structure Defoe's narratives deeply so that readers will value the illocutionary functions of speech, imagine the potential harmony of secular and religious values, and listen more attentively to their voices and interior monologues which Defoe equates to listening to the voice of Providence.

By interpreting the dialectic of his texts through the methods of semiotics and discourse analysis, I explicate his words cumulatively and incrementally while trying to minimize biographical speculations. By offering a few long citations, I trust that readers will gain a stronger sense of the linguistic richness of his diverse voices. Because his fictional and non-fictional works contain multiple perspectives, I take his major texts at several reprises rather than pretending to give them once-and-for-all readings. Defoe is a major author because of the entertaining and absorbing ways in which he consciously and intuitively faces literary and moral problems. By examining the contrarian qualities of his books, I seek not to impose a false orderliness on his corpus. The recent and admittedly incomplete revision of Defoe's canon highlights the need for eclectic critical methods. My first book on Defoe, written long before the major revisions of his canon appeared, outlined traditional contexts in which his fiction might be read. *Daniel Defoe's Moral and Rhetorical Ideas* holds that his fictional and non-fictional writings manifest philosophical subtlety, religious intelligence, rhetorical skill, linguistic inventiveness, and fictional purposiveness. The present study takes a less-travelled route in demonstrating that his fiction is related stylistically and conceptually to his moral and religious outlook. My main claim is that he was inspired by a shrewd sense of ambivalence and paradox and that his fictions require a criticism that values polar thinking and dialectical expression. Hence the epigraphs on the frontispiece, the relevance of which I return to throughout because they offer provocative insights into creation, God, spiritual exercise, ethics, and narrative. By describing how Defoe exploits polar thinking, I argue that contraries, whether defined as narrative devices, material dualities, or theological paradoxes, are as basic, if not more so, to his writing than verisimilitude, empirical observation, and religious orthodoxy. By shunning formal distinctions between non-fiction and fiction because of his dominant concern for posterity and future readers, Defoe more easily promoted his dialectical views of expression, narration, and identity, views which anticipate aspects of postmodern narrative practice and theory. By focusing on his contrarian imaginary, my study freshly approaches the relevance to the history of the novel and to narrative theory of the dynamic relations between literary technique and theology. Defoe's inventive fictional practices embody principles that furthered and even goaded the subsequent development of narrative, as the ideologically antagonistic adaptations of the Crusoe story by Muriel Spark, Michel Tournier, and J.M. Coetzee in the latter half of the twentieth century bear witness, a topic taken up in my coda.

A Bibliographical Note

As Paul Alkon in a 2002 review article said, Defoe scholars must appreciate the two major editorial ventures that have brought and are continuing to bring this author more fully into the present, if in unique ways. The Pickering edition in forty-four volumes groups his works variously according to topical and generic principles, while the Stoke Newington edition is presenting single texts through the contextual efforts of editorial teams. Neither edition is complete, the Pickering edition not fully embracing Defoe's journalism and the Stoke Newington edition having produced but few volumes. Setting aside the relative inaccessibility of the editions on account of their cost, Alkon doubts that they will advance appreciation of Defoe's "best works" as "autonomous artifacts," which for general readers should, he maintains, be freed "from bondage to history." While his view that nothing makes *Robinson Crusoe* "altogether a piece with Defoe's other writing" or "locates it as an inevitable expression of its time" is opposed by the present study's opposition to categorical distinctions between fiction and non-fiction, I share Alkon's belief that, since Defoe is somewhat "invisible," biographical speculation provides no firm ground on which to make unassailable decisions about what he wrote and published.

As P.N. Furbank and W.R. Owens, perhaps the most authoritative commentators on his oeuvre admit, bibliographers are "doomed to face" insoluble problems given the lack of external evidence for the authorship of many of his works, including those most commonly said to be his, that is to say, his "novels." Nonetheless, in *Defoe De-Attributions*, they challenge the inclusion of 252 items of the 570 titles in John Robert Moore's *Checklist of the Writings of Daniel Defoe*, often because of the vague impressionability as well as logical implausibility with which the tradition of scholarly attribution has claimed to identify internal evidence. While one must recognize their arduous detective work into publishing history, one must at the same time acknowledge that bibliography – far from an exact science since it employs speculation into degrees of probability and possibility – must rely on linguistic and literary sensibilities to the extent that the book trade's records from which it draws are imperfectible and ultimately indeterminable. Still, in addition to remaining open to "compelling internal evidence," Furbank and Owens frankly and scrupulously admit to changing their minds about a given work they had removed from Moore's list. However, in *The Canonisation of Daniel Defoe*, following the lead of the economic historian Peter Earle, they say the task of critics is "to search for the true connection" between "two Defoes," the composer of the novels and the author of the more numerous non-fictional works. Alkon's argument that there is no real Defoe to be detected rejects the conceptual desirability of seeking such a connection. Moreover, from the perspective of literary theory, Furbank and Owens rely not only on the traditional yet dubious distinction between fiction and non-fiction but also on a dualistic and reductive view of his authorship, a dualism challenged explicitly and implicitly by my study. If such distinguished scholars understandably uphold positivistic notions of biographical consistency to further claims for a consistent bibliographical identity, from the viewpoint of Defoe's textual operations, their stance limits the plurality of his voices, discounts the dialectic between his narrative disclosures and concealments, and ignores his polarity thinking, which repeats, extends, and reverses narrative discourse in ways that defy the laws of contradiction. In the face of their syntactically vague claim that he wrote "improvisatory sentences," my study applies lexical, grammatical, rhetorical, and semiotic analyses to his works in the hope that my application of these methods mostly to his undisputed, if anonymous, works may extend considerations of the nature of internal bibliographical evidence. That being said, I never press a case for bibliographical attribution or de-attributions. Again, when I occasionally draw on bibliographical claims which differ from those of Furbank and Owens, I always indicate my sources in notes. In particular, I rely on the sensibility of Maximillian Novak, whose works I have respected for many years despite disagreeing with aspects of his secular viewpoint. To the degree that one is obliged to recognize the community of Defoe scholars past and present rather than any one authority, I sometimes refer to different editions of the "same work" in notes. Given ongoing controversies about Defoe's bibliography, I mostly cite either original editions from which I took notes when studying in libraries with major holdings or modern editions which adhere to eighteenth-century printing conventions.

I close this preface by recalling the inspiring example of Charles Darwin, who, far from being discouraged by the incompleteness of the fossil record, based the origin of the species and natural evolution on theorizing that very incompleteness. I trust that readers of this volume will find its journey into Defoe's *imaginaire* or moral imagination a fresh and innovative exploration into the creative mentality of this "world author."

R.J.M.
Edmonton, Alberta, 2012

DANIEL DEFOE

Contrarian

Chapter One

Contraries: Linguistic, Narrative, and Theological

We never see the true State of our Condition, till it is illustrated to us by its Contraries.[1]

This statement by Robinson Crusoe with its first-person plural pronoun and absolute negative offers a generalization that stems from personal retrospection of fallibility yet presumes to speak for all readers. This insight into the limits of perception and cognition is voiced passively: truth about the human condition is reached only through acknowledgment of its imperfectibility, the contrariety of circumstances, and the polarities of experience. Crusoe's pithy and epigrammatic contention is a key to the genius of Daniel Defoe, to what the French would call his imaginary. In his direct and oblique commentaries on human life, Defoe favours the ebb and flow of imagination and privileges recursive and ironical rather than linear and rational thinking. In establishing the critical tradition that emphasized Defoe's verisimilitude and that found his realism believable because artless, Sir Walter Scott looked down on his predecessor's linguistic and conceptual genius. Besides attributing "rusticity of thought" to him, Scott described his language as "loose and inaccurate, often tame and creeping, and almost always that of the lower classes of society." Despite feeling impelled to "read every sentence and word upon every leaf" of Defoe, Scott judged his forebear to be no conscious stylist because he could not "have changed his colloquial, circuitous, and periphrastic style for any other, whether more coarse or more elegant."[2] Setting aside the social condescension and class consciousness in his survey of Defoe's writing, we may wonder why, despite his fascination with Defoe's texts, Scott was dull to the verbal, situational, and conceptual ironies that permeate his predecessor's non-fictional and fictional works.

We may better appreciate Defoe's verbal and imaginative creativity if we regard his texts less from the standpoint of literary realism and more from linguistic and cognitive perspectives.[3] By this route, we may reach a sense of how his verbal redundancy, rhetorical amplification, and mental expatiation complement each other. Defoe exploited polysemy and semantic vagueness because he knew that language, while consisting of plural registers and codes, is itself but one of many codes. If we apply discourse analysis and semiotics to his texts, we shall see why, far from seeking to create rules which define literariness and delimit genres, he either eschewed or transgressed such rules because of his imperative need to express voices and personas that would appeal to diverse audiences and convert them into a coherent readership. Since he did not treat reading as an unproblematic activity because he grasped that it has a history of its own, linguistic, historicist, and cultural theories of textuality serve better than formal realism to explain how he derives authenticity from personal, political, and mythic strategies.[4] Hence, this study extends previous applications of narratology and reader-response theory to the semiotic procedures motivating his narrative achievements.[5]

As I aim to demonstrate, Defoe exploits the instrumentality of ordinary language because he understands that, since reading is subject to history, he is obliged to create readers by endowing them with new habits. This authorial impulse may be approached via J.L. Austin's theory of speech-act theory and performative meaning. The core of Austin's theory is that statements cannot be simply true or false because they perform meaning and actions in the moment of their articulation. To Wolfgang Iser, Austin's theory attempts "to describe those factors that condition the success or failure of linguistic communication," factors that, while addressing the "pragmatic nature of language," may be applied to the reading of fiction, which may be regarded as "a linguistic action in the sense that it involves an understanding of the text, or of what the text seeks to convey, by establishing a relationship between text and reader." In her application of Austin's theory of discourse analysis, Mary Louise Pratt refutes literature's linguistic autonomy and pretended transcendence of "the ordinariness of ordinary language." To Pratt, "the 'literariness' of novels" is "not 'literary' at all" but belongs to a "more general category of speech acts" that, "like all behavior, are correctly or felicitously performed only if certain conditions obtain." Given Austin's "context-dependent linguistics," Pratt argues that literariness resides not in a text's "message but in a particular disposition of speaker and audience with regard to the message, one that is characteristic of the literary speech situation." Since "our daily discourse is full of other kinds of fictive speech acts," she holds that literature is not the only medium that puts invented speech acts on display.[6] Her sense of textuality includes objects of study "such as historical events, institutional practices, or cross-cultural relationships" which, like written works, are to be read as "systems of signs to be deciphered and interpreted, rather than as realities to be recorded."[7] A major implication of ordinary-language philosophy, then, is that readers will respond fully to all kinds of texts only by recognizing that the latter absorb, collect, and store a range of contexts. This concern with reader response, which, as we shall see, was a preoccupation of Defoe's, is underscored widely by current literary theory. Thus, Terry Eagleton declares that since semiotics is "a theory of communication which includes a theory of cultural organization, a theory of cognition and semantic memory, and a theory of perception," literary texts, being "'code-productive' and 'code-transgressive' as well as 'code-confirming' ... may teach us new ways of reading, not just reinforce the ones with which we come equipped."[8] Another implication arising from discourse analysis is a warning to critics to question the procedures of literary history, including biographical assumptions about authorial agency. That is to say, semiotics warns us to guard our distance in relating to authors and characters by recognizing how much language delimits their agency because it is the medium in which we live and preconditions our linguistic performances. To Jacques Lacan, language, "like the unconscious, is an impersonal system outside the subject's control – a system from which the subject is irrevocably alienated."[9] This being the case, criticism, far from expecting to discover textual and authorial consistency, should concern itself with uncovering and assessing how authors deal creatively with linguistic and semiotic circumscriptions. Robert Scholes voices the implications of this perspective for readers when he claims that, since an "author is not a perfect ego but a mixture of public and private, conscious and unconscious elements, insufficiently unified for use as an interpretive base," one must grant irony to be the figure "that must always take us out of the text and into codes, contexts, and situations." Since double vision is required of readers and since irony traces "the dialectic between *signifier* and *signified* which, of necessity, takes us outside of the text and forces us to postulate the existence of a semantic structure which governs the encoding procedure both in history and in literature," it may be the chief means of testing the coherence of Defoe's imaginary.[10]

*****

Polysemy, a common device in Defoe's fictions, conveys his awareness that words do not have singular meanings or stable references even in apparently precise contexts. The nouns and nominal phrases which his characters and narrators employ form a basis on which he appeals to readers through lexical plurality and semantic vagueness. The substantives expressed by characters and narrators denote material reality variably, thereby exposing the arbitrary as distinct from natural conventions of naming. Besides sensing that verbal expansiveness generates discursive gratification, Defoe's protagonists know that things cannot easily be denoted by single words or names.[11] To Defoe, reference in the actual or fictional world is never simple or direct; besides compounding it, he renders it oblique for the sake of both fictional pleasure and conceptual integrity.[12]

Consider Crusoe's habit of describing his island's geography and animals with correlative nouns. When he refers to a "Creek or River" (51), a "Rivulet or Brook" (142), a "Tortoise or Turtle" (86), and a "Flock or Herd" (163), his polysemy raises questions about synonymy in readers' minds. The seeming equivalence of substantives invites us to doubt the precision of nouns and exactitude of names. This doubt grows when Crusoe's correlative nouns and nominal phrases offer definitions or afterthoughts, as when he speaks of a "Neck or Inlet of Water" (48), a "Bank of hard Sand, or rather Earth" (49), and "Embers, or live Coals" (123). These correlatives seem paradoxical because they both differentiate and fuse material phenomena, treating nature generically and specifically at the same time. Since correlatives also apply to things which Crusoe uses or makes, they mediate contrary mental attitudes. When he plans his escape from Barbary, he gets hold of "Rusk or Bisket" and a "Parcel of Twine or Thread" (21). On the island, he does not distinguish between "Plank or Boards" (49), "Fence or Fortress" (59), "Shovel or Spade" (73), "Spindle or Axis" (74), "Spear or Weapon" (87), "Pestle or Beater" (122), "Squab or Couch" (152), and "Chark, or dry Coal" (177). He compensates for his lack of a "Scythe or a Sicle" with one of his "Broad Swords or Cutlasses" (117). Synonyms also apply to what he ingests; he speaks of "Succades, or Sweetmeats" (192) and of the "Bread" or "Bisket" he finds in the first wreck (133). Such nominal doublings are not a semantic feature limited to the experience of a castaway. Before he reaches the island, Crusoe refers to "Lance or Dart" (30) and to "Writings or Covenants" (40). He generates ambivalence from proper names and prepositional phrases when he mentions "the River *Gambia* or *Sennegall*" (29) and speaks of setting a course "towards the *Canary* Islands, or rather between those Islands and the *African* Shore" (18). Verbal and nominal ambivalence governs his narrative and descriptive modes as when, about coming ashore, he says a wave "landed me, or rather dash'd me" (45) and when the "Entrance or Door of a Cave [is] not really any Cave or Way into the Rock at all" (58).

Defoe's sense of what it means to belong to a speech community and perform speech acts was acute.[13] Since his protagonists are more or less alienated from society, he exploits the paradoxes of denotation and connotation for ironic purposes. Things on Crusoe's remote island have more than one name because denotation renders words simultaneously distinct and equivalent, specific and generic, and because most lexical items have historically evolving connotations.[14] Since transferred meanings occur in natural language and daily discourse, Defoe was aware that figures of speech both resist native speakers and allow them scope for creativity. How he exploits this semantic dialectic is illustrated by the multiple names Crusoe assigns to the shelters he finds and builds on the island and by the ways in which his polysemy involves familiar with exotic and domestic with foreign connotations. The diction with which he describes his dwellings, if easily appropriated, is also intractable. At one moment, he domesticates nature and pretends that his primitive island is civilized. At the next, he must admit that it resists him and his European viewpoint.

The first night on the island he spends in a tree in which he sleeps comfortably despite his fear of wild animals. He calls the tree his "Appartment" (48). He later applies this noun to his elaborately contrived shelter or "Fortification" on the occasion when he tells the victims of the mutiny how he has survived (258). When he begins to build this shelter, after debating whether to have "a Cave in the Earth, or a Tent upon the Earth," he irresolutely decides to have both (58). This ironical non-decision, in aiming at harmonizing the man-made with the natural, entails viewing what he constructs with further variability. If his "Home" is always a "Tent" and "Cave" (100), it is also a "House" since he furnishes it with some boards "like a Dresser" on which to order his

"Victuals" (75) and because he raises "Rafters" which he "thatch'd or cover'd ... with Bows of Trees" (67). Its rude domesticity is improved by military defensiveness: he goes beyond domesticating his hillside by seeing his "Fence" as a "Fortress" (59) and his "Pale" as a "Fortification" (67). His "Habitation," besides being a "Room or Cave" (74), is also a "Storehouse" (67), a "Warehouse or Magazin" (74), and "Barns" (123). Beyond assigning his shelter domestic and military values as well as mercantile and agricultural connotations, Crusoe fancifully seeks orderliness by endowing it with the biblical term "Habitation" (98).[15] Yet, if it affects orderliness, diction resists his fancifulness. If his shelter serves as a "Kitchen, a Dining-room, and a Cellar" (74), it remains a "Vault, or Cave" (178) and "Cavity, or Grotto" (179). If it becomes a "Castle," it stays a "Hutch" (208) and even degenerates into a "Cell" (174) and "Prison" (269). At one moment his shelter conforms to his fancy, at the next it resists his psychological needs and social affectations. Far from domesticating and aggrandizing the natural scene, his denotations are challenged, if not contradicted, by connotations.[16]

When he calls his abode a "Castle" and "Hutch," opposing connotations in the lexical field of building would appear to oblige Crusoe to see that antonyms inevitably recoil on synonyms. But his linguistic acuity is not as keen as his creator's. On asking readers to decide whether his sojourn on the island was "my Reign, or my Captivity" (137), Crusoe does not realize, as readers likely do, that it is both and that his proffered choice is beside the point unless one were to grant him a political existence.[17] Antithetical phrases that he applies to the island highlight antonyms, as when he calls it "*the Island of Despair*" (70) and "my beloved Island" (139), or "a planted Garden" (99) and an "uninhabited Wilderness" (113), and describes his outlook as "a dismal Prospect" (62) and a "tollerable View" (63). Lacking full awareness of the semantic reciprocity of synonyms and antonyms, he never achieves an assured narrative viewpoint. Since built and natural phenomena are not simply themselves in his experience, his denotations and connotations are diffuse, his unsteady lexical style often endowing his narrative assertions with an ironic recoil. Semantic broadening and narrowing, melioration and pejoration, appear in such close proximity that the island never becomes a stable context for sense transference.[18] When he approaches the victims of the mutiny "thro' my little Grove," he says in an aside that it had become "a very thick Wood" (249). Lexical contraries are an aspect of things he makes. When he cooks "some very good Broth," he immediately reports that, since it lacked "Oatmeal" and "several other Ingredients," it is not the broth he wanted it to be (121). Such qualifications regularly undermine his assertions. With regard to his "Taylering" or rather "Botching" (134), he describes making a "Pair of open-knee'd Breeches" from "Goat–Skin" (149). But he retracts the noun "breeches," saying that he actually made a "Pair of some–things," that is to say, breeches that do not merit that specific designation. To emphasize that these clothes are beyond categorization, he uses multiple similes which further disperse meaning. His "some–things" are "like *Pantaloons*," "like Buskins," and like "Spatter–dashes." Conveying indeterminacy, these similes show that he lives in a realm in which simple and established comparisons do not apply.

Far from being literal-minded, Crusoe seeks the "Similitude or Fitness" between things when he measures the footprint against his own (158). In describing the island as having a "constant Verdure, or Flourish of *Spring*" (99), he juxtaposes visual and acoustic denotations with qualifiers of distinct temporal ranges. But, more often, he muddles transferred meanings. The green space in front of his cave he first calls "the Green" (58), in the next breath saying it is "like a Green" (59) so that his simile counters his metaphor. Yet he still aggrandizes the "green" by giving it "the Nature of a Terras" (60). Similar verbal irony that arises from the unresolved tensions between literal and metaphysical reference recoils on his physical and mental actions. After reporting that he "came to an Anchor," he undoes this specificity by describing the substitute he had made: it is "a kind of an Anchor [from] a Piece of broken Graplin" (138). When he reports that "the dreadful reproaches of my Conscience" first "extorted some Words from me, like praying to God" (90), he qualifies those words: he cannot say "they were either a Prayer attended with Desires or with Hopes." The simile is undone by the lexical clash between specific and generic terms. These examples show how verbal irony produces narrative recursiveness: Defoe rhetorically complicates lexical items so that they turn back on themselves rather than project a linear narrative mode.

Defoe is less interested in depicting physical setting by specific terms of space and time than in making it convey Crusoe's ambivalent moral and spiritual condition. That his isle is "*the Island of Despair*" (70) and "my beloved Island" (139) reveals how his cultural outlook wavers. If, because the island is remote from Europe, he looks upon it as different from and better than civilization, he also denies its difference and superiority by imposing traditional political criteria on it. As we detail later, he assumes the roles of lord of the manor, prince, and generalissimo.[19]

For now it is enough to recall that he presents the island as both a "Country" over which he rules as "Emperor" (128) and a colony which he administers with a "Commission" under the British crown (275). Far from seeing the island on its own terms, he views it from alternating political illusions. If he learns to make things from scratch and to appreciate the value of labour independently of European civilization, he duplicates material processes which he observed in England and relies on the tools which he takes from shipwrecks without which he would have been a "meer Savage" (130). His imaginative sense of the island lacks stability and coherence since he does not grasp how culturally determined his ideas of space and time are. That his sense of the island is both fanciful and factual reveals how Defoe deploys lexical and rhetorical polarities to make relations between action and character intriguingly problematic. It is a compelling paradox that Defoe's narratives succeed in appealing to readers because his characters and narrators struggle, not wholly successfully, to be storytellers.[20]

Although *Captain Singleton* is less innovative than *Robinson Crusoe,* this account of piratical and mercenary exploration is nonetheless informed by discursive ironies because Defoe correlates nouns and phrases to render material and mental phenomena strange and familiar.[21] Occasionally Singleton's correlatives emphasize his different stances as character and narrator, as when he judges fellow mutineers "void of Counsel, or, as I now call it, Presence of Mind" (54). More often, they expand geographical or technical definitions, as when he refers to "the Inhabitants or Natives of the Island" (21), a "Cutler, or Worker in Iron" (27), "*Monsoones,* or Trade-Winds" (28), and "a little Cove, or Inlet" (67). If such synonymous phrases approach redundancy, correlatives also make the strange familiar and the familiar strange. In the middle of Africa, the band of adventurers comes to what they regard as a sea rather than lake, Singleton writing of its "Shore, or Water–edge" (103). Phenomena the adventurers encounter evade categorical definitions so that the narrative often provides second and contrary thoughts. When they kill and eat a "creature like a Goat," it turns out to be "no Goat" (92). Passing through a barren, uncharted region, they see only a "few Trees or rather Shrubs" (105). New territories afford neither stable perceptions nor lucid similes. At one point all Singleton can report is that "the Earth was pretty full of green Stuff, of one sort or another" (91). What is as true for Singleton as for Crusoe is that what humans see and create outside constitutional society has little determinate status. On being cast ashore, Singleton lives in "a kind of a Tent … or rather a

Hut" (14). Journeying across Africa, he and his fellows transport "Hutts or Tents" (82). Objects that might strike readers as antithetical do not appear so to the narrator. Material processes involve imprecise substitutes. When the pirates proof a ship, they do so with "a Sort of Stuff" that serves for "Pitch" (43). There is a strange familiarity in things the adventurers provide for themselves: to walk on burning sands, they make a "sort of Shoes" that Singleton calls "Gloves for our Feet" (48) or "Foot-Gloves" (123).

That irony and paradox induce readers to observe and then to look past the unreliability of characters and narrators owes much to Defoe's deployment of syntactical balance and epigrammatic antitheses. His narrators occasionally speak with such grammatical pithiness that narrative polarities are forcefully brought home to us. When Singleton says "we were upon *a* Voyage and *no* Voyage, we were bound *some* where and *no* where" (32), the equipoise of irresolute action and escapist adventure is inescapable. Singleton reinforces this contrariness in the same paragraph through these balanced clauses: "as we went every Day nearer the Sun, the Sun came also every Day nearer to us." The almost inane redundancy of this expressive formality shows that grammatical precision advances narrative irony to undermine conventional expectations of adventure. The following correlative clauses show that the relation between the adventurers and the white man they encounter is less that of discoverers to discovered than one of reciprocity: "as we were a Relief to him ... so he was equally a Relief to us" (128). Further narrative polarities that derive from syntax are evident when Defoe treats numerals and adverbs vaguely in order to induce readers to probe narrative illusion.[22]

Like Defoe's other fictions, *Captain Singleton* regularly presents numerals correlatively. The girl who lets young Singleton be seized by gypsies is "Twelve or Fourteen Years old" (1). One voyage round Madagascar takes a "Month or six Weeks" (39), Singleton in the next breath saying it took "many Weeks" (40). Adverbs and adverbial phrases marking time and place often lack antecedents. When Singleton talks of joining the pirate band in its efforts to kill natives in the tree or "wooden Castle" (209), he uses the phrase "*about this time*" with no limiting context (210). His reference to place can be as vague, as when he says "so we put into *Cadiz*, that is to say, we came to an Anchor in the Bay" (140). The prepositional phrases may be equivalent adverbially, but readers know that pirates could never have docked in that port. Settings are rendered vague by syntactic tensions between verbs and adverbs, as in the following example concerning Ceylonese natives who approach the pirates' stranded vessel: "they, as it were, surrounded us on that Side," standing in a "Half Circle, or rather three Fifths of a Circle" (230). Here overstatement undoes the denotation of "surround," while modifying phrases counter the hyperbolic main clause.

Semantic vagueness stemming from syntactical reversals applies to human agency from the start. The young Singleton is "dragged about" by a woman he calls mother, yet not only is she not his mother but he declares that he wanted for nothing from her (2). The clash between being "dragged about" and "wanting for nothing" is a curiously offhand equivocation. More striking is the equivocation when Singleton says, "Captain *Wilmot* made me, or rather I made my self, Captain" (153). For it doubly affects our sense of the agency of Wilmot and Singleton; it partly establishes praise of Singleton's leadership in the face of Wilmot's debased captaincy while beginning to expose Singleton for upholding conventional ideas of adventure which William Walters the Quaker opposes strenuously. From the start Defoe also proleptically heightens readers' sense of the narrative future by syntactically emphasizing other figures of speech. Take euphemisms, for example: Singleton as narrator does and does not elucidate them. Referring to his first "Adventure," he says that he "found Means to secure, that is to say, to steal about twenty Moydores" (5). Continuing to explain his roguery, he says he was able to "take Care of my Master's Man and to furnish myself" better than others on the ship. But he does not always acknowledge euphemisms; in the next breath he talks of having "snipt" the ship's stores for himself without further comment (6).

Defoe's figures of speech alert readers to how grammar and etymology lie at the conceptual base of narrative polarities, the figures training us to appreciate the evasive wit of narrators. Oxymoron, since it involves syntactic balance and logical antithesis, signals Singleton's narrative cleverness. Thus, he says that for himself and the band of adventurers it was "a happy Kind of Disappointment" that their digging for gold was not immediately successful; slow progress let them dispose of it without the political strife to which pirate bands were so often subject (96). Yet when litotes and hyperbole are joined to oxymoron and paradox, the latter figures reveal Singleton's narrative cleverness to be sleight of hand, as when he claims the band had many "pleasant Adventures with the wild Creatures" (88). The adventures are terrifying: "to allay our Joy" lions, tigers, and elephants are menacing every night (92). If animal voices make "Musick," it is "far from pleasant" and "very disturbing" (100). As he recounts "all sort of such Wilderness Musick" (90), his figures alert us to the ongoing ambivalence and duplicity of his narrative.

The coexistence of semantic vagueness and figurative schemes concentrates readers' attention on narrative unreliability, which is further evidenced when Singleton blames himself for keeping "no Journal" (9) of his early life.[23] This fault matches his later refusal to learn navigation, which prevents him from describing the "Latitudes or Distances of any Places we were at" (39). Supposedly constructing his narrative from collective memories, he avoids reconstructing them: "The Journal of their Travels is too long to enter upon here" (133). Still, he facetiously refers to his fellow pirates ending "their Journals at the Gallows" (139). This metonymy signals a callous superiority which reminds us that Singleton encounters the world and self equally inconsiderately. Of one territory he reports that it is "barren enough," but it produces "a Crop in less than three Months Growth" (132). In one breath he calls himself a "hardned" rogue yet reports having a "Pang" of conscience that he has never had before (258). When he begins to have "other Thoughts of my self, and of the World, than ever I had before," he is governed by an "unthinking Temper" (265). After the roguish William has "settled my Mind to more prudent Steps," Singleton is still "little better than a distracted Fellow," filled with thoughts of suicide and the "dreadfullest Despair" (267).

Given the contrariety of Defoe's syntactical and lexical styles, it is to be expected that, far from creating precise settings, determinate plots, and single-minded characters, his narrative mode ignores the neoclassical unities.[24] The temporal setting of *A Journal of the Plague Year* is not restricted to the London of 1665.[25] In addition to the "Fire" of 1666 (35), later historical phenomena, such as urban growth, are prominent. The narrator writes to the moment in discussing Providence "now the Contagion is over" (75), often distancing himself from "those days," as when he refers to the first newspapers (1), notes that far larger "Throngs of People" have settled in the metropolis since the Restoration (18), and opines that "*Spittle-fields*" was in 1665 a fifth of its size "now" (19). That the setting is the London of 1722 – the book's publication date – and of 1665 entails a double-time scale typical of Defoe's narratives. Moreover, the *Journal* is generically mixed: the Saddler's text is a daily journal and retrospective memoir. An editorial note gives the burial place of the "Author of this Journal" (233) to convey that he wrote in the distant past from a concern for posterity in case "the like Distress should come upon the City" (94 and 118). Yet the Saddler claims that "most of this Work" is based on "Memorandums" collected during the plague (76). He rewrites them selectively: he excludes the name of a suicide since the family is "now flourishing again" (81) and claims to hold back "private Meditations" for his "private Use." He repeats that his "Meditations upon Divine Subjects" are "profitable" only to himself (77). Whereas his account is full of religious reflections, it ends in the face of the return of "all manner of Wickedness among us" by citing a verse from his "ordinary Memorandums" (248).

A double-time scheme governs *Roxana*. Its title page sets the protagonist down in the reign of Charles II, a historical context that is confirmed when Sir Robert Clayton, who died in 1707, becomes her financial adviser. Yet Roxana first arrives from France at the age of ten in 1683 and marries at fifteen when James II was about to abandon the throne.[26] Subsequent chronology means that, when Roxana organizes the masquerades and dances before the king, she does so in 1723, when masquerades were popular for the first time. In *Roxana,* then, the protagonist reaches the pinnacle of her sexual career in the reigns of Charles II and George I, this double-time scheme enabling Defoe to fault the political culture of past and present courts. His narrators often present ambivalent and wide-ranging temporal settings that address Defoe's readers from both inside and outside a span of years.

Ambivalence sometimes affects Defoe's presentation of place. The incoherent ending of her autobiography, in symbolizing Roxana's deteriorating spiritual condition, shows that she cannot harmonize spatial setting and story. Her two accounts of leaving England for Holland do not cohere. The first reveals her confused desire to emigrate; she resolves "upon Nothing" while manoeuvring her husband to consider living away from London or abroad (243). She does not mention her tormenting daughter Susan when preparing for a possible voyage. The second account, which details Susan's relentless pursuit of her in England, emphasizes Roxana's solitariness and inability to converse with her husband, her Quaker friend, and her alter ego, Amy. Roxana's haunted sense of self and shapeless autobiography correlate to her vagueness about place.[27] Her conflicted impulses – to leave England and to hide in the English countryside – reveal that she has habituated herself to avoiding purposeful deliberation and steady reflection to the point of self-destruction.

That Defoe's linear and episodic plots are also repetitious and circular is a narrative polarity that heightens the contrariety of action and agency. The voyages in the two sections of *Captain Singleton* start and end inconclusively: the circularity involved heightens tensions between motive and purposelessness in Singleton and his fellows. As we have seen, the group of mutineers is and is not committed to travelling: "we were upon *a* Voyage and *no* Voyage, we were bound *some* where and *no* where" (32). Likewise, Singleton is both indifferent to and zealous about his captaincy. His indifference derives from his sense that he can adopt "no Side" in debating goals. Having "no Home" since all the world is "alike" to him (35), he lacks political and spiritual purpose. Yet, when on the journey across Africa he is "forced to command" (54), he is a competent leader. When he becomes a sea captain in the second part of the narrative, his ingenuousness always clashes with his skill as piratical trader. By depicting Singleton's constantly varying sense of environment, action, and self, Defoe undermines popular assumptions about adventure stories and defies readers' imaginative participation in them: thus, Singleton's restless life and erratic narrative both depreciate and displace "the flaming Stories of Captain *Avery*" (154), the notorious pirate romantic legends about whom Defoe was concerned to scotch on several occasions.[28]

Moll Flanders's repetitious, cyclical movements expose her purposive action to irony.[29] Born in "*Newgate*" (7), she is later imprisoned in "that horrid Place!" (273). Her "Frolick" as "a Countess" to Oxford (61) and trip to Lancashire to marry a rich husband collapse the difference between her holiday excursions and mercenary adventures: each journey is self-entrapping. On her ultimate return to Colchester, the families in which she was raised are "all dead or remov'd" (267). Her "Country rambles" are circular (268). Her trip to Virginia – which she calls her "Rambles to *Virginia* and back again" (127) – with its coincidental incest ends with her return to England and prostitution. That she later thinks transportation to Virginia can be a new start – as if she were going there for the first time to establish a new family life – is exposed when she hypocritically takes up with her former family. Despite her propaganda, the "New World" (312), not new to her, offers no fresh start but anticlimax. She returns to social isolation in England, for, if discovered, Jemy will hang.

For Defoe, fresh starts, distinct middle actions, and defined endings are sources of irony and of mythical implications, not determinate stages in plot development. He prefers going over old ground, repeating discontinuities, and concluding indeterminately to show actions recoiling on agents and to explore polarities of causation and motivation.

His stories imply that divine omniscience converts perverse complaints and desires into agents. The storms that cast Crusoe on the island and Roxana on the English shore are illustrative. Crusoe self-indulgently thinks that in Brazil he lived "just like a Man cast away upon some desolate Island" (35) and Roxana "secretly wish'd, that a Storm wou'd rise" and drive the ship voyaging to Holland "over to the Coast of *England*" (122). Both are displaced by undisciplined impulses which narrative turns into emblematic punishments. This ironic yet extended sense of divine agency partly explains Defoe's wish to close his fictions in irresolution. Although Crusoe's island experience teaches him to value society, when he returns to England he cannot actualize what he has learned. He sets off on his travels again because still driven by a supernatural agency that he constantly testifies to but cannot grasp; he is "inur'd to a wandring Life" and unable to "resist the strong Inclination" to revisit the island (304). He never reconciles competing impulses. On the island he is afflicted by contrary motives. Even after repenting, he is discontent, as evident when he gets lost and wanders around "very uncomfortably for three or four days" (111). His self-contained efforts at contentment are undone when the shipwreck makes him "weep like a Child" about his social alienation (113). By making Crusoe acknowledge conflicting impulses, Defoe ironically heightens the contrariety of motivation. On seeing the savages on his side of the island and the need to conceal his works by making everything seem "wild and natural" (182), Crusoe must realize both that "*the Fear of Man*" (163) is terrible and that the prospect of having his wish for society granted dulls the "Edge of his Invention" (167). He never assimilates the tension between social and private motives, which is why, despite relying on Providence and the mutiny for escaping from the island, he fails to anticipate that the mutineers will undo his creative work there.

Action is frustratingly circular for protagonists. Roxana knows that dancing in the Turkish costume endangers her by gratifying her vanity, yet she still talks about it compulsively. While trying to conceal her past, she wears the costume for her husband and the Quaker, making it a clue by which Susan may track her.[30] Colonel Jack's five marriages manifest a self-destructive impulse. That he remarries his first wife, who secures a pardon for his treasonable conduct, accentuates his self-entrapping agency. Promising his fourth wife not to join the Jacobite Rebellion, he restrains himself for a while but risks all by advising the rebels.[31] Like Roxana's, Jack's past haunts him. Avoiding recognition by flight to Havana, he is imprisoned by the Spanish authorities.

Escaping, he trades illicitly with Spanish merchants only to be forced into "Retirement" among them (301). If Jack's accumulation of wealth and insecurity exposes personal and political faults, the Saddler's restlessness indicates society's failings. Confined like other citizens in the face of death, he ventures into the streets: staying "within Doors" for a fortnight at the height of the plague, he "cou'd not hold it" (103). Moving "freely about the Streets," he may not endanger himself (58). But his fluctuating stasis and movement symbolize conflicts between private and public values. Several times he reports that shutting up infected houses had "good Success" (37) and constituted a "publick Good" (48). Yet he reiterates that it did not "answer the End at all" (53) and did "little or no Service in the Whole" (71). Through the Saddler's oscillating viewpoints, Defoe praises and blames the public policies of 1665 to suggest that better ones must be adopted in 1722.[32]

Readers easily see that Defoe's characterization is founded on polarities. For he treats the relations of character and narrator dialectically. The first-person form in which protagonists not only tell their stories but are agents in them is experimental to the extent that his narrators identify with and condemn their former selves in hard-to-predict ways. Since the syntactic and cognitive distance between characters and narrators constantly shifts, the protagonists never attain a fixed perspective. Sometimes identifying with their former selves, they dissolve narrative distance and time, while, at other moments, by condemning themselves out of hand and denying integrity to those selves, they render their narratives judgmental and abstract. To Homer Brown, the narrators repeatedly assert and lose their identity and sense of selfhood because of Defoe's alertness to the sacrificial symbolism entailed in both narrative actions.[33] To complicate this matter, the narrators often undermine their narration by commenting on their inadequacies and inviting readers to improve their texts. To Defoe, narrative viewpoint inheres less in the representation of fixed identity than in processes of textual retrospection and prolepsis: tensions between recounting the former self and addressing readers pull the narrating selves in contrary directions. If narrators maintain a distance on their former selves and undermine their capacity to make judgments, they also uphold judgments which they made as characters. Thus, Moll condemns the men of the Mint for putting "a Rape upon their Temper to drown the Reflections" (65), and Roxana, decrying fool husbands, urges: "Never, Ladies, marry a Fool" (8). Moreover, occasionally identifying with former emotional manoeuvres, narrators lead readers to question those gaps between disclosure and concealment which undermine simple ideas of narrative reliability. Polar relations of characters and narrators train readers to be moral critics: that Defoe's creatures are reliable and unreliable places interpretative duties on us.[34] In the words of Lincoln Faller, "Defoe's novels are rich in gaps, dark patches, all sorts of loose ends," because, being intent on depicting "the isolation of the individual subject," he emphasizes the failure of characters and narrators to communicate with others and themselves so that readers will give meaning to his texts which they bring by way of "'reflection.'"[35] Far from making fiction mimetic, Defoe asks us to improve his fictions by meditating on them; as Moll says, the "Moral indeed of all my History is left to be gather'd by the Senses and Judgment of the Reader" (268).

Defoe's discursive and narrative polarities invite readers to find his characterization absorbingly problematic. Since his characters are both wordless and verbose, they stand in a curious relation to the speech community and to speech acts by which they might bring themselves more fully into being. As explorers of strange physical and mental territories who cannot always find words for things and experiences, they, unlike a William Dampier, are uncomfortable in their worlds and with themselves.[36] When Crusoe cannot name "vast great Creatures" (24) or "a large Bird that was good to eat" (73), his inability to classify things limits his sense of material reality and personal identity. Defoe questions his characters' travel motives and their manner of facing up to phenomenal and spiritual uncertainty by stressing their dullness to maritime facts. On shipboard Crusoe does not know the meaning of "Founder" (12) and swoons when a gun is fired as a distress signal; Moll does not know what is meant by a "Main-mast" (105); and Jack does not understand "the Geers, as they call'd it" and "the *Cat-a-nine-tales*" (113).[37] The much-travelled Moll claims towards the end of her account that she did not learn the meaning of "Geographical" until underway with her autobiography (327). Ignorance of the languages of law and social hierarchy also reveals how much reality is closed to characters. Moll is unsure about "the Magistrates, as I think they call'd them" (10), and she and Jack misconstrue terms of gentility and rank. Besides showing their disengagement from social and spiritual reality, their occasional wordlessness indicates how removed they may be from the political and cultural forces that govern linguistic meaning. Vagueness with words and names is not overcome at the close of their autobiographies. When she forgets the name of "the largest River in *Ireland*," the Shannon (319), and admits that she never learned the names of other "great vast Waters" (330), Moll's poor sense of geography and the world is inseparable from the ineffectuality that stems from cultural illiteracy and spiritual anomie.

Since his narrators may be lost for words and verbose while sometimes alert to nominal conventions, Defoe can better convey how perspective depends on one's standing in the speech community. To this end, narrators comment on verbal usage, pointing out names and idioms which they do or do not use and with which they are or are not familiar. The following examples come from Moll's commentary: "she was call'd Down, as they term it, to her former Judgment" (8); "my Nurse, as we call'd her" (10); "my Obstinancy as he call'd it" (41); spinsters "impatient of their present State, resolve, *as they call it,* to take the first good Christian that comes" (75); "in black and white, *as we say*" (158); "my little Income, as I call'd it" (158); "all those Women who consent to the disposing their Children out of the way, *as it is call'd* for Decency sake" (173); "make a Figure as the World calls it" (189); "very far from what we call being in drink" (236); "I could not forbear going Abroad, *as I call'd it now*" (253). Such examples, which generally suggest that discourse precedes and creates reality, could be multiplied a hundredfold. More particularly, Moll's verbal commentary shows that, if she largely speaks and writes in the first person singular, she does not always do so. Her remarks on naming which distinguish between first and third person and between first person singular and plural pronouns show that she does not possess a fixed perspective or single, characteristic voice. The phrase "call'd Down," which refers to her mother, she uses in a remote way, distancing herself from idiom and other speakers. Yet, in the phrase reporting that her proprietary attitude to her nurse was shared with fellow pupils, she speaks as a member of a group. The two phrases place her singularity and identity under scrutiny. One notes that the first-person form of discourse is variable: far from being fixedly singular, it expresses plural viewpoints and conveys multiple aspects of the narrator's identity. One further notes that parenthetical remarks on naming place the narrators' former and present selves in polar relations to the speech community. Moll's subject pronouns assert that she voices public idiom while guarding her private idiolect, that she shares in but is critical of the speech community, and that she does not understand yet rejects social codes. Finally, one recognizes that, far from discriminating between characters and narrators by having the former speak as outsiders and the latter as insiders, characters may talk as insiders and narrators present themselves as outsiders.[38]

The protagonists' fluctuating relations to the speech community reveal that, inasmuch as grammar conveys agency, syntax may undo their pretended uniqueness and degrade their narrative reliability. Consider Crusoe's description of his journey with Xury and Colonel Jack's account of his adventures with Captain Jack.[39] Both narratives juxtapose singular and plural first-person pronouns so that the main characters come across as alternately active and passive. At moments, Crusoe and Colonel Jack are differentiated from their fellows; at others, not. Alternating pronouns heighten their statements about being inferior to their subordinates, as when Crusoe and Jack declare respectively that Friday and the Tutor are better Christians.[40] The unstable pronouns and passive constructions invite us to probe the identity of characters. Moreover, syntax implicitly queries the narrators' sense of composition. When Crusoe reproduces the journal he wrote on the island, his preterite soon becomes a past continuous tense because he intervenes between his writing and readers, editing and expatiating upon his text, unwilling to let it speak for itself.[41]

If, as this example attests, narrators are presented as impulsive and deliberate writers, they also have a contrary sense of narrative sequence and its future. They claim their accounts have a strong order and natural logic. Crusoe says that he "must go on with the Historical Part of Things, and take every Part in its Order" (222). Besides often forestalling the narrative future and thwarting readers' expectations of surprises, narrators hold back details until the proper place in the story arrives, as when Crusoe announces he "shall give a full Account" of how he improved his cave "in its Place" (62). To a degree, they write as if story is independent of them and historically fixed. Yet, they refer to the narrative future as much in the subjunctive as in the indicative mood, as much in the passive as in the active voice. Describing the value of making his habitation undetectable, Crusoe reports that it "may be observ'd hereafter upon a very remarkable Occasion" (76). This forecast is both tentative and provocative. Singleton likewise says that certain facts about a family he has aided "may be worth reading, if I have room for it in the Account" (270). He does not include such facts. The narrators have a vague as well as precise sense of the boundaries of story; they all write as if they have not fully determined what they are going to include once they have started writing. In addition, while they appear to be both first-time and one-time writers, they consider composing further books. Although Moll emphasizes her "own Story" and not Jemy's (301), the idea that his life would make a "much more pleasing History"

(304) prompts her to think of "making a Volume" of his life "by itself" (339). That the narrators speak in polar terms about realizing the narrative future confirms that readers will know that they are not engaging with uncontestable narrative illusions or naive realism. Two more examples of this ironic foreshadowing will, perhaps, clarify its rhetorical function. When Roxana reports that, although her husband has left her forever, she might have occasion to write about him, her indicative and subjunctive moods conflict. That she not only sees him again but spends time and money spying into his life while withholding herself reminds readers to monitor the constant tension between revealing and disclosing in her narration.[42] Because Colonel Jack speaks as contrarily about the narrative future, it is not surprising that, after he dismisses his first wife from his story, she becomes crucial to its denouement.[43]

As members of the speech community who are clear and unclear about verbal mediation, Defoe's narrators rationalize their lives according to plural fictional modes. But, in struggling with their autobiographies, they make story itself an important narrative sign. Like the others, Colonel Jack voices conflicting ideas of story. On the one hand, story is what happens to him and he participates in it. On the other, it is what he possesses; it marks him off from other people and history. Yet, try as he might, he cannot reconcile these modes. His story is inseparable from those of his two brothers: it is "our Story" (5). Yet, in telling of Major Jack, Colonel Jack promises readers "the process of [the Major's] Story" (6). Still, he concentrates on his "own Story," which is "the main thing" he has "to set down" (17). This leads him to exclude what is "no part of my Story" (88); he declares that Captain Jack's does not belong "to Mine" (95). He tries not to tell the former's story but continues doing so. He declines writing a "Journal of the Wars" (215), claiming that the Old Pretender's failed mission to land French troops in Scotland in which he participated "belongs very little to my History" (223), but, since it does so belong, he compulsively details military conflict. He keeps declaring his intention to be strictly autobiographical but finds himself – partly because of his need for identity and partly from his pride in being an untutored historian – giving long accounts of Captain Jack and the European wars. Just as he does and does not control the order of his narrative, so he cannot subordinate context to text or adhere to a strictly personal concept of story.

The narrators' divergent stances on their lives are accented by how they perform as writers and speakers. On the one hand, they view their lives as printed texts to which they apply phrases that emphasize abbreviation, shorthand, highlighting, and accounting. Through such repeated terms as "in short," "in a word," "as above," they emphasize the process of transcription and spatial layout, a process that requires brevity, straightforwardness, and recapitulation in consideration of readers. That is, they convey the impression that they are poring over their texts as if book production were formally detachable from themselves and as if their identities were unassailably solid. But, equally often, as will be variously elaborated in later chapters, they find writing heavy going: they fault themselves for not having written memoirs that would make composition authentic and they belittle their expressive powers.[44] By disparaging their texts and by complaining that their identities are poorly substantiated, they appear to write to the moment and, paradoxically, to imply the need for fuller texts that will project a truer sense of themselves.

Defoe heightens the paradoxes of authorial competence by having narrators speak as if they were audible and as if readers were interlocutors or members of an immediate audience. The colloquial aspects of narrative voice, such as frequent affirmations about writing and insistence on personal authenticity, in pulling us close warn us not to get too close. The habitual narrative assertions that "you may be sure" or "you may easily see" ironically signify that trustworthiness is dubious. This is so because the narrators invoke plural audiences and distinct readerships: Moll and Roxana address women as well as general readers, and Jack, who like Moll expatiates upon transportation to the colonies, includes the criminal classes among his readers. Since the rhetorical appeals of narrators range widely, readers cannot avoid noticing how audience is both fragmented and generalized. Tensions between colloquial and written modes further signal Defoe's wish to give first-person narrative multiple points of view.

Neither in experience nor in storytelling do the protagonists grasp material reality or attain psychological equilibrium. Had they done so, Defoe would have betrayed his sense of narrative dialectic. When Crusoe for the third time repeats his account of landing on the island, we learn that, if on the first day he experiences "Despair of any Relief," on the next he feels "some Comfort" (70). In telling the "Particulars over again" (69), he accentuates less the redundancy than the selectivity of his accounts, both sapping mundane details and building up their reality. In the tension between withholding and revealing details, Defoe exploits the notion that, just as perception is variable and unsteady, so narration is subject to conceptual fatigue and arbitrariness. Because his characters live stories yet as writers cannot seize the relation of text and context, because they often speak about story in the way that only narrators might be expected to do, and because his narrators are speakers as well as writers, Defoe makes his characters' and narrators' struggles with story into ways of engaging reader response. His fictions are recursive since he knows that narrative is most powerful when thrown back upon itself. His characters' and narrators' polar attitudes to audience, story, and writing allow him to emphasize narrative's mediating functions so that readers may enjoy his fictions as incomplete systems of competing signs.[45] Only partially reliable as must be the case, his narratives require to be improved and even reconceived as they are read. In so performing, readers never feel superior since narrative dialectic recalls us to our fallibility as moralists: the linguistic and narrative signs which rouse us to our roles as readers preclude superiority on our part.[46]

*****

The discursive realm in which Defoe's fiction and non-fiction operates exploits linguistic and narrative contraries since he upheld a stance on Christian theology that, far from being determined by a rational sense of logical contradictions, subordinated the latter to a holistic spiritual vision. This claim flies in the face of the many Defoe critics who deny him religious sense and metaphysical intelligence in their commitment to secular concepts of literariness and to fixed notions of genre.[47] However, the most compelling critic of his criminal novels stresses that Defoe prevents readers from drawing "facile inferences" from his texts by restoring "the relationship between men and God to a proper disequilibrium."[48] The following excerpt from a dialogue in *Due Preparations for the Plague* offers a starting place from which to show that Defoe elaborated a dialectical approach to theology that relied on the "doctrine of mingling opposites":

> *1st. Bro* You talk upon Contraries, you are all Mysterious.
> *2d. Bro.* You may call it Mysterious if you will, but 'tis a Blessed Truth, tho' 'tis a mysterious Thing to those that understand it not: No Repentance, no Humility, no Tears like those that are rais'd by an humble Sense of infinite undeserved forgiving Grace: and no Joy, no Satisfaction of Soul, no Rejoicing, nay, Triumph of Soul like the Joy that is founded in Sorrow, founded in Repentance.[49]

The second brother argues that humility and triumph, tears and rejoicing, are necessarily existential aspects of faith in response to his brother's denial of reciprocal coherence to them. In his *Dictionary* Samuel Johnson gives the primary definition of a contrary as a thing of opposite qualities. His secondary definition draws on the field of logic because it holds that one contrary may refute another. But, since logical contraries are antagonistic propositions, the falsehood of one cannot make the other true. From this standpoint, contraries are contradictions that yield no positive truth. Acutely aware of the distinction between logical and alogical contraries, Defoe makes the second brother see that contraries operate like Heraclitus's "attunement of opposite tensions": they are the most divergent members of a singular set – polarities and opposites subsumed within one classification. By analogy with how Isaiah's God creates light and darkness, the second brother's spiritual contraries embrace conflicting states because they are mutually informing.

Defoe often employs logical contraries to expose political and ecclesiastical contradictions. In *The Free-Holders Plea against Stock-Jobbing Elections of Parliament Men*, impersonating a yeoman, he decries the "Wisdom of late Parliaments" in establishing the old and new East-India trading companies. The two companies, pointlessly made to rival one another, are "two Contraries" absurdly "upheld by the same Authority."[50] Fourteen years later in 1715, he more directly disparages parliamentary debates about occasional conformity in Queen Anne's reign. While the public may have been gulled into thinking the toleration of Dissenters was the matter of discussion, "the Arcana of the Quarrel were as remote from the Pretences of it, as two Contraries may be supposed to be," because the "Statesmen on both Sides" were mere jugglers bent on taking power to themselves and away from the monarch.[51] In *The Conduct of Christians Made the Sport of Infidels*, Defoe's persona, Kara Selym, an enthusiastic convert to Islam, with amusing logicality exposes theological conflicts in the Church of England arising from the Bangorian controversy. To Selym, two "Reverend Fathers" of the church oppose each other with equal "Obstinacy, and Fury; affirming, with the greatest Imprecations, two Contraries, one of which only can be true."[52] Nonetheless, the alogical sense of "contrary" more often informs Defoe's works with polarity thinking and upholds Johnson's definition of that term as "a thing of opposite qualities," a sense upheld by the *OED*, which calls contraries "things the most different of their class." Thus, when the persona in *The Lay-Man's Sermon upon the Late*

Storm says that "Contraries, may Illustrate but Contraries never Incorporate," Defoe implies that, although contrary attributes and qualities cannot be dissolved into single essences, that very impossibility renders them informative and revelatory.[53] Since he held that, because the Creator alone can resolve contraries into essences, belief in Him renders contraries intelligible to humans.

That Defoe's theological concerns led him to develop a dialectical theory of expression and cognition may be clarified by the remarks of a nineteenth-century author who, in voicing one of that period's most acute observations of Defoe's narrative methods, elaborated Johnson's alogical sense of contraries. Early in *Elements of Rhetoric*, Richard Whateley, the distinguished churchman, argues that fictional verisimilitude is necessarily paradoxical. For him, *Robinson Crusoe* is an "admirable fiction" because it conforms to Aristotle's "paradoxical maxim, that impossibilities which appear probable, are to be preferred to possibilities which appear improbable." In Whateley's view, had Crusoe "been represented with that half-brutish apathetic despondency, and carelessness about all comforts demanding steady exertion, which are the really natural results of a life of utter solitude," his story would have been less natural. Its realism stems from Crusoe's energy in the face of alienating circumstances. To Whateley, fiction writers must derive probabilities from impossibilities to foster credible generalities rather than actual particularities. Motivating this dialectical prescription is his tenet that the contraries fall into the rhetorical class of analogy. In his words, "Contraries must have something in common; and it is so far forth only as they *agree*, that they are thus employed in Argument. Two things are called 'Contrary,' which, coming under the same class, are the most dissimilar in that class. Thus, virtue and vice are called Contraries, as being, both, '*moral habits*,' and the most dissimilar of moral habits." In this manner, Whateley recovered the argument from contraries that was formulated by Aristotle and adopted by pedagogy since ancient times; in dealing with analogy, potentiality, and comparable sets of phenomena, the argument provided a major source of topical amplification. The following passages from Aristotle prepare us to recognize Defoe's strategical ways of presenting rhetorical rather than logical contraries for the benefit of readers:

> if of two contrary things it is possible that one should exist or come into existence, then it would seem that the other is equally possible; for instance, if a man can be cured, he can also be ill; for the potentiality of

> contraries, *qua* contraries, is the same. Similarly, if of two like things the one is possible, so also is the other. And if the harder of two things is possible, so also is the easier ... And if a thing is possible for those who are inferior, or weaker, or less intelligent, it will be still more so for those whose qualities are the opposite.[54]

Aristotle here posits a logic of ordinary conversation different from formal logic because the former requires that existential contraries not preclude one another. Thus, polar states of human health have an equal potential, just as easy and difficult tasks are equally achievable by people with lower and higher capacities. For Aristotle, such discursive contraries refer to states or conditions that are implicated, that is to say, folded into one another.[55]

In the years before writing his major political journalism in the *Review*, Defoe began to exploit contrarian arguments so as to make his cultural commentary more pointed. For example, in *Advice to All Parties*, he equally expresses surprise and trust that society remains unified despite its ever-increasing sectarianism when he declares that "The World is made up of a Conjunction of Contraries, and the Harmony is the more Admirable."[56] One of his early satirical strategies was to aggravate human contradictions before subsuming them under a transcendent perspective. In the *Review* itself, he often presents High-Church and Jacobite propaganda as powerful because baseless in order to turn its threats back on its partisans.[57] His initial stance in many numbers is to profess helplessness before the crushing contradictions of political discourse:

> One Great Man says one thing, and another says the contrary; one Talks and Prints; another Writes, and it is printed; the Queen Speaks and Prints, and these things Clash with one another; What shall poor Authors do? 'tis impossible for us to reconcile Contraries, and make Arguments out of Contradiction.[58]

Such self-dramatizing stances suggest that Defoe cannot translate contradictions into contraries. But he usually proceeds to disavow his defensive incapacity because it is his "Business" to take the "Discourse" of political opponents "apart." He causes such discourse to implode by moving rapidly between litotes and hyperbole and by mixing oblique and direct expressions in ways that recall the epigraph from the Gospel of Mark: thus to heighten the responsiveness of readers, Defoe insists that "the Meaning of Authors ought no more to be always understood, than Authors that have no Meaning, ought to be regarded."[59] His accounts of political order arising from disorder remarkably encourage a theological sense of contraries in numbers of the *Review* which celebrate the Protestant legacy of King William and promote the 1707 Act of Union between England and Scotland.

In the first case, he argues that those who speak of the King "without some Extasie" devalue English liberty and betray their "*English* Extraction." Here he implicates praise of William with fidelity to the English constitution and condemnation of those who would betray it, for there

> can be no just Reflection upon the former Dangers he rescued this Nation from, without due Excursions in Honour of his Memory; and would Men justly measure things by their contraries, it would appear in this, that you never find the other Gentlemen Reflecting with Regret upon the late Times, but they sincerely Curse his Name.[60]

While the relation between polar thinking and "just Reflection" is the subject of my next chapter, it is clear here that Defoe illustrates his practice of rhetorically co-opting political enemies: that the king deserves reverence is confirmed by his detractors' curses. Defoe's understanding that praise and blame are rhetorical contraries insists that defamation proves the King's glory. Those who decry his achievement "Illustrate it by Instances of its contrary ... since no Man can desire a greater Testimony than that of the Enemy."[61] The case of the Union (for which Defoe was an agent in Scotland), in fulfilling William's commitment to the Protestant Succession, affords another occasion in which dialectical thinking implicates a theological appreciation of contraries.[62] Convinced that "Never did Contraries better illustrate" than in the Union, Defoe makes it a symbol of God's unique power to reconcile opposites. Providence, the final cause of the Union, reconciled "many wonderful concurring Circumstances ... jarring Causes, illustrating Contraries" and "conquer'd the implacable Spirit of the two most violent Extremes in Contrari[e]ties in the World, strict *Calvinism* and *High-Flying* Passive Obedience."[63] Only "invisible and inscrutable Providence" could have effected this "Coalition of Interests"; only the "*Digitus Dei*" can "master radicated Prejudices" and "reduce refractory and direct Contraries."[64] The Union images divine creation since "the Harmony of its Order is produc'd from the Connection between the most different and incongruous Elements." In the Union, as in creation, Providence brought "Contraries, not only to illustrate, but to support and subsist one another." Resistance to the Union was not merely overcome but transformed by God's entry into history to defy human logic and appropriate political process:

> Every Step taken against it, lifted it forward; rabbles and tumults rais'd to scare it, quicken'd it; Banter and Jest on one side, made the other serious and steady; every Extreme mov'd towards it as an Engine, in which the Wheels have contrary Motions, and yet all tend to carry on the main Design of the whole.

The simile of the backward motion of opponents propelling the Union forward like wheels on axles and the paradox that its enemies helped bring the Union into being illustrate the dialectic inherent in this argument from contraries.

Before I continue to analyse Defoe's theological application of contraries to political history, it is worth recalling that dialectical images were available to him from a literary tradition in which cosmology and physics revolutionized concepts of matter. For example, that planetary motion is progressive and regressive figures in John Dryden's treatment of genre in *Of Dramatic Poesy: An Essay*, when Neander, in distinguishing between French and English dramatic plots, draws on the analogy of "the orb of the fixed stars, and those of the planets." For "if contrary motions may be found in nature to agree, if a planet can go east and west at the same time, one way by virtue of his own motion, the other by the force of the First Mover, it will not be difficult to imagine how the under-plot, which is only different, not contrary to the great design, may naturally be conducted along with it." The poetic licence which cosmology afforded Defoe is apparent when he applies this double planetary motion to define the tradesman's conscientious conduct:

> The Tradesman, all Life and Spirit, like a Planet, is continually in a brisk Motion; and whether direct or retrograde, he always has his double Revolution round his own Axis, and at the same Time progressive too: He has his annual and his diurnal Motion; by the last he influences his Shop, and immediate Correspondence; and by the first his Encrease in Stock, and the general gain of his Business, which he casts up annually for his compleat Satisfaction.[65]

As we shall see, Defoe's interest in the dialectic manifest by natural phenomena moves his imagery beyond analogy to a trust in God's continuing presence in creation. Admitting that he is remote from the divine authorship that reconciles contraries, he still describes Providence's agency in doing so. Limited to using contraries by way of illustration, he yet views them with prophetic insight: "my Business is to eye the Designs Heaven has had in all these things, to finish his own mighty Decrees, and bring forward the Determinations of inscrutable Providence." Certain that God employs evil as well as good agents, Defoe scrutinizes intersecting religious and secular forces to show that Providence brought about the Reformation in Britain "by and out of the concurrent Circumstances of the Passions and Follies of Men, nay, and even their basest Vices also." The Reformation, he contends, was founded on Henry VIII's evil agency because in the Creator's mind "the very worst and wickedest of Men's Designs shall concurr to bring to pass the best and greatest of his glorious Works."[66] Defoe extends this theological sense of contraries to current affairs, when, despite his disgust with the King of France, he champions Louis XIV's proscription of duelling: "No Argument can perswade me that a Great Action is one jott the less so, for being brought to pass by a Person, we don't like."[67]

Defoe's commitment to society's progress explains why, as a polemical writer embroiled in sectarian conflicts, he increasingly adopted transcendent stances by voicing arguments for contraries. He had cherished the hope that society might discard aspirations for uniformity and totalitarian ideologies because he saw no necessary bond between spiritual harmony and theoretical unanimity:

> our Principles have no Manner of Concern in our civil Peace, why may we not brew the same Malt, and drink the same Ale, and sit at the same Table, and enjoy all Sorts of Sociable and Gentleman-like Familiarity; and not be always comparing our Creeds, or capping Principles; our Opinions in Religion are not at all absolutely necessary Ingredients in our civil Peace; we may be Comrades and Neighbours, we may be Partners in Trade, in Offices, nay in Beds, and not at all of a Sortment, either in our Religious or in our Politick Opinions.
>
> Nay, let me carry it farther, we may go to heaven without a Union of Principles; *The Unity of the Spirit* is formed in the *Bond of Peace*, not of Parties; and this Unity of the Spirit may be found without a Union of Principles.[68]

But experience taught him both that party spirit was not to be overcome by directly expressed ideals of social harmony and that political strife rendered straightforward didacticism ineffective. He knew he had to stop simply repeating his tenets because he was aware of "the foolish Banters" of envious critics who depreciated his quoting of himself in the hope of "instructing and informing one honest-meaning ignorant Person." In defending this early reliance on topical repetition, he asserted his appreciation of "the Rules of Language" and "Rules of Writing." That he repeated in the *Review* what he "had in other Pieces printed before" did not mean he was "barren of Invention." Rather it showed he was conscious of diverse speech communities. He justifies his repetitiousness by rhetorically asking "do not our Ministers preach the same Sermons to different Audiences?"[69] He realized that pulpit oratory had to employ plural lexical registers and modes of discourse. Thus, in *The Complete English Tradesman*, he compares the problems of commercial and theological jargon: "A Tradesman ... like a Parson, should suit his language to his auditory; and it would be as ridiculous for a Tradesman to write a letter fill'd with the peculiarities of this or that particular trade, which trade he knows the person he writes to is ignorant of, and the terms whereof he is unacquainted with, as it would be for a Minister to quote St. *Chrysostome* and St. *Austin*, and repeat at large all their sayings in the *Greek* and the *Latin*, in a country church among a parcel of ploughmen and farmers."[70]

Despite his decision not to become a professional preacher, Defoe's critical sense of pulpit oratory enabled him to forge a dialectical and rhetorical style that faced up to both the diversity and the perversity of audiences and readers.[71] Bearing in mind one author's apology for the Quakers, he compares audience responses to it and to his own writing:

> Those they were wrote for would not read them; those they were wrote against did not value them; those that read them did not understand them; those that understand them did not like them; those that lik'd them would not buy them; his Friends would not vindicate them, his Enemies would not trouble themselves to answer them, and he that wrote them did not believe them; and all this, but the last, was from the Character of the Author.
>
> Just thus goes it with our Addresses – Those you make them FOR are not fond of them, those you make them AGAINST laugh at them, those you make them TO do not value them, those that sign them do not understand them, those that understand them do not like them, those that like them do not believe them – And all this from the Character of the Party.[72]

In Defoe's eyes, there are fundamental problems with publication and written communication, the overriding issues being how to obviate the contradictory behaviour of the public and how to create a coherent readership. That party spirit and sectarianism degrade discourse explains why Defoe feels he must go beyond conventional didacticism and pulpit oratory in the *Review* and employ a rhetorical dialectic to sustain theological paradoxes. The following paragraph further illustrates how systematic was his pained awareness of society's evasion of speech acts and performative meaning:

> We have such odd Mixtures of Contradictions, and of opposite Circumstances among us, both in Religion, Morals, and Politicks, at this time, that it is very difficult for a Man that can see an Inch before him, not to be surpriz'd at every sort: What a checker-Work is among us? Much Charity, no Religion! much Religion, little Charity; much publick Talk, no publick Spirit; much publick Spirit, no Temper; much Zeal little Knowledge; much Knowledge little Zeal; good Philosophers, no Christians; good Neighbours, no Politicians; good Christians, no Conjurers; much Honesty drown'd in little Passions; much Sense blinded with little Prejudices, and much Passion and Prejudice, with little Reason; much Ignorance for want of little Information; little Information for want of much Patience; great Temper, little Judgment; great Judgment, no Temper; great Christians, much Unbelievers; great Believers not much Christians; some believe every Thing, and fall out with no-body, others believe nothing, and fall out with every-body; some unite with those that persecute them, and others persecute those that unite with them; some break Faith with those that trust them, and others trust those that break Faith with them; here we abjure those we adhere to, and there refuse to abjure those we resolve to divide from, and to reject: Here force Men to swear, that fear an Oath, there connive at their not swearing, who value not their Oath; here we sell Property to preserve Religion, there sell Religion and all its Professors, to preserve Property; to-day we banter our Friends, to-morrow ourselves, and in both banter Heaven.[73]

Far from remedying social and moral fragmentation, ecclesiastical institutions had, in Defoe's mind, hastened the degradation of public discourse by adhering to traditional philology. Thus, he condemns the "abundance of Learned Fools … and Ignorant Wise Men" who boast of their "Letters" and "Load of Learning" while lacking "the common necessary Acquirements, that fit a Man either for the service of himself or his Country." One minister he knows, "a Critick in the Greek and Hebrew, a Compleat Master of the Latin," writes blushingly bad letters, preaches soporific sermons, and publishes nauseating books. A "Master of Languages, and buried in Letters," he "cannot spell his Mother Tongue, knows nothing of the World, and has never look'd abroad." Such learning makes Defoe "covet to be Illiterate rather than thus a Scholar."[74] Holding that clerical learning often betrays divine purposes, he elaborates a theological view of language that prizes plainness above learned affectation, studied redundancy, and vociferous profundity. He takes

> Plainness to be the Perfection of Language, and being explicit, the true Design of Providence, in giving Man a Voice, and Words to speak by; he that studies to speak deeply, studies, and takes a great deal of Pains to do just nothing, and as *Job* says, *Darkens Counsel by Words without Knowledge*[.][75]

However, if linguistic efficacy is a divine gift, verbal plainness involves more than conforming to prescriptive rules: "The *English* Tongue is Entirely govern'd by Custom, and the Authority of General Usage, supersedes *Grammar*, Literal Constructions, and all the Power of *Syntax*." The evolution of English is leaving the classical languages behind; "the very Beauties of our Expression" derive "from those very things which are the Deformities in other Languages." The plainness of English is paradoxical because custom has legitimized mixed metaphors in compound nouns and phrasal verbs, as in "an Iron Rolling-stone, a Silver Inkhorn, a Stone Horse-block" and "stand still, sit up, say nothing, hold your Tongue." Logically incoherent, these are effective "Figures of Speech, more than all the Systems of Rhetorick ever prescrib'd."[76]

Defoe studies idiomatic usage and semantic processes since he believes that he will educate readers to the creative aspects of discourse through the dialectic in ordinary language. To him, communication is a social action and interlocutors engage in transactions because articulating words entails the sharing of codes which is potentially either genuine or pretentious. The following passage about purchasing garden plants taken from *The Complete English Tradesman* confirms his sense that verbal usage entails transactional behaviour because speakers exist within semiotic systems whether they know so or not. If they do know so, they are less subject to delusion and deception because their knowledge focuses more on referential processes than on seeming products.

Those who do not know so will be gulled by others because they impose on themselves.

> Thus if you go to a Garden to buy flowers, plants, trees and greens, if you know what you go about, know the names of flowers, or simples, or greens; know the particular beauties of them, when they are fit to remove, and when to slip and draw, and when not; what colour is common, and what rare; when a flower is good, and when ordinary; the gardener presently talks to you as to a man of art, tells you that you are a lover of art, a friend to a Florist, shews you his Exotics, his Green-house, and his stores; what he has set out, and what he has budded or inarch'd, and the like: but if he finds you have none of the terms of art, know little or nothing of the names of plants, or the nature of planting, he picks your pocket instantly, shews you a fine trimm'd fuz-bush for a juniper, sells you Pinks for Painted Ladies, an ordinary Tulip for a rarity, and the like: Thus I saw a gardener sell a gentleman a large yellow Auriculas, that is to say, *a run-away*, for a curious flower, and take a great price; it seems the gentleman was a lover of a good yellow, and 'tis known that when nature in the Auricula is exhausted, and has spent her strength in shewing a fine flower, perhaps some years upon the same root, she faints at last, and then turns into a yellow, which yellow shall be bright and pleasant the first year, and look very well to one that knows nothing of it, tho' another year it turns pale, and at length almost white: This the gardeners call a run-flower, and this they put upon the gentleman for a rarity, only because he discover'd at his coming that he knew nothing of the matter. The same gardener sold another person a root of white painted Thyme for the right *Marum Syriacum*, and thus they do every day"[77]

Defoe's approval of alogical and idiomatic metaphors and exposition of semiotic transactions are fundamental to his theological interest in the semantic polarities integral to ordinary language. As early as *An Essay upon Projects* in 1697, he differentiated between usage and sense, claiming that, while custom arbitrates usage, reason judges sense. This distinction resembles what semanticists see as diachronic and synchronic sense development. Defoe claims both that history governs how verbal conventions change over time and in different speech communities and that there is a universal system of signification in discourse. He puts it this way: custom is "our best Authority for Words" and "Reason must be the Judge of Sense in Language." He applies religious similes to this semantic distinction by saying that, if words are "like Ceremonies in

Religion," sense "like the Essentials, is positive, unalterable." For him, vocabulary changes according to regional dialects and national histories while there is a "direct Signification of Words, or a Cadence in Expression" which is universal and absolute.[78] Given the importance of cadence to his fictional and non-fictional narratives, we return to the topic of linguistic dialectic in the second section of chapter 8.

Social reform and spiritual progress were inconceivable to Defoe unless semantic polarities and theological paradoxes could be brought to bear on mental and imaginative experience. In his account of how Crusoe's discourse refers to the experience of human nature, Graham Martin contends that prose and poetical references exist in a polar relation for Defoe because the world's plenitude is not reducible to "rigid formulas." In Martin's eyes, Defoe understood the capacity of discourse to mediate detailed, dense, and imaginative references simultaneously. Martin's sense of the role Defoe's texts impose on critics recalls the stance of David Lodge, who insists that novelists are no less verbal artists than poets because novels and poems derive equally from ordinary language. In arguing that the textual analysis of prose fiction is a "disguised form of paraphrase," Lodge relates the instrumentality of paraphrase to polar thinking:

> Whenever we try to express our understanding and appreciation of a literary text, we are obliged to state its meanings in different words; and it is the *distance* between the original words and our own words, when the latter are brought to their maximum of sensitive and articulate responsiveness that we feel the uniqueness of the writer's achievement.

The critic who best explains the necessity and the imperfectibility of paraphrase is Frank Kermode, for whom contraries are essential to hermeneutics since narrative comprises a "radiant obscurity" and since interpretation is "bound to fail." Consequently adequacy rather than perfection should be the goal of critics: to "be blessedly fallible, to have the capacity to subvert manifest senses, is the mark of good enough readers and good enough texts." Kermode highlights the parabolic nature of narrative because parables "proclaim truth" like a herald but conceal it "like an oracle." Explicating my epigraph from St Mark, Kermode argues that parables are "about everybody's incapacity to penetrate their sense" since they function by obliging insiders to recognize they are elaborately "being kept outside." When Defoe discusses the limits on satirical expression required by decency, he speaks in a manner close to Kermode's stance on parables: Defoe says he must "talk in the dark, and reprove by Allegory and Metaphor, that People may know, or not know what I mean, just as it may happen."[79] His tenet that inclusive classification rather than exclusive logic attains fundamentally imaginative truths explains why he preoccupies himself with polar aspects of physical, mental, and spiritual phenomena. In asserting that such phenomena are neither invariable nor fixed by observation, he underscores the inherently ambivalent potentialities of creation and subordinates materialism to irony and single images to plural perspectives.[80] In John Macquarrie's terms, Defoe may be seen to present a "thoroughly dialectical interpretation" of the polar aspects of human life which fits "philosophical theology."[81] His fascination with polarities may be also brought into focus by Dietrich Bonhoeffer's view of how theologians ought to reconcile Christ's opposing attributes. Urging them to admit the limits of christological discourse, Bonhoeffer claims that a self-critical theology "prohibits the setting up of any statement on its own, and allows a statement only if it is qualified and supported by its contradictory opposite."[82] Bonhoeffer's stipulation fits the second brother's account of repentance in *Due Preparations*: the tears of true repentance are superlatively happy yet derive from unmerited grace; spiritual satisfaction stems from unchangeable regret. These theological contraries require the imagination to apprehend the numinous and validate parabolic mystery. Repentance and grace, while equally essential, relate reciprocally to each other. What the second brother's account produces opposes simplistic and singular relations: if repentance must be earned, grace cannot be merited, and spiritual satisfaction does not transcend remorse but confirms its reality. Thus, the second brother prescribes and endows divergent but necessary ideas with a mutually informing reciprocity.

The second brother's polar connection of repentance and grace typifies Defoe's fictional worlds as much as his theology. Like William Shakespeare and Blake, he holds that opposing ideas are mutually informing in all realms of creation. Friar Laurence's words among my opening epigraphs testify to the contrary functions of good and bad things and to the dynamic and reciprocal tensions between vice and virtue, and Blake's proverb equates the vitality of creation to its unpredictability.[83] Detailing the vagaries of psychological and social experience, Defoe's fictions present such topics as loss of consciousness and moral insensibility in ways that confirm his dialectical sense of private and public life.[84] His fictions show how people who degrade themselves and devalue society approach true identity and spirituality, like Job, through their negativity.[85] Since repentance is a single act of volition stemming from spiritual retrospection and a continuous daily practice never to be perfected, Defoe invents extremely variable contexts and endows characters with volatile psychological features and erratic narrative conduct.[86] An ironic aspect of their secular conduct is their religious behaviour: unable to realize their spiritual potential, they unconvincingly see themselves as religious and harshly condemn themselves as irreligious. This ironical reflexivity obliges readers to admit to experiential ambivalence. If his characters approach truth by glimpsing secular and spiritual tensions, what contraries reveal to them is so limited that they cannot be said to win a vision that transforms their awareness of, and agency before, contradictions.[87] But their limitations entertain readers. Since characters and narrators are further from and closer to truth than they know, their contradictions may be significant contraries to readers who recognize the author's innovative derivation of spiritual values from secular life.

Readers of Oliver Goldsmith's *The Vicar of Wakefield* (1766) and Laurence Sterne's *A Sentimental Journey* (1768) will recognize that Defoe's innovative dialectic led to no dead end in narrative practice. Goldsmith's and Sterne's priestly narrators are rhetorically engaging precisely because of their fallibility and the discrepancies between their preaching and their questionable self-assuredness. Dr Primrose and Sterne's persona are flawed centres of narrative self-consciousness, Goldsmith and Sterne no doubt having appreciated the contraries of blindness and insight in Defoe's texts. Of course, Henry Fielding was the chief agent to mediate narrative dialectic to his successors. Although he used Defoe's accounts of Jonathan Wild as a source for his political satire based on this gangster, he admitted no familiarity with his predecessor's techniques. However, his theory of moral dialectic in the opening chapter of Book Ten of *Tom Jones* recalls Defoe's stance. In this chapter, Fielding eschews "Models of Perfection" because he will not condemn a character as bad because it is not perfectly good. He holds that characters of "angelic Perfection" and of "diabolical Depravity" in "any Work of Invention" will overwhelm readers' minds with "Sorrow and Shame." For readers will despair of living up to the former pattern and with respect to the latter will be ashamed to partake of a nature that can be so degraded. Only characters who have "enough of Goodness" and "little Blemishes" will move well-disposed readers to "Admiration and Affection." Fielding concludes that "nothing can be of more moral Use than the Imperfections" in mixed characters because they create a "Kind of Surprize" that lingers most in "our Minds."[88]

If Defoe may be viewed by literary history to be in line with his successors' concern with reader response, it may still be the case that later fiction writers neither did nor could grasp the scope of his rhetorical, narrative, and theological dialectic. For his fictions uncover in psychological states, seemingly remote from faith and theology, latent spiritual ideas. If he judges his characters and obliges readers to condemn them, his narrative implications are optimistic since he seems to hold that no mental condition lacks spiritual potential. The corollary of his refusal to treat theology straightforwardly is his fiction's experimental optimism: it is worth reiterating that theological paradoxes are narrative resources for Defoe. Repentance is a useful contrary – "a thing of opposite qualities" – not only because it is a theological paradox but also because it is validated by characters who testify to it even as they fail to exemplify it. Since the soul experiencing repentance triumphs yet is sad and knows the joy of transformation while remaining burdened with the irremediable past, the struggling penitent, whose religious fulfilment is nominal yet who sees that spiritual progress is a constant battle which he or she is not joining, is a powerful example because of failing to embody theological ideas while apprehending and esteeming them. Defoe embeds theological contraries into his narratives because polarities inhere in a religious outlook on the world and because creation and individuals are attunements of opposites. To Defoe, physical and psychological realities are informed by contraries. Hence, in *Conjugal Lewdness,* he says that even ideal marriage partners will encounter marital problems since "Flesh and Blood is a Composition of Contraries and inconsistent Humours."[89] If good people never get free from original sin, Defoe has another reason for treating faith as an inescapable struggle: as the noblest human action, faith never transcends the individual's imperative to battle natural perversity.[90]

Since contraries inform all material and immaterial phenomena, Defoe implicates the corporal and spiritual realms, folding them into each other in ways that transcend mere analogy. In letter 77 of the first volume of *A Collection of Miscellany Letters,* he says:

> It is an Observation in natural things, that those which we call most delicate, are subject to the greater Corruption; and I cannot but think the Observation may be carried into the moral World: Thus Religion, the noblest

> Exercise of the Soul, may degenerate into the lowest Degree of Superstition, and is capable of the basest Hypocrisy. And, indeed, it is rationally to be accounted for, since the highest Virtues are opposite to the deepest Vices; and so Love, the most generous Passion of the Soul, admits of such debased and abominable Abuses, that a Pen, tolerably modest, would blush to point out, and a Reader, not thoroughly past Decency, would colour to meet with.[91]

Like Shakespeare's Friar Laurence, Defoe holds that the most highly structured material phenomena are most susceptible to degradation: the more valuable things are, the more worthless they can become, and vice versa.[92] This reciprocity of the good and bad aspects of material reality upholds Aristotle's law of contraries: the more distant the good and the bad, the closer, paradoxically, are they related. Since the law of contraries applies to the moral habits of humans, the ties between virtues and vices become stronger as the gap between them widens. The most valuable tendance of the soul, if distinct from the basest conduct, is yet inseparable from it. Religion opposes superstition, but, since the former may degenerate into the latter, they are related ontologically: contrary moral impulses make virtues and vices opposites that exist in the same dynamic classification.

As a religious writer, Defoe presents spiritual tendance and self-abasement as contraries in many texts. For example, in *The Family Instructor* of 1718 he declares that the "lower you are in the Esteem of your Penitent Thoughts, the nearer you are to the Gate of Hope."[93] One attains enlightenment through the dual process of failing to comprehend and of learning that human understanding is fallible. That it is difficult yet essential to grasp how contraries operate in and between all categories of material and immaterial reality caused Defoe's writing to employ methods that resemble the *via negativa* of visionaries.[94] Crusoe suggests as much in this chapter's epigraph when he claims that "we never see the true State of our Condition, till it is illustrated to us by its Contraries; nor know how to value what we enjoy, but by the want of it."[95] Trust in the mutuality of presence and absence clarifies why the maxim, "Experience teaches best, when dearest bought," appears in the political work of which Defoe was most proud.[96] In the *Review*, he discusses his need to depict extreme physical and psychological states of deprivation and negligence: he wants to be "a Painter good enough to represent in Lively Colours, the Operations of Nature, when agitated by Violent Passions" and to paint "Convulsions of Soul" at moments of great loss since he knows "no bitterer part of Humane Anguish, than the clear Sense of some most Exquisite Benefit lost by some most Intollerable Oversight, and Neglect, sold for some Toy, and the Opportunity of possessing it refus'd [f]or some Sordid and most Despicable Trifle."[97] Crusoe's prescriptions for conversation in *Serious Reflections* are the stronger for negative experience: he is the "more particularly sensible of the Benefit and of the Pleasure of [Christian conversation], having been so effectually mortify'd with the Want of it" (75). When cast ashore in the Bay of Bengal by the crew that turns against him for censuring their pointlessly cruel killing of 150 natives on Madagascar, Crusoe says, speaking with narrative irony, that he "had the particular Pleasure, speaking by Contraries, to see the Ship set sail" without him.[98] As marooned owner of the ship, Crusoe does not regret reprimanding the crew for their cruelty to indigenous people: his material loss reflects a moral gain. Defoe's characters often celebrate in their autobiographies principles which they have failed to actualize or embody. Having increasingly experienced the gap between immoral conduct and moral impulses, they try to work out their repentance by structuring their confessions for their own and society's good. But, as they do not cope with the contraries of experience, so they fail to master them in writing. Yet their inability to compose life stories that reach a spiritual plane is instrumental to readers' autodidacticism. Defoe asks us to appreciate, through the deficiencies of characters and narrators, the reciprocal operation of psychological and spiritual contraries.

Letter 89 of the first volume of *A Collection of Miscellany Letters* confirms Defoe's way of arousing readers to spiritual awareness. After observing in Friar Laurence's vein that bees make honey by feeding on poisonous plants, he says that the example of "virtuously wicked" people may "quicken" to good those who are "remiss and indifferent." The latter, "directly the Reverse of the former," are "wickedly virtuous."[99] His antithetical oxymora preclude moral dualities: while good people may be bad since not actively good, bad people who serve good purposes are good in their badness. On account of the contrary relations of vice and virtue, his characters and narrators are never simply bad or good. Defoe makes this point in *A System of Magick* when he comments that

> Of so much Force is Ironical Righteousness, that the blackest Agents are fittest to be made the brightest Examples of it; since also the greatest and best Principles are often illustrated by their most infamous, and consequently, by their compleatest Contraries.[100]

Here he tightens the dialectical relation of negative exemplification and positive principle to sharpen readers' moral awareness. Appreciation of the argument from contraries led him not to base fiction on simple mimetic models, since he realized that truth is best exemplified by imperfect images of the good and best represented by examples of the bad which exemplify the good. The paradoxes in this passage suggest why Defoe opposed literal-minded ideas of cognition, as will be demonstrated in the next chapter. For now it is enough to consider a passage in *The Family Instructor* of 1718, which upbraids conventional explanations of how we acquire moral and religious sense:

> it is a Testimony to the Divine Original of Religion, that it is not the Effect of Priestcraft, or of the Prejudices of Education; clamour'd into our Heads by Nurses, and whipt into us by School-mistresses, Mothers and Pedagogues while we are little, and then whin'd into us by the Parsons, as we grow up: That it is not owing to the Mechanism of the Spirit, working by the Artifice of Words upon the Senses and Passions; but that a religious Awe of GOD, a religious Abhorrence of Evil, and a religious Rectitude of the Desires and Affections may be, and oftentimes is, wrought in the Mind, not only where no Example, Instruction, or other Prepossession intervenes to attach the Mind; but even in opposition of the evil Examples of Parents and Instructors.[101]

Here Defoe delimits an innate predisposition to moral and religious sense – a predisposition open to but not determined by social and institutional forces – that is activated when an individual reads and meditates in opposition to those forces. In implying that innate ideas arise in the mind despite negative environments, Defoe saps one of the foundations of Lockean psychology.[102]

It will surprise no one that Defoe applied the law of contraries to aesthetic experience. Thus, in *A Tour through the Whole Island of Great Britain,* he describes with enthusiastic reluctance the site in Derbyshire on which Chatsworth House stands. One travels to the "most beautiful palace in the world" over a "difficult desart country," looking down at the house and "most pleasant garden" from a "frightful height." Having crossed a "comfortless, barren, and … endless moor," one stands on a "precipice" to look down into "the most delightful valley." However, "If contraries illustrate, and the place can admit of any illustration," the clashing imagery of plateau and valley "must needs add to the splendor of the situation, and to the beauty of the building."[103]

*****

To James Joyce and Virginia Woolf, the claims made on behalf of Defoe's fiction and non-fiction in this chapter would not have seemed unusual. Both authors recognized his unique contributions to fiction. Joyce thought Defoe original because he was unhampered by literary models. In a 1912 lecture at the University of Rome, he said Defoe was the "first English author to write without imitating or adapting foreign works, to create without literary models and to infuse into the creatures of his pen a truly national spirit, to devise for himself an artistic form which is perhaps without precedent." To support his view that Defoe was an original writer attuned to England's nationhood, Joyce maintains that "The whole Anglo-Saxon spirit is in Crusoe: the manly independence; the unconscious cruelty; the persistence; the slow yet efficient intelligence; the sexual apathy; the practical, well-balanced religiousness; the calculating taciturnity." Yet more relevant to the present study is Joyce's sense that Defoe had a gift for prophecy and that this gift properly baffles critics. Joyce was content that *Moll Flanders* "reduces contemporary criticism to stupefied impotence." What stumped critics is that beneath "the rude exterior of his characters" there is "an instinct and a prophecy." Joyce emphatically claims that Defoe's prophetic appeal may be more significant than that of Saint John the Evangelist.[104] Woolf, writing in 1919, rated *Robinson Crusoe* and *Moll Flanders* among the "indisputably great" novels, because Defoe's narrative talents transcend conventional notions of conscious artistry. For Woolf, his impersonality as an artist was what really mattered because it generated a collective kind of representation. Of *Robinson Crusoe* she says that it "resembles one of the anonymous productions of the race itself rather than the effort of a single mind." Aesthetic opacity rather than clarity accounts for the greatness of Defoe's novels: they are repositories of phenomenal weightiness and elemental richness that oblige readers to a certain sifting and refining. "He seems to have taken his characters so deeply into his mind that he lived them without exactly knowing how; and, like all unconscious artists, he leaves more gold in his work than his own generation was able to bring to the surface." For Woolf, Defoe's chief virtue was in dealing with the "important and lasting side of things" rather than "with the passing and trivial." He does this because "he achieves a truth of insight which is far rarer and more enduring than the truth of fact which he professed to make his aim."[105]

Upholding the insights of Joyce and Woolf, this study argues that Defoe intuitively grasped the recursive and reflexive nature of narrative because he valued reader response highly. It attests to his narrative experimentation and philosophy by probing how he incorporates contraries into his fiction and non-fiction to clarify humanity's spiritual needs. In elaborating the notion that narrators gain critical and subversive power, Defoe advances the opposing notion that the solitariness entailed by this power may delude and harm them. But that he examines the disadvantages as well as advantages of fantasy and authorial power hardly exhausts his compositional dialectic. If his fictions criticize society, they also serve as public documents. This instrumentality underscores another contrary: narrative, even if it draws more on social experience than fantasy, may as much undermine as reinforce identity. The coexistence of documentary functions and autobiographical ironies confirms that narrative remained ambivalent in Defoe's mind. His narratives have a rich textual plurality because, as he dramatizes how rationalization devalues narrators' expository structures, readers are diverted from condescension by the contrary processes involved in reading and interpretation. The inadequacies of narrators are never sufficient grounds for despising them.

The textual richness of Defoe's fiction obliges readers to appreciate the tensions between and in experience and fantasy. To reiterate what my preface claims, the dialectical purposefulness that inheres in his linguistic, narrative, and theological contraries shows that his narrative experiments and moral imagination warrant continued assessment, as Starr opines, when, after noting that Defoe's "moral outlook" is flexible, independent, and vigorous because it refuses "steady allegiance to any single legal or moral code," he says that Defoe's attitudes are "less exclusively Puritan" than they are taken to be, and as Furbank and Owens suggest when they state that Defoe had "a powerful imaginative feeling for dilemmas."[106] Indeed, his fictions do not mirror early eighteenth-century life simply. They reflect a keen, polemical curiosity about the institutional and spiritual forces at work in society and show that, seeing these forces in tension with one another, he gave them an educative and engaging form through the medium of fiction.[107] His narratives are richer for his belief that fiction and non-fiction exist in a dialectical relationship. My final chapter details this relationship by analysing the contrary values that he gives to the concept of voice. By emphasizing that naming things and classifying reality make point of view dynamic, he suggests that humans have plural voices.

His protagonists hold internal dialogues with themselves as well as speaking monologues aloud. Their mixed speech forms, in displacing conventions of sound and silence and of spoken and unspoken words, invite readers to probe the involvement of psychological and spiritual insight. Textual ambivalence and narrative unreliability are vital to readers' sense of Defoe's trust in fiction and of his teasingly problematic exploration of relations between consciousness and conscience. The incomplete stories his characters live and his narrators tell, their interestingly, even exquisitely, limited self-awareness and moral sense, show that Defoe trusted that fiction arises from humanity's mixed and conflicted nature and that it compensates for human nature positively as well as ironically.

Chapter Two

Just Reflections

I found just Reflections were the utmost Felicity of human Life.[1]
I leave the Readers of these things to their own just Reflections.[2]

In chapter 1 I began to argue that Defoe is a verbal artist committed more to expressive than logical language and a rhetorician with an acute sense of the reciprocity of semantics and ontology. The present chapter extends this argument by showing that he would have understood what Walter Ong calls the "residual primacy of orality in culture."[3] That Defoe adopts the ancient, pre-literate voices of prophet and preacher – a claim elaborated throughout my chapters – allows him to express transcendental truths by way of contraries or "depth paradoxes." Philip Wheelwright uses this phrase when showing how expressive language challenges "the universal applicability of the law of non-contradiction." To Wheelwright, depth paradoxes best approach the mysterious, many-sided nature of being without distorting it.[4] The aspect of residual orality which I treat in this chapter involves the rhetoric of copiousness and amplification – what modern linguistics terms redundancy.[5] Partly because of his appreciation of orality, Defoe habitually and knowingly made his expository style depend on repeating words and phrases. On account of his schooling and subsequent admiration of oratorical writers such as Dryden, Defoe knew that repetition endows words with incremental sense and referential extension.[6] Through repetition, he broadens denotations, dramatizes connotations, and processes empirical and abstract terms in order to subordinate philosophical to religious usages. His multitudinous repetitions of the phrase 'just reflections' is the focus of this chapter since they heighten dialectical themes in his fiction and non-fiction and exemplify how his texts shape the cognitive responses of readers.[7] If "just reflections" designate spontaneous mental reactions, they also denote the moral processes that govern self-consciousness and spiritual meditation. The phrase's semantic range exemplifies Lodge's contention that "the perception of repetition is the first step towards offering an account of the way language works" in novels and supports his claim that "the notion of a radical discontinuity between the language of poetry and the language of other kinds of discourse" precludes recognition of the function and intrinsic value of words in fiction, a mistaken notion that can be amended only by understanding that paraphrase and semantic explication are legitimate forms of critical analysis.[8]

*****

As the epigraphs suggest, Defoe's characters may happily experience "just Reflections," but, since they may also be mentally confused and spiritually unfulfilled, they invite readers to think reflexively in their stead. Besides making "just Reflections" preoccupy characters and narrators to facilitate the responsiveness of readers, Defoe constantly repeats the phrase to bind secular conduct to religious knowledge and to subordinate epistemology to theology. This occupation signals his wish to unsettle pretensions about what the mind may learn and how it learns.[9] He spurned claims that ideas are solely empirical – that they arise only from bodily sensations and self-contained cerebrations. On behalf of innate ideas, he details connections between psychological and spiritual experiences and depicts highly emotional and surprisingly numinous states because of what they reveal about how mental awareness of religious truths both falters and flourishes.[10]

If, as Maximillian Novak has shown,[11] Defoe was well-read in political and economic theory, he looked at science and religion in contrary ways because he could not single-mindedly admire contemporary philosophy, as this typically facetious passage from *The Consolidator* evidences:

> No Man need to Wonder at my exceeding desire to go up to the World in the *Moon,* having heard of such extraordinary Knowledge to be obtained there, since in the search of Knowledge and Truth, wiser Men than I have taken as unwarrantable Flights, and gone a great deal higher than

> the *Moon,* into a strange Abbyss of dark *Phenomena,* which they neither could make other People understand, nor ever rightly understood themselves, witness *Malbranch,* Mr. *Lock, Hobbs,* the Honourable *Boyle,* and a great many others, besides Messieurs *Norris, Asgil, Coward,* and the *Tale of a Tub.*[12]

The whimsical persona here adopts a Menippean stance on the metaphysical overreaching that leads to heterodox views of terrestrial reality. He also facetiously suggests that, having unsuccessfully entertained "many Projects" for bringing "regular thinking" to natural philosophers, his only solution is to get the "Model" of a "thinking Engine" from the lunar world, an engine which will

> screw up the Will, the Understanding, and the rest of the Powers ... bring the Eye, the Thought, the Fancy, and the Memory, into Mathematical Order, and obedient to Mechanick Operation; help *Boyl, Norris, Newton, Manton, Hammond, Tillotson,* and all the Learned Race, help *Phylosophy, Divinity, Physicks, Oeconomicks.*

Without such "a mechanick Chair of Reflection," natural philosophy will not improve.[13]

Such irony is motivated by Defoe's scepticism about claims for the progressive evolution of human nature: "*Humanum est Errare,* whether in this World or the Moon, 'tis all one, Infallibility of Councels any more than Doctrine, is not in Man."[14] Humans delude themselves with rational systems. Compulsive overreachers, they fall back onto negative philosophical views and infidelity:

> Men affecting to search into what is impossible they should clearly discover, learn to doubt, because they cannot describe, and deny the Existence because they cannot explain the Manner of what they inquire after; as if a thorow impossibility of their acting by their Sense upon Objects beyond its Reach was an Evidence against their Being.[15]

The tenet that ontology transcends empiricism could not be more strongly expressed. When humans pretend to solve cosmological and theological problems, they get lost in heterodoxy: "Men by nice Reasoning, may distinguish themselves into, and out of any Religion, or any Opinion; especially, when they think to reconcile every part of their Religion to their Reason."[16] Rational theology is delusory: those who pore "upon the Sacred Mysteries of Religion with the Mathematical Engines of Reason" reach conclusions that are merely "incoherent Stuff."[17]

Defoe did not mock scientists who admitted the limits of rational empiricism and worked within networks of Christian gentility that prized civil conversation over philosophical disputation.[18] He upheld the genteel civic humanism of "Sir Isaac Newton, Mr. Lock, the great and truly honorable Mr. Boyl" in order to decry the "ignorance and folly" of the hidebound gentry who expressed the "most riveted aversions to learning and improvement in the very face of an improving and knowing age." True men of science, argued Defoe, were agents of "polite learning" at home and in "the whole Christian world" where they were justly famed "for the highest improvements in the sublimest studyes."[19] He singled out Robert Boyle since he was "not a gentleman only, not a man of birth and blood as to antiquity onely, but in degree also, being of noble blood and of one of the familyes that has the most enobl'd branches of any in England and Ireland."[20] Boyle's aristocratic lineage and religious sensibility were instrumental to his scientific prowess; he was an agent of progress because he embodied traditional social values. He was an exemplary Christian philosopher who, together with Francis Bacon, rescued learning from scholasticism by studying aspects of nature that lend themselves to cause-and-effect analysis even as he recognized that God limits empirical inquiry to recall mankind to His infinite power.[21] Boyle saw that natural philosophy deals only with second causes and that

> The Christian begins just where the Philosopher ends; and when the Enquirer turns his Eyes up to Heaven, Farewell Philosopher; 'tis a Sign he can make nothing of it here.[22]

Defoe's endorsement of scientific education is heightened by his celebration of Boyle's view "that an industrious and skillful Enquirer might spend a long Life in the Study of a single Mineral, without discovering all its Qualities." After stressing that "the Fields of Knowledge" are so "wide-extended" that no one "has Strength to labour the whole," Defoe voices an equally sceptical and theological attitude towards natural philosophy:

> Learning is no more than refin'd and polish'd Ignorance. Its true End and Design is to assist in contemplating God in his glorious Attributes, and beholding him in his wonderful Works: To confess him to be omniscient, and to humble our selves in his Sight, declaring we know nothing.[23]

From this contrarian perspective, whereas science progresses gradually, human nature does not. To Defoe, only by working within an informed ignorance can scientists advance in spiritual awareness.[24]

Feeling no less fallible than anyone as regards reasoning power, Defoe did not always present himself humbly. Not only did he dramatize himself in prophetic tones that he turned on his religious community but also he tended to depreciate philosophical authorities and minimize his intellectual indebtedness.[25] Consider the following claim in *The Consolidator*, which, in its commentary on a fractured, self-destructive religious denomination conveys an alienated yet superior insight:

> What Blindness, *said I to my self*, has possest the Dissenters in our unhappy Country of *England*, where by eternal *Discords, Feuds, Distrusts* and *Disgusts* among themselves, they always fill their Enemies with Hopes, that by pushing at them, they may one time or other compleat their Ruin; which Expectation has always serv'd as a means to keep open the Quarrel; whereas had the Dissenters been United in *Interest, Affection* and *Mannagement* among themselves, all this Heat had long ago *been over*, and the Nation, tho' there had been *two Opinions* had retain'd but *one Interest*, been joyn'd in Affection, and *Peace at Home been rais'd* up to that Degree that all Wise Men wish, as it is now among the Inhabitants of the World in the Moon.[26]

On the other hand, his upbringing in dissent, besides habituating him against respecting persons and deferring to authorities, undoubtedly motivated him to pretend to be a self-determining spokesman.[27] In the realm of jurisprudence, he venerated Hugo Grotius yet upheld the latter's ideas of political resistance not because they were "affirm'd" by Grotius or "by any greater Authority, but because they are first Principles."[28] In the realm of political philosophy detailed in *Jure Divino*, his precise admiration of Algernon Sidney is remote from his formulaic allusions to Locke. In this poem, which bases political theory on scriptural history, he mentions Locke once, and this in a footnote that also refers to *Oceana* (the tract by James Harrington) and Sidney.[29] In another footnote, he treats Sidney with a respect that corresponds to his celebration of Boyle's aristocratic civility:[30]

> *Algernon Sidney*, an Ancient Branch of the Noble Family of the *Sidneys*, and Brother to the then Earl of *Leicester*, drew out a true System of Original

> Power, and the stated Bounds of Government and Subjection by the Laws of God, Nature and Reason; and tho' it might be design'd for the Press in answer to Sir *Robert Filmer*, it was not yet perfected or finish'd for the Press, nor had it been exposed to View; but the Manuscript being seized, and the Subject examin'd, it was thought fit instead of answering him with the Pen, to answer him with the Axe, and conquer his Argument by the Extent of that very Power he exploded.

Grimly sarcastic, Defoe adds that this "Admirable way of disputing" means that "Arbitrary Power is only to be defended by Arbitrary Power, and Passive Absolute Subjection can only be exemplifyed by it self." Sidney's defence of political liberty remains "unanswerable." Those who "cut off his head, meerly because they could not answer his Book," were feeble orators "who afterwards own'd the Doctrine to be true, which they put him to Death for, and practis'd the very same thing which he was murther'd for defending." In sympathetically heralding the unjust death of this political martyr whose republicanism he did not share because of his appreciation of "patriarchally divine kingship," Defoe implies his greater distance from Locke's political liberalism.[31]

He could not have remained other than distant from Locke because he was appalled by how easily the latter's rationalism could be translated into atheism by deists such as John Toland.[32] A defender of the social benefits of reasonableness, Defoe participated in an intellectual movement led, among others, by Bishops Butler and Berkeley, that emphasized the moral and spiritual insufficiency of reason as a norm for civil conduct.[33] Although aware of Locke's works, he infrequently cited them because the philosopher's Arianism severed Christian ties between charity and justice.[34] His moral distance from Locke is particularly evident in the preface to *Jure Divino,* where he subsumes political philosophy under theology and champions "the Native Rights of Conscience" rather than viewing natural rights in a secular way. To Defoe, natural rights are necessary evils rather than positive goods.[35] Hence, he bases his call for toleration on theological rather than rational grounds:

> Christians of what Denomination soever, being Orthodox in Principle, and Sound in Doctrine, have a Native Right to Liberty of serving God, according to the Dictates of their own Consciences, and ought to be Tolerated, provided they behave themselves peaceably under the Government, and obedient in all other things to the Civil Magistracy of the Country in which they live.[36]

As Manuel Schonhorn says, by grounding political theory in scripture, Defoe moves "in a direction contrary to Locke's antimonarchicalism."[37] Hence, the preface to *Jure Divino* critiques heterodox evasion of Christian principles which are "so plain, so visible in Scripture, so explicit in our Creeds and Confessions of Faith." As a result,

> if a Man denies the Nature, Being, or Attributes of God, the Resurrection of the Body, Futurity of Rewards and Punishments; the Divinity, Conception, Birth, Death, Resurrection, Ascension and Intercession of our Redeemer; his delegated Power of Judgment and Retribution: the Power, Operation and Efficacy of the Holy Spirit, and the Mystical Union of the Trinity; if any Man denies the Necessity of Faith and Repentance, and the Salvation of a Soul, only by the Purchase and Merits of a Redeemer,

such a man is a "Disciple of that *Jezabel*, who calls her self a Prophetess, and who ought not to be suffered, that is, Tolerated, in the Church of Christ."[38]

Given his theological resistance to empiricism, republicanism, and abstract natural law, it is not surprising that Defoe's fictional and non-fictional texts dramatize questions about the nature and scope of reflection.[39] For Defoe, reflections involve much more than the series of mental operations that Locke defined in his attack on innate ideas when he argued that, far from being equivalent to conscience and religious identity, consciousness is the duration of ideas in the mind. Indeed, Defoe shows that Locke's progressively deductive mode by which simple reflections become compounded and complex does not match how people actually think. To Defoe, "just Reflections" are more than mirror images or perceptible signs. The adjective "just" signifies "appropriate and legitimate," not "mere" or "pure." His usage of the phrase brings it closer to moral judgment and spiritual meditation.

Defoe moves far beyond the view that ideas of sensation passively received by the mind are the ground out of which the faculties arise. To Locke, as a child grows and its cognitive awareness develops, simple ideas of sensation and reflection become compounded and complex. This progressive ideology did not convince Defoe, as much as it failed to impress Gottfried Leibniz and David Hume.[40] For experience does not necessarily lead to "just Reflections." Defoe's characters and narrators may testify to "just Reflections," but these at best are nugatory and evanescent: they may not be substantiated by self-examination or instantiated by writing. Characters and narrators may fail to attain personal and spiritual integrity by being too easily distracted by sensuous imagery and too much governed by naive percepts to embody the requisite dialectical awareness.[41] Narrative implications arising from "just Reflections" invite readers to see that Defoe subordinates realism of presentation to philosophical realism.[42] Far from intensively transcribing daily experience as he sometimes claimed, he plumbs tensions between human and divine ideas, his fiction delving into the chasm between the two. That he endows "just Reflections" with profane and theological meanings complicates his practice of literary representation. The polar meanings he attributes to reflection carry him beyond epistemological concern with how the mind knows its operations as a result of processing ideas of sensation.[43] If reflection occasionally signifies to Defoe reception of sensuous images into consciousness and rational analysis of material reality, it also denotes the rise of moral impulses, the insights of conscience, and the intuition of spiritual truths. Defoe further expands the denotations of reflection by making it convey the individual's capacity to expatiate, generalize, and improve ideas, a capacity entailing oral and written discourse. The person who truly reflects does not merely grant the spiritual aspects of nature, self, and society but comes to moral action and sensibility by scrutinizing all experience, transcribing it, and trying to improve it for others.[44] Reflection is mental, social, and discursive conduct that entails the reflexive expression that is instrumental to autobiography and the self-examination that fortifies ethical norms.

Narrative dialectic magnifies the polysemy of "just Reflections." To return to the epigraphs: they show that Defoe's narrators do and do not enjoy them. Reaching them, they discover spiritual truth; only glimpsing them, they urge readers to realize them. Reflections are unsteady: less to be possessed than constantly sought, less to be arrived at in certainty than to be reached for in doubt. Since his narrators do and do not attain "just Reflections," Defoe can ask readers to perform acts of interpretation based on their inconsistencies and contradictions. In judging his fictions, we cannot absolutely decide whether his characters are reliable or untrustworthy. For we must grant that they have their faculties about them and that they mirror physical, and reflect upon mental, reality authoritatively – to a degree. We must also grant that his narrators, at moments, reach an ample sense of reflection. For narrative and ontological reasons, those moments are brief and fleeting. The dynamics of story and the nature of being let Defoe represent that what his characters reflect is both reliable and unreliable since such contrariness best induces readers to make fuller reflections.

By embedding the polysemy of reflection into his texts, Defoe derives spiritual patterns from incremental verbal repetition and conforms his narrative strategies to theological concepts. If we see the meanings of reflection as a narrative resource, we may grasp why he presents characters and narrators dialectically and why their unsteady perceptions and conceptions invite us to ponder human agency and religious morality.[45] That they do and do not attain "just Reflections" is hermeneutically important. As they live and think about living, they do not grasp the contraries inherent in the material and spiritual realms partly because they cannot step outside the oral and narrative discourses which mediate their being. Apprehending contradictions rather than comprehending contraries, they convey to readers the grounds of moral agency and identity. In this, they are devices whose uncertain spiritual insights implicate theological into narrative dialectic so that this intricate reciprocity may render the act of reading fiction as challenging as it is entertaining.

*****

In *Robinson Crusoe*, the keyword "reflection" highlights Crusoe's stance on the physical and spiritual realms, revealing the processes by which he grows in experience and conscience to be unsteady yet reciprocal. The youthful confidence manifest in his early seafaring owes much to evasion: less traveller than wanderer, he shuns patriarchal and divine authority. His evasiveness about repentance is inseparable from a wavering selfhood. The first storm he encounters prompts him to "Vows and Resolutions," but once it has passed he forgets "Repentance." His next voyages evade the impulses aroused by the first storm.[46] Fear of drowning in that storm elicits "Reflections" on "past Conduct," yet, as soon as the "Sea was returned to its Smoothness of Surface and settled Calmness by the Abatement of the Storm," he "drowned all my Repentance, all my Reflections upon my past Conduct," letting the "Current" of "former Desires" bear him away (9). By correlating the polar states of the sea – tempestuousness and calmness – to Crusoe's spiritual condition, Defoe implies that his first reflections are spontaneous impulses to do with self-preservation rather than accurate and rational observations. Perversely internalizing the external world, his reflections ignore the dynamic tensions between physical and spiritual life. In surrendering to the "Current" of old desires and drowning incipient reflections, Crusoe is passive and active over against the sea while sloughing off the ironic parallel. Readers thereby see that he is as dull to phenomenal as to metaphysical reality, as unfamiliar with the language of navigation as with that of prayer. He will not spiritualize the language of navigation.[47] Although, as narrator, he reports that his hardened thinking is typical of sailors, the narrative conveys his unique perversity: claiming to have drowned his reflections, he still experiences "Intervals of Reflection" (9) which he treats negatively as "Fits" of "Distemper" (10). As character, he thought he had won a "compleat Victory over Conscience," but as narrator he warns that "another Trial" on his next voyage forced him to acknowledge his "Deliverance." If reflections are temporarily evaded, they cannot be suppressed since consciousness is a latent form of conscience. Crusoe would negate conscience, but consciousness recoils against such wilfulness. Hence, on the next voyage he remains alienated from marine life and navigation. Besides being ignorant of the word "Founder," his heart dies within him when "called to the Pump," and he is shocked to see "the Master" and "the Boat-Swain" at prayer because they expect the ship to sink. Although he works "heartily" at the pump on his turn, he falls in a "Swoon" when the ship fires a "Gun as a Signal of Distress" (12): his "Heart was as it were dead within" him, "partly with Fright, partly with Horror of Mind and the Thoughts of what was yet before" him (13). He manifests a curious blend of ignorance and anxiety. A stranger to maritime and spiritual discourse, he is both ready and unready for group action. Powerless to obey "Loud Calls from my Reason and my more composed Judgment to go home," he is passive before "some such decreed unavoidable Misery" that drives him "forward against the calm Reasonings and Perswasions of my most retired Thoughts" (14).

Crusoe's limited capacity to ponder his inconsistent actions and unsteady will power arises partly from a refusal to scrutinize the possibility that human agency is subject to temporal cycles governed by Providence. Having fallen from being "a Merchant to a miserable Slave" among the Moors of Sallee (19), he repeats the cycle of rising and falling when, as one of a group of Brazilian plantation owners, he leads a slaving venture only to be shipwrecked. As narrator, he comments that "abus'd Prosperity is oftentimes made the very Means of our greatest Adversity" (37). However, discontent with Providence as much as enterprise motivated him to become a slaver: he thought life in Brazil worse than being cast away on a desert island. Hence, he urges readers to "reflect that when they compare their present Conditions with others that are worse, Heaven may oblige them to make the Exchange, and be convinc'd of their former Felicity by their Experience." He concludes that it is "just" that "the truly solitary Life I reflected on in an Island of meer Desolation should be my Lot" (35–6). The slaving venture perpetuates his spiritual rebellion; remaining "the wilful Agent of all my own Miseries," he "double[s] the Reflections" upon himself (38). Heeding little the cycle of rising and falling, as character he makes himself more vulnerable to Providence by obeying "blindly the Dictates of my Fancy rather than my Reason" (40). On the island, his meditative powers continue to wane. After the wreck breaks up, he does enjoy the "satisfactory Reflection" that he salvages as much as he can (57). But his fretful discourses deprecate Providence; tears run down his face as he expostulates aloud about why "Providence should thus compleatly ruine its Creatures." If "something always" returns "to check these Thoughts, and to reprove" him and if this "something" which he calls "Reason" expostulates with him "t'other Way" (62), this vague recoil suggests a double awareness that might make reflection the object of reflection. That is, if his thinking is not reflexive, it testifies to potential mental recursiveness and still registers religious impulses. But that he will not develop his reflections makes them more disturbing. He admits he lacked "divine Knowledge" and was not only "wicked and prophane" but also possessed "a certain Stupidity of Soul, without Desire of Good, or Conscience of Evil" that made him act "like a meer Brute from the Principles of Nature, and by the Dictates of common Sense only, and indeed hardly that." Metaphysical dullness about bodily preservation stops him looking "inwards towards a Reflection" (88). Feeling a "meer common Flight of Joy," he looks on his preservation "without the least Reflection upon the distinguishing Goodness" of God (89). His low-grade, semi-conscious discourse sees him speaking to himself with the "Voice of meer Fright and Distress" (90). Knowing "not what my Tongue might express" and speechless after his "Exclamation" for divine help, he is visited by an exact recall of his father's warning that if he left home God would not bless him. This recall prompts him to speak: "Now, said I aloud, My dear Father's Words are come to pass" (91).

But re-articulating his father's scriptural words enables him neither to look inwards nor to develop an exegetical sense because he cannot integrate speech and reflection. When he continues to repine, "Conscience presently check'd me in that Enquiry, as if I had blasphem'd," speaking to him "like a Voice" (92). Conscience renders him speechless: he "was struck dumb with these Reflections, as one astonish'd, and had not a Word to say, no not to answer myself" (93). Biblical deliverance does not move him: "The Words were very apt to my Case, and made some Impression upon my Thoughts at the time of reading them, tho' not so much as they did afterwards; for as for being deliver'd, the Word had no Sound, *as I may say*, to me; the Thing was so remote" (94). He is metaphorically and metaphysically deaf. His meditations seem externally imposed: "I was, as it were, made to ask my self such Questions as these, viz. Have I not been deliver'd, and wonderfully too, from Sickness?" (95). Reflections "extorted some Words" from him "like praying to God," the simile indicating that his prayers are vague, disembodied, and unwilled. Far from processing his reflections out of a spiritual sense, they aggravate his spiritual pain, as the following simile conveys. In his "greatest Composures" of mind, the "Anguish" of his soul breaks out "like a Storm" (113).[48]

Since this dissociation of mind and soul is not repaired when he claims to have found grace through repentance, Crusoe's remorseful self-criticism does not lead to a reflexive tendance of soul, which his attitudes to material reality illustrate. His inventiveness does not thoughtfully inform how he regards the world. When he builds the *periagua*, his mind is so intent on the voyage he aspires to make that he has not the "least Reflection" about getting the vessel down to the sea (126). He learns about the intractability of nature by default. By approximately reproducing the processes of bread making, he does win the "just Reflection" that things are valuable only as they are useful (129). But he simplifies and misrepresents life on the island by way of consoling himself rather than working at his repentance. As we saw, he dignifies island life by appropriating to it the language of European civilization. That he also applies pejorative terms to it shows that he experiences contrary emotions that escape his full awareness. When he ponders the gap between his hopeless and enjoyable prospects, his trust that things will evolve for the better is merely a desire for contentment. Ironically, he views the island less in terms of spiritual contentment than from an unthinking drive to reproduce a society he never appreciated. His reflections remain unstable long after his repentance because Defoe's dialectical sense of the claims of body and spirit imposes on his protagonist the need to realize the profound reciprocity of speaking and thinking. On the positive side, Crusoe sees that his island life is better than he deserves, and his "terrible Reflections" on his sins yield a trust in divine grace and delimit hope that his repentance may be acceptable to God (132). Using the Bible to appreciate the miracles that have sustained him, he tries to be thankful for his lot by "conversing mutually with my own Thoughts" and even with "God himself by Ejaculations." But, on the negative side, he does not properly rate "the want of Conversation" (136). Whereas Defoe values conversation in the Pauline sense of 'way of life,' Crusoe limits it to mean "absence of fellow humans" because he is still unable to integrate the needs of body and soul and to balance action and contemplation.

His meditative thinking regresses when the footprint forces on him the recognition that life in a state of nature lacks a legal constitution and social contract and tempts him to destroy all he has built and to hide himself from threatening strangers. If he overcomes superstitious reactions to the footprint, cheerful that he had not seen it earlier, he is overwhelmed by "terrible Thoughts" about what might have happened had the cannibals found his boat. These undisciplined thoughts, "rowling upon my Mind," rack his imagination (155). The reflections that help him trust in Providence oppress him with his solitariness in a strange land. As narrator, Crusoe meditates on the humility he gained from these polar reflections: Providence protected him from the cannibals without awareness on his part of either the protection or the cannibals. The humility that disables reflections arising from sensations leads him to acknowledge spiritual impulses: when "Sense, our own Inclination, and perhaps Business has call'd to go the other Way, yet a strange Impression upon the Mind, from we know not what Springs, and by we know not what Power, shall over-rule us to go this Way" (175). In conceding spiritual notions of identity, he seems to testify to innate ideas. The many "Reflections" he draws from his impressions lead to a "certain Rule" of following "those secret Hints, or pressings of my Mind." However, although his appreciation of "secret Dictates" enhances his "Reflection upon the Folly" of his youth when he ignored these strange hints, he still desires to flee his divinely appointed station (195). He enjoys "many very profitable Reflections" on the gap between past enjoyment and present fear (196). He happily accepts humanity's lack of omniscience and inability to read the future. But he fails to explore the *via negativa* and the dark night of the soul. Nor does he delve into imperfectibility and the insight that comes from blindness. As his story ends, the various forms of his reflections, far from being integrated, become dispensable or are trivialized. There is no time to reflect on "the first sound of a Man's Voice" when he rescues Friday, who must be allowed to behead his enemy (204). His "merry Reflection" about his island being a flourishing kingdom is pure fantasy (241). Back in England, he is no steadier: his "several Reflections" on his circumstances are unsustained; they emphasize his social alienation and religious superficiality, confirming the anticlimactic quality of his narrative and life (279).[49]

While the incremental repetition of "just reflections" is less common in *Captain Singleton* than in *Robinson Crusoe,* when it does occur it does so in association with schemes of bathos and anticlimax that confirm Defoe's refusal to assign linear progress to fiction because he wanted readers to contemplate both narrative reflexivity and the endless cycles of human self-entrapment. An alienated child, Singleton alienates himself from society. His tenuous upbringing and seafaring adventures sink him in circumstance and hypocrisy. While he criticizes institutions and debunks the romance of the outlaw's life, his life and text suffer from an inability to face up to personal and social contradictions. The early pages of his autobiography alert readers to his erratic memory and questionable authority; as he tells us, "you may be sure I kept no Journal" (3). His first religious thoughts arise when he observes the sun worship of the tribe that transports the adventurers' goods across Africa. But these thoughts are short-lived and prejudiced; they are displaced by coarse "Reflections" about being glad not to have been born among such "stupidly ignorant and barbarous" creatures. He is untroubled with "Qualms of that Sort for a long time after" (61). The next occasion when he might religiously bind reflection to sensibility occurs during the gale off the coast of New Guinea that nearly sinks the vessel he is commanding. A "Flash, or rather Blast of Lightning" so shocks the air that it seems as if the ship has been hit by a broadside. The "terriblest Clap of Thunder" is like the "Blast of a Hundred Thousand Barrels of Gunpowder" (194). Only Quaker William remains composed enough to keep the vessel from foundering: the crew is terrified, and Singleton is all "Amazement and Confusion." He views his "Horrour" through "the just Reflection of my former Life," feeling "doom'd ... into eternal Destruction" and convinced that "God had taken me into his immediate Disposing." But his reflection is partial; it lacks "the moving, softning Tokens of a sincere Penitent." He is "afflicted at the Punishment, but not at the Crime, alarm'd at the Vengeance, but not terrify'd at the Guilt, having the same Gust to the Crime" (195). If fear of God moves him to relate his past to his present, spiritual lethargy hardens him to the self-image the storm exposes. The stricken ship is his emblem; it is an external mirroring an internal horror. But Singleton and his crew do not apply that emblem's meaning to themselves:

> we were all somewhat like the Ship, our first Astonishment being a little over, and that we found the Ship swim again, we were soon the same irreligious hardned Crew that we were before, and I among the rest. (196)

Singleton's unsustained self-examination leads nowhere but to materialistic indifference.

Although they recur, his penitential impulses are aimless. The interpolated story of Robert Knox's nineteen-year imprisonment on the island of Ceylon highlights this aimlessness. For Knox finds comfort in "God, who is the Father of the fatherless, and hears the Groans of such as are in Captivity" (241). Faith renders Knox content to "dwell in a strange Land where there was to him a Famine of God's Word and Sacraments, the Want of which made all other things to be of little Value to him" (243).[50] When Singleton says he is "a Kind of Charity School-Boy" with "no Desire of going any where" and insists he is "at Home" anywhere because he has "no where to go" (256), he parades his aimlessness. As narrator, he stresses his impenitence: his retrospection will not embrace spiritual paradoxes. Boasting of his roguery and indifference to native land and contemplation of death, he is pricked by conscience, which warns him that he will regret his words. Although this is the case, he continues, to the end of the narrated action, to delay relating ideas of self and time: at the close, he admits that the "Time of my Reflection" has not yet come. He refuses to think about ultimate things even in the face of William's provocative paradox that it is "because Men live as if they were never to dye, that many dye before they know how to live" (258). He excuses himself from spiritual effort by saying he cannot make reparations to all the victims he has plundered. He discounts the consolation in William's argument that restitution must wait on opportunities presented by God. Because he dramatizes his social alienation to avoid spiritual self-examination, Singleton cannot conclude his story. Refusing to read positive signs in his few, negative reflections, neither he nor his story reaches a spiritual denouement. Both are as anticlimactic as in *Robinson Crusoe* because Defoe wants his narrative and theological polarities to habituate readers to self-criticism and to consider how much reflection must entail the psychological processes which consolidate spiritual identity.[51]

The theoretical and narrative bases that support anticlimax and structure reader response in *Moll Flanders* seem firmer than in the life stories of Crusoe and Singleton because Defoe extends the semantic range of "just reflections" and elaborates the religious bonds between reflection and reflexivity by intensive psychological dramatization. He invites readers, implicitly and explicitly, to recognize through his protagonist that the life of the mind is more inclusive than she ever knows. Although Moll is persistently tactical and calculating, her thinking is rarely meditative. Since her consciousness and sensibility are unintegrated, readers learn that emotional responses to her fiction necessarily involve them in reflexive thinking: Moll's story induces them to conceive anew the reciprocity of cerebration and imagination. Defoe effects this recognition through the polar relations he creates between Moll as character and Moll as narrator. Neither as character nor as narrator does Moll stop thinking, but her contradictory reflections do not entail reflexivity. She lacks steady self-consciousness because she disperses her selfhood. As narrator, she does and does not identify with her former self; as character, she sometimes foretells her later self but sometimes denies it existential scope. She first turns reflection on herself when the elder Colchester brother seduces her with gold. Viewing the gold "with very little solid Reflection" (25), she reiterates his fine words about marriage without analysing them. Hence, she regrets being bound to him when his younger brother courts her: she "repent[s] heartily" but experiences no "Reflection of Conscience" (31). As individual agent, she blames her secular thinking. But, when she finds the men of the Mint "a Subject of strange Reflection" since they put a "Rape upon their Temper" to avoid their "Reflections," she adopts the role of social commentator (64–5). This moral superiority implies the possession of a spiritual outlook which, as narrator, Moll often tells us she lacked.

That Defoe assigns contradictory reflective capacities to Moll is further evident when she discovers her incestuous marriage to her brother by penetrating her mother's autobiography and its narrative obfuscations; refusing to be distracted from the truth, she insists that her mother look deeper into her life story and deduce fuller meanings from it. But, when she tells her mother that she has "most serious Reflections" about continuing to live with her brother, her stance is strategic rather than moral; a "Riveted Aversion" that has "no great concern about it in point of Conscience" impels her to detach herself from him (98). If not "Hypocrite enough to feign more Affection to him" (99), she still overstates her moral stance, as is clear in the rapidity with which she succumbs to economic necessity at Bath, that "Place of Gallantry," where she calls herself a "Woman of Fortune, tho' I was a Woman without a Fortune" (106). This evasive play with verbal ambivalence exposes her sense of moral dialectic to be merely shallow. The "many sad Reflections" she has in Bath stem from the diminution of her capital. Far from making her thoughtful, material need causes her to wait on something advantageous (106). Seeking to attract decent males, she displays a low-grade sense of reflection based only on monetary calculation and social illusion. Setting her cap at men of good name, she is simply bent on avoiding the "least Reflection," by which she means notoriety and ill-fame (107). Her contradictory thinking about, and inconsistent conduct with, reflection yield implications that widen the gap between her vices and virtues, while enforcing their reciprocity.

Moll's relationship with the Bath gentleman who keeps her illustrates Defoe's awareness of what psychological and moral harm abuses of reflection produce. As soon as she gains security from becoming his mistress, she starts to fear that "just Reflections of Conscience" will stop him keeping her. In "this happy but unhappy Condition" she bears three children. Aware of how conscience generally informs sensibility, she possesses reflections, not with enough conviction to change her conduct, but sufficiently to become deeply anxious. Hers are doubly secondary: first, instead of applying them to herself, she applies them speculatively to the gentleman in his absence; second, she forgets them in his company. Her reflections about reflection form no searching introspection; they remain "secret Reproaches" of conscience (120). Yet, when the gentleman develops a "religious Abhorrence" of their relationship, Moll sees that his "sad Reflections upon his past Life of Gallantry, and Levity" constitute "sincere Repentance." In granting that his "Reflections were just," Moll potentially shares them. But, in continuing to extract money from him, she will not share them. At this point, appropriately, given how contradictory her reflections are, she leaves "the Readers of these things to their own just Reflections," trusting they will make them more effectually, since she is an "indifferent Monitor" (126).

Moll the narrator does not convert her contradictions into contraries because that role is left to readers. That she is dull to narrative contradictions and only partially makes just reflections constitutes the formal means by which Defoe implicitly reinforces her explicit invitations to readers. That we are urged to make connections when Moll as character and narrator fails to do so encourages us to work at imagining the relation between the psychological and spiritual meanings inherent in reflection and the reflexive practices required by the search for a healthy identity. When Moll abandons the banker to marry Jemy, she has "some Reflections" about forsaking the faithful citizen (143), but she succumbs to the "glittering show of a great Estate" (144). Her fortune hunting and false conformity to Catholic rites block her self-awareness so that her sense of reflection becomes more contorted. When, upon marrying the banker, she sees Jemy, her "Mirth" is interrupted and she is frightened to "Death." Her "first sensible Reflection" is self-defensive; she is glad that her new husband is not present to notice her shock (185). A groundless fear that he has returned to insult her, this reflection exposes her desire for personal concealment and her ongoing deception of society. When Jemy commits a highway robbery, she distracts the "Hue and Cry" to cover his escape from the "mob Gentry" (186). The more she distorts reflection the more she avoids self-criticism. As a thief, she contemplates the poverty of her victims, but material necessity deafens her conscience and hardens her heart against "Reflections" (193). They still arise but wear off ever more quickly, becoming less reflexive and more self-destructive. If she admits not having true reflections, this reflexivity is a matter of insincere repentance and criminal rationalization as in the instance of telling herself that she has given "a just Reproof" to negligent parents whose child she has robbed (194). As her crimes mount, she is shocked by her own hardening, namely, "to a Pitch above all Reflections of Conscience or Modesty" (202). She is "beyond the Power of all Reflection" when she steals from the family in the burning house yet claims to be touched "to the very Soul" (206). This contradiction shows that emotional sensitivity is not necessarily reflexive. Moll's sense of her inhumanity does not lead her to make reparation. Because she tells herself, after each criminal act, that she will commit only one more, her reflections are nugatory. However, we are not asked to judge Moll's contradictions without noticing those of other social types. The baronet who fears contracting venereal disease lies with Moll again when he finds she is safe. His "just Reflections" keep him away only until they wear off (237).

If incarceration in Newgate does not improve Moll's reflective conduct, it manifests growing self-criticism; in widening the gap between character and narrator, prison heightens the implicit reciprocity of those roles. As character she simply regrets imprisonment, allowing Moll the narrator to comment on her laxity: the former Moll did not regard her time as "given for Reflection upon what was past" (278), and she failed to connect reflection to repentance. While her guilt was heavy enough to have impressed anyone with "the least power of Reflection," she degenerated to the point of tolerating Newgate: she sank below remorse. Her ideas of heaven and hell remained minimal; they were no more than a "bare flying Touch, like the Stich or Pain that gives a Hint and goes off" (279). This seems the nadir of her identity. But Defoe treats her loss of awareness contrarily: Moll retains a critical point of view and a residual moral sense. In blaming herself for Jemy's degeneration, she discovers a capacity for perceptual and cognitive recovery. Sympathy for him leads to her "first Reflections" upon the "horrid detestable Life" she had led (281). With this sympathy comes guilt. As this flows in, she renews her distaste for her birthplace; disgust with Newgate brings self-disgust. If these "first Reflections" are sound, they restore her to herself only partly. She connects thinking to identity, entertains a retrospective sense that carries her beyond material circumstances to a "kind of view into the other Side of time," and relives images from the past. In renewing these images, she glimpses the interdependence of consciousness and conscience. Heightened lexical awareness confirms her incipient theological perspective. Her "extended Notions" of the word "Eternity" signal a potential for connecting reflection to spiritual self-analysis: her "Reflections" on eternity convey "of meer Course" an idea of repentance (287). Contrarily however, while words mediate her renewed sense of self, she cannot express this sense. She disclaims analysing the impressions made on her soul: "it must be the Work of every sober Reader to make just Reflections on them" (288). Again, Moll invites readers to win a clearer insight into material and spiritual reality. Not expected by the minister to sustain the relation between reflection and repentance, Moll, as narrator, acknowledges the validity of his fears for her relapse: they are "not without Cause" (294). Her final reflections imply the inevitability of relapse and ask readers to look beyond her supposed penitence to the reasons for its dubious nature.

By contrast with Moll, H.F., the narrator of *The Journal of the Plague Year,* is a model of reflection since he openly admits the dilemmas of a commentator who, in the face of regulatory and moral contradictions, tests society's collective thinking and examines how much its institutions may be said to be thoughtful and reflective. The multiple meanings of reflection embedded into his self-aware commentary directly shape readers' responses to the presentation of society's political and religious reflexivity. Although he claims to have withheld his "Meditations upon Divine Subjects" (77), his comments on the plague and government policy are inseparable from his spiritual autobiography. To H.F., as to William in *Captain Singleton,* mortality entails a traditional paradox: death destroys, but thoughts of death are "wholesome Reflections" since they led to the closure of entertainment venues, such as theatres, "gaming Tables, publick dancing Rooms, and Music Houses" that had begun "to debauch the Manners of the People." Still, in his mind, reflections on death were not "rightly manag'd" by the local government. Had they been, London would have become a "second *Nineveh*" and penitence been more widespread. Sadly, "a quite contrary Extreme" befell "the common People"; fear drove them to "extremes of Folly" (29). Having asserted that reflections on death proved wholesome, he concedes they were not adopted by the populace: common folk were "stupid in their Reflections" because they resorted to superstition and magic. His contention that reflections on mortality are wholesome is reinforced by details that refute the universality of polarity thinking. This irony grows when H.F. expresses sympathy for the poor by reporting that those who repented of crimes were left alone to suffer the pangs of conscience since church ministers were few and far between and since, because there was often "no Body surviving to record" their confessions, they were deprived of spiritual solace. If in general the people did not repent, many did, yet were unable to sustain their religiosity, not through folly, but through ecclesiastical desuetude. That the poor did and did not repent and that they did and did not enjoy serious religious reflections is a narrative contrary that binds the difficulty H.F. has in generalizing about the plague to his humanity as a commentator. His uncertainty only seemingly opposes his prescriptions, for the two are reciprocally integrated. It is vital to readers' sense of moral dialectic that H.F., besides condemning the poor, confesses his sympathy for them in "serious Awe and Reflection" (34).

H.F.'s contrarian sensibility equally propels personal and political activism. After meeting a bereft man who has lost wife and children to a burial pit, he sheds "Tears in the Reflection" (63). He then visits the inn where three men who mocked the bereaved man are drinking. While consoling this man, H.F. confronts the scoffers. By deflecting their anger to himself, he soothes the grieving man, forewarns the scoffing atheists about the divine punishment that will visit them, and validates the sincerity of his conscience and proselytization: he makes the contemplation of death wholesome to himself. In observing the suffering around him, he experiences the "full Power of Reflection" and registers the deepest "Impressions" in his "Soul" (171). His sensibility makes his writing about death socially critical and politically constructive. Condemning urban development that desecrated the graves of plague victims, he voices outrage at the devaluation of death: "with some Reflection" to provoke readers to moral inferences, he reports that "dead Bodies were disturb'd, abus'd, dug up again, some even before the Flesh of them was perished from the Bones, and remov'd like Dung or Rubbish to other Places" (231). Given that latterly built memorials cannot remedy the disturbance of burial grounds, H.F. declares that the ritual understanding that the dead are always with us has both great political and religious significance.

Defoe's semantic and narrative polarities with regard to "reflection" in *Colonel Jack* invite readers to respond to a marginalized character whose lack of formal education and selfish aspirations yield positive implications about how citizens should be politically responsible to the Hanoverian regime. At the start of this fiction, the relation of narrator to character is distant and close in order that readers' assumptions may be unsettled. By its end when this relation is less volatile, readers are encouraged to respond religiously to the protagonist's spiritual challenges. Looking back to when he first bought food and clothes with his criminal gains, Jack as narrator stresses his former self-deception: happy in his imagination, he was ignorant of "greater Felicity" (16). The young Jack experienced no "Grief or Reflexion," because he naively equated the purchase of necessities with gentility.[52] Yet, in his alienation, besides suffering extreme anxiety about securing his money, he was obliged to confront his reflexive ignorance. Far from being totally self-deceived, he felt impelled to rectify the damage caused by his thieving. He enjoys "Satisfaction" as a "Natural Consequence" of making "Restitution" to a poor widow, subsequent "Reflection" telling him he ought to compensate all his victims (87). But this thought wears off, because he is not encouraged by his environment to develop his innate impulses and because his reflections do not become retrospective. The dialectic underlying Jack's independence and neediness strengthens Defoe's narrative contraries: Jack does and does not stand apart from society, which is and is not supportive of him.

Jack is slow to understand the ties between identity and morality. After being transported to a New England plantation, he has the mental space to examine his past but fails to reach a stable sense of self. On the plantation, his reflections on having been brought into the "miserable Condition of a Slave" neither involve "clear Judgment" nor stem "from Conscience." He simply assumes them to be impressions from "some strange directing Power" (119). But he does not address them as spiritual intuitions. Having become a plantation owner who appreciates being "in the World" free from crime, he lacks reflective satisfaction because he cannot shut out images from his past: "like Reflections upon Hell," these images show that, if liberated from crime, he has not freed himself from its mental and spiritual ramifications. He does not explore the possibility that reflections may have a source in Heaven or Hell. Nor does he contemplate the feasibility of innate ideas and spiritual mediation. He does not see, as readers do, that reflections are not simply properties of the conscious mind. His capacity for "making a right Judgment" does not admit "serious Religious reflections"; it derives from "meer Reasonings" from himself and his superficially genteel code (156).

The paradox that loss may constitute gain is a motif by which readers may assess Jack's ultimate failure to employ reflection as a means of self-correction and moral insight. That he is "secretly easie" and takes "a kind of Pleasure in that Dissaster" when a ship transporting goods purchased with his criminal gains is lost indicates a latent capacity for reflection (157). But his vague sense of gentility impedes him from contemplating providential dispensations. By contrast, his Tutor rejoices in the punishment meted out to his crimes. In accepting responsibility for his past, the Tutor displaces its haunting images and applies his "feeling and affecting Sence" of sin to himself and to social criticism. His commentary on prison life admits that he had no serious reflections when in the Newgate at Bristol and that, whenever reflections came, he evaded them by resorting to "Wine and Company." Coherently analysing this penal episode enhances the Tutor's belief in the divine purpose of his punishment even as it induces him to satirize the system by which he was punished. His reformed sense of self generates enlivening moral contraries: "delightful Sorrow" binds righteousness to penitence (164–5). Although this discourse of loss and gain unsettles Jack's complacency, Jack will not internalize his Tutor's paradoxes because a "Dead Lump" lies on his heart (165). He knows his Tutor's "Reflections are certainly very just" (168) and realizes that his ingratitude to Providence might return him to destitution. But he lacks penitential faith and a "Fund of religious Knowledge" (171). When punished with exile among the Spanish, he does not look back to the good in his life yet declares "just Reflections" to be "the utmost Felicity of human life" (307). In exile he improves upon his life by writing his memoirs, which helps him look back with pleasure and develop some "due Reflections." But readers are asked to make "the same just Reflections" which he should have made.

Jack's negative experiences and deficient explications are the grounds for readers' positive inferences, Defoe's semantic broadening of "reflection" enabling them to convert images of personal loss and moral decline into their own imaginative and spiritual gain. As narrator, Jack declares that his misfortunes as character will benefit readers if they seize the opportunity to improve on inconsistent and low-grade reflections. By putting inadequate "Reflections" into writing, Jack enjoins readers to make better ones: his account gives "Room for just Reflections of a Kind which I have not yet made" (307). His text is incomplete in the sense that he has neither worked out his final viewpoint nor fully interpreted his experiences.[53] By contrast with the beginning of his autobiography where the wide gap between character and narrator modulates sympathy for the young Jack, at the end the narrator undermines himself by emphasizing the inadequacies of his viewpoint.[54] With "a just Detestation," he has learned "as *Job* says, *to abhor my self in Dust and Ashes*."[55] In Jack's mind, readers will assume their inferential advantage over him if they have "the Temper of Penitents." Because they are "at Home," resting in the security of society and religious faith, they may draw "penitent reflections" from his text (308). Their social and spiritual trust will let them read his past better than he himself can; they will rewrite his story. He cannot reflect fully because he remains alienated from the society for which he has written his life. But readers will improve his autobiography if they develop a polar appreciation of secular and spiritual reflections.

The necessity for readers to draw inferences from narrative contradictions and to develop a dialectical sense of reflection is yet clearer in *Roxana,* for Defoe's polarity thinking in this fiction transforms psychological into metaphysical problems similarly to Graham Greene's depiction of the intensely destructive self-loathing of Pinkie in *Brighton Rock*. From the beginning, Roxana is an intelligent and principled young woman whose personal and social experiences are so intense that the relation between her roles as character and narrator is extremely close and detached. This tension between her two selves alters in the course of her autobiography on account of her cognitive and expressive regression: her identity and textual control disintegrate in tandem. The preface advises readers how to respond to her limited reflexivity; it states that, in censuring herself, her self-criticism "*guides*" readers to "*just Reflections*" and to the "*Noble Inferences*" to be drawn from her story. Yet she does reflect: "*the Reproaches of her Conscience*" are never quieted by the "*unexpected Success*" of her wicked life because the voice of her conscience will not be silenced. Her reflective potential is evident, the preface suggests, since "*she makes frequent Excursions, in a just censuring and condemning her own Practice*" (2). She analyses her resistance to conscience and admits to spiritual frustration, these insights confirming that vicious pleasures are not worth the pain of incomplete repentance. Her life story yields two grades of "*just Reflections*": the ones glimpsed by character and narrator and the ones available to the reader. The first convey spiritual lapses; the second "*guide us to just Reflections in the like Cases*" (2). By deducing reflective improvements from her self-criticism, readers will mediate their own lives through Roxana's text.

This fiction's reflexive didacticism is absorbing because Defoe's dialectical treatment of material pleasure and mental pain deepens the paradoxical reciprocity of the character's gains and losses. Quite steadily Roxana the narrator represents her former self as unable to grasp, let alone reconcile, the contradictions inherent in identity and social existence. While she lived "merrily, and as happily" with the landlord-jeweller, "dark Reflections ... came involuntary in, and thrust in Sighs into the middle of my Songs." A "heaviness of Heart ... intermingl'd itself with all my Joy" (48). She hid these "loose Reflections" and "dark Intervals" from him, to her "utmost" trying "to suppress and smother them" in herself (49). Her reflections are "dark" and "loose": melancholic, irrepressible, and undisciplined. She is not "without some just Reflection" when her "Vanity" is satiated by becoming the prince's mistress (74). But her anxiety and loneliness are heightened by this reflection which neither counteracts her predisposition to wickedness nor improves her moral will. When she preaches to the prince about honouring marriage vows, she knows that her preaching obliges her to discontinue being his mistress, yet she cannot will to do so; her reflections are not "strong enough to go that Length" (82). They are retrospective, not prospective; they come "too late." The prince has "just Reflections" also only after his princess's death when they cannot affect his behaviour to her (103). Defoe's repeatedly contrary presentation makes reflection instrumental to readers' sense that this broad mental category is ineffectual unless cognition leads to moral action. Since Roxana hinders reflection from guiding her conduct and prevents her self-awareness from being fully reflexive, she exemplifies the extent to which moral knowledge may be advanced by a wicked character. Confronted by polar images of her, readers both sympathize with, and remain aloof from, her.

Reflections haunt Roxana increasingly because she is less and less able to admit their moral agency. The affair with the prince fills her with "many dark Reflections" about being an "Instrument in the Hand of the Devil" (102). She admits she snared the prince and obstructed his reform. Dark thoughts inhibit her relations with the Dutch suitor who thinks her pious. When he "very prettily order'd his Discourse, between serious Reflection and Compliment," she has "too much Guilt to relish it." She turns "it off to something else" and deflects his witty sentiments (137). When she grows tired of whoredom, moral exhaustion "brought some just Reflections upon me, relating to things past," but "there was not the least Hint in all this, from what may be call'd Religion or Conscience, and far from any-thing of Repentance" (200). One reflection takes the form of an internal dialogue in which a voice of "somebody" asks her "the Question" why she continues to be a whore (201), but she develops "no Impressions … of that Kind which might be expected from a Reflection of so important a Nature, and which had so much Substance and Seriousness in it" (203). The "little Consequences" that flow from this limited reflexivity make her think she can present herself to her children as "fit to be own'd" by keeping her past life a secret and controlling how she reveals herself to them. Since she will not view the contradictions of her agency as moral contraries, her reflections are inevitably "very sad," as when the "bitter" recognition that her daughter does not know her is the "more agreeable." Although she seeks "some Figure of Life" in which not to appear "scandalous to my own Family," readers know that her hope is vain (206). Her low-grade reflections enter her conscience less and less while she experiences their destructive power more and more.

Defoe induces readers to draw inferences from Roxana's inadequate reflections by steadily widening the gap between her impulses and will: her autobiography itself yields "Reflection" because of the tensions between her ongoing sinfulness and retrospection. The past recoils on her through reflection's autonomy. When she marries the Dutch merchant and acquires the titles she covets, her "prosperous Wickedness" is "afflicting"; the more she looks at the past, the more "black and horrid" her sins appear (243). The conduct to which she is prompted by "Reflections" tends to be pessimistic. Pondering the "Justice of Heaven" leads her to expect her ill-gotten gains to be blasted, so she keeps her wealth from her husband's (260). Despite claiming to enjoy with him a "regular contemplative Life" and "all humane Felicity," reflections "prey upon" her "Comforts" and gnaw "a Hole" in her "Heart" (264). That her pleasures become pains and her gains become losses are paradoxes which self-degradation prevents Roxana from viewing as inevitable polarities. Still her failure to recognize paradoxes validates readers' polarity thinking. Yet, when she feels undone by being exposed to her daughter, Roxana is also glad since this feeling leads to "some very good Reflections" about the "Justice of Providence" (297). No one is so bad that she cannot glimpse the relation between psychological and moral contraries. She enjoys occasional religious reflections because, while arising from self-discipline, they offer themselves independently of that discipline. Thus, she reflects that "Sin and Shame" are "like Cause and Consequence" because people cannot conceal the first or avoid the second (298). If ideas about human self-destructiveness and Providence's operation through the contraries of human nature do not save Roxana, they are signs which Defoe wants readers to grasp imaginatively as well as inferentially.

*****

The exquisitely detailed processes that present Roxana's psychological and spiritual decline depend on Defoe's incremental verbal repetition and semantic broadening of "reflection." He can so fully elaborate the ebbing and flowing of Roxana's consciousness because his commitment to polarity thinking enables him to show that ideas in the mind are too variable and dynamic to yield an enduringly stable sense of identity. His presentation of narrative contradictions and moral contraries in *Roxana* tellingly illustrates his conceptual interest in the pluralities of selfhood and in the dynamic tensions between the past and the present that challenge Lockean epistemology and promote sacramental attitudes to material reality. These claims may be substantiated by seeing that the multiple meanings of reflection exemplify a persistent concern for reader response and polarity thinking in Defoe's non-fiction, as a brief survey of three of his major conduct manuals, *Religious Courtship*, *The Complete English Tradesman*, and *Conjugal Lewdness*, will attest.

The word "reflection" is as instrumental in *Religious Courtship* as in *Roxana* for inducing readers to explore the reciprocity of cognition and spirituality. In this guidebook, a fashionable suitor is rejected by a young woman who loves him but despises his indifference to religion. The suitor loves her but does not respect her reflective sensibility. He perceives his folly when, in courting a second woman, he recognizes the pattern of his conduct to the first. Seeing his attitudes embodied in the second, he breaks off the courtship, motivated by the "just and natural Reflections of his own Reason." The self-improving thoughts that stem from the suitor's reflexivity deter his conventionally lax conduct, make him examine the code of gentility to which he unthinkingly conforms, and oblige him to see that true gentility and Christianity are mutually sustaining. But these analytical results of reflection yield no spiritual awareness. This arises only after a poor tenant instructs him about prayer. Once the suitor-landlord values the "mental Voice" that injects words into his soul, "comforting Reflections" and a "kind of inward Peace and Satisfaction" fill him. Reflection, from beginning in moral impulse and rational analysis, becomes spiritual grace, Defoe embodying in this process the contrary that reflection is both natural and learned, that it spontaneously arises within the suitor yet must be explained to him.[56]

The suitor does not soon renew his courtship because Defoe endues reflection with further significance. Since the first young woman equates reflection with grace, the suitor's task of remedying his declared indifference is difficult. Despite grieving the loss of her suitor, the young woman's "only comfortable Reflection" is that she is delivered from religious indifference. The suitor gets her to accept him only after a long train of narrative coincidences. As we shall see in later chapters, much of *Religious Courtship* concerns society's attempts to overcome the young woman's distrust of her suitor's conversion. An old clergyman, among others, must endorse it with "some very handsome Reflections." Still, the suitor is daunted by the "just Reflection" that his former indifference must be offset steadily by social and religious conduct. In *Religious Courtship*, reflection, in denoting moral impulse, rational self-examination, and grace, invites readers to make inferences about the necessary integration of secular and religious conduct.[57]

That the necessary moral regulation of business practices is a major concern of *The Complete English Tradesman* owes much to how Defoe employs "reflection" to refer to the voice of conscience when reprimanding commercial misconduct. In this concern, he critiques Bernard Mandeville's easy paradox that private vices constitute public virtues and argues that productive commerce depends on tradesmen's self-discipline. Thus, he warns the tradesman who thinks he need not treat his shop as the centre of his world that such self-deception will recoil on him, there being "no fraud against his own reflections" since "a man is very rarely an hypocrite to himself."[58] This insistence that no man can deceive his own conscience recurs when, after criticizing the modish, expensive, and wasteful fitting up of small shops, Defoe tells larger businesses to apply the same "just reflection" and to resist "the humour of the times." To Defoe, ledgers and account books should incorporate reflection as much as spiritual autobiographies do, because tradesmen must see themselves as members of a principled community. By keeping books, no matter how discouraging, shopkeepers will know how they stand and be better able to make the "just reflections" that will keep them clear of bankruptcy and to maintain honest relations with fellow tradesmen. Since he is troubled by the "very melancholy Reflection" that businesses overstimulate consumerism, Defoe emphasizes that tradesmen must obviate such allegations by cultivating moral reflections. They must reconcile how they appeal to the vanity of customers to their consciences; they must grow their trade with "Caution" and "sedate Reflection." They should avoid rationalizing their trade since they must bear in mind that their own "Days of reflection" may not be far off. Defoe offers himself as a model: tradesmen are advised to make "the like just Reflections" he has done in discouraging vice and luxury. By apparently refuting the Mandevillean paradox that citizens' vices are tradesmen's virtues, he can more energetically insist that readers find his account of the moral dangers in trade "worth our Reflection" and draw "many useful Inferences" from it.[59]

Defoe expatiates on reflection in his non-fiction because he was troubled by the evasiveness inherent in reasoning. He thought that people tend to abuse reflection when considering both private and public matters since reflexive thinking invites self-deception. His unease with storytelling arises partly from his sense that it is inseparable from conventional forms of rationalization. Hence, he often insists that shame is the recoil of reflection. In *Conjugal Lewdness,* he stresses that shame alone will rouse people from their sexual vices. Unless made to feel shame, they will excuse those crimes: far from examining vice, they prefer to tell stories which imaginatively re-enact their sins and reinforce public immorality. Guilty "once in the Fact," they accumulate guilt by acting it "again in the Reflection" (334). Storytelling may be a morally destructive performance: it may be a self-gratifying way of warding off repentance and recommitting sin in the telling. For Defoe, neither reflection nor story should consist of mere representation or reenactment. He held this view from his earliest writings, as *The Shortest Way with the Dissenters* shows. When his hysterical persona imagines that posterity will chide his generation for refusing to wipe out the Dissenters, he betrays a total blindness to rhetorical and narrative contradictions. He represents a powerful group that claims to be threatened by its helpless victims: sparing the disadvantaged minority, he claims, will destroy posterity. Certain that such "Reflections" are "just," he conveys how illogical and fanatical, how unreflecting and unreflexive, they may be.[60]

The painful realization visited on Defoe by hostile reactions to *The Shortest Way* was that, far from in tune with reader response, he had to improve his rhetorical invention in order to induce audiences to reflect positively on his writing.[61] If one barrier in his way was his dubiety about both story and logic, one route open to him was to accommodate narration to reflection through a dialectic that aggregated his appreciation of orality and textuality. Versed as he was in the Bible and pulpit oratory, he was as literate in philosophy and science. Not only did he try to work out how to appeal to the oral foundation of literate mental habits, but also he appears less to have rejected the basis of reflection in logic than to have discovered how reflection may transcend rationality in the name of theology.[62] As we have seen in this chapter, his textual incorporation of reflection illustrates the precedence his polarity thinking takes over generic distinctions between fiction and non-fiction. *Serious Reflections*, the work which we explicate in the next chapter, shows that his polarity thinking makes a major contribution to narrative theory by elaborating his contrarian ideas about speaking and writing. This apology for *Robinson Crusoe* and *Farther Adventures* treats narration and reflection dialectically. Its preface calls *Robinson Crusoe* an "imaginary Story" and a "just Allusion to a real Story" and proposes that its narrative details are fictional and analogic, fanciful and referential [A5r]. This is no single-minded view of verisimilitude. *Serious Reflections* employs the polysemy of reflection to justify narrative discourse. Although "our own Reflections ... may often err, often be prepossess'd," Defoe draws "just Reflections" by relating storytelling to spiritual meditation, basing textual integrity on how theology informs narrative (12, 120).

Chapter Three

Serious Reflections: An Apology for Faith and Fiction

I have many things to say, but you cannot bear them now.[1]

If the Obstinacy of our Age should shut their Ears against the just Reflections made in this Volume upon the Transactions taken Notice of in the former, there will come an Age when the Minds of Men shall be more flexible, when the Prejudices of their Fathers shall have no Place, and when the Rules of Vertue and Religion justly recommended, shall be more gratefully accepted than they may be now.[2]

The coda to this chapter explores Defoe's polar discussion of the literary methods and reputations of John Wilmot, Earl of Rochester, and Milton, showing that his contrary stances to these authors imitate prophetic modes of discourse. If, as the epigraphs above suggest, Defoe adopts prophetic stances in a range of texts, he does so precisely in *Serious Reflections*, which acknowledges cultural resistance to forensic oratory and appreciates that speaking and hearing do not necessarily accord with each other. He often spoke like a prophet because he observed that his contemporaries chose to be deaf to the semantic extensions of "just Reflections" which the previous chapter has analysed. Indeed, his rhetoric incorporates several aspects of prophetic discourse as defined by Abraham Heschel. For one thing, by addressing future as well as present audiences, Defoe seems to invoke a whole people as he invests himself "in what he says and in what is going to happen to what he says." For another, his language is "luminous and explosive, firm and contingent, harsh and compassionate, a fusion of contradictions" that aims "to conquer callousness" and "to revolutionize history." For yet another, Defoe "alienates the wicked as well as the pious, the cynics as well as the believers, the priests and the princes, the judges and the false prophets." The final aspect of Heschel's account of prophetic conduct that fits Defoe's rhetoric is his awareness that in dealing with relations between God and man contradiction is inevitable: "Escape from God and return to Him are inextricable parts of man's existence. Conformity to logical standards is not characteristic of man's conduct, which is why contradiction is inherent in prophecy."[3]

Defoe imitates the provocative withholding and disclosing of Old Testament prophets because he does not trust in the preparedness of audiences to receive his paradoxical messages. Thus, in *Serious Reflections,* he elaborates ideas about belief and fiction through theological contraries, given what John Richetti calls his constant opposition to secular philosophy.[4] As an apology for fiction, *Serious Reflections* manifests a cognitive and aesthetic sensibility that enhances appreciation of Christian hermeneutics while dramatizing problems in winning sympathetic readers. In promoting his uniquely polar outlook, he admitted the barriers that impede authorial originality. He was aware that his contrarian mind-set was not received wisdom and that he needed a conceptual frame of reference in which his narrative and theological speculations might prove harmonious. Knowing his authorial discourse had to be somewhat in tune with the speech community, he conveys in *Serious Reflections* his tenet that no text can stand alone or speak simply and transparently for itself.[5] In this, as in other works, he takes up a series of topics again and again, his repetitions over-determining their reception given the problems of shaping reader response.[6] At the same time, since he believes that cognitive awareness depends on grace and revelation, he presents interpretation as both clear-cut and mysterious, as not only rationally lucid but also conditionally recursive.[7]

My second epigraph, taken from the preface to *Serious Reflections,* anticipates a future in which readers will respond to Defoe's works flexibly, a time when religious wisdom will overcome sectarian resistance.[8] Other voices he employs in *Serious Reflections* are those of a preacher keen on pulpit oratory, a theologian dubious about rational philosophy, and a critic for whom the Bible is the ultimate source of literary truth. If he sometimes disclaims preaching because he doubted its rhetorical efficacity, he still addresses readers as a spiritual authority. Understanding how his self-effacing and authoritarian stances complement one another clarifies his theory of fictional dialectic. Like

Kermode in his exegesis of the Gospel of Mark, Defoe approaches fiction as he does faith – as insider and outsider.[9] With rhetorical contrariness, he charges the generality of readers with unconcern for religion to induce in them theological sense. If prophetic closeness to the divine alienates him from the public, he dramatizes his alienation to goad citizens towards fellowship. The contrary stances he applies to characters and narrators, he also applies to himself and readers. Far from righteousness simply governing his voice, he relies on the interaction of theological and narrative dilemmas. Hence, the preface to *Serious Reflections* claims that the island in *Robinson Crusoe* was invented to move readers because

> Facts that are form'd to touch the Mind, must be done a great Way off, and by somebody never heard of: Even the Miracles of the Blessed Saviour of the World suffered Scorn and Contempt, when it was reflected, that they were done by the Carpenter's Son; one whose Family and Original they had a mean Opinion of, and whose Brothers and Sisters were ordinary People like themselves. ([A6v])

Since Christ's miracles were discounted by those in his community, only a remote setting will provoke readers through defamiliarization; narrative forms and categories must transcend the recognizable. Since the narrative in *Robinson Crusoe* contains factual and autobiographical elements, Defoe had partly to conceal them so that they might retain potential didactic power: "There even yet remains a Question, whether the Instruction of these Things will take place, when you are supposing the Scene, which is placed so far off, had its Original so near Home" ([A6v]). In Defoe's mind, the setting in *Robinson Crusoe* admits that neither the prophets nor Christ moved those to whom they were familiar. Since the prophets were dishonoured by their peoples and Christ was spurned by those who saw Him merely as a carpenter's son, readers must be addressed in parables – with oblique and analogous, rather than direct and immediate, stories. Defoe's prophetic tones realize that he could not make biblical vision a straightforward paradigm for reaching audiences. He knew he had to present the setting of *Robinson Crusoe* contrarily: to get close to readers he uses a distant scene and to provoke them to examine their mundane lives he gets them to imagine a strange land. *Serious Reflections* moves readers by stylistic and conceptual polarities: relying on the Bible and insights gained from voicing spiritual truths, the text reveals how foundational to narrative is a theological awareness of the necessary tensions between secular and religious values.

The multiple, often conflicting, stances in *Serious Reflections* are most evident when Defoe speaks ambivalently in his own as well as in Crusoe's voice.[10] He and his protagonist variously occupy the subject position since the apology for Crusoe's story requires Defoe to defend his own as well as his persona's authorship. Sometimes it is unclear which voice is speaking. That he drops the guise of impersonation seems clear when his commentary draws together ideas about spiritual reform that he had been pondering since his earliest writings.[11] Yet, *Serious Reflections* is an effective apology since at times Defoe upholds biblical perspectives; at others, he declines to do so. At times, he supports natural religion; at others, he questions it. Polarities dominate his discussions about how people should react to reason, revelation, and Providence. By no means does he always exploit polarities; sometimes he laments them. He nonetheless confronts them in his tenacious desire to link secular and religious ideas. This tenacity yields valuable implications for fiction.[12] His promotion and criticism of religious ideas together with his variable rhetorical techniques indicate an alertness to secular pressures on theology. *Serious Reflections* illustrates how narrative form may be derived from the dialectical tensions between religious and secular values.

Its first chapter, "Of Solitude," paradoxically contends that Crusoe's solitary experience is socially meaningful; in several stages, it relates spiritual meditation on the island to public discourse so that readers will not interpret the island as a monastic retreat. Defoe's first stage emphasizes the universality of solipsism and hedonism: perceptual isolation and psychological self-centredness are a bar to altruism and sympathetic knowledge of other people:

> The World, I say, is nothing to us, but as it is more or less to our Relish: All Reflection is carry'd Home, and our Dear-self is, in one Respect, the End of Living. Hence Man may be properly said to be *alone* in the Midst of the Crowds and Hurry of Men and Business: All the Reflections which he makes, are to himself; all that is pleasant, he embraces for himself; all that is irksome and grievous, is tasted but by his own Palat.
>
> What are the Sorrows of other men to us? And what their Joy? Something we may be touch'd indeed with, by the Power of Sympathy, and a secret Turn of the Affections; but all the solid Reflection is directed to our selves. Our Meditations are all Solitude in Perfection; our Passions are all

> exercised in Retirement; we love, we hate, we covet, we enjoy, all in Privacy and Solitude: All that we communicate of those Things to any other, is but for their Assistance in the Pursuit of our Desires; the End is at Home; the Enjoyment, the Contemplation, is all Solitude and Retirement; 'tis for our selves we enjoy, and for ourselves we suffer. (2–3)

The metaphorical references to taste, "Relish" and "Palat", and the repetition of "reflection" implicitly abandon Lockean psychology and emphasize that solitude is an existential condition. The point is that mental isolation need not be cultivated in hermitages or on quests because it is a psychological given, the only remedy for which is discourse with self and God. Hence, this "Silence of Life" is not "afflicting" as long as "Man has the Voice of his Soul to speak to God, and to himself." The second stage of Defoe's argument holds that this meditative discourse is a prerequisite of social converse: "That Man can never want Conversation, who is Company for himself; and he that cannot converse profitably with himself, is not fit for any Conversation at all" (3). By contrast, hermetic retreats devalue "Converse with Mankind"; they do not yield spiritual solitude since humans cannot be "entirely given up to conversing only with Heaven, and heavenly Things" (6).[13] Hermetic societies distort human nature and forget that social and spiritual experiences are reciprocal and complementary. Defoe spurns the "apparent Mortifications" of retreats in human and theological terms: withdrawal from society constitutes "a Rape upon human Nature" and a "Breach of Christian Duties"; "Hermit-like Solitudes" devalue secular living by rejecting the truth that society is where "Christian Communion, Sacraments, Ordinances, and the like" gather full meaning (7). Spiritual solitude is attained only by those who see that society is the medium of faith and that sacramental experience operates most significantly in the secular realm.

The reciprocity of social converse and spiritual solitude lies behind Defoe's polar concern with the particularities of material reality and their symbolic function in fiction. The preface to *Serious Reflections* theorizes such narrative flexibility when, about Crusoe's insular entrapment, it claims that "'tis as reasonable to represent one Kind of Imprisonment by another, as it is to represent any Thing that really exists, by that which exists not" ([A5v]). That Albert Camus made this sentence the epigraph of *La Peste*, his symbolic novel about an imaginary plague in Oran, North Africa which intermittently reflects both the German Occupation of France and the author's a priori metaphysical view of the problem of evil and necessity of suffering in the world, shows that Defoe's intellectual desire to extend the psychological into the theological realms was recognized by one of the leading novelists of the twentieth century and that he exerted a greater influence on later novel writing than is usually recognized.[14] Camus's opting for intermittent symbolism over sustained allegory appears to confirm Defoe's dialectic of concrete and abstract meaning.[15] Certainly, Crusoe's island is viewed from the perspective that material reality more endangers the isolated individual than the resident of society. His "forc'd Retreat" evinces the "anxiety" of "Circumstances": his deprivations were "very unsuitable to heavenly Meditations" (7). Once his basic needs were met, insecurity produced "Extremities of Fear and Horrour." Lacking "all manner of Temper," he was not "fit for religious Exercises." Isolation impeded spiritual solitude. Comparing the island experience to hermetic societies whose religious practice is removed from "the ordinary Course of Life" (7), Defoe argues that the mastery the soul must win over itself cannot arise from ignoring bodily, psychological, and social needs: spiritual solitude depends on exterior as well as interior factors. One pre-condition of spiritual solitude is that material circumstances must not aggravate the passions:

> Divine Contemplations require a Composure of Soul, uninterrupted by any extraordinary Motions or Disorders of the Passions; and this, I say, is much easier to be obtained and enjoy'd in the ordinary Course of Life, than in Monkish Cells and forcible Retreats. (7)

Inner composure requires material needs to be met by society. Spiritual discipline may transcend physical circumstance but its pre-condition – composure of soul – stems from social security. Spiritual solitude is achieved only if the soul's superiority is maintained in the course of engagement with corporal transactions. Convinced that getting the soul into its "superior Direction and Elevation" (8) is more important than monastic rules and a cloistered life, Defoe presents spiritual solitude as a tendance of soul that acknowledges material reality. This religious binding of immaterial to material values explains how the fictional island addresses religious problems arising from social alienation.

On the basis that spiritual identity requires an integration of secular and religious values, Defoe expatiates on interior moral conduct. The notion that spiritual growth best takes place in society is extended when he defines what "absolute Mastership" over sin entails. Sin is as much a matter of having wicked desires as committing evil deeds because "a vicious Inclination remov'd from the Object, is still a vicious Inclination, and contracts the same Guilt, as if the Object were at Hand" (8). Citing Christ in Matthew 5:28 to the effect that a man who lusts after a woman commits adultery, Defoe insists that, when a man merely fantasizes about fornication, he commits adultery:

> so it will be no inverting our Saviour's meaning to say, that he that thinketh of a Woman to desire her unlawfully, has committed Adultery with her already, though he has not looked on her, or has not seen her at that Time; and how shall this thinking of her be remov'd by transporting the Body? It must be remov'd by the Change in the Soul, by bringing the Mind to be above the Power or Reach of the Allurement, and to an absolute Mastership over the wicked Desire; otherwise the vicious Desire remains as the Force remains in the Gunpowder, and will exert it self when ever toucht with the Fire. (8–9)

From this ethically rigorous viewpoint, immoral ideas are spiritual misdeeds which may be obviated only by the self-restraint to which secular society is partly instrumental. Whereas such discipline restrains moral fallibility and spiritual self-destructiveness, hermetic institutions simply remove humans from existential tensions between mental actions and moral self-regulation.

> All Motions to Good or Evil are in the Soul: Outward Objects are but second Causes; and tho' it is true, separating the Man from the Object, is the Way to make any Act impossible to be committed; yet where the Guilt does not lye in the Act only, but in the Intention or Desire to commit it, that Separation is nothing at all, and effects nothing at all. There may be as much Adultery committed in a Monastery, where a Woman never comes, as in any other Place, and perhaps is so: The abstaining from Evil therefore depends not only and wholly upon limiting, or confining the Man's Actions, but upon the Man's limiting and confining his Desires; seeing to desire to sin, *is to Sin*; and the Fact which we would commit if we had Opportunity, is really committed, and must be answer'd for as such. (9)

This passage shows why Defoe's stance on moral behaviour is a contrary one. To him, actions are as much notional and internal as they are bodily and external. If material fact and social circumstance do not directly cause moral good or ill, self-regulation cannot proceed without the medium of secular public discourse. The individual, vulnerable to self-seduction, needs society to offset his limited self-knowledge. Society establishes "Rectitude of Life" and enhances the soul's resistance to temptation. While the recluse is susceptible to fallibility since "our own Reflections ... often err" and are often "prepossess'd," the citizen has companions, conversation, and books to guard his spiritual identity (10). Good company mediates religion because social discourse and spiritual truth conform to each other. Society matters spiritually because, by reinforcing the discipline of individuals, it obliges them to experience the complementarity of secular and religious values. Spiritual solitude is a civic concern given the equivalence of interior and exterior life, the ideal harmony of private and public values, and the reciprocity of faith and good works.

The following passages later in *Serious Reflections* exemplify the contrary theological stances that Defoe adopts on good works and faith because they help to integrate secular and religious values. In the first he begins by asking rhetorically: "What is Religion to me without Practice? And altho' it may be true, that there can be no true Religion, where it is not profess'd upon right Principles; yet that which I observe here, and which to me is the greatest Grievance among Christians, is the Want of a religious Practice, even where there are right Principles at Bottom, and where there is a Profession of the Orthodox Faith" (155). Thirty pages afterwards, he upholds "a rich unbounded Grace, that rewards according to itself, not according to what we can do; and that to be judged at the last Day according to our Works, if literally understood, would be to be undone, but we are to be judged by the Sincerity of our Repentance, to be rewarded according to the infinite Grace of God, and Purchase of Christ, with a State of Blessedness to an endless Eternity" (187).[16]

Defoe's polar insistence on creed and conduct and on the reciprocity of material and spiritual truths helps readers to interpret the island and to understand the theological foundation of his literary tenets. By denying both that spiritual solitude entails aloofness to society and that it is simply a private matter, he can more readily defend the case that a reading of the island be based on the dialectical relation of faith and good works and more pointedly argue for an interpretive model that rejects solipsism, positivism, and naive assumptions about romance. Claiming that a person may enjoy "the blessed Calm of his Soul" without an "Affectation of Reservedness" (11), since he will be as little distracted by society as helped by religious retreats, Defoe urges readers to see that relations between the individual and society and between the person and his conscience are dynamic rather than categorically distinct. To clarify this, Crusoe affirms that, since returning to England, he has experienced St Paul's "wrapt up State" (12).[17] This biblical allusion validates the claim that numinous experience is not at odds with social life and that, while the soul may be translated, it never transcends material reality. The allusion also sets up an amusing critique of implausible conventions in the genre of the saint's life:

> Man is a Creature so form'd for Society, that it may not only be said, that it is not good for him to be alone, but 'tis really impossible he should be alone: We are so continually in need of one another; nay, in such absolute Necessity of Assistance from one another, that those who have pretended to give us the Lives and Manner of the *Solitaires*, as they call them, who separated themselves from Mankind, and wander'd in the Desarts of *Arabia* and *Lybia*, are frequently put to the Trouble of bringing the Angels down from Heaven to do one Drudgery or another for them; forming imaginary Miracles, to make the Life of a true Solitair possible; sometimes they have no Bread, sometimes no Water, for a long Time together; and then a Miracle is brought upon the Stage, to make them live so long without Food; at other Times they have Angels come to be their Cooks, and bring them Roast-meat; to be their Physicians, to bring them Physick, and the like: If Saint *Hillary* comes in his Wanderings to the River *Nile*, an humble Crocodile is brought to carry him over upon his Back; tho' they do not tell us, whether the Crocodile ask'd him to ride, or he ask'd the Crocodile, or by what Means they came to be so familiar with one another: And what is all this to the Retirement of the Soul, with which it converses in Heaven in the midst of infinite Crowds of Men, and to whom the nearest of other Objects is nothing at all, any more than the Objects of Mountains and Desarts, Lions and Leopards, and the like, were to those that banish'd themselves to *Arabia*? (12–13)

Here Defoe mocks authors who, in the process of celebrating the lives of hermits and solitary saints, undervalue individuals' dependence on society by spuriously turning angels into domestic creatures, such as bakers, cooks, and doctors, and by ludicrously making crocodiles providers of ferry services. In addition to deriding the application of mundane details to saints' lives, Defoe debases narrative formulas that displace naturalistic description while catering to superstition and gullibility. In order to stress that meditation is not purely an ascetic practice and that society has immanent spiritual value, he turns to 2 Corinthians in which Paul insists that grace through prayer is the means of spiritual growth "without the Help of artificial Mortification" (16).[18] Since religious retreats are neither necessary nor sufficient conditions of numinous experience, Defoe reiterates that spiritual growth is achievable within society. Since on the island Crusoe does not achieve full spiritual development, readers are invited to correlate secular and religious values by treating his narrative in terms of spiritual discourse.

This explains why "romance" is presented in *Serious Reflections* negatively and why Defoe thought hard about viewing it positively. In the preface, he admits to being stung by detractors of *Robinson Crusoe* and *Farther Adventures* who reject their truth value as "all a Romance" ([A2v]). *Serious Reflections* grants the widespread view of romance's triviality when Defoe says that a false story spread by a self-important narrator is "a brooding Forgery" and a "Chimney-Corner Romance" (117). In the final section of *Serious Reflections, A Vision of the Angelick World,* he curbs visionary enthusiasm by urging that "the highest Raptures, Trances and Elevations of the Soul, are bounded by the eternal Decree of Heaven and let Men pretend to what Visions they please, it is all Romance, all beyond what I have talked of above, is fabulous and absurd, and it will for ever be true, as the Scripture says, not only, *those Things are hid from the Eye,* but even from the Conception" (*Vision* 44–5).[19] Theological limits to cognition make romance a term that exposes spiritual pretensions. Yet, when the family in *A New Family Instructor* debates "the Reading or not reading Romances," Defoe dramatizes tensions between negative and positive uses of the term. The sister opposes reading them "as a Diversion, there being no possible Pleasure in reading a Story which we know to be false, but related as if it were a Truth." To her, "the writing or publishing a Romance, was a Lye; so, of Consequence, the reading it, that is to say, the reading it as a Diversion, or with Delight, must be the same." But her brother makes the counter-statement that "where the Moral of the Tale is duly annex'd, and the End directed right, wherein it evidently accords; the enforcing sound Truths; making just and solid Impressions on the Mind; recommending great and good Actions, raising Sentiments of Virtue in the Soul, and filling the Mind with just Resentments against wicked Actions of all Kinds: … in such Cases, Fables, feigned Histories, invented Tales, and even such as we call *Romances,* have always been allow'd as the most pungent Way of writing or speaking; the most apt to make Impressions upon the Mind, and open the Door to the just Inferences and

Improvement which was to be made of them." Still, he makes "a kind of Proviso at the End of his Discourse, against approving of such Fables and Romances as are usually the Product of the present Age, having no such moral or justifiable End attending them."[20]

If he denigrates contemporary fiction, the brother's apology for narrative as a rhetorical instrument for grounding readers' moral, philosophical, and spiritual inferences accords with how Defoe embeds the reciprocity of personal and social identity into his discussion of "conversation" in the third chapter of *Serious Reflections*. Here the word signifies St Paul's "way of life" as well as verbal discourse.[21] By conjoining the word's secular and religious senses, Defoe continues to exercise how readers should respond to Crusoe's island. First, he claims that moral conversation is "an Emblem of the Enjoyment of a future State" since "*suitable Society is a heavenly Life*." Yet, if conversation is man's "most compleat Blessing" as an image of the afterlife, it is also "one of the Peculiars of the rational Life" (75). It is both transcendent and immanent. Second, he elicits conversation's immanence via another polarity: while he who is intent on good conversation needs society, society needs him because good conversation produces admirable citizens. This polarity shows that faith and civility are reciprocal, if not identical: "Wit is as consistent with Religion, as Religion is with good Manners" (81). Citing Ephesians 4:26, Defoe says good conversationalists are the only ones who can "*Be angry and sin not*" (76): articulate persons are most forgiving because most self-critical. Adapting St Paul's advice in Philippians 2:3, "*be Affable, be Courteous, be Humble, in Meekness, esteeming every Man better than our selves*" (83), Defoe emphasizes that conversation advances both social harmony and individual spirituality.

His analysis of debased conversation, in addressing problems with storytelling, theorizes the mutual inclusivity of ordinary language and literary discourse. Since it has "received a general Taint" (88), conversation will be reformed not by legislation but by speakers whose converse is the means and end of reform. Conversation is debased by those who disjoin secular and religious values and subject theology to social ambition. With "fancied affected Capacities," they make sacred doctrines a "common Subject" so as to appear witty. They vulgarize the "Divinity of the Son of God, the hypostatick Union, the rational Description of the State Everlasting … the Demonstrations of undemonstrable Things" in self-aggrandizing talk (88).[22] Their witty eminence degrades public mores by abusing theology: they strip Christ of his divinity and deny the hypostatic union "because they cannot distinguish between the Actions done by him in his Mediatorial Capacity, in Virtue of his Office, and those Actions, which he did in Virtue of his Omnipotence and Godhead" (89). They deserve castigation because they spurn the Trinity for not conforming to their rational notions.

Defoe's linkage of debased conversation to narrative's secular norms confirms his preference for dialectical exposition. Having declared that reform may be left to moral speakers, he creates rhetorical energy by conceding that such reform is problematic. He says he must treat modish conversation in secular ways since most readers doubt or deny the Scriptures and since "Divinity is not my Talent, nor ever like to be my Profession" (94). This disclaimer accords with neither his prophetic tones nor his biblical allusions.[23] Despite admitting that scholastic language is "not the way of talking that the World relishes" and that "talking Scripture is out of Fashion" and despite claiming to address "Men that have nothing to do with God, and desire he should have nothing to do with them" (95), he will not adhere to an exclusively secular viewpoint. For he holds that no wise person who respects his ancestors and his humanity will deny the operation of conscience. Nor will he justify vice to himself or deny that vicious talk is brutish. These categorical negatives are rooted in theology, Defoe affirming that natural reason yields conviction about God's existence and that no sensible man needs more demonstration than he finds within himself since there is "a *tacit* Sense of the Deity … lodg'd in the Understanding that is not stifled without some Difficulty, and [that] struggles hard with the Fancy, when the Party strives, to be more than ordinary Insolent with his Maker" (101). His defence of conversation insists on intuitive awareness of God's existence and on conscience as an innate principle.[24]

That secular experience cannot evade innate ideas is crucial to Defoe's narrative theory since this tenet correlates private and public meaning, defends introspective awareness, explains the anthropocentric causes of immoral expression, and defies the modish reduction of theology. So, he mocks those who, believing God to be "as they please to make him," regard Him to be "a fine well bred good natur'd Gentleman like Deity." In their complacency, they cannot accept that He damns to eternity and that He allowed the Jews to crucify Christ. They view the Bible as "a good History," the "Miracles of the New Testament as a Legend of Priestcraft," and Christ's story as "a meer Novel" (101). Such reductive attitudes, fostered by popular views of narrative, devalue the Bible and deny its uniqueness: degraders of conversation and the Bible refuse to see that upholding the reciprocity of secular and religious values is a moral imperative.

The complementarity of private and public values explains why Defoe's prescriptions for conversation involve self-regulation and institutional authority. On viewing debased conversation from the double perspective of church and state, he promotes legislative efficacy, which he earlier set aside. Claiming that Arian and Socinian heresies govern fashionable talk, he examines public morality from the stance of the ecclesiastical establishment: people who leave church during the *gloria* or sit through the doxology out of disbelief in Christ's divinity should be punished by statute. Such abuse of the liturgy is debased conversation. Having formerly granted that legislation cannot reach individual speech, he now urges that it apply to conduct which defies orthodoxy: legislation ought to defend the church.[25] Since conversation is debased by abuse of institutional worship, the "Civil Power" must preserve worship from "the horrid Invasion of Atheists, Deists and Hereticks," as it does the "Publick Peace" from "Free-booters, Thieves, and Invaders" (102). This insistence on the complementarity of church and state reflects Defoe's complex sense of symbolic action: worship and creed are crucial to the identity of individuals and society. From this stance, since government legislates against vices, it should penalize those who ridicule doctrines concerning salvation, the crucifixion, and Gospel revelations. Urging the state to eliminate heresy by penalizing conversational modishness, Defoe trusts the legal system to encourage spiritual discourse.[26] In thus connecting legal and religious tenets, he does not address non-conformist readers in a soothing manner.[27]

That debased conversation is aggravated by sexual impropriety confirms his sense of the complementarity of private and public values and upholds his belief that verbal expression is a form of conduct. In attacking "Bawdy, that Sodomy of the Tongue," he extends biblical imperatives (105).[28] His first targets are the unmannerly aspects of "lewd Discourse": he contends that, while modesty is less a virtue than an effect of the Fall, lewd discourse, which exposes what modesty conceals, saps custom. Citing Genesis 3:7, he holds that, while nakedness is the effect of Adam and Eve's sin, shame is the effect of their nakedness. This distinction between sin and shame critiques lewd talk in terms of both natural morality and theology: shame, a form of natural wisdom, is a sign of penitence, while lewd speech signals evasion of "Original Degeneracy" (107). If customary opposition to lewd talk is a "Badge of original Defection" (108), religious values are embedded into custom.

His ultimate charge against lewd discourse being that it inhibits the reciprocity of religious and secular values, Defoe next relates lewd talk to oral storytelling, explaining why the secular motives of stories are harmful. He argues that storytellers are usually so involved in their stories that they ignore probability: "so tickled" with narrative invention, they are "blind to the Absurdities and Inconsistencies of Fact in Relation" (112). Impelled by the need to entertain in social prominence, authorial self-gratification dulls their narrative sensibility and moral accountability. Storytellers subject themselves to irony by sapping their identity. Irony traps narcissistic narrators since psychological and social impulses render their storytelling self-perpetuating. If witnesses to the events they relate, they narrate with growing inaccuracy, deluding themselves about their reliability. The cost of narrative entertainment is high; storytellers debase accurate representation and social converse. While he distinguishes stories based on authentic inventions from those that do not pretend to be factual, applying the term "Parable" to the latter, one sees that the potential ironic rationalizations of storytelling inhere in the narrators of all his major fictions.

Serious Reflections shows that Defoe disparages stories told with omissions or amplifications as if they have "no real Original." In his mind, the foundation of narrative lies in the necessary tensions between particular experience and general meaning, for only stories so based can fortify social converse. Biblical texts inform this prescription. Applying 1 John 1:8, "the Truth is not in them," to storytellers intent on self-gratification, Defoe implies that they damage social trust, as is the case when he cites Ephesians 4:25, "*Let every Man speak Truth unto his Neighbour*" (116–17).[29] His narratives reinforce the Christian community since they are parables or "allusive all[e]gorick" histories that generate salient truths. In wanting narrative to serve society and conversation, he did not conceive of that service simplistically. If "Parable" seems not to fit his narrative practice, that he equates it to "allusive all[e]gorick History" shows that he extended its meaning: it incorporates fact and analogy, particular and general truths, along with ambivalence and paradox (115). This semantic extension recalls the prefatory declaration which refutes those who charge that *Robinson Crusoe* is a romance invented to impose on the world: "I *Robinson Crusoe* being at this Time in perfect and sound Mind and Memory, Thanks be to God therefore; do hereby declare, their Objection is an Invention scandalous in Design, and false in Fact; and do affirm that the Story, though Allegorical, is also Historical" (A2v).[30]

The miscellaneous closing chapters of *Serious Reflections* are experimental because they elucidate Defoe's narrative theory and parabolic practices with increasing recursiveness. These chapters illustrate Starr's important observation that Defoe imposes on his protagonists and himself dilemmas that arise from casuistry's need to explore rather than to reconcile multiple viewpoints. For Starr, casuistry renders narrative inconsistency irrelevant given the difficulty of articulating generalizations in the context of probability and uncertainty.[31] Indeed, the final chapters of *Serious Reflections* deal again with such topics as the relation between Christianity and civility and between faith and good works from contrary perspectives that renew Defoe's moral and religious satire and enable him to heighten his prophetic tones.

In its survey of world creeds, the fourth chapter presents relations between natural and revealed religion and between faith and good works contrarily. It begins with Crusoe's dialogue with a gentlewoman who wonders if there is a universal religion based on "the Light of Nature." Slow to reply, he ponders whether faith and worship originate from "one and the same natural Principle," deciding that spiritual and practical devotion are not equivalent (124). Crusoe then considers that, if pagans may win immortal life since they have not sinned against "saving Light," heathenism might be a blessing: to be born a Christian may not be so (127). Recoiling from the idea that Christianity condemns more people than paganism, he finds it impious to hold that, if savages are to be damned for lacking revelation, God damns those who cannot know Him. Such theological dilemmas open up satirical and narrative implications.[32] Unable to draw propositions from the polarities of revealed and natural religion, Crusoe turns to polemical ideas but must face up to recursive ironies. Judging the Barbary Moors' inhumanity, he says that revealed always displaces natural religion and that Christianity has a "*Civilizing* Influence," if it has no "*Saving*" one. Since Christianity operates "upon the Manners, the Morals, the Politics, and even the Tempers and Dispositions" of people, leading them to "true Methods of Living," revealed religion has secular benefits. Since Christianity teaches men "to live like Men, and act upon the Foundations of Clemency, Humanity, Love, and good Neighbourhood, suitable to the Nature and Dignity of God's Image, and to the Rules of Justice and Equity" (129), revealed religion yields more secular benefits than natural religion. He contends that the Romans were uncivilized despite their imperial achievements. But, if he dispraises natural light by contrasting heathen life to the secular refinement of Christians, his stance on pagans is unstable. Sympathy with them finds no real difference between cannibalism and the European refusal to give quarter in battle, when he calls how savages eat one another "a kind of martial Rage" rather than "a civil Practice" (132). Insistent that the cannibals he encountered were humane and easily civilized, Crusoe modifies his view that Christianity is inevitably civilizing. His defence of natural light arising from the cannibals' predisposition to sociability discomfits European civilization.

He similarly exploits natural religion when he castigates Christianity after decrying Chinese civilization. Decrying modish admiration of China, he calls that nation's theology a "Rhapsody of Moral Conclusions" (133), adding that its idolatry is less rational than that of Greece and Rome. China's religion renders its "State Maxims and Rules of Civil Government" futile, its people's "gross Ignorance in the Notion of a God, which is so extremely natural" denoting a "Nation unpolish'd, foolish, and weak, even next to Ideotism" (137). Its natural light is degraded by Confucianism, Crusoe affirming that the heathen have "fallen from the knowledge of the true God, which was once, as we have Reason to believe, diffused to all Mankind" (147). In granting heathens natural light, he treats it as congruent with revealed religion – as if the two might be equivalent. But this view highlights the "gross things" done by "Nations, who profess to have had the clear Light of Gospel Revelation": if heathens betray natural light, Christian nations more culpably betray divine revelation. By re-establishing distinctions between natural and revealed religion after having collapsed them, Crusoe also reverses himself by holding that Christianity is not inevitably civilizing. In prophetic anger, he denounces the contradictory behaviour of Christians more harshly than he does that of the Chinese: he laments that "preposterous Enthusiasms" and "gross Absurdities" cause Christians to behave barbarously and superstitiously "as if Religion divested us of Humanity" (147). Some "common receiv'd Customs of Christians" are so scandalous they "would be the Abhorrence of Heathens" (149). After disallowing natural light to China, he faults Christian betrayal of revelation as objectionable to that light. Maintaining that pagans once possessed natural religion, he heightens satire of Christians by suggesting that, besides having betrayed revelation, they lack natural light. Far from theologically reconciling natural and revealed religion, his satire gathers polemical energy from the polar process of contrasting and comparing secular and religious values.

Appalled by the doctrinal strife of Catholics, Protestants, Lutherans, and Huguenots, Crusoe argues that ecclesiastical sectarianism severs creed and conduct. His satire of sectarianism heightens the polar relations of good works and faith, rendering these tenets antithetical yet complementary. First, he dissociates creed and conduct: there is a "Want of a religious Practice, even where there are right Principles at Bottom, and where there is a Profession of the Orthodox Faith" (155). Faith guarantees good conduct in neither nations nor individuals. Second, he shows that faith without good works is as unacceptable as good works without faith. He attacks the conduct of the English because their tenets may be sound, but their conduct is overrefined and uncharitable: making the Bible their rule of faith, they overzealously dispute doctrines. As his satirical commentary unfolds, it increasingly unsettles theological disputes about faith and good works. Sectarian differences, far from being "*Essential, Doctrinal, and Fundamental*" (179), should be abandoned, allowing good works and faith to delimit one another. Since it cannot resolve theological contraries, such as relations between "eternal Decrees" that determine history and the "Efficacy of praying" that modifies creation, faith must be tempered by charity. The satire of sectarianism, if apparently favouring charitable conduct, implies the mutually informing contrariety of faith and good works.

This contrariety invites readers to see themselves under the aspect of divine omniscience: as theological contraries, faith and good works show that belief and conduct transpire ultimately in the realm of spirituality that defies human categories. Thus, the premise that "Negative Virtue is Positive Vice" (180), underlying Crusoe's sense that a good man can be bad, shapes reader response by insisting that our awareness relate itself to the divine mind. The negative Christian abides by the letter of the law but will not see himself in that context. This self-assured Pharisee belittles religion: he pulls off "his Hat to God Almighty now and then, and thank[s] him, that he has no Need of him." Pride is "the Opiat that doses his Soul even to the last Gasp," and

> it is ten thousand to one, but the Lethargic Dream shoots him thro' the Gulph at once, and he never opens his Eyes till he arrives in that Light, where all things are naked and open; where he sees too late, that he has been a Cheat to himself, and has been hurry'd by his own Pride in a Cloud of Negatives, into a State of positive Destruction, without Remedy. (182)

As we saw with regard to moral contraries in chapter 1, the "negative good Man" makes himself a victim of contradictions. He desires a good name yet shuns good works. "A good Name, is indeed a precious Ointment, and in some Cases is better than Life," but "it must be a good Name for good Deeds, or otherwise, a good Name upon a bad Life is a *painted Whore,* that has a gay Countenance upon a rotten, diseased, corrupted Carcass" (182).[33] Since the Pharisee covets the effects of the imperatives he belittles, he reduces himself to a lesson in fallibility and to an object of ironical wordplay. "He is no Drunkard, but is intoxicated with the Pride of his own Worth." Too proud to pray to God, he thinks nothing of abasing himself to win social respect; "he is a Man perfect in the Circumstances of Religion, and perfectly a Stranger to the essential Part of Religion" (185–6). His external notions of self and conduct ignore how living under the aspect of eternity should prevent him from justifying himself in his own eyes and from imagining he can win a good name in God's. His pride and slavish obedience to the letter of the law stem from refusing to see good works and faith reciprocally and from failing to subordinate selfhood to divine omniscience. He does not see that good works necessitate faith, that grace "rewards according to itself, not according to what we can do," and that fulfilment depends on "Sincerity of Repentance" (187). Trusting in natural light alone, the Pharisee will not grant its polar relation to revealed religion. By contrast, the Publican enjoys a better spiritual condition, his awareness of sin leading him to value faith and good works reciprocally: this positive Christian knows that, if good works are necessary to reputation, faith is essential to the self-knowledge that makes reputation significant. Through Crusoe's exposure of negative Christianity, Defoe heightens the mutually informing aspects of good works and faith: the imperative of good works chastens people with their imperfectibility but instils faithfulness in them. Theological polarities reveal why humans should have a contrary sense of identity: such polarities inform how individuals should address selfhood.

The prophetic stance on spiritual experience in the latter parts of *Serious Reflections* asks readers to look past the letter of the law and to consider how divine omniscience affects narrative sensibility by testing how Providence's impingements into daily life extend polar ideas about material reality and spiritual identity. Defoe's former correlations of secular and religious values are unstrained by contrast with his later exacerbation of theological dilemmas. The more he discusses spiritual experience, the more variable his viewpoint becomes: he accepts and transcends theological definitions with increasing volatility. His oscillating treatment of spiritual vision remains, however, crucial to understanding his narrative energies and dialectical presentation of self and mind.

Having told readers not to be wrapped up in religion, in chapter five he urges them to study the operations of Providence since they are too satisfied with "the general Knowledge of religious Principles, and the common Duties of a Christian Life" (204). Were they to train to open themselves to revelation, they would aid society as well as themselves. Were they to balance revealed knowledge and natural light, they would make the "strait Path easy and pleasant to themselves" and be "useful to others by the Way" (204). Defoe points up this balance by citing the Bible to prove that listening to the voice of Providence is fundamental: Proverbs 2:3–4 declares that religious knowledge is to be hunted like treasure. In citing Psalms 33:6 to show that "the whole Trinity" upholds the world, he insists that the voice of Providence is a proper spiritual quest since natural religion, as revealed in the Bible, "intimates the Necessity of a Providence guiding and governing the World" (207). He further discusses Providence as a rationalist, social commentator, preacher, and scholastic theologian as well as a prophet because multiple voices afford him imaginative scope in relishing challenging ways of interpreting it. On the one hand, Providence is "determin'd, and determines all other things for our Advantage" (209); on the other, "notwithstanding the Crimes of Men," it "is actively concern'd in no Evil" (210). The world is governed benignly, but men remain independent moral agents so that Providence cannot be said to determine crimes. Only because they have contradictory notions of natural and revealed religion do they blame Providence for what it cannot cause. That it informs "every Circumstance of Life" does not mean it determines individual moral choice (211). It imposes necessity upon events and causes but leaves the individual free to deserve rewards or punishments. This distinction between determinism and free will means that Providence must be reverenced without either supine passivity or enthusiasm and that, far from limiting moral agency, it obliges the prudent, according to Proverbs 22:3, to foresee and avoid evil. For Defoe, the theological contraries inherent in Providence fortify, rather than sap, identity.[34]

The literary value of Providence evolves from his discussion of its voice. In explaining how Providence makes itself known and interpretable, he employs modes of identity and communication that resist single-mindedness and adopt plural views of selfhood and reality.

Rejecting the allegation that its voice is indirect, he asserts that it could not be clearer: humans may obey its "secret Dictates, as far as Reason directs, without an over superstitious Regard to them, any more than a total Neglect" (213). Yet, its voice, if accessible to reason, is mysterious. Only within the context of an ineffable spiritual order can it be a matter of reasonable faith that Providence has "the supreme Direction" of personal as well as general affairs and that those who ignore its voice neglect the welfare of their souls. While he supports this paradox by referring to arguments from natural religion and to texts such as Matthew 10:30 which announce God's concern with the most minute things that befall men, he grants that not all natural events can be attributed to divine agency.[35] This being so, Christians must read the spiritual meaning of events through meditative habits. To listen to the voice of Providence, the individual's sense of theological polarities must lead to an interpretive ability that comes from continuous spiritual self-awareness: he must subject "his Mind to a constant Obedience to the Dictates" of Providence, give "an humble Preference to it in all his Conclusions," and wait "the Issues of it with a chearful Resignation" (215). Recognizing that particular providences are divine emanations that generate public and private meanings leads in turn to a sharper awareness of the dialectic that informs an individual's sense of reality.

Since Providence speaks in the historical record as well as to individual souls, particular providences include dates – the "Concurrence of Events" and "periodical Times" – because secular history is spiritually symbolic.[36] Because Providence speaks in polar terms, anniversaries in the Civil War and Glorious Revolution are not only items of public record but also signs obliging individuals to develop retrospective awareness concerning worldly rewards. Again, from a polar viewpoint, if "Eminent Deliverances in sudden Dangers" are a "just Call upon us to Repentance" (220), they do not exclude attention to secular reality:

> for as we are to trust Providence with our Estates, but to use at the same Time, all Diligence in our Callings, so we are to trust Providence with our Safety, but with our Eyes open to all its necessary Cautions, Warnings, and Instructions. (221)

The interconnectedness of private and public providential signs reveals that material and spiritual meanings are and are not controlled by humans, are and are not determined by God. From this complex stance, Defoe spurns as atheists those who either abandon their worldly concerns to Providence or feel they can ignore tokens of blessing and punishment. Rejecting the spirituality of mundane experience, they shun the contrary that the "Sufficiency of Gospel Revelation" proves the need to interpret all aspects of daily life in terms of God's ongoing revelations. Defoe emphasizes the need to view secular life in visionary terms by appealing equally to biblical and experiential evidence. Whereas Hebrews 2:1, Matthew 28:20, and Acts 10:11 show that God is concerned with "Conduct in the inferior Life" and that He manifests His concern in secular reality (225), listening to the voice of Providence improves with practice. It may, at first, be precariously subjective, but we can take "such Notice of the several Providences, that happen in the Course of our Lives, as by one Circumstance to learn how to behave in another" (227). This development of spiritual vision shows once more how and why Defoe uses polar aspects of life and cognition to delimit faith. That we cannot reconcile God's freedom to enter nature and history with the immutability of His wisdom or connect Providence's alteration of nature's course with His unchanging agency involves contraries that fruitfully defy intellectual systems. Since theology cannot explain why Providence has "a spontaneous Power of acting" (231), individuals may find in their limited intellect a source of faith. Providence is less the object of systematic study than a subject which, in endowing people with a "Sense of a future State" and getting them to detect spiritual meaning in secular reality, authenticates faith by both limiting and expanding human awareness (232). Thus, for Defoe,

> there is a manifest Difference between acknowledging the Being and Operations of Providence, and listning to its Voice, as many People acknowledge a God, that obey none of his Commands, and concern themselves in nothing of their Duty to him. (236)

Since listening to Providence ideally integrates psychological and spiritual identity, Defoe, as we shall see, incorporates the voice of Providence into his fiction because, in helping to embody the reciprocity of secular and religious ideas, it also validates his narrative dialectic.

The sixth chapter of *Serious Reflections*, in discussing a holy war against paganism, strikingly exemplifies how he derives narrative rules from religious dialectic. For, while his call for a holy war opposes paganism on political and biblical grounds, it attacks European sectarianism, too: talk of conquering paganism subserves the reform of Christianity. He begins by zealously citing the prophecy in the second chapter of Isaiah that "*the Knowledge of God shall cover the Earth, as the Waters cover the Sea*" (240). Next, he expounds three New Testament texts confirming Isaiah's view that the Messiah's kingdom shall be exalted above all nations.[37] Then, after surveying the world to see which nations are Christian and which pagan, he concludes that Christianity exists meaningfully only in Europe. He then proposes that Christian nations, rather than warring with one another, should vanquish paganism. By dominating the world, Christian princes would fulfil biblical prophecy, be agents of Providence, and compassionate men's souls. They would also reform their nations. Moderating his zeal, he refuses to idealize force: "the Business of Power, is to open the Way to the Gospel of Peace; the Servants of the King of the Earth are to fight, that the Servants of the King of Heaven may preach" (252). Force would merely destroy pagan rites.[38] Defoe distinguishes imposing creeds from preparing pagans for religion since force is inimical to the "Nature of Religion" (254). Further, were Christians to impose creeds by force, they would simply perpetuate sectarianism.

At this point, Defoe's militancy takes high polemical risks. In further justifying war, he claims that pagans, being governed by the devil, lack natural light and that Christians may effect the decrees of Providence. The first claim counters his former statements that pagans have natural light; the second suggests Providence can be advanced by humans. However, he upholds providential authority by arguing that the secular and religious realms conform to each other and that unprincipled wars may serve Providence. His example is the Roman invasion of Britain: the Romans did not conduct a just war, being simply interested in conquest,

> yet God was pleased to make this Violence be the kindest Thing that could have befallen the *British* Nation, since it brought in the Knowledge of God among the *Britains*, and was a Means of reducing a heathen and barbarous Nation to the Faith of Christ, and to embrace the Messias. (255)

Here he seems to be saying that, if man's worst intentions may serve Providence, his best ones, manifest in a holy war, must be acceptable to God. This presumptive argument heightens the sense that he aims to make readers both more and less sure about moral action. By arguing that, if Christians direct their hostilities at pagans, they will arrive at religious fundamentals and appreciate how much faith contributes to secular happiness, Defoe implicitly apologizes for his polemical hyperbole and recursive thinking. By insisting that Christians will become more tolerant and better governed by "higher Principles" in their relation with the non-Christian world, he once more implies that theological dialectic and rhetorical flexibility are complementary.

A Vision of the Angelick World sheds more light on the metaphysical substrate of Defoe's theory of fiction because it questions biblical examples of spiritual insight through its dialectic of natural and revealed religion, the resulting implications about cognition and imagination yielding powerful contraries about literary reality and narrative procedures. Rather than presenting a singular vision of the afterlife, *A Vision* seeks "to conceive justly" the converse between spirits and humans and to convey "Ideas of the invisible World" that "may not be confused and indigested." Defoe begins by insisting upon the limits which scripture itself imposes on interpretations of heaven and hell. He is not concerned about the "Locality of Bliss and Misery" because, since "we are to BE, we must have a *where*" and because scripture asserts simply that "*Judas* is gone to his Place" and that "*Dives* in Hell ... saw *Lazarus* in *Abraham*'s Bosom" (2).[39] In its vagueness and lack of details, scripture avoids making a "positive Declaration" of the "Company" in Heaven and Hell. Indeed, its narratives of important scenes are questionable because non-specific. This is the case with the account of the disciples' fright at seeing Christ walk on the water: "One would have thought such Men as they, who had the Vision of God *manifest in the Flesh*, should not have been so much surpriz'd."[40] Far from a prayer, their cry to God represents superstitious distrust of Him; it was either an appeal to man for help against the devil or an appeal to the devil himself. Their conduct suggests that "to see a Spirit, seems to be an Allusion, not an Expression to be us'd literally, a Spirit being not visible by the Organ of human Sight" (3). The stories of Christ's appearance to the two disciples on the way to Emmaus and of the request of the mother of Zebedee's children to Christ to let them sit on his right and left hand in Heaven are similarly questionable because of their simplistic and misplaced sense of spirit.[41] These stories provoke Defoe to turn to other biblical accounts in order to insist that spiritual essence is materially imperceptible but conceptually true and that it is determinable by rational, figurative, and existential experience. Thus, he finds proof of God's converse with man through the medium of spirits in the episode of the Witch of Endor who had a familiar spirit which she called up as an apparition of Samuel to preach righteousness to Saul.[42] Defoe reinforces his criticism of simplistic notions of spirituality by making Crusoe admit that he suffered from a "Hypochondriack Delusion" which made him see spirits where there were none (6). About the goat dying in the cave he confesses that he "felt Apparitions, as plainly and distinctly as ever I felt or saw any real Substance in my Life" (7). After so depicting Crusoe's diseased imagination, Defoe reasserts certainty about spiritual converse:

> we are all able to bring Evidence of the Existence of the Devil from our own Frailties, as we are to bring Evidence of the Existence of God from the Faculties of our Souls, and from the Contexture of our Bodies. (12)

Bodily awareness and introspection into the structure of our souls are a form of natural religion that validates extrasensory intuitions and generates proof of the communicative presence of the devil and God. Even evil deeds validate spiritual presence, for "Harmony between the Inclination" and the "Occasion" when humans sin indicates the informing reality of the evil spirit (13).

Yet Defoe limits the devil's informing presence in order to sustain his oblique explication of spiritual converse. Thus, he argues that the devil's agency is as narrow as it is wide. Tacitly citing James 1:14, "*A Man is tempted when he is drawn away of his own Lusts, and enticed,*" Defoe insists that, while the devil may cunningly match "alluring Objects to the allurable Dispositions" (13), he does not cause moral guilt. If seduced by the devil, humans still effect their own seduction! By holding that humans cannot blame the devil for their sins, he distinguishes spiritual vision from superstition and equates the latter with moral rationalization.

Defoe's contrary perspectives on revealed and natural religion are remarkable when he next argues that spiritual converse involves biblical communication via dreams since the "Converse of Spirits" can never simply be the object of rational analysis (14). In the context of holding spiritual reality to be less the object of philosophical calculation than of religious sensibility, he views God's warning to Joseph to go to Egypt as confirmation that dreams are a spiritual medium.[43] After citing other biblical stories proving that God used dreams through the "Ministry of Spirits," Defoe insists that this spiritual transmission still obtains:

> when any Notice for Good, or Warning against Evil, is given us in a Dream, I think 'tis no Arrogance at all for us to say, the Angel of the Lord appear'd to us in a Dream. (16)

He appropriates biblical words to stress the naturalness of spiritual converse since the New Testament dispensation did not displace the

Old Testament's model of God's relation to mankind. By appealing to readers' retrospection about the prescience of dreams, he is adamant that natural religion is a matter of existential experience:

> If I may speak my own Experience, I must take leave to say, That I never had any capital Mischief befel me in my Life, but I have had Notice of it by a Dream; and if I had not been that thoughtless unbelieving Creature, which I now would caution other People against, I might have taken many a Warning, and avoided many of the Evils that I afterwards fell into, merely by a total obstinate Neglect of those Dreams. (17)

These deferential, conditional, yet assertive and categorical tones mediate the polarities of spiritual converse: Crusoe's repeated failures to act on dreams prove that they operate as spiritual converse. Recursive ironies explain why this converse is natural if not rational and scriptural if not natural. Such recursiveness, being essential to the argument that dreams are not simply the devil's devices but convey the voice of Providence, justifies the view that "the Consummation of the typical Law" did not displace prior revelation and that the Holy Spirit does not render dreams redundant. Defoe's dialectic of natural and revealed religion holds that the New Testament does not promote a single model of spiritual reality: St Paul's conversion by Ananias and St Peter's meeting with Cornelius, the devout centurion, constitute "eminent Instances of God's giving Notice of his Pleasure to Men, by the Interposition or Medium of a Dream" (18).[44] Both stories show that God has employed dreams as revelations "since the Expiration of the *Levitical* Dispensation, and since the Mission of the Holy Ghost" (19). These biblical exegeses yield narrative implications that challenge systematic theology.

Defoe's dialectical treatment of spiritual converse delivers important points about vision and imagination. Undogmatic about what experiencing the invisible world means, he recognizes that people open to spiritual converse must have imaginations "addicted to realizing the Things" they perceive (24). Yet, if individual perceptual disposition is as instrumental to spiritual converse as are superior agents, this disposition is not unproblematic because the imagination, when the soul is more than "ordinarily agitated," may produce "Lunacy and Distraction." Only when the mind is strong enough to digest the infinite ideas of the "extended Fancy" is the soul

> capable to act strangely upon the Invisibles in Nature, and upon Futurity, Reallizing every Thing to itself in such a lively Manner, that what it thus

> thinks of, it really sees, speaks to, hears, converses with, etc., as livelily, as if the Substance was really before his Face. (25–6)

Here Defoe's cognitive psychology bases reality on the reciprocity of imagination and spiritual experience. Whereas he denounced hermetic societies for concentrating on things spiritual, he now holds it desirable for people to be "continually elevated above the very Thoughts of human Things" (27). The visionary state is important less for percepts than for transcendence: detaching himself from worldly temptation, the seer realizes the emptiness of human wisdom. Creation is not opened up by rational approaches to matter: the seer recognizes "the Emptiness of our modern Notions, that the Planets [are] habitable Worlds" (29). By decrying the plurality of worlds, Defoe subordinates rational optimism to the uniqueness of creation.

To Defoe, ineffable vision is apprehensible only if the individual honours material reality by exercising the reciprocity of natural and biblical revelation through spiritual imagination. While Crusoe saw armies of good and evil spirits hurrying about the invisible world, he disclaims seeing "into any Part of the World of Light" (32), since the soul's highest raptures are "bounded by the eternal Decree of Heaven." With Luke 19:42 in mind, he insists that heavenly visions are hidden from conception: it is sinful to form ideas of Heaven and Hell "other than as the Scripture has described them" (45). Hence, he does not equate vision with personal growth: images of the angelic world neither change him nor produce knowledge of futurity. But they do lead to ontological insights. Thus, the contrary treatment of spiritual converse upholds the polar tenet that natural light transcends materialism as long as it respects biblical revelation.

Defoe's reluctance to specify the content of visions and to systematize spiritual converse heightens the complementarity of secular and theological values by which he advances his theories of spiritual identity and narrative realism. He affirms that, while "*strong Impulses* of the Mind" (47) are "certain Intelligence of Things unseen, because they are given by Persons unseen," they are "directed for the Advantage of Life" (52): spiritual insight yields implications for practical living; it glimpses terrestrial, not celestial, futures. Yet, he treats the self-awareness produced by that insight as religious. This converse is no substitute for grace and divine revelation, but, in aiding daily life, it sustains doctrinal verities: listening to spirits certifies immortality and guarantees the favourable disposition of Providence towards mankind. It gives existential proof of the individual's spiritual identity and defies atheism. Since it is one of the "many undeniable Testimonies in the Breasts of every rational Being to prove his Existence" (63), this converse complements revealed religion and orthodox theology. Its narrative relevance is exemplified by the story of atheistic students that closes *A Vision*. One student converts after hearing voices telling him to repent and believe. Although the voices belong to a pious old man and a zealous fellow student and not to spirits, Defoe explains that they are "directed from Heaven," if "not immediately spoken from thence" (83). But he subordinates this explanation to his claim that Providence superintends such coincidences, its superintendency in no way degraded by the mediation of fallible human agents. Circumstances, being instruments of Providence, reveal the conformability of natural and revealed religion. Defoe ends his story of the students by doing what he does throughout his fiction: he claims that secular facts are best read by spiritual contemplation since the former are most meaningful in the context of the latter.

*****

The two poets to whom Defoe alludes in *Serious Reflections* to clarify his dialectical stance on narrative and theology are the Earl of Rochester and Milton, poets whom over his long career he represented similarly and contrarily. In an essay in the *Review* that treats music allegorically by developing synaesthetic senses of harmony, he places these poets among the greatest of writers when he declares that music affects "the Eye, and the contemplative part of the Soul, as well as the Ear" because

> there is Musick in every beautiful Building, every delicious prospect, every fair Object; All the regulated Life of a just and pious Man is Musick in the Eye of the Observer; the Eloquence of the Orator, the Lines of the Poet make Musick in the Soul; who can read *Virgil, Horace, Ovid, Milton, Waller* or *Rochester,* without touching the Strings of his Soul, and finding Unison of the most charming Influence there? The beauteous Works of Providence are all Musick to the observing Mind; when we view the Heaven, the Work of his Hands, the Moon and the Stars which he has made, what Musick is there, is the Contemplation.[45]

Milton and Rochester's poetry like a bow touches the strings of readers' souls, the resulting music being spiritual meditation. Although allusions to the poets in *Serious Reflections* usually present them as positive archetypal figures, Defoe, as we shall see, enjoyed making them out to be heterodox icons in other texts.

The first allusion to Rochester is to line 158 of *A Satyr against Reason and Mankind*: "For all men would be cowards if they durst."[46] This line illustrates Defoe's view that it is "false Bravery" for a man to face a cannon rather than to confess his sins: "all Shame is Cowardice, as an eminent Poet tells us, That all Courage is Fear, the bravest Spirit is the best qualify'd for a Penitent" (28). Here Defoe transforms Rochester's materialist denigration of metaphysics into an apology for spiritual heroism. Later conceding that Rochester "turn'd all Matters of Faith into Ridicule, burlesqu'd upon Religion it self, and made Ballads and Songs on the Bible" (100), Defoe is comfortable citing the poet since he recanted his "Infernal learning" on his "Death Bed" (99–100).[47] The second positive allusion to Rochester in chapter four of *Serious Reflections* is to lines 127–8 of *A Satyr*, the poem's Hobbesian stance stressing human degeneracy and moral self-destructiveness: in contrast to the mutual respect of animals of the same kind for one another: "Man for baser Ends, such as Avarice, Envy, Revenge, and the like; devours his own Species, nay, his own Flesh and Blood, as my Lord Rochester very well expresses it" (122).[48] The hypothetical trenchancy of the poem's third and fourth lines in which Rochester imagines being incarnated in an animal rather than human body – "*A spirit free to chuse for their own share / What Case of Flesh and Blood they please to wear*" – is later appropriated by Defoe's spiritual perspective in *A Vision*, the foundation of its anti-materialism being that "Matter cannot act upon immaterial Things" (60).[49] Thus, Defoe cites Rochester to fortify the claim that there is converse "between Spirits uncased or unembody'd, and Souls of Men embody'd or cased up in Flesh and Blood, as we all are on this side Death" (*Vision* 14). The poet's reductivism is again later made to accentuate contrarily Defoe's emphasis on the reality but ineffability of that converse: "the Restraint of our Souls in the Case of Flesh and Blood we now wear not admitting it, and not being able to familiarize those Things to us; Man being by no Means, in his encorporated State, qualified for an open and easy Conversation with unembodied Spirit" (*Vision* 42).

The tenet that spiritual converse is real yet beyond rational verification also lies behind Defoe's two allusions to Milton in *A Vision*, these allusions ostensibly concerning the metaphysical problem of how evil entered the world. After wondering whether Milton is right to attribute envy of mankind to Satan or whether Providence appointed the devil to be a "continual Disturber for divine Ends," Defoe says that the matter is "to us unknown" and unknowable, such "Secrets" being lodged "much higher, than Imagination" can go (32). Yet, in questioning the "Height" to which imagination carried the poet when he entered the "Abyss of Satan's Empire" and formed the "Palace of *Pandemonium,*" he accepts Milton's notion of spiritual temptation since it defies empirical models of cognition:

> who forms Ideas in the Mind of Man? Who presents beautiful or terrible Figures to his Fancy, when his Eyes are clos'd in Sleep? Who, but these insinuating Devils. (*Vision* 40)

Here Milton helps Defoe to resist Lockean epistemology and to promote the mind's proclivity for both imaginative and spiritual experience.

If we look further into how Defoe exploits the works and reputations of the two poets in allusions, we see that not only does he treat them as polar types but he also exploits them as individuals whose polar attributes enhance his literary identity: from this point of view Rochester is a vice figure whose atheism serves Defoe's religious dialectic, and Milton is a practitioner of the religious sublime whose heresies expose false ideas of imagination and spirituality.[50] In the early *Reformation of Manners: A Satyr* published in 1702, Defoe depicts them as polar opposites. He calls Rochester "matchless" for leading "one long Debauch of Thirteen Year" but reports that he has forty times more readers than Milton. Linking Rochester to "*the Lewd,*" he associates the less popular Milton with "*the Sublime.*" Contrarily, in the late *The Compleat English Gentleman,* he seriously calls Rochester "great" and somewhat ironically describes Milton as "sublime."[51] In *Jure Divino,* Defoe declares with pointed ambivalence that "In Wit and Crime the late Lord Rochester was hardly ever outdone by one Man in the World." Then he goes on to mythologize the poet's duality:

> The Image of Pan too admirably suits the late Lord *Rochester;* Pan was Painted, half Man, half Goat; his upper Parts the Man, and his lower Part the Beast: Nothing can suit the Character better; he had a head fill'd with the refined'st Wit, but the Vices of his other Part were Brutal and Intollerable justly suited to the representation of a Goat, and abhor'd by all Good Men.[52]

Yet, what enabled Defoe to adopt Rochester's identity was the poet's rhetorically demonstrative self-consciousness that the *Review* often exploits and imitates. Thus, Defoe discountenances a rival journalist by insisting he ought "to joyn my Lord *Rochester*'s Confessions to his Penitential, – *I am a Rascal, that thou knowest*!."[53] He chides another politician by redirecting the depiction of the hound, Jowler, in *A Satyr* and its invective against Sir Thomas Meres, praising the poet's "powerful Way of Reasoning" even as he facetiously calls Rochester "That Dog in a Doublet."[54] The poet helps Defoe clarify his ideological position as one who wants the Church of England to continue to *"hold the reins of Government"* even as he begs it to *"extend her Charity"* to those like him who *"cannot Conform."* To those "Warm Gentlemen" who treat non-conformists "as Enemies" and "whom no Argument will reach, no Courtesie oblige, who will Damn the Author and His Work, in spight of Argument, Sence, or Manners," he directs Rochester's verbal defiance of critics of his poetry: *"I count your censure Fame."*[55] Unable to uphold the occasional conformity of Dissenters, he takes to himself Rochester's definition of "a Plain Dealer" who because he speaks "home and Impartially" inevitably purchases the curse of both sides.[56] As he says elsewhere in the *Review*, again citing A Satyr, "I never expect, but that according to Rochester, the *Turn-Rounds* will all agree to call me *Turn-Round*."[57] In the *Review* then, as in many other texts, Defoe identifies his experience as a beleaguered and misunderstood writer with the notorious authorship of Rochester, in the process justifying his conversion of a wicked figure into a positive icon.

The process by which he celebrates and appropriates Milton's expressiveness even as he charges him with abusing poetic licence and orthodox theology, while it appears to reverse the stance by which he blames and praises Rochester, nonetheless reveals much about the narrative dialectic through which Defoe upholds spiritual values. There are extrinsic reasons why he was as critical of Milton as of Rochester.[58] Defoe would have known that Toland, the radical deist, besides writing Milton's biography because he shared the poet's republicanism, joined the secret society that Milton founded to memorialize the regicide of Charles I.[59] Defoe gave Sidney pride of place in *Jure Divino* because the latter's republicanism spurned Milton's support of regicide.[60] Although influenced by the commonwealth principles of Charles Morton, headmaster of Stoke Newington Academy, when looking back at the manuscripts of his school exercises in politics Defoe claimed nothing was taught or encouraged "that was Antimonarchical, or Destructive to the Government, or Constitution of *England*."[61] As Frank Bastian says, "much of Defoe's intellectual development was independent of the formal instruction provided by Morton's

Academy."[62] His contrarian explication of faith and good works and arguments for the reciprocity of secular and religious values in *Serious Reflections* suggest why Defoe did not share Milton's disenchantment with politics which, according to N.H. Keeble, is manifest in Christ's defiance of Satan's expediency in Book II of *Paradise Regained*.[63] Whereas Milton transferred hopes for the "Good Old Cause" into a concern for salvation based on individual moral psychology, Defoe not only constantly upheld arguments for a mixed constitution but increasingly argued for the necessary constitutional role of the crown. While not spurning Milton's concern with moral degeneracy, he upheld the role of monarchs as moral exemplars, which is why he depicts pirates contrarily and excoriates them for seeing themselves as kings in their outlawry. Avery's "new Colony" collapses because his reputation as "King of Madagascar" is built on unfounded military strength and because he hypocritically sustains an egalitarian republic, being secretly intent on abandoning his fellow pirates and gaining reintegration into European society. Captain Misson, the utopian founder of Libertalia, may be "a perfect Deist" who thinks "Miracles, both in the New and Old Testament, inconsistent with Reason" and who sees no difference between ecclesiastical states and "secular Principalities," but he fills his head with patriarchal notions about every father being "the Prince and Monarch of his Family" and about reigning as "Sovereign of the Southern Seas." His regal absolutism renders him subject to contingency when the natives of Madagascar decimate his kingdom.[64]

Defoe's intrinsic opposition to Milton is explicable in terms of the latter's radical evasion of scriptural authority. While deeply appreciating the poet's expressive powers, he depreciates his myth making. Milton's verbal expressiveness appeals to Defoe's sense of cognitive and moral development and of spiritual identity. When in *Mere Nature Delineated* he argues that Peter the Wild Boy's insensibility to the world proves he is not fully human, Defoe alludes to lines 48–55 of Book III of *Paradise Lost* in which the blind Milton prays for "celestial Light" to shine in him so that he may tell of things invisible to mortal sight:

> Nature seems to be to *him*, like a fine Picture to a blind Man, ONE UNIVERSAL BLANK, as Mr. *Milton* very beautifully expresses it; he sees the Surface of it, but seems to receive no Impression from it of one Kind, or of another: He looks on the infinite Variety, with a kind of equal Unconcernedness, as if every Object were alike, or that he knew not how to distinguish between Good or Evil, Pleasant or Unpleasant.[65]

Here Defoe contrarily transposes Milton's moving prayer for inspiration into an image of the nadir of insensibility: the wild boy neither receives impressions from things nor experiences pleasure or pain. Another example of his admiration of Milton's verbal power germane to the polar exploration of the natural light of peoples unreached by Christianity examined earlier in this chapter is the passage, including the phrase "Naked Majesty," from Book IV of *Paradise Lost* in *Conjugal Lewdness*. However, after lauding Milton's account of the prelapsarian innocence of Adam and Eve in the Garden of Eden to argue that primitive virtue exists "to this Day in the untaught Savages in many Parts of the now known World," Defoe rejects "Pretences for going naked" in Britain that were practised by radicals during the Civil War. To Defoe, these pretences are

> a meer Chimera, an Enthusiastick Dream, seldom attempted but by a Sect of Madmen, worse than Lunatick, who, heated with a *religious Phrenzy*, (the worst of all Possessions) pretend to Nakedness as the Effect of their Innocence, at the same Time making it a Skreen to all Manner of Lewdness and Debauchery.[66]

These words match what Keeble refers to as the desuetude of nakedness as a spiritual sign: opposing millenarian radicalism, Defoe upholds the orthodox view that theological primitivism is sexually hypocritical. If he distinguishes here between Milton and sectarianism, his contrarian outlook does not always do so. Later in *Conjugal Lewdness*, he applauds Milton's account of ideal married love but rejects his promotion of divorce.[67] To Defoe, marriage is a sacred, not a social, contract: he refutes Milton's view that marriage may be dissolved on the basis of incompatibility.

His extensive focus on Milton's unorthodoxy clarifies how Defoe bases literary theory on theology and biblical hermeneutics, as evident in his contrary stances on Milton's presentation of evil entering creation. In Book VII of *Jure Divino*, he applauds Milton's account of Satan as the originator of sin and seducer of Eve in *Paradise Lost* Book III, calling it "very admirable." In the same book of *Jure Divino*, "*Milton's Pandemonium*" is said to result from "the deepest laid Thought" that has "ever appear'd in print"; the poet is "so Masterly a Genius" that his expression of "Original Crime" is unsurpassed in the English language.[68] But in *The Political History of the Devil*, "*Milton's Pandemonium*, tho' an excellent dramatick performance" is called "a meer trifling sing-song business, beneath the dignity of *Chevy-Chase*." The "fine spun thought" of having Satan refuse the Messiah's authority and turn rebel from thwarted expectations of being chief general of the heavenly forces is "strain'd too far." Ignoring that the Son of God had no power over heaven and earth until after the Resurrection, Milton forgets that Satan's motives for rebellion are beyond comprehension. If metamorphosing Satan and his angels into monsters requires the "human fancy" to "draw pictures," invention motivating "all the beauteous Images and sublime expressions in Mr. *Milton*'s majestick Poem," his poetic licence should not have trivialized the ineffable and abused biblical theology. Defoe challenges the presentation of Satan as "sovereign elevated Spirit and Monarch of Hell"; Satan could not have been affronted by the creation of the Son of God in Heaven because God did not create the Son before Satan fell and before He created the world. Milton's narrative ascription degrades the Incarnation and the Resurrection. That Milton represents Satan "in the person of his Image and Creature man" is another blasphemous abuse of poetic licence.[69]

Defoe's belief that rhetoric should serve rather than oppose theology intensifies his attack on Milton's poetic licence: the poet's imaginative excesses are betrayed by wordiness and hyperbole. His "Towring Fancy" exceeds that of "*Ovid* in his *Metamorphosis*" since he pretends to compliment God "with a flux of lofty words, and great sounds." Milton's rhetorical indecorum is further manifest in his turning the Devil into "a very fine story" and Jesus Christ into a "*je ne scay Quoi*," this aesthetic catch-all Defoe's synonym for nonsense and a reminder of how in *Serious Reflections* he scorns deists who turn the Bible into "a good History" and Christ's life into "a meer Novel" (101).[70] When he points out that in "one line" the poet has Christ "riding on a Cherub, and in another sitting on a Throne, both in the very same moment of action," temporal theology and narrative plausibility equally move him to fault Milton. They oblige him to add that Milton has Christ address his saints in Heaven "when 'tis evident he had none there; for we all know Man was not created till a long while after; and no body can be so dull as to say the Angels may be called Saints, without the greatest absurdity in nature." The narrative amplification that presents Christ putting his saints "in two several Bands, and of differeing Persons and Species" is also unjustifiable and redundant. This fault is sustained when Milton has Christ draw up his army in warlike order, with the angels and saints forming distinct legions as if the one were infantry and the other cavalry, only to announce that they will not have to fight because He alone will engage the rebels. The amplification undoes itself and overlooks that "there were no Saints at all in *Heaven* or *Earth* at that time; GOD and his *Angels* fill'd up the place; and till some of the *Angels* fell, and Men were created, had liv'd, and were dead, there could have been no *Saints* there." In facetious retaliation, Defoe insists that "Saint *Abel* was certainly the *Proto-Saint* of all that ever were seen in *Heaven*, as well as the Proto-martyr of all that have been upon *Earth*."[71]

Another Milton "Blunder" was to give Hell a fixed location and "a being before the Fall of the Angels" and to present it "opening its mouth to receive them." This inexcusable poetic licence goes beyond illustration in pretending to divine knowledge. While "Poesie may form Stories, as Idea and Fancy may furnish Materials, yet Poesy must not break in upon Chronology, and make things which in time were to exist, act before they existed." Granting Milton the freedom to create fanciful settings, "to make Hills and Dales, flowry Meadows and Plains (and the like) in Heaven; and places of Retreat and Contemplation in *Hell*," Defoe also concedes his right to present the "Absurdities" of the "*Angels* a dancing in *Heaven*" and "the *Devils* a singing in Hell." But he disallows the making "their Musick in *Hell* to be harmonious and charming," this imagery being "incongruous, and indeed shocking to Nature." Since Milton's images, far from respecting ineffable essences, are confused, they are properly "disallow'd by all the Criticks of what tribe or species soever in the world." To Defoe, Milton's poetic licence is both distracting and evasive; it will not pose fundamental if unanswerable questions. It fails to ask how Satan "came to fall, and how Sin came into Heaven." It will not question how "the spotless seraphic Nature" came to "receive infection" and how this contagion spread. Variously phrasing the issue of the origin of evil thus, Defoe states that Milton "is in the dark about it, and so we are all; and the most that can be said, is, that we know the fact is so, but nothing of the nature or reason of it." Narrative continuity obliged Milton to assign "some cause or original of the *Devil*'s Rebellion," but, while his design is "well laid," it lacks "two Trifles call'd *Truth* and *History*." Its decoration may be "noble and great" and its invention unobjectionable, but "the Plot is wrong laid," being "contradicted by the Scripture account." According to the Bible, Christ was announced in heaven "from Eternity," not after the Fall of the Angels. But, since Milton's heterodoxy places Christ's annunciation in heaven rather than from eternity, it "lays an avow'd foundation for the corrupt Doctrine of *Arius*, which says, there was a time when Christ *was not* the Son of God."[72]

Defoe tolerates Milton's story of the Archangel's formation of a party of rebel angels for two reasons: scripture says that God expelled them from his holy habitation; and, since humans do "merry" things in the devils' name, they manifest the latter's influence on daily life. What he will not tolerate is Milton's claim that the devils are locked up in Hell with the key kept in Heaven. This claim is absurd because the scriptures declare that the devils will be eternally confined in the future when Satan "shall be *reserved in chains of darkness*." For Milton to propose that Hell is "a *local* Confinement" from which Satan escapes by knocking off his fetters is a low idea. The Book of Job confirms that the devil is abroad: when Satan presents himself among Job's neighbours, God's question as to where he had come from implies that the devil is a "prisoner at large."[73] Thus, the devils exist in a "State of Liberty to act." Further evidence that Milton was no visionary comes from the fact that he explains nothing about how Satan knew that mankind had been created and how he sought out Adam and Eve, these topics remaining a "Matter of just Speculation." Indeed, the poet does well not to speculate about how Satan learns that "the Almighty Creator had form'd a new and glorious Work." But Defoe speculates to uphold his metaphysic of hell: perhaps "the *Devil* having, *as I have said,* a Liberty to range over the whole Void or Abyss, which we want as well a Name for, as indeed Powers to conceive of; might have discovered that the Almighty Creator had form'd a new and glorious Work." To Defoe, Milton does better in imagining that Satan takes on the shape of a toad to whisper seduction to the sleeping Eve, because dreams may be induced in sleepers by whispering to them. This psychological reality which applies to sleeping and waking imaginations means that the poet is not indulging in licence when he depicts the devil as a powerful toad, for Satan has the "same Facility" to "prompt our Thoughts, whether sleeping or waking" since to "dream, is nothing else but to think sleeping." Facetiously turning this apology for Milton against empirical philosophers, Defoe reminds readers that "we have abundance of deep-headed Gentlemen among us, who give us ample Testimony that they dream waking."[74]

*****

As the explication of *Serious Reflections* and the analysis of allusions to Rochester and Milton show, Defoe applied polar perspectives equally to issues of theology and the imagination partly because he was acutely troubled by ecclesiastical conflicts and literary pretensions while, at the same time, remaining hopeful about the social importance of biblical and spiritual sensibilities. Accepting that religious writing dominated the book trade, he believed that biblical discourse should be a substrate of all genres within the literary system.[75] He was content to locate his theory of fiction within this context. For him, literary history could not be only secular because textual criticism derives from biblical hermeneutics. Yet Defoe the contrarian challenged as well as upheld this context, as readers are about to see in the next chapter's study of his biblical allusions, which are as experimental as they are traditional, as realistic and graphic as they are symbolic and emblematic. I reserve for the final chapter a deeper analysis of the impact of his psychological and cognitive ideas upon his narrative theory, only hinting here how analogy is crucial to this theory.[76] Near the end of *A Vision*, he states:

> It is then our Felicity, that the Converse of Spirits, and the Visions of Futurity, are silent, emblematick, and done by Hints, Dreams, and Impulses, and not by clear Vision and open Discovery. (43)

This emphasis on oblique spiritual learning harmonizes with the statement in the preface to *Serious Reflections* that so much appealed to Camus: "'tis as reasonable to represent … any Thing that really exists, by that which exists not" ([A5v]). It also matches his criticism of Islam when he decries the Koran for deriving paradise from ideas of sensation, that is, by making "only a heaven of Sense" (*Vision* 45). His view of the obliqueness of spiritual vision conforms to the following claim about how experiential analogies are limited only if we take his polarity thinking seriously:

> We can Form no Idea of any Thing that we know not and have not seen, but in the Form of something that we have seen. How then can we form an Idea of God or Heaven, in any Form but of something which we have seen or Known? By what Image in the Mind can we judge of Spirits? By what Idea conceive of eternal Glory? Let us cease to Imagin concerning it, 'tis impossible to attain, 'tis criminal to attempt it. (*Vision* 46)

This admonition is less opposed to empiricism than concerned to emphasize its restrictive effect on imagination. However, as the next chapter shows, Defoe's biblical allusions resist the limits he imposed on the literary imagination and spiritual vision by exploiting poetic licence.

Chapter Four

Biblical Allusions as Narrative Resources

Son. Dare any one, after all this, say, that it is improperly, and in a Metaphor, that Jesus Christ is called *The Son of God*, and that there is no essential Difference in the thing as ascrib'd to him, or as it is ascrib'd to other Creatures?

Daugh. Or that he is called a Son in no other Sense, than as the same Title is given to Angels, to Kings, and to Magistrates?

Fa. The Difference lies here, just as it is between the Extremes of Contraries; one least, t'other greatest; one a Son from Eternity, the other a Son of Two or Three Days; or, as is between the Creator and the Creature; one a Son of God, worshipp'd and ador'd as God, by Angels and Men, the other a Son of God, who, under the glorious Title, or rather under the Shadow of it, contains all the Impotence, Weakness, and Infirmities inseparable from a Creature.[1]

The explication of *Serious Reflections* in the previous chapter has shown that Defoe employs several voices and polar stances in order to validate storytelling and to root narrative's purposive functions in the Bible and Christian doctrines. Oral and published fictions mediate for him dialectical tensions between religious and secular values, between spiritual and material circumstances. Speaking as prophet, preacher, and explicator, he challenges standard interpretations of texts and understandings of the imaginative processes involved in reading, seeing the scriptures and church doctrines as dynamic and problematic rather than dogmatically stable. In arguing with himself and adopting polar stances on spiritual vision, he blurs the discursive boundaries between himself and Crusoe, his persona, to make his authorship self-effacing and hard to follow. In the same way that he denies ultimate literary authority to Rochester and Milton, the two poets whom he most often cites, his rhetorical contraries and polar thinking render his personal testimony provocative rather than simply authoritarian. His biblical allusions in *Serious Reflections* compound his textual multivalency; sometimes their sources are provided, sometimes not; sometimes they are singular, sometimes they are typologically joined. Given his interest in cognitive psychology and in the ambivalent operations of spiritual insight, sometimes they are conflated with the dictates of natural law, and sometimes they defy those dictates. The present chapter further probes why the Bible is foundational for Defoe and why he both respects it literally yet adapts allusions by rewording them and taking them out of context. For Defoe, the Bible is both an exceptional text and an accessible medium of revelations; if its words are to be read literally, they are also to be taken anagogically because they signify immanence and transcendence. Far from treating the Bible only single-mindedly, Defoe cites it plurally and inventively to defy atheism and to unsettle unorthodox creeds.

In her brilliant responsiveness to Defoe's "radical ambivalence," Sandra Sherman finds in his texts a "new kind of narrativity" explicable in terms of his participation in a print culture that was increasingly reliant on financial credit and on a speculative, precarious sense of the future. From the stance of historicist materialism, Sherman argues that "Defoe is a phenomenon of discourse, not an authorizing will located outside and prior to language."[2] Necessarily, she sets aside the metaphysical and theological sensibility with which Defoe theorizes the harmony of material and spiritual values, not heeding what Christopher Hill sees as the centrality of the Bible to "all spheres of intellectual life" in the seventeenth century.[3] Since the Bible continued to be embraced by radicals, it menaced ecclesiastical orthodoxies, Hill claiming that all "heresy originates from the Bible, because the Bible itself is a compilation, a compromise." Conscious of both the repressive and enthusiastic abuses of the Bible, Defoe, as we shall see, treated it "as the ultimate authority on economics and politics no less than on religion and morals."[4] Unsurprisingly given his habitual contrarianism, he regarded the Bible as the master text because, among other things, it narrates the fallibility of the disciples and explicates christology by means of paradox.

The epigraph at the head of this chapter represents the rhetorical climax of a discourse about the inapplicability of metaphor to Jesus of Nazareth in *A New Family Instructor*. Christ is beyond metaphor because He is the ultimate and most perfect contrary: He is the eternal and the historical son; the omnipotent creator and the creature who stands in for humanity's impotence. His divinity comprehends this theological dialectic because the propriety of the word "son" as applied to Him depends on anagogical thinking that transcends polysemy or allegory. The semantic integrity of "son" when Christ is its referent is unique, his deity incomparable with other heavenly and earthly powers – with angels, kings, and magistrates. Defoe often attacks the rational theology of Deism, Socinianism, and Unitarianism because, by variously denying this transcendence, those ideologies belittle the anagogical significance of *"the Son of God."*[5] That is, they ignore the absolute idealism in the theological contraries of that phrase. Christ is the Son of God because He is the eternal cynosure of creation, the only creature that images God's divinity as it enters history, and the sole being with the capacity to stand in for humanity. Hence, the conversation in *A New Family Instructor* elaborates "how This *Son of* GOD is understood in the New Testament, and how he is distinguish'd from those that are called Sons of God in Allegory and Metaphor." With John 10:38 in mind, the father explicates how Christ speaks of "the incorporate Union between the Father and himself" when He says "The Father is in *me,* and I *in him.*" The father insists that "to be in God, is an Expression no Man can assume; nothing can be so but what is Divine":

> To be *in God,* is to *be God;* whatsoever is *in God, is God.* In him there's no Accident, no Quality; but whatsoever is *in him,* is of his Essence, and of his Substance. *This Son* therefore being in the Father, is really, and essentially, and substantially GOD, as the Father is, and must be so essentially.

This explication of Christ's divinity is important for several reasons, not the least of which is that His absolute contrariness makes Him the foundation of typology. Thus, the father, alluding to Christ's claim in John 10:28 that He gives "eternal Life" to mankind, asks rhetorically:

> Can a Man lay down his Life for the Sins of other Men? Can the Life of a Man be a Ransom for the World? Is there any one Scripture that intimates a Parity? He is indeed called our High-Priest entering into the Holy of Holies, by Way of Allusion to the Annual Atonement, and as an Explanation of the Type and the Thing typify'd; but it was the Divine Person of Christ alone, which could make an Equality or Proportion between the Type and the thing typify'd, and could make the Price paid be equal to the Purchase.

To further deflate theologies that view Him as human, Defoe emphasizes that, while the Gospels present Him through Old Testament types, as in allusions to Aaron's priesthood, all biblical narrative, whether prophetic or historical, has Christ as its foundational referent:

> there's not an eminent Action, or Person, but is one way or other a Type or Representation of the Messiah; not a Prophesy, but one way or other relates to him; not a History, but one way or other points to him.

A New Family Instructor offers a progressive, reader-oriented interpretation of the Bible. Far from denying the evolution of biblical hermeneutics, this work relates exegetical tradition to ongoing divine mediation. While God reveals himself "in a wonderful Manner, by little and little, one Age after another; the Church sees her Doctrines form'd under the Hands, and by the Pens of Men enlighten'd by heavenly Inspiration, *Prophets, Apostles, Evangelists,* whose Works put all together, make up the Body of the Scriptures." Still, it is "GOD and not *Man,* who speaks throughout the whole Book, and who was the first true Author of it."[6]

For Defoe, the Bible serves readers as both history and myth: as the supernatural Christ saves mankind by having taken on human flesh, so God authored the scriptures through human agents to offer Himself perpetually in the text to readers. Paradoxically, the text is self-contained and open, because continuously mediated by God in His direct appeal to individuals: "the Scripture is a daily Revelation, and the Spirit of God, who is promised to lead us, is a daily Inspiration."[7] The *Family Instructor* of 1715 emphasizes how typology affects bible reading when a naive male child obliges his lapsed father to explain this Protestant tradition: "*Why,* the Bible is the Word of God, it was dictated by Inspiration of the Spirit of God; when you read the Bible, you are to believe that God speaks to you in the Words you read; *this is his Voice.*" Later, the son's naivety stings the father into more fully explaining the historical plenitude and contemporary significance of the Bible:

> *Child,* the Bible is your Rule of Life, tho' the Spirit is the secret Instructor; the Scripture is the Key of Instruction; there you are to learn how God is to be worshipped; how to order your Conversation aright … There you have an Historical Account of the whole World, of its Creation, the Fall, the first Condemnation of it, to a general Deluge, typical of the great Deluge of God's Wrath, which shall drown all ungodly Men for ever: There

> you have the History of God's Church from the Beginning to the Fullness of Time, and the fulfilling Old-Testament Types, and Old-Testament Promises.

The Bible mythically gathers into itself all reality; not only does it contain all the past but its typology opens up the future. Reading the Bible not only recreates the cosmos but provides intimate spiritual contact with the Creator.[8] The sacred waits to enter the profane through the bible reader's imagination. Biblical revelation is not simply historical, for typology involves seeing how things are moving forward according to the plan in the Creator's mind.[9] Biblical typology is mythical – essential and creative: it renews the world and the rites by which the world is realized.

A fine account of typology that helps to contextualize Defoe's views is provided by Gerald Bruns's focus on the hermeneutics by which "earlier biblical materials were rewritten in order to make them intelligible and applicable to later situations." For Bruns, the Bible is "a self-glossing book"; its parts "relate to one another reflexively, with later texts, for example, throwing light on the earlier, even as they themselves stand in the light of what precedes and follows them." As a self-interpreting and self-effacing text, the Bible impedes attempts to reconstruct its textual history and to postulate original intentions. Being prophetically oriented towards the future, it resists historical criticism that regards textual understanding as simply progressive. Addressing itself to the "time of interpretation," the Bible must always be newly appropriated. To read involves constant remaking. In such terms does Bruns explain "midrash" – a "reflexive and reciprocal" understanding in which readers take the text to themselves, understand themselves in its light even as their situation illuminates the text which consequently discloses itself freshly. Midrash permits readers to sustain the openness of revelation to their own history. To Bruns, Christian typology is "absolutely continuous with midrash," being "rooted in the figure of Jesus as the sectarian midrashist who appropriates the sacred text, seeing its meaning in its application to himself."[10]

Defoe's interest in the self-interpreting, intertextual hermeneutics of the Bible arose from a growing antipathy to sectarianism. Why, he kept asking, were the British such intemperate bible readers? *Serious Reflections* states that there are "more several Communions or Communities of religious Kinds in England, than in all the other Protestant Countries in the World" because interpretive conflicts push "our religious Broils to the Extremity" (173). In the Dissenting Academy at Stoke Newington, where he trained to be a Presbyterian minister, he learned to apply the Bible to all aspects of life, having early committed to memory the Pentateuch because of his family's fear that the Reformation might be undone with the Restoration of Charles II. So, if he appreciates that Britons take "the Scripture to be the great Rule of Faith, the Standard for Life and Doctrine," he dislikes their excessive zeal, as *Serious Reflections* shows:

> we flie thither and search for ourselves, not having Popery enough to expect an infallible Judge, nor Indifference enough to acquiesce in the Judgment of the Clergy; and perhaps a little too tenacious of our own Interpretation, even in things we are uninstructed about.

To recall the "Separations and Schisms" that arose "during the bloody intestine Wars in the Years 1640 to 1656" when "Liberty" was "given to all Opinions to set up themselves" would only lead to "more Division" (174). His remedy is to "exercise more Charity in our Disputes, that we might differ more like Men of Temper, and more like Christians, than we do" (175). A visionary trust that "all our unkind, unchristian, unneighbourly, unbrotherly Differences" will have no place in Heaven should instil ecclesiastical and hermeneutic moderation:

> we shall see, that there have been other Flocks than those of our Fold, other Paths to Heaven than those we shut Men out from; that those we have excommunicated have been taken into that superiour Communion; and those we have plac'd at our Left-hands, have been there summon'd to the Right-hand. (176)

Many "contradicting Notions and Principles, which we thought inconsistent with true Religion," will turn out to be "reconcilable to themselves, to one another, and to the Fountain of Truth." Doctrinal disputes about the relation between the fixedness of divine law and the efficacy of prayer in bringing about changes will be seen to be reconcilable theological contraries:

> All the Difficulties in our Conceptions of things invisible, will then be explain'd; all the Doctrine of the Immutability of the divine Councils will then be reconcilable to the changeable Events of things, and to the Varieties often happening in the World: The Unchangeableness of the eternal

> Decrees will then appear; and yet the Efficacy of praying to God to do this, or not do that, to pardon, forgive, spare, and forbear, which we now say is inconsistent with those unchangeable Decrees, shall be reconcilable to that Unchangeableness, in a Manner to us now inconceivable. (177)

*****

Defoe's belief that the Bible is the master text motivated him to exercise the typological sensibility of readers. Despite having declined to enter the ministry, he neither forsook pulpit oratory nor allowed his expansive curiosity about the world to displace his knowledge of biblical hermeneutics. His wide-ranging experiences with commercial enterprise and journalistic polemics led him to apply the Bible to his surroundings in an eager, if self-dramatizing, manner.[11] All his non-fictional and fictional texts combine traditional and innovative, historical and typological stances to the Bible in order to provoke creatively religious responses in readers. His inclusive apology for the Reformation in *A Tour through the Whole Island of Great Britain* is a fine example. Its topographical and economic survey includes praise of Protestant martyrs along with ecclesiastical satire. He lauds the Reformation for re-instituting "the primitive simplicity of the true Christian profession" and for dismantling monasteries that had forsaken "the Christian pattern prescrib'd in the scriptures." While he lauds Pope Gregory, "a true primitive Christian Bishop of Rome," for sending St Augustine to convert England, he charges later archbishops of Canterbury with having "plagued, insulted, and tyranniz'd over the Kings of England" under "that usurp'd honour of Universal Bishop." Decrying Catholicism's institutional power, Defoe rejoices that Henry VIII despoiled Cardinal Wolsey of Hampton Court and Whitehall, "monuments of ... excessive pride," and purloined the "immense wealth of that prelate, who knew no bounds of his insolence and ambition."[12] By contrast, he reveres martyrs "in the Marian tyranny," such as Dr John Hooper, the Bishop of Glastonbury, and "that glorious martyr, Dr. Ridley," the Bishop of London, whose names he jointly honoured more than twenty-five years earlier in *An Enquiry into the Occasional Conformity of Dissenters*.[13] He expressed this admiration a few years before the *Tour* in *Serious Reflections*, where he differentiates between basic tenets of faith and ritual modes of worship in order to clarify the Reformation's primitive Christianity:

> Bishop *Ridley*, and Bishop *Hooper*; the first, a rigid Church of *England* Bishop, the other, almost a Presbyterian, or at least a Calvinist, like *Peter* and *Paul*, differ'd hotly, and withstood one another to the Face, in the very Beginning of the Reformation: But when they came to burn for their Religion, Fire and Faggot shew'd them the Reconcilableness of all their Disputes; convinc'd them, that it was possible for both to hold fast the Truth in Sincerity, and yet entertain differing Notions of the Rites and Outsides of the divine Œconomy, and at the Stake they ended all their Disputes, wrote healing Letters to one another, and became Fellow-Martyrs and Confessors for that very Profession which was so intermix'd with Censure and Dislike before. (178–9)

This passage is preceded by one describing the consensus building of the primitive churches recorded in the New Testament in the face of interpretive schisms and Roman persecution:

> When they did differ in any Particular Points, they wrote healing Epistles to one another, contended with Modesty and with Charity, and referr'd willingly their Notions to be decided by one another. They did not separate Communion, and excommunicate whole Churches and Nations, for a Dispute about the Celebration of *Easter*, or unchurch one another for the Question of receiving and re-baptizing of Penitents, as was afterwards the Case. The Furnace of Affliction burnt up all that Dross, the Fury of their Persecutors kept their Minds humble, their Zeal for Religion hot, and their Affection for, and Charity to one another encreased as their Liberty, and their Numbers were lessened. (178)

Defoe honours the sacrifices made by the Early and Reformation Churches that made them models of communal and ecclesiastical toleration. His ongoing wish to reconcile biblical interpretation to Christian conduct explains why he transposes motifs from *Serious Reflections* to the largely secular *Tour*. In the latter, he visits Hadley to "see the place where that famous martyr, and pattern of charity and religious zeal in Queen Mary's time, Dr. Rowland Taylor, was put to death." Since "veneration for his memory … is a more lasting monument" than "a tomb of marble," Taylor, he claims, will live "in the hearts of the people … as long as this island shall retain the Protestant religion." Naturally, his trust in the symbolic power of collective memories is sometimes disappointed. Thus, if Oxford University was the home of "our first reformers and martyrs," Defoe regrets that at Lutterworth, the "birthplace of honest John Wickliff," the townsfolk have forgotten the Oxford scholar and "first preacher of the Reformation in England … born amongst them."[14] But equally naturally, he records signs of primitive Christianity in action. He is cheered by Dorchester's harmonious Anglicans and Dissenters, who meet in "civility and good neighbourhood, like catholick Christians, and men of a catholick, and extensive charity," the adjective "catholic" signifying ecclesiastical inclusiveness. Occasionally, he is tolerant of Roman Catholics. For example, he is content that a community at Winchester follows St Benedict's rule since they live "to the highest degree, obliging among their neighbours."[15] Such broad-mindedness informs his literary sense of the Bible, as when he admires the "scripture elegance" of the scholar-translators of the King James Bible.[16] Still, his appreciation of the text's primitive appeal disallows its transposition into local dialect. At Martock, a scholar reading his lesson "a little oddly in the tone of the country," takes the verse, "I have put off my coat, how shall I put it on, I have wash'd my feet, how shall I defile them?" (Song of Sol. 5:3), and vocalizes it as "Chav a doffed my cooat, how shall I don't, chav a wash'd my veet, how shall I moil 'em?" This "dexterous dunce" may be "diverting," but his idiomatic transposition offends Defoe's sense of the difference between ignorance and primitiveness.[17]

*****

Thoroughly grounded in typological hermeneutics and ecclesiastical history since the Reformation, Defoe frequently hid his distaste for abusers of the Bible and pretended to distance himself from his ministerial training so that he might more powerfully transpose biblical allusions while celebrating the scriptures' universal applicability with cunning obliqueness.[18] His seeming reluctance to foist biblical perspectives on unbelievers generates extreme tonal swings in his authorial rhetoric. As noted in the previous chapter, the following disclaimer in *Serious Reflections* serves to direct readers' attention to his contrary performance in the whole text:

> I shall not pretend to invade the Province of the Learned, nor offer one Argument from Scripture or Providence; for I am supposed to be talking to Men that doubt or deny them both. Divinity is not my Talent, nor ever like to be my Profession, the Charge of Priestcraft and Schoolmen would not lie against me; besides, 'tis not the way of talking that the World relishes at this Time; in a Word, talking Scripture is out of Fashion. (94)

For example, after demeaning himself as "a very mean Expositor of Texts," he explains why Felix trembled before Paul in Acts 23:25, transmuting self-disparagement into an exegesis fit for the pulpit (191). The "Scriptures upon all Occasions," he insists, present faith and repentance as "two *Hand in Hand* Graces"; there is "not one Mention of Faith in the whole Scripture, but what" recommends faith "to our Admiration, and to our Practice." For faith is

> the Foundation and the Top-stone of all Religion, the Right-hand to lead, and the Left-hand to support, in the whole Journey of a Christian, even thro' this World, and into the next: In a Word, 'tis the Sum and Substance of the Gospel Foundation (193).

The architectural and pilgrimage imagery supplementing the classical references to the Graces in seemingly complying with those who mock the Bible actually inverts its complicity.

An even more subtle ironic reversal is achieved by a disclaimer in *An Essay on the History and Reality of Apparitions* which upholds "the Humours of the Day" to please readers only to transform modish conformity and authorial compromise into *topoi* that justify mediating scriptural truth through perceptual and cognitive fallibilities:

> Well, we must comply however; the Humour of the Day must prevail; and as there is no instructing you without pleasing you, and no pleasing you but in your own Way, we must go on in that Way; the Understanding must be refin'd by Allegory and Enigma; you must see the Sun through the Cloud, and relish Light by the help of Darkness; the Taste must be rectify'd by Salts, the Appetite whetted by Bitters; in a word, the Manners must be reform'd in Masquerade, Devotion quicken'd by the Stage not the Pulpit, and Wit be brighten'd by Satyrs upon Sense.[19]

Apparently, literary mediation must accept the indirectness of "Allegory and Enigma." For no one can look at the source of light, the sun, without being blinded; the darkening effect of clouds makes light visible; taste for the absolute, stimulated by bitterness, must be improved by saltiness; reform of manners and religion will be effected more by theatrical illusion than by pulpit oratory; and moral intelligence will be heightened by satire of sense perception. After lamenting that spiritual truth cannot be apprehended immediately, Defoe treats this lament ironically, his dismay at promoting the Bible to resistant readers turning to exposition of his trust in polar ways of doing so. Again, in *A System of Magick,* when he complains that "light-headed Readers" with "Wits too volatile for this remote Story" will find biblical chronology "too grave" a subject, he pretends to drop it to "oblige Folly" yet admits he will displease "truly wise and solid Heads." By appearing ready to uphold "that most fashionable Custom of writing most of that which is pleasant, and least of that which is profitable, so willing is your humble servant to be a Man of Mode," this pretended alliance with bad encourages good readers.[20] This self-dramatization as complicit and beleaguered author confirms that biblical allusions require mixed narrative modes.[21] One such mode places implicit alongside explicit allusions, while others adapt and compound allusions.[22]

Defoe's allusive practices confirm that his narrative theory is based on the Bible's divine immanence since God addresses readers and converses with them by mediating Himself to individual consciences. The theory is supported by the tenet that humans retain a divine spark since the Fall is remediable to a degree. *Serious Reflections* claims that insofar as honesty "is found upon Earth, so much of the first Rectitude of Nature, and of the Image of God, seems to be restor'd to Mankind" (32). Consequently, Defoe derides rational materialism by promoting double vision and spiritual discourse: "the Reason of the Creation" is not "to be found in the Study of Nature, on the Surface of our Earth" (*Vision* 28). Thus, he calls readers to admire the world through meditation, through that "Silence of Life" when "a Man has the Voice of his Soul to speak to God, and to himself" (*Serious Reflections* 3).[23] Paradoxically, divine immanence justifies parabolic and allusive invention with the Bible. When presenting the "grand Principles upon which all Religion depends" by the "glorious Text," Psalms 33:6, he adds parentheses: "by the Word (*God the Son*) of the Lord (*God the Father*) were the Heavens made, and all the Host of them, by the Breath (*God the Holy Ghost*) of His Mouth" (206–7). This adaptation distinguishes between Christ as incarnate word, God as speaker in His creation, and the Holy Spirit as inspiration. This exegesis of the Trinity links the "Voice of God" to the "voice of Nature" since God's Providence is "the silent Voice, *if it may be allowed me to call it so,* of his managing Events and Causes" (216). The "Voice of God in his Work" shows that "his immediate Voice from Heaven, is not entirely ceased from us, though it may have changed the Mediums of Communication" (225–6). Readers with "a Sense of a future State, and of the Œconomy of an invisible World" may engage "with the acting Part of Providence" through inferences achieved by double vision (231–2, 237). They may "look upon the Things of Life with the same Eyes, as we shall do when we come to the Edge of Time." Double vision – "when one Eye can as it were look back on the World, and the other look forward into Eternity" – elevates spiritual solitude into seeing "more with half an Eye" and judging "better at first Glance, than we can now with all our pretended Wisdom and Penetration" (*Vision* 27). Such vision is blessed: it is "our Felicity, that the Converse of Spirits, and the Visions of Futurity, are silent, emblematick, and done by Hints, Dreams, and Impulses, and not by clear Vision and open Discovery" (*Vision* 43). Such signs are "Words spoken to the Mind, tho' not to the Ear" (*Vision* 48). They are "directed from Heaven," if "not immediately spoken from thence," since God "may appoint Instruction to be given by fortuitous Accidents, and may direct concurring Circumstances to touch and affect the Mind as much, and as effectually, as if they had been immediate and miraculous" (*Vision* 83). Double vision reveals the sacred manifesting itself in the profane and thereby encourages allusive reading.

*****

Far from constricting the plural and dynamic points of view in his non-fiction and fiction, Defoe's appreciation of the Bible and its genres enhanced his creative flexibility. His various allusions to the Book of Proverbs, a "wisdom text," in *The Complete English Tradesman* illustrate this flexibility, as it allows him to promote trade and to prescribe mercantile codes.[24] Since he decries sloth in business, warns that the sluggard shall wear rags, and promises the diligent wealth and influence (Prov. 18:9, 23:1, 10:4, and 12:24), Solomon is a monitor to tradesmen as well as an apologist for trading practices. Blaming inflation on buyers, Solomon permits traders to overcharge (Prov. 20:14) and argues that Heaven creates wealth as a commercial incentive (Prov. 10:4). To dignify "the royal patron of industry" when warning that the "*Tradesman that is a lover of pleasure, shall be a poor man*" (Prov. 21:17), Defoe inserts "tradesman" into the text, excusing his addition as follows: "I hope I do not wrest the scripture in my interpretation of it, I am sure it agrees with the whole *tenor* of the wiseman's other discourses." By boldly adapting the text of the Book of Proverbs, Defoe derives from it rules that dignify trade paradoxically. He applies "*The borrower is servant to the lender*" (Prov. 22:7) to tradesmen, urging them to "bow down ... and worship" buyers as idols, this rule of trading humility inverting the proscription of idolatry in Leviticus 26:1.[25]

His biblical allusions often endow Defoe's trading rules with a polar flexibility that not only shuns dogmatism but also sometimes converts typological into secular analogies. Hence, while a trader must "confine himself within his own sphere," it seems that politicians will always "converse with Tradesmen," since *"a man diligent in business … shall stand before princes"* (Prov. 22:29), for, if traders need not converse with politicians, politicians need to converse with traders. Further upholding the trading middle way, the text, *"he that loves pleasure shall be a poor man,"* warns traders not to shut their shops out of devotional zeal (Prov. 21:17). Here tradesmen are cautioned against self-indulgence while being advised not to subordinate business to religious observances. Defoe's contextual transposition of biblical texts in his defence of trade and the middle way often employs images that compound literal, satirical, and typological reference. For example, when he says that innkeepers might intoxicate clients by "putting the Bottle to their Neighbour's Nose," he adds – with comic particularity – "Nose" to Habakkuk 2:15. He further defends trade with surprising obliqueness by applying David's confession – "I said in my haste, All men are Liars" (Ps. 116:11) – to its detractors. His typological images render tradesmen both butts of and vehicles for satire. If he chides them for loading "their wives with the blame of their miscarriage" like "old father ADAM, *tho' in another case*" (Gen. 3:12), he also argues that trade would improve were the urban poor to be sent to the country to "get their Bread as *Adam* did, by the Sweat of their Brows" (Gen. 3:19). In these instances, typological similes deflate both their customers and tradesmen. When comparing tradesmen's refusal to let apprentices serve customers to "*Laban*'s usage of *Jacob, viz.* keeping back the beloved *Rachel,* whom he served his seven years time for, and putting him off with a blear-ey'd *Leah* in her stead" and when equating dandies' "Pye-ball'd party-colour'd" dress to Aaron's golden calf, Defoe turns typological into secular metaphors, his ironic reversals clarified when we recall that, if customers lower themselves as idolaters, tradesmen are advised to idolize customers.[26]

Defoe applies allusions to commerce ambivalently partly because he despises those who hypocritically single out tradesmen for not doing as they would be done by and for not taking "our Saviour's Rule for a Standard of Uprightness" (Luke 6:31). Since no one embodies this "Golden Rule" of morality, he recalls Christ's words to the youth who thought he had fulfilled the commandments (Matt. 19:20): until the youth gives everything to the poor, his integrity remains incomplete.

Since no one can match this youth, Defoe adapts Matthew 10:16: "A Tradesman should be wise as the Serpent, but he should be innocent, that is, *Honest* too as the Dove." Yet, in so excusing tradesmen, he holds them to high standards since the trading community is not necessarily harmonious. Thus, about the injunction to *"live peaceably with all Men"* (Rom. 12:15), he says that the "blessed Apostle's Rule" applies most "to a Tradesman." Moreover, since rich traders typically condemn unsuccessful ones, he cites the parable of the boastful Pharisee in Luke 18:11 in which Christ favours the humble Publican who acknowledges his failings. He likens boastful tradesmen to Nebuchadnezzar, who claimed to have created his own majesty (Dan. 4:30). Since he was chastened by divine threats, superior tradesmen are advised to wait on divine calls.[27]

Typological allusions in *Due Preparations for the Plague* more dramatically raise awareness in the mercantile community about how it should subordinate professional reality to spiritual life.[28] The family in this guidebook is "religiously Educated," but, whereas mother and daughter make "Eternal Life" their "chief Business," the two sons are engrossed in trade. A "faithful Monitor," the daughter is a type of Mary Magdalene – one of "her Sister Preachers." Her brothers dismiss her words as *"Idle Tales"* (Luke 24:11): unaware that the phrase by which they demean her is scriptural, they are linked ironically against their knowledge to doubters of the Resurrection, Defoe hinting that the brothers will ultimately be converted, a wish expressed by their mother, who cites Hosea 6:1, "Thou hast smitten and Thou wilt bind us up," to proclaim that the plague inspires repentance. She also cites Jonah 4:11, in which God justifies sparing Nineveh to encourage her family to see that what happened to Nineveh is a type of what should come to pass in London. Jonah 3:10 supports her view that Londoners must imitate the people of Nineveh in securing God's forgiveness. But the stubborn elder son quotes Jonah 3:5 with its prediction of Nineveh's destruction within forty days to claim that Jonah needlessly disturbed Nineveh. Why should Londoners, he asks, fall on their knees like the people of Nineveh and put on sackcloth? Whereat the mother tacitly cites and connects Matthew 3:2 and Psalms 112:7. The first text shows that, when John the Baptist urged repentance on the grounds that the kingdom of Heaven is nigh, he did not frighten the people, and the second, *"He shall not be afraid of Evil Things, whose Heart is fixed, trusting in the Lord,"* aims at inducing her son to trust that God renders the heart unafraid of *"Evil Tidings."*[29]

Dialectical tensions between explicit and tacit and between conscious and unconscious allusions in *Due Preparations* increasingly generate dramatic implications in the dialogue which more deeply embed typology. The siblings' growing awareness that they unknowingly as well as knowingly cite the scriptures, thereby embodying God's Word, fortifies typology by applying it to a secular, urban setting and reinforces the importance of auto-didacticism. When for the first time the sister, anguished by her elder brother's apathy, asks "How shall our Hearts endure, or our Hands be strong, in such a Day as that?" she gives voice to Ezekiel 22:14 without acknowledging the biblical source, partly since news of the plague makes her swoon. Recovering from her fainting fit, she accepts the coming of the plague, tacitly citing Matthew 11:26: "'Tis the Lord ... let him do what seemeth good in His sight." Submitting to Providence yet disparaging her own spiritual preparations, she disclaims preaching, typifying Defoe's contrarian didacticism which makes exemplary characters demean themselves.[30] This didacticism is reinforced when the younger brother laments the elder's apathy – "O *Brother*, whose Heart can endure, or whose Hands be strong in the Day that God shall deal with them" – for this repetition of the verse from Ezekiel demonstrates the sister's positive effect on her younger brother and testifies to familial bonding. Tensions between explicit and tacit allusions build when the younger brother alleges to his sister that his brother "puts the Evil day far from him." Humility prevents her telling her younger brother that he is unconsciously alluding to Amos 6:3. More intent on the elder's conversion than on exegesis, she repeats Matthew 11:26 tacitly as before: "We are to say, it is the Lord, let Him do with us what seems good in his Sight." Her silence about the biblical source again ironically heightens her authority: suppression of scriptural provenance endows her with spiritual authenticity. Shunning self-righteousness, she encouragingly tells her younger brother that he judges himself too harshly. Citing the prodigal's story to show that God always accepts penitents (Luke 15:17), she again disclaims being a preacher; if, as she says, the parable simply enters her head, Defoe suggests that God speaks through the textual implications.[31]

The dialectic between faithful uncertainty and unrealized spirituality becomes clearer when, as his sister soothes his worries about repentance, the younger brother comforts himself. When she proclaims the nature of grace, "The Preparation of the Heart is of the Lord" (Prov. 16:1), he admits his belief in this verse. When she cites seven texts concerning God's invitation to turn to Him, he quotes Joel 2:12–13, verses which, having studied in his faithlessness, he knows convey the same message.[32] Finally, sister and brother explicate the texts mutually. Their explication is spiritually powerful since they transcend dialogic convention and enclose themselves in typology. Humbling *"themselves greatly before the Lord their God,"* they become types of Manasseh, whose story is told in 2 Chronicles 33. Their dialogue is more than domestic and allusive because it extends scriptural awareness into typological vision. Their reading is spiritual since the texts which they assemble perform religious self-criticism and mutually faithful encouragement.[33]

H.F., the saddler-narrator in *A Journal of the Plague Year*, gains authority as a social and political commentator because, looking beyond his vocation in trade, he constantly debates with himself about how typology should be applied to his nation in a time of extreme trouble. When he refuses to flee the plague and rejects his brother's reading of Matthew 27:40, "Master, save thy self," since Christ spoke "in another Case quite different" (9), he denies his brother's analogical extension of the verse. On the other hand, he justifies his calling to trade by opening himself to biblical revelation: his familiarity with Psalms 91:7–10 causes other verses, such as his "Times were in his Hands" (Ps. 31:15), to come spontaneously to mind (13). His studied and casual allusions heighten his "Call" and "Intimations from Heaven" (10). That God mediates himself in history and scripture inspires H.F. to invent policies for population dispersal and civic administration and to authenticate them by critiquing and upholding typology. When he says that London has been "designed by Heaven for an Akeldama, doom'd to be destroy'd from the Face of the Earth" (Acts 1:19 and Gen. 7:4), he reads the Old and New Testaments as self-glossing and concludes that, since God punishes nations as well as individuals, social policy must acknowledge the deity (19). Yet he condemns a Quaker for crying doom "like *Jonah* to *Nineveh*" and shouting "O! the Great, and the Dreadful God!" (Jon. 3:4 and Dan. 9:4), subordinating typology to his belief that social harm lurks in street preachers' enthusiasm (21). Since after thundering against "false Prophets" by citing Matthew 7:15, he alludes to Jonah 3:5–10 to claim that, had Londoners fallen on their knees, "we might have been a second *Nineveh*," his promotion of typology reveals his wish to harmonize prophecy and policy (29). That prophecy may reinforce social planning is clear when about maternal plague victims he opines that "it might well be said as in the Scripture. *Wo! be to those who are with Child; and to those which give suck in that Day*" (Matt. 24:19), Christ's words about the end of time creating sympathy for pregnant and lactating women. H.F.

leaves "this Admonition on Record" so that mothers will be the first to receive public assistance in future plagues (118).

To expose apathy to public administration, H.F. embeds typological awareness into his story of the three poor men who flee London. That the plague is "an armed Man" (Prov. 6:11) underscores their sensibility and shows that they flout regulations responsibly (120). John, the leader, cites 2 Kings 7:3–4 to compare the threesome to the lepers of Samaria; the two groups trust equally in Providence (124). When John begs residents of Epping not to shut their "Bowels of Compassion," his allusion to 1 John 3:17 implicitly warns that God punishes those who do not aid the poor (143). When the threesome receives a bushel of wheat, Joshua 5:11 proves their integrity: they eat "parched Corn, as the Israelites of old did" (144). H.F.'s narrative perspective on the need for reform, in its constant balancing of fact with supposition and sympathy with judgment, justifies the proper use of typology. Thus, he regards allegations that citizens fleeing London had "an evil Eye" and wilfully infected rural people as an abuse of Mark 7:22 by those prejudiced against the metropolis (154). His urban perspective questions the restraints imposed on householders and excuses their assaults on watchmen, by saying, in the words of Psalms 7:16, that the latter's "Mischief was upon their own Heads" (156). To H.F. as a metropolitan, civic regulations require an improved correlation of natural and divine causation, since the "Agency of Means" and divine intervention halt the plague, God choosing to "stay his Hand" (2 Sam. 24:16 [171]).[34] Such a correlation yields tonal poise: he will not affirm that all enthusiasts perished, but many must have gone "to their long Home," evil days implicating divine punishment (Eccles. 12:5 [178]); nor will he assert that no charitable people died, for the Lord must have saved them (Prov. 19:17 [211]). Since "the immediate Finger of God" halted the plague (Exod. 8:19 [244]), "the Help of Man" being "Vain" (Ps. 6:11 [245]), H.F. minimizes the sectarianism that returned with the end of the plague, because "the Scripture commands us to judge the most favourably, and according to Charity" (Matt. 7:1–2 and John 7:24 [235]). If the nation has a poor typological sense, his is strong: the English, like the Israelites, forget God's help, but he behaves like the leper who turned back to Christ (Ps. 106: 12–13 and Luke 17: 12–17 [247–8]), his scripturally informed actions inviting readers to view social imperatives through biblical analogies.

Perhaps the most striking example of Defoe's dialectical dramatization of biblical allusions in conduct books which applies figural thinking to domestic and professional life arises from the patriarch's rejection of typology in *Religious Courtship*.[35] This father, whose spiritual evasiveness dominates this text, prevents his daughters from choosing marriage partners because he will not recognize their "Light." He will not grant his youngest daughter a negative voice because he will not let her "stand in her own light."[36] An avowed unbeliever, he denies his conscience even as it pricks him. His youngest daughter, while loving her suitor, values spirituality more; she knows that romantic love may "be a Snare" to her soul.[37] Whereas, to the father, only hypocrites "talk Scripture," his daughters obey their late mother's injunction, "*Be not unequally yoked*" (2 Cor. 6:14), hoping to respect patriarchy when their father and spouses honour religious instruction.[38]

The youngest daughter's suitor, spurned by her as "*one of God's Enemies*" (Ps. 83:2–5), gradually puts himself in a positive typological light by developing a reflexive discursiveness. Hearing himself in the inane words of a second mistress, he is horrified by "his own Picture." His horror mounts when two rakes who, like him, claim to be "*mighty good Christians*" abuse religious sensibility. However, in his new discursive self-consciousness, he heeds an aristocrat who argues that Paul's appearance before Agrippa, Festus, and Sergius Paulus shows that gentility and Christianity are conformable. The aristocrat's exegesis of Acts 25:13–14 and 13:7 leads the suitor to feel "under the Curse of Darkness in the midst of Light."[39] Subsequently, the suitor learns from William, a poor tenant, that light is accessible to him. When William tells him that, where much is "*given*," much is "requir'd" (Luke 12:48), the landlord grants that William's "Treasure is in Heaven" (Luke 12:33): this reciprocal allusiveness reveals that the faithless suitor converses allusively with a pious inferior. William then articulates a series of integrated allusions which demonstrate that hermeneutic intelligence resides in the poor and uneducated: he declares that few rich people are called, that the poor are rich in faith, and that it is hard for rich men to enter the kingdom of heaven (1 Cor. 1:26, Jas. 2:5, and Matt 19:23). Then he provides offsetting verses which announce that the promise is made to all, that God blesses those whom He causes to approach Him, and that they shall live who seek the Lord (Exod. 20:24, Ps. 65:4, and 69:32).[40]

William's biblical intelligence emblematizes spiritual gentility; to his textual expositions he joins sensitivity to emotional signs. He detects a "*longing earnest Desire after*" God in the landlord's wretchedness. As a result, he encouragingly compounds other allusions: those who hunger and thirst after righteousness shall be filled, the longing soul shall be satisfied, and God will fulfil the desires of those who fear him (Matt

5:6, Ps. 127:9, and 145:19). Moreover, he cites reflexive texts in which he can include himself, as when he says "we must pray, that we may be taught to pray" (2 Chron. 16:9). When he goes on to compound allusions, namely, the natural desires of the heart are evil, every good gift comes from above, and once a good work is begun God will perfect it (Gen 6:5; Jas. 1:17; Heb. 13:21), he argues that impulses to pray are divine. The dialogue between landlord and tenant confirms this because, when he urges William to speak without deference and reminds him that death does away with social distinctions, the landlord unconsciously cites Romans 3:22. That this statement takes biblical form symbolizes spiritual progress: his words are becoming prayerful. Appropriately, William adapts the text of Proverbs 16:1: "The preparation of the heart and the answer of the tongue, is from the Lord." His addition of the second phrase elucidates William's belief that prayer occurs when God hears His motions in souls and touches hearts of bible readers. Psychological apperception is for William as important to prayer as liturgical formality:

> earnest Desires are really Prayers in their own Nature; sincere Wishes of the Heart for Grace, are Prayers to God for Grace: Prayer it self is nothing but those Wishes and Desires put into Words, and the first is the essential Part; for these may be Words used without the Desire, and that is not Prayer, but a Mockery of God; but the Desires of the Heart may be Prayers even without the Words.

To William, God answers desires that He forms in souls, whether vocalized or not, for such desires are the "Voice of his own Spirit and Grace." The heart moved by the Bible may silently express itself thus: "*Lord! make good this Word to me! Lord! draw my Heart to thee! Lord! help me thus to seek thee.*" To William, this "*mental Petition* is Prayer as well as Words; and is, perhaps the best mov'd Prayer, and the best exprest in the World." Never having read the Bible, the landlord nonetheless voices scriptural allusions that symbolize God's speaking in him. Defoe lingers on the paradox of wordless, interior expression. After William explicates the relation of faith and unbelief in John 20:31 and Mark 9:23–4, the dialogue briefly becomes internalized. The landlord silently says amen to the text from Mark, and William hears the landlord's unspoken voice. At this point William explicitly recognizes the landlord's spiritual progress, which is confirmed by God's voicing biblical words in him![41]

By contrast, the father's dogmatic allusiveness undoes his faithless patriarchalism because of his sister-in-law's subtle interpretive powers. At first, he asserts the "original Command of God, that Children should obey their Parents" (Exod. 20:12 and Eph. 6:1). Refusing to reply in kind, she urges that parents cannot evade God's law. Next he cites Caleb's promise of his daughter Achsah in marriage to him who will smite Kirjathsepher (Josh. 15:16). The sister-in-law, mindful of Numbers 30:5, grants that the Bible gives fathers power over daughters without explicitly alluding to the text that fathers cannot force them to marry. Yet, when he defends himself by claiming to embody the text, "*Be angry, and sin not*," she counters Ephesians 4:26 with verse 13: "*Let all Bitterness and Wrath be put away from among you*." Her verse evinces the "genuine Interpretation" of his: since both texts specify conduct to strangers, self-correction applies most to parents' treatment of children. Her exegesis makes her brother-in-law admire her as a "healing Preacher."[42]

The tedious narrative route which the suitor must take before becoming an eligible marriage partner confirms Defoe's view that indifference to the Bible and typology are best avoided since hard to repair. Hence, he heightens narrative contraries by allusions in the denouement of the first section of *Religious Courtship*. The suitor is ideal except for his religious indifference. He is the only man the youngest daughter wants as a husband. But she refuses to be yoked to one who says to the Almighty "*Depart from us, we desire not the knowledge of his ways*" (Job 21:14). Yet the moment she makes this declaration, the suitor, who, readers know, is on the way to reformation, rides by unseen. Because her eldest sister and aunt know that they cannot simply report what they have heard about his penitence, they lay it up in their hearts, the allusion to Luke 1:66 emphasizing that his former hypocrisy creates communal, domestic, and psychological problems. When the eldest sister reveals the suitor's repentance, she claims that her discovery made her heart burn within her, just as the Saviour's speech on the road to Emmaus did to the disciples (Luke 24:32). This typological image of revelation leads the youngest to take her suitor's penitence as blessed.[43]

That *Moll Flanders* was published in the same year as the last three titles discussed above might suggest that biblical allusion and exegetical licence enrich this fictional autobiography. In fact, biblical allusions effect emblematic patterning in all of Defoe's fictional plots. Moreover, his allusions confirm that, far from being a textual fundamentalist, he adopted an experimental stance on scriptural references that privileges spiritual over positivistic readings. Throughout his fictions, the ironies entailed by allusions invite readers to look into and beyond the typological imaginations of his protagonists.

Moll's allusions recoil on her since she hardly internalizes the catechism and the Bible's cultural heritage at all. Despite her churchgoing, she is "not Nice in Point of Religion" (142). The penitence towards which the minister moves her by "proper Quotations of Scripture" (287) is unrealized since she cannot "repeat the excellent Discourses of this extraordinary Man" (289). She neither digests nor re-imagines his sermons. Prompted to "real signs of Repentance," she guards her evil ways as shown by her unresponsiveness to Jeremiah 23:22 and Jonah 3:10 (287). Since such texts escape her full attention, ironies sap her allusions. Courted by the younger Colchester brother, she trusts the elder will save her from social contempt; she saw "the Cloud" but did "not foresee the Storm" (30), 1 Kings 18:44 conveying her dissociated sensibility and blindness to Providence. She fittingly blames herself when she describes her lust for the elder brother and insists that she enticed herself into sin (Matt. 5:28 [59]) and when she admits that luring the draper into marriage caught her in the "very Snare" of deceit (Ps. 9:16 [60]). Yet these allusions point up those by which she blames others and minimizes her own sins, as when she condemns the "Sons of Affliction" in the Mint (Prov. 31:5 [64]) and generalizes the baronet's lust by depreciating drunkards who, catching venereal diseases, go like an ox to the slaughter until a dart strikes their liver (Prov. 7:22–3 [226]). Such allusions heighten her spiritlessness when faced by her banker-husband's vacuity and when attempting to bribe witnesses keen to testify against her. They also unsettle her projected narrative future. Of her unconcern at a fellow's incarceration, she says her "Measure was not yet fill'd up" (Matt. 23:32 [204]). This allusion to Christ's judgment of the children of those who killed the prophets shows by prolepsis how she re-enacts sins and afflicts herself.[44] Like Pontius Pilate, she washes her hands of misrepresenting herself to Jemy (Matt. 27:24 [146]), and she and the baronet venture "too near the brink of a Command" against adultery (Eccles. 3:29 [116]).

The negative implications arising from Moll's allusions put readers on their exegetical guard. Consider how she excuses Mother Midnight's lying-in facility as "an Error of the right Hand" but insists she "has gone to her place" (Job 18:21): merely glancing at the godless woman's fate, Moll belittles divine justice, saying tritely that Mother Midnight is inimitable (170–1). Similarly, when she meets her son in Virginia, she exposes herself to blame as she attempts self-exculpation. Her "very

Bowels" move towards him (Song of Sol. 5:4), her suppositious maternal feelings – "yearnings of Soul" – linked to the test in 1 Kings 3:26 in which the true mother gives up her child (322). Since she has sacrificed nothing, her claim to be a noble mother could not ring less true. Her attempts to apply typological images to herself are no more persuasive. When she claims to face "the Gates of Destruction" (193) and to be "ingulph'd in Labyrinths of Trouble" (204), she is merely histrionic. If poverty throws her "into the Mire" (Job 30:19 [203]) and criminal insensibility makes her a long-used "Pitcher" certain to break (Eccles. 12:6 [241]), dramatic irony reduces her images to clichés.

Defoe invites readers to take up figural hermeneutics and to question the typological imagery which Colonel Jack and Roxana employ when they pretend to tragic faith. The preface to *Colonel Jack* announces that the penitent "*shall be return'd like the Prodigal,* and his latter End be better than his Beginning" (2). This compound allusion to Luke 15:11 and Job 42:2 is repeated when, about being kidnapped to Virginia, Jack says his part was "harder at the Beginning, tho' better at the latter End" (118), and when his wife, a slave on his plantation, says that, after a tender "Beginning," her "End" was "with the Prodigal brought to desire Husks with Swine" (258). These repetitions function distinctly: Jack's allusion signals spiritual poverty, while his wife's parabolic reference substantiates her penitence. Not until he finds a tutor in Virginia does Jack study the Bible and apply it to the former self that readers have long encountered. But he remains a poor reader and interpreter. As a child pitied for rags and praised for gentility, Jack laid "up all these things in [his] Heart" (8). This allusion to Luke 1:66 does not fit John the Baptist's status as the one who fulfils the prophets to the nameless waif's genteel pretensions. When Jack later reapplies this text to his illicit trade with Spaniards, laying up directions for it in his "most secret Thoughts" (290), his distance from prophetic models is greater. If allusions sometimes uphold Jack's moral potential, as when he excuses a drunken slave for not, like Noah, knowing the power of spirits (Gen. 9:21 [135]) and when he shares his Tutor's sense of repentance as the "delightful Sorrow" described in 2 Corinthians 7:10 (165–6), most allusions express his material and contingent concerns. When a ship transporting goods bought with his criminal gains is lost, he is glad: his honest wealth will be harmed neither by "fire in [his] Flax" nor by a consuming "Moth" (Josh. 15:14 and Matt. 6:19 [157]). By simply contrasting honest and ill-gotten wealth, Jack does not relate ethical to religious sense, for the first allusion points to Solomon's being moved by God to burst bonds as weak as flax burnt with fire while the second categorically opposes worldly and spiritual treasure. He does admit he cannot turn gratitude to the plantation owner into a "higher obligation" since he cannot imitate the Pharisee of Luke 18:11. Instead, he reads Matthew 18:30 defensively even after realizing that "not a Hair of our Heads shall fall to the Ground without [God's] Permission" (170). Knowing that God might "take away again his Wooll, and his Flax" and return him to wretchedness, he is unmoved by Hosea 2:9 (171). The irony of his situation – his apathetic lack of discipline in the face of biblical knowledge – is clarified when he cites Acts 8:31. Despite his Tutor's efforts to promote the Bible as the "sure Fund of Instruction," Jack uses this text to declare that he has no one to help and guide him (171). That he exaggerates his solitude while asserting false claims to tragic faith is an irony that dominates the close of his anti-climactic autobiography. In a "distemper'd Fancy" raised by anger at his second wife, he exposes himself by citing Solomon's dictate that jealousy is "*the wrath of a Man*" (Prov. 6:34 [225]). He further degrades himself by possessing "an evil Eye" (Mark 7:22 [226]) and granting the spiritual truth of "the Text, that it is not good for Man to be alone" (Gen. 2: 18 [233]). While two references to Romans 11:15 show that respect for his wife teaches him that "A faithful Counsellor is Life from the Dead" (268) and that her pardon is a "kind of Life from the Dead" (275), he himself disclaims spiritual regeneration, closing his account as a faithless victim. Having lived "without God in the World," he abhors himself "in Dust and Ashes," far from tempering Ephesians 2:12 with Job 42:6 (308). His hopeless sense of futurity inhibits him from listening harder to the voice of Providence and to his own inner voice.

As in *Colonel Jack* so in *Roxana*: self-dramatizing allusions recoil on the protagonist and ultimately signify damnation. Despite calling for sympathy in the face of tragic suffering, Roxana victimizes herself with her allusive conduct. In poverty-stricken distress, she likens friends to "Job's three Comforters" so as to affect heroic loss (Job 2: 11–13 [17]). Comparing herself to Job exposes her to narrative irony; when lust for titles makes her consider deserting the Dutch merchant, gratitude to him vanishes "*as if it had been a Shadow*" (235). The fault implied by her adoption of Job's voice (Job 14:2) is the more profound given her brother-in-law's conscientious urging of his wife to be charitable to Roxana's children, since giving to the poor is lending to the Lord (Prov. 28:27 and 19:17 [22]). Sensitive to Solomon's commercial analogies, the brother-in-law applies the phrase the "Bowels of Compassion" to his extended family because of the wise man's dictate that those who shut their ears to the poor will themselves be unheard (23). The narrative shows the brother-in-law to be prophetic since Roxana hides herself from her offspring and corrupts those on whom she relies. If eventually deceived into marrying her, her Dutch lover resists her free-love ideology of marriage because he will not give up "Soul as well as Body, the Interest of this World, and the Hopes of another" (1 Thess. 5:23 [157]). He will not lead himself into temptation by cohabiting with her on her terms (Matt. 6:13 [158]). Roxana does not similarly draw on the Bible even when she replaces natural-law with common-law arguments. In refuting Amy's legitimization of cohabitation with the landlord, Roxana opposes her maid's reading of Genesis 30:1–8 by making Amy also lie with him (39).[45] Pledging to care for offspring of this liaison, Roxana corrupts her maid into imitating Rachel and tasting the bitterness of misapplied scripture.

Roxana's self-dramatization leads her to drink deeper of this bitterness. Facing starvation, she sees herself as "one of the pitiful Women of Jerusalem" who ate their children, but she fails to see that Jeremiah's words are prophetic, not literal (Lam. 2: 20 [18]). Although she describes the landlord's relief as "Life from the Dead" (Rom. 11:15), she perversely seduces him (30).[46] Her allusiveness becomes blasphemous when she calls herself "despis'd, and trampled on by all the World," since Isaiah 53:3 prefigures the Messiah (37). Again, when she tells herself that she submits to the landlord for "a Morsel of Bread" (38), the ritual hospitality of Genesis 18:5 and Judges 19:5 suggests that she falsely sees herself ensnared by goodness. That biblical typology serves her histrionic self-image is again apparent in her dealings with the prince. A "poor desolate Woman," she abases herself "at his Feet" (61). Since Esther fell at Ahasuerus's feet to protect the Jews (Esther 8:3) and since Mary fell before Christ trusting He could save her brother (John 11:32), Roxana's exploitation of the language celebrating figural women is transparent. When the prince drops her, she compares herself to Mary the mother of Jesus: he did not "send me empty away" (110). That she so incongruously likens the prince's material compensation for his sexual licence to God's love for Mary heightens her allusive perversity (Luke 1:53).

Roxana finds it impossible to cite the Bible constructively with regard to sexual relations. When she comments on rejecting and accepting the Dutch merchant, her allusions are increasingly negative. She rejects him because she contends that a wife is no more than an "*Upper-Servant*" (148).[47] Equating marriage to self-abasement, she takes the life of

Israelite slaves in Exodus 21:5–6 as her model. She agrees to marry the merchant with no altered conviction but with a "Copy of my Countenance" (233). In her mind, becoming a wife means playing the part of an upper servant and embracing "the Family as a House of Bondage." Her sense of Jewish slavery demeans the typology of the Exodus (Exod. 13:3 and 14). When she nearly rejects the Dutch merchant again, she says "it was very well my Heart fail'd me" (Ps. 73:26 [236]). Glad that weakness like David's stops her returning to the reformed prince, she abuses biblical symbolism rather than contemplate that God might be supervising her life. Her increasing abuse of biblical symbols is apparent when she fears adding her wealth to her husband's. At this prospect she trembles like Belshazzar (Dan. 5:6) and describes her powers of corruption in terms of a moth, a caterpillar, and fire in flax (Matt. 6:19, Isa. 33:4, and Judg. 15:14 [259]). No wonder she admits to a secret hell within, "a Dart struck into the Liver" (Prov. 7:23 [260]). At this stage of her autobiography, her most positive allusion transpires when she urges Amy not to hurt a hair of Susan's head (Matt 5:28 and Luke 21:18 [273]).[48] But the inefficacy of this allusion confirms that her abuse of the Bible serves to heighten readers' sensibility. Haunted by her daughter's "Evil Spirit," Roxana claims to find "a *Bitter* in all my *Sweet*" (310), Defoe inviting us to recall that the hungry soul finds every bitter thing sweet but the full one loathes honeycomb (Prov. 27:7) and that bitterness and sweetness are reversed for those who confuse evil and good (Isa. 5:29). Cursed by an evil spirit sent by the Lord (1 Sam. 16:14), Roxana persists in calling life sweet. But, in failing to grasp the polar relations between bitterness and sweetness, she approaches insanity more nearly, the most desperate and self-destructive of Defoe's narrators (264 and 310).

While Roxana subjects typology to courtly decadence, Crusoe comes to rely on the Bible in the New World, isolation from Europe allowing him to become allusively sensitive. His compulsive desires to explore the world mean that he avoids taking his father's biblical advice. Crusoe senior promotes the middle station of life based on Solomon's view that a "just Standard of true Felicity" is "to have neither Poverty or Riches" and that one can taste "the sweets of living without the bitter" (Prov. 30:8 [4–5]). If the father's wish for the son not to suffer the extremes of life justifies Crusoe's rejection of paternal advice, it explains why, on the island, Crusoe must repeatedly ask: "How can [God] sweeten the bitterest Providences?" (148). His spiritual task is to recognize Providence's reconciliation of experiential contraries. But this task further defines itself over against his rejection of typology. His first experience of a storm at sea prompts him to return like the "true repenting Prodigal" (Luke 15:11 [8]), but his second leads him to doubt that, were he to return, his father would be "an Emblem of our Blessed Saviour's Parable" and kill the "fatted Calf" (Luke 15:23 [14]). By evading patriarchal typology, Crusoe becomes an anti-type. So, the captain who blames his ship's loss on Crusoe's flight from home and unjustified presence on board, recalls that Jonah asked to be thrown overboard for his sins (Jon. 1:12 [15]).

Crusoe changes his attitude to typology on the island because Providence furnishes him with "three very good Bibles" (64). But, before he can read them properly, he must renew his speaking and listening. When he first attempts to pray, his prayers lack the "Grace of God" since they arise from the "Voice of meer Fright" and "Hurries of my Soul." His challenge is to sensitize himself to internal dialogue because, "like a Voice," conscience renders him "dumb with ... Reflections" and leaves him "not a Word to say" (88–93). Before speaking to himself he must, paradoxically, experience speechlessness: he must go beyond linguistic convention to realize that the Bible's words have "no Sound" to him. Its words make "a great Impression upon" him only after he takes them "in a different Sense" that entails winning "a true Scripture View of Hope" (94–6). He is guided "to things of a higher nature" when "constant reading the Scripture, and praying to God" (97) leads to "Communications of [God's] Grace to my Soul" (112). From studying the Bible "thrice every Day," his "very Soul" blesses God every time he opens it (114). Condemned to a "silent Life" which requires him to accept that he is being punished by the lack of social discourse, he trusts that he is promised deliverance, Psalm 50:15 causing him to imitate the children of Israel (94–6 and 156–7). After he habituates himself to the question "*Can God spread a Table in the Wilderness*?" he voices texts that he has not yet read, such as those which glorify divine deliverance and contain the blind men's prayer for mercy (Acts 5:31 and Matt. 9:27 [96]). Spontaneous and unconscious allusions evidence divine conversation in him and confirm his typological acceptance of the Exodus. By taking the children of Israel as a model, he hopes to survive in the wilderness. The Bible induces religious observances in him: on the anniversary of being shipwrecked, he fasts and prostrates himself until "the going down of the Sun" (Josh. 1:4 [103]) and, since Providence fills his Table (130), he celebrates nature's plenitude (Ps. 78:19 [148]).

Besides assigning his protagonist positive allusions, Defoe employs ironical ones throughout. Since the cedar from which he makes an immovable canoe is larger than those in Solomon's temple, Crusoe's resistance to Providence is counterpoised with the patriarch's praise of God (1 Kings 5:6 [126]). Crusoe may claim to be supported by miracles "as great as that of feeding Elijah by Ravens" (1 Kings 17: 4–6 and Mark 10: 22 [132]), but his claim sustains neither his conduct nor his narrative. Nor does he wait on the Lord, as he claims (Ps. 27:14 [157]). Like Saul threatened by the Philistines, he feels forsaken when he learns about the cannibals' visits to the island (1 Sam. 28:15 [159]). Far from crying "to God in [his] Distress," he lives in "the constant Snare of the Fear of Man" (Prov. 29:25 [163]). Hiding in caves "like one of the ancient Giants" (Gen. 6:4 [179]), he abandons himself to violent fantasies and only slowly realizes that the so-called savages' "Light" is their "Law" (Rom. 2:14 [210]). Far from teaching the Bible to Friday, Crusoe admits that Friday is "a much better Scholar in the Scripture Knowledge" (221).[49] Indeed, Crusoe's biblical sense remains unsteady. He does not foresee that lack of food might make the island's inhabitants rebel like the children of Israel (Exodus 16:3–4). About Providence's increase of his wealth, he "might well say" his "latter End" exceeds his "Beginning" (Job 42:12 [284]), but his return to England yields neither personal nor spiritual composure. The parallel he draws with Job reveals how habituated he is to rootlessness: the blessing of wealth does not lead to spiritual integrity. When he departs from England again, the gap between his biblical allusions and mode of life shows readers that exegesis and spiritual self-examination are always to be improved, always to be renewed.

*****

To uphold the Protestant tradition of Bible reading established by the Reformation, Defoe could not have made Crusoe, his most positive exemplum, an ideal hero. That would have betrayed the literary dialectic and rhetorical inventiveness that perpetuate biblical spirituality in all his non-fiction and fiction. In that Crusoe's story is historical and allegorical, literal and figurative, combining explicit and implicit biblical allusions, it employs polar allusiveness like most of Defoe's works. In showing that the encompassing context for his writings is the Bible's evolving interpretative history, his authorial self-effacement enjoins participatory roles on readers who are invited to respond to his texts by extending their sense of the Bible as the foundation of all texts. Defoe honours the Reformation by inducing readers to train their imaginations to detect biblical words so that they may recognize such words and tones in their own communal and inherited speech.[50] He heightens the applicability of the Bible to the mundane world so that readers may discover, if not recover, the accessibility of prayer and the power of spiritual vision.

Chapter Five

Political Impersonations and Cultural Implications

LIBERTY is the Glory of an *Englishman*; 'tis as Natural to him to desire it, as 'tis lawful to him to maintain it; 'tis his Inheritance, purchas'd with the Blood of his Ancestors, and as 'tis his Portion, so 'tis his Pride; but 'tis with an *Englishman* about his Liberty, as 'tis with many of them about Popery; there is a kind of national Aversion among them to Popery; 'tis the universal Scare-crow, the Hobgoblin, the Spectre with which the Nurses fright the Children and entertain the old Women all over the Country, by which means such horror possesses the Minds of the common People about it, that I believe there are an 100000 stout Fellows, who would spend the last Drop of their Blood against Popery, that do not know whether it be a Man or a Horse.[1]

Defoe's prophetic and typological allusions to the Bible detailed in the previous chapter prepare us to analyse how and why he relates political ideology to positive and negative aspects of religion and theology. As the text offering ultimate authority to the dialectic of transcendence and immanence in private and public discourse, the Bible functions for Defoe as the substrate of society because it provides categorical imperatives not only to the vocations involved in commerce and trade but also to politicians and theorists of government. As a believer in God's absolute authority, he promoted monarchy over republicanism, often ironically embodying his belief in personas whose doctrines were, at one extreme, not far removed from leaderless and institutional anarchy and, at the other, time-serving and atheistic forces intent on sapping monarchical power for their political advantage. In defending kingship in the reign of George I, he refused to subordinate his polarity thinking and double vision to political ideology: a Dissenter and Whig, he refused especially after 1714 to adhere to the rhetoric of Dissenters and Whigs, because of, as Schonhorn sees it, his growing discontent with governmental developments in the Hanoverian era and his critique of political illusions:

> The progress of Defoe's political thought reveals that he saw English liberty endangered by the grasping power of the new parliamentary interests. He grew to understand that England's deliverance by William and his Protestant hero's reign had not settled the dangerous and incipiently destructive struggle for political domination that is the history of his Stuart century. Post-Revolution shibboleths of limited monarchy, king-in-parliament, balance of power, and co-ordinate government – these Defoe understood as smokescreens that were meant to obscure the growing domination of parliaments.[2]

As the epigraph above shows, Defoe happily decried the slogans one might have expected him to cherish. In the words of Roy Porter, the concept of liberty based on Locke's theory that "political legitimacy could spring only from consent" became a "Whig mantra." But the epigraph derides that mantra by satirizing the religious superstition and popular culture which absorbed it. By 1724 when he published *The Great Law of Subordination Consider'd*, Defoe assailed Whig political theory given what he saw as the corrupting power of finance, public debt, patronage, and professionalized armed forces on parliamentary procedures, as we are about to detail.[3] Despite being an apologist for trade and commerce, Defoe rejected the Whig view that liberty is the "cradle of culture," his Augustinian sense of human depravity leading him to uphold traditional notions of monarchical authority and social hierarchy. In the epigraph from *The Great Law of Subordination Consider'd*, the analogy between national glorification of liberty and hatred of Roman Catholicism categorically links both to the prejudices of popular culture. The unthinking populace assumes that liberty like their hatred of Roman Catholicism is a natural principle inherited in their blood. The analogy between the two prejudices implies that liberty, like the religious phobia, functions like a scarecrow, hobgoblin, or spectre. Liberty, far from being an intelligent ideal, is an irrational, self-destructive slogan for the nation. Twenty years or so before, in *The True-Born Englishman*, which joins patriotic and cultural pride to xenophobia, Defoe had learned how to mix blame and praise in modes that defy prejudices about racial purity.[4] But here his attack on liberty is more harshly presented so that he might subordinate it to orthodox religious principles. Thus, in the paragraph after the epigraph he demeans the popular notion of liberty by sexual innuendoes:

> Liberty is a word of Endearment, 'tis the Hereditary Favourite of the People; 'tis the Nation's Mistress, I was a going to say it was the Nation's Whore; in a Word, 'tis talked of by every-body, valu'd by every-body, and understood almost by no-body.

After reiterating that "English Liberty ... is as blindly espous'd" as Popery is hated by a nation that mistakes both "in the grossest manner," he argues that liberty of conscience and the press are among "several Sorts of Liberty, which are grossly abus'd" since they have become thoughtlessly ingrained in the culture. His point is that, if the concept of liberty upholds freedom of religious conscience, it does not permit atheism. If "Persecution for Religion" is intolerable since "conscientious Christians" ought to be left "to worship God in the Manner which they believe to be most agreeable to his Will, and most edifying to themselves," there should be limits to religious liberty, for it is "grossly abus'd, when 'tis made use of to protect those who deny all Reveal'd Religion; who, instead of a *Liberty* in Religion, claim a *Liberty* to be of no Religion at-all." The toleration extended to Dissenters for "Religious Liberties" does not reach to "harden'd Consciences" who "*worship no God at all.*" Those who assert the liberty to blaspheme God, deny the Redeemer, and mock religion are "unsufferable"; "both by the Laws of God, and of all Christian Nations, [they] ought to be punished," there being "nothing of Religion or Conscience" in their case. For similar reasons, he finds the liberty of the press a "Parallel Case in this very same Constitution, and Government." Thus he defends restrictions on the press, because the English are unjustifiably proud that "every Man is at Liberty to Print and Publish what he pleases":

> the Government frequently take up both *Authors* and *Printers*, if they Print any thing offensive, or against the *Administration*; or if they publish any Personal Reflections, the Person injur'd if these Reflections are unjust and slanderous, has a Right to prosecute the Publisher and Author, and will have his Remedy at Law.

Having experienced such prosecution, Defoe speaks both feelingly and obliquely about the negative effects of the Whig ideology of liberty upon individuals and society.[5]

His satire of Whig ideology operates by a more subtle dialectic in *Mere Nature Delineated,* which blurs distinctions between court and popular culture for religious purposes. The preface, declaring that "*our modern Men of Mode*" are the "*Objects of a just Satyr,*" apologizes for "*a little Appearance of Levity.*"[6] With ironic blandness, Defoe impersonates a natural philosopher who voices polar suppositions about whether Peter the Wild Boy has a soul and is human or not, suppositions that equally generate satirical implications. The persona's ostensible subject, having grown up in a state of nature, lacks speech and social awareness. Apparently sympathetic to George I's wish to nurture Peter, the persona mocks the court's progressive benevolence, since the Wild Boy is merely "a Thing in human Shape." The story that he was raised by forest animals is untenable because humans, unlike beasts, cannot survive in the state of nature. Man, insists Defoe,

> cannot rest on the Ground, or roost in the Bushes; the Trees that are the Habitation of the Fowls, and which cover the other Creatures, scratch and hurt him; He must have a House to live in, or nothing; he cannot Burrow like the Rabbit, or earth himself in a Den like the Badger: They are warm and secure from the Weather … but the poor naked, tenderskin'd Brute of Human Kind, must have a House to keep him dry, Cloaths to keep him warm, and a Door to shut him in, or he is lost.[7]

Humans, despite their degeneracy, "can't throw off the Soul, or its Faculties." "Royal Compassion" may suppose Peter to "have a Soul, the Image of his glorious Maker," but the youth is "demented" and lacks "the Faculties proper and particular to a Soul" and to "human Society, the Heaven of Life!" If he does have a soul and prefers "the Brutal sensitive Life" when he "must see and know" that life among Christians is "much happier than that of the Woods and the Forest," the implications "upon the present inspir'd Age" are vast. In choosing "to continue silent and mute, to live and converse with the Quadrupeds of the Forest, and retire again from human Society, rather than dwell among the inform'd Part of Mankind," Peter shuns the models of development at court. Still, the persona coyly feels the problem of Peter's unchanged conduct may be solved by again supposing him "Soul-less, his Judgement and Sense to be in a State of Non-Entity." A lack of "rational faculties" must explain why the "Surface" of "Nature" gives him no impressions of "one Kind, or of another": he "looks on the infinite Variety [of nature], with a kind of equal Unconcernedness, as if every Object were alike, or that he knew not how to distinguish between Good or Evil, Pleasant or Unpleasant." The only other solution to his arrested development lies in court culture. Living at court could not remedy his cognitive unresponsiveness because a "Plague of Dumbness" has "over-spread" courtiers in England and Europe. Statesmen embody "this Kind of Dumbness" and are "justly ranked among the Mute Part of the World" since they are "famous in their Generation, for making long Speeches, and saying nothing." If Peter "appears at Court with some Vivacity in his Countenance," it must be because of his "Joy at seeing so many Images there, whose Purity of Sense suits them to himself."[8]

At this point in the satirical exposition, Defoe's persona links the dullness of courtiers and parliamentarians to their Jacobite predispositions by turning Peter into an "Emblem of Court Fools" that will "illustrate several other Species of Fools." Hence, Peter might well liaise with the Pretender abroad because his defects qualify him to serve "in divers Capacities, to the Advantage of all Sides." He might also represent the Pretender in England, for

> he would have a vast Advantage in that Employ, more than most of the Emissaries, or Agents, they could send over, would be able to obtain; namely, That he might act with all possible Security against our Laws, or the Resentment of our Government, go and come, see and be seen, and give very little Offence; for that it is a known Maxim in a wise Part of our Law, *That a Fool cannot be guilty either of Murther, or Treason.*

Moreover, Peter is blameless for lacking religious awareness since he could acquire none in London.

> Can any one learn Religion in this Town! Or come to the Knowledge of Him of whom they can receive no Notions from any about them? Who should teach him the first Notions of Religion here? Shall he be taught Religion by its Contraries?

Since courtiers and parliamentarians are negative religious models, they afford Peter no spiritual guidance: "Swearing among the Beaus and Fops" yields no positive notion of religion. Since Peter's "organick Powers" have been stunted, he could not deduce religion from their "horrid and execrable Blasphemies." To gratify "Sceptical, Deistical, Ante-Enthusiastick readers" who are never at "Pains to make Pretensions to Inspirations or Revelations of any kind," the persona refuses to specify how Peter might be instructed in "the Principles and Practice of Christian Knowledge," but he prods other readers by taking it "for granted, that his Instructors shall gradually instill the Christian Knowledge into his Soul by constantly blending it together, and joining it to every other Branch of their Instructions." In then claiming that his satire applies only to "foreign and remote Countries," the persona exposes British governmental theory and practice in a Swiftian vein:

> our own Statesmen, Ministers, Counsellors, and Politicians (except such as are out of Office and unemploy'd) ... are all out of the Question; nothing but Praises and Panegyricks attend them; they are all wise, honest, just, generous (may they be always so) abusing no-body, and no-body abusing them; which last, however, if they escape, they will have more to boast of, than most honest Statesmen that ever went before them; but this is a Digression in order to be rightly understood only.

This facetious irony leads to the exposition of Defoe's governing political idea: the decline in respect for monarchy will be repaired only if the "Kings of the Christian World" learn to govern by acquiring "the Art of Reigning without Favourites" and becoming "their own Prime Ministers." Were they to stop being "Deputies to their upper Servants," they would reduce the number of "State Fools," lead the public "to see with their own Eyes," and induce princes to "answer for their own Mistakes" rather than for "the Mistakes of their Ministers."[9]

This emphasis on monarchical authority is heightened by Islamic allusions the satirical power of which will be explored further at the end of this chapter. In Turkey, claims the persona, where the "Emperors are Men of Pleasure" and, taken up with "Luxury and Indulgence, wallow in their Sensualities, and dwell in their *Seraglio*, effeminated with Women, and surrounded continually with their Whores," the Grand Viziers are the political authorities. But, in Christian realms where kings are not "Idols, or Gods of their People, but the Fathers of their Country," nothing increases "the mutual and joint Felicity, both of Sovereign and Subject, like the personal Administration of their Princes." England has always done best when its monarchs have not relied on "Tools call'd Favourites." However, when a Grand Vizier "makes a false step," his error is not inconvenient, because all the "Grand Seigneur" does is "whip off his Head" and install another favourite. Were this way of dealing with "Politick-Riders, and Christian *Viziers*" adopted in Christendom, such a "wholsome Severity" might make "Arbitrary

Governments much easier to the People than they are." The oxymoron, "Christian *Viziers*," confirms how *Mere Nature Delineated*, by turning the Wild Boy into an emblem of courtly modes, amusingly upholds Defoe's prescriptions for monarchy.[10]

Such prescriptions inform *Memoirs of a Cavalier*, a fictional autobiography published six years before *Mere Nature Delineated*, the earlier work offering revisionary insights into the reign of Charles I and the Civil War by celebrating monarchy and decrying theocracy.[11] In the Cavalier's eyes, Charles I "always took the best Measures, when he was left to his own Counsel" (221). But his army was plagued by "Crouds of Parsons," the "Camp and Court" being full of "Clergymen" (123). The king did not realize that the "*Clergy was resolved if there should be no Bishop, there should be no King*" (227). Nor did he see that both Anglican and Dissenting clerics "made Religion rather *the Pretence* than *the Cause* of the War" (165). On the continent, the Cavalier appreciates the separation of church and state. Like Roxana, he finds the "stupid Bigotry" at Rome "irksome"; the "entire Empire the Priests have over both the Souls and Bodies of the People" signals a "Meanness of Spirit." Again like her, he thinks the "Civil Authority" at Venice has "a visible Superiority over the Ecclesiastick" (34).[12] An undogmatic royalist, the Cavalier agrees with the removal of Charles I's "evil Counsellours" but does not grant that "all the Powers and Prerogatives of the Crown should devolve upon the Parliament" (143). Hostile to the seditious "Clamours of the People," he believes the Civil War might have been avoided had Charles understood "the Management of Politicks" (21). An idealistic non-partisan, he promotes a mixed constitution that privileges moral leadership and humane power: anticipating the Glorious Revolution, he lauds the heroism of Gustavus Adolphus, King of Sweden, and General Fairfax. The former was self-disciplined and accessible to his subjects. Creating order in society, he inspired reverence with his energy and spirituality. Despite opposing General Fairfax's ideology, the Cavalier admires his strength and humanity: "No Man in the World had more Fire and Fury in him while in Action, or more Temper and Softness out of it" (265).

*****

As *The Great Law of Subordination Consider'd*, *Mere Nature Delineated*, and *Memoirs of a Cavalier* suggest, after 1720 Defoe no longer trusted that the Hanoverian era would effect the constitutional renewal he had projected in 1715 when he wrote in *Strike while the Iron's Hot* that

> It cannot be deny'd, but that the People of *Great Britain* have now another Opportunity put into their Hands, to settle and establish themselves upon right Foundations, and to stop all the Gaps, at which the Mischiefs of our late Evil Government has broken in. Certainly no Nation ever had two such Opportunities, one on the Neck of another, to fix their Liberties and fortify the Defence of their Constitution, as this Nation has had. They have now had Six and Twenty Years Experience.[13]

This statement's measured syntax with its idiomatic forcefulness and architectural imagery holds that, since executive actions had lately betrayed the Revolution of 1688, constitutional renewal would transpire only if members of parliament were to improve the "Provision against the Exercise of *Arbitrary Power*" by the monarch, disclaim the Jacobite tenet of "Divine Hereditary, Indefeazable Right," define toleration against the High-Church view of it as mere "Exemption from Penalties," educate Dissenters to their rights, and reassign the "Power of making Peace and War" so that ministerial abuse of national interests will cease. While arguing for legislated penalties against seditious Tory clergy for meddling in state affairs, Defoe more generally assails the "Tyranny of Party" and the "Bondage of Prime Ministry." Hence, his tracts after 1714 call for constitutional renewal by espousing multiple viewpoints rather than partisan ideology. Thus, for Schonhorn,

> Daniel Defoe is a writer as complex and as contradictory as any we can read in English literature, and thus there are many Defoes. And there is one Defoe for whom "modern" or "Lockean" political paradigms have been misleading Procrustean formulas. They have obscured some distinctly idiomatic aspects of Defoe's political Revolutionary and Hanoverian Whiggism.[14]

In denying that Defoe's refusal to be a single-minded Whig is atypical, Schonhorn cites H.T. Dickinson's view that "an essential aspect of Whiggism was its suspicion of the executive." In the years following George I's accession, Defoe faced a maze of political issues that led him to invent voices that surpass in intricacy the mixed modes of idealization and satire he created in *Jure Divino* and the *Review*. His Georgian tracts advance the techniques of impersonation and ventriloquism that he had exploited in *The Shortest-Way with the Dissenters*, even though such techniques had earlier caused him financial and psychological distress.[15]

One reason why he expanded his range of impersonations was that Queen Anne's death on 1 August 1714 ushered in years of constitutional instability.[16] While the 1701 Act of Settlement had stipulated that succession to the throne should pass to the House of Hanover, resistance to King George led, on his coronation day, to riots that lasted beyond the election campaign of January and February 1715 so that, by the end of July, Habeas Corpus had been suspended and the Riot Act had been rushed through Parliament. The election aggravated the instability. At Anne's decease, the Tories held a large majority in the House of Commons, which they expected to hold by rousing voters with the slogan "the church in danger." But a 240-seat majority disappeared into a Whig victory of 65 seats. Spurred by this reversal, the Whigs sought reprisals against the late Queen's ministers and contemplated obliterating the Tory opposition. The Jacobite Rebellion of September 1715 encouraged this aggression by providing the Whigs with justification for the Septennial Act of 1716 that, in prolonging the life of Parliament by four years, robbed Tories of the prospect of an election in 1718. Hard on the demise of Tory opposition came the surprising Whig schism. When Whigs fought Whigs, internecine strife heightened the secularization of political life.[17] Bitter conflicts over the relation of religion and politics increased dissension in 1716 and 1717 when Benjamin Hoadly, Bishop of Bangor, promoted the subordination of church to state. Factionalism was intensified by the Jacobite plot of 1718, by debates about religious rights and persecution of Dissenters leading to the repeal of the Occasional Conformity and Schism Acts in 1719, and by the financial crisis of the South-Sea Bubble in 1720.[18]

In defending the Hanoverian Succession as a confirmation of the Revolution of 1688, Defoe emphasized the juncture of constitutional and religious values and attacked interest groups which menaced that integration.[19] While he served Whig administrations after 1714 by sapping opposition to them, neither coercion nor partisanship stifled his rhetorical flexibility.[20] Habituated to turning his pen on Tories, Jacobites, and High-Churchmen, he also turned it on Whigs, Low-Church Anglicans, and Dissenters in certain circumstances.[21] So, while he maintained the political and religious stances of his early journalism, he modified those stances by moving away from contract theory and elaborating the myth of the warrior-king.[22] Upholding the Glorious Revolution in George I's reign presented Defoe with occasions to develop his sense of irony, impersonation, and narrative contraries and to realize a growing independence of thought. Keen to integrate secular and religious values even as he argued for the separation of church and state, he experimented with political stances. The necessity of supporting Whigs exercised his abilities to present issues from contrary viewpoints. That he had to write indirectly as well as directly on behalf of Whigs meant that he gained expressive powers from impersonating Tories more subtly – and more defensively – than he had in *The Shortest-Way with the Dissenters*. The licence to temper Tory criticism of Whig administrations required him to be strategic when imitating Tories. By disclaimers, ambivalence, and suggestive vagueness, he turned impersonations of Tories into attacks on Whigs with impressive flexibility.

While he viewed George I's rule as the theoretical embodiment of the Protestant Settlement and bulwark against Jacobitism, he acknowledged personal motives: loyalty to Robert Harley and belief in his former patron's political moderation made him resist the Whigs' vindictiveness against the Earl of Oxford. This partly explains the gap between the stridency with which he discredited the Tories before the election of 1715 and the equanimity with which, after the election, he sometimes argued for their comprehension into political life. Fiercely opposed to Jacobites as he was, he saw the worth of trying to comprehend them after the Fifteen ingloriously petered out at Preston.[23] His reactions to the Bangorian controversy are similarly contrary: whereas he adopted Hoadly's views in order to deflate High-Churchmen, he satirized the bishop for promoting the secularization of politics. That his contrary stances are understandable is not to suggest that he confronted political strife with ease. The polarities by which he tried to deal with it reveal that rhetorical inventiveness was hard won. One mode by which he distanced himself from strife was the impersonation of Quakers. By adopting their voices, he freed himself from Whig and Tory propaganda.[24] The stance of Quakers – theoretically principled outsiders to politics – let him treat both Whigs and Tories ironically. At the same time, his worldly Quaker personas are amusingly untrue to their sect's ideals. The way he exploits their dialect and disgust with political corruption while he laughs at some of their tenets, the way he makes them spokesmen for moderation while he comically exploits their mannerisms, evidences the thought-provoking contrariety inherent in his impersonations. Since his Quaker personas are shrewd commentators on the political system, he can more effectively apply narrative contraries to defend the constitution and reconcile secular and religious values. At one and the same time a propagandist for the Whigs, an ironic defender of Tories and Jacobites for and against the Whigs, and an author wishing to stand back from political confusion, Defoe achieved in the early Georgian years a rhetorical flexibility instrumental to his developing sense of fiction.[25]

*****

Queen Anne's domineering, disunited ministers caused Defoe to seek rhetorical space in which to renew the dialectic by which he related politics and religion. He found such space in impersonations of the voices, mannerisms, and pacific tenets of Quakers. The titular ambivalence of *A Friendly Epistle* illustrates this point.[26] Its persona berates Thomas Bradbury, a Dissenting Congregationalist, who called for vengeance on the Queen's ministers by arguing on behalf of the lawfulness of taking up arms against tyrants. Bradbury's inflammatory pulpit oratory is belittled as misplaced. The persona leaves vengeance to the Lord: mistrustful of human justice, he urges preachers to exemplify forbearance rather than excite vengeance. Since "*the Wrath of Men worketh not the Righteousness of God*" (James 1:20), the Quaker says that calls for justice lead to injustice and that those who have the "Power to interpret Laws, or strain and extend the Ordinances of the Land to their own Purposes" often call right wrong. Despite his political and judicial indifference, he ratifies George I's choice of ministers because they oppose the Pretender and he maintains that Jacobites would deserve death should they restore the Pretender. Besides defending the constitution, the Quaker tells Bradbury to preach against the degenerate times with its growing number of theatres in which the populace "embrace the Works of Darkness" and the nobility avoid "the Paths of Truth." The Quaker's case against playhouses only vaguely resembles Defoe's views.[27] More germane to this study are the risks of stirring up antagonistic reactions that his impersonations incurred in the communities that his satire both imitated and challenged. Thus, this tract's polar ideological stances made Quakers fearful of governmental reprisals, and the Dissenters felt threatened from within by a member.[28]

The following three tracts confirm that Defoe's polemical impersonations of Quakers retaliate against prominent controversialists by exposing their ideological inconsistencies. In March 1715, Defoe published *A Sharp Rebuke from one of the People Called Quakers*, which charges the high-flying Henry Sacheverell with stirring up political strife by – far from granting that dissenting forms of worship are legal – conceding only that Dissenters are not subject to state violence and judicial penalties. Saying the high-flyer hides his "Persecuting Spirit" under "wholesome Severities" and critical of his Jacobitism, passive resistance, and campaign for King William's assassination, the persona views Sacheverell's attacks on George I as sour grapes for the displacement of High-Church clergy in 1688.[29] This Quaker, in defending the Revolution Settlement, apologizes for George I's patriotic and religious sensibility from a stance that goes against his sect's tenets.

While he approved of Hoadly's assault on theocracy, Defoe mocks the bishop for decrying Dissent through the Quaker persona of *A Declaration of Truth to Benjamin Hoadly*.[30] This Quaker first praises the bishop for denying that men have authority to join their power to "the Right Hand of Jesus" since He needs no partners. But then he ironically recognizes Hoadly as a candidate for conversion: once illuminated by "Heavenly Light," he will join "the Friends." The Quaker relates the bishop's authority to the Friends' theory of subordination: they obey superiors who demand subjection in the Lord but not those who demand it in matters unrelated to God's will. The bishop's opposition to priests who usurp Christ's power already conforms to Quakerism. Aware of the chasm between worldly Hoadly and unworldly persecuted Quakers, Defoe proposes with ironical anarchism that the latter are models for the bishop. His zealous persona holds that, if Hoadly continues on his path, he will be "assisted by the Spirit of Truth to pull down and overthrow the whole Power, Hierarchy and Constitution of that People who call themselves *The Church*." By separating from the "Usurpers of unrighteous Authority," he would overthrow both Low- and High-Church. Yet, he will not see that his "Robes of Distinction" are tokens of "that usurp'd Power" he condemns. The Quaker further exposes his contradictions:

> thou shouldst not delay any longer joining thy self unto the Lord's People, whose Cause thou hast already so worthily pleaded: For why shouldst thou not cause thy Life and Doctrine to conform unto each other?

Hoadly must cease being an ecclesiastical "Ruler," if his words from the "Speaking Place" are true. The periphrastic avoidance of "pulpit" marks a turn from mock deference to sharp criticism: the Quaker warns the bishop he will not be able to join the Presbyterians given their belief that human laws bind the conscience and that reward and punishment affect the "Succession of Officers." Contrarily, this Quaker violently threatens Hoadly's complacent orthodoxy to advance ecclesiastical calm and Protestant unity.[31]

By endowing his Quakers with revolutionary stances and ideological inconsistencies, Defoe enjoys making them into mouthpieces of political and religious extremes. His goading of Hoadly in *A Friendly Rebuke to One Parson Benjamin* is a brilliantly comic example.[32] This Quaker reports that the bishop's fellow priests spurn the controversies he provokes. Upholding Hoadly because his tenets erode his authority, the persona finds it odd that the bishop should attack others for their contradictions. Benjamin does not see that he vindicates the view that a minister is "an unscriptural Employment of Humane Invention, imposed upon the Faithful, neither of Divine Original, or vested with Divine Authority." Since the "Discipline belonging to the Ecclesiastick Constitution, as it is settled by the Lay-Powers among us, is not a Christian Discipline," the Quaker wonders how Benjamin can bring himself to conform to this "*Not Christian Discipline.*" Nor can he understand why Benjamin, whose office commits him to peace, loves controversy: he is serving his own glory since his "worldly Instruments, and the Arts of [his] fancy'd Rhetorick" clash with the tenet that his Master's kingdom is "not of this World." Benjamin erratically vindicates Christ's kingdom through controversy, because he implies that this kingdom may be aided by human power, while also holding that "no Humane Power can claim any Right to interpose in the Government of that Kingdom." Rhetorically trapping Hoadly, the Quaker speaks with succinct brilliance:

> Doubtless Friend, if no Laws, no Constitutions are concern'd to interpose in the Government of Christ's Kingdom, no Power is wanting to support or maintain it; but as Christ alone has the Right of Legislature, which thing I allow, so he has Power sufficient to extend its Influence in the Hearts of his Subjects; to diffuse the Knowledge of his Will, and to produce an Universal Obedience in his Subjects to those his Laws if he thinks fit to have it so.

The Quaker's political analogy defies Benjamin's theology: if Hoadly believes in Christ's heavenly agency, he engages in debates irrelevant to "the Kingdom of Jesus." He fails to see he has provoked a massive reaction against himself and inflamed the public by not recognizing how party prejudice infects his arguments. To the Quaker, as to Defoe, partisan writers reach only a limited readership. Hoadly's ecclesiastical illogicality, besides sapping his authority, foments strife among Anglican clergy and weakens church hierarchy. Like Defoe too, the Quaker faults Hoadly's view of occasional conformity given its vague latitudinarianism. Since Christians must obey the dictates of conscience, the Quaker is appalled the bishop remains in the church after conceding that its persecution of Dissent usurps Christ's authority. Hoadly's lack of charity makes him "*a Sounding Brass, and a Tinkling Cimbal.*"[33] That the Schism and Occasional Conformity Acts are to be repealed contents the Quaker since they have degraded public morality, but he grants Hoadly no credit. Again like his creator, the Quaker maintains that the Dissenters may not benefit from the repeals since conforming with one congregation for "pretended Conscience" and with another for "Worldly Enjoyment and Advantage" is "Vile and Hypocritical."[34] The repeals may undo the Dissenters' "true Sincerity" and entice them back to the Established Church, which Hoadly's championing of their liberty likely aimed to do. The Quaker simply hopes that King George's concern for the "Peace and Tranquility" of his people will effect principles superior to Hoadly's. While he dislikes congregational schisms, the Quaker upholds denominational differences because they testify to genuine liberty of conscience.

Defoe's Quaker personas with their contrarian stances as religious outsiders and political insiders illustrate the rhetorical licence with which in the reign of George I he defended the Revolution Settlement, these impersonations exploiting rapid topical transitions and as quickly transforming praise into blame and vice versa. The remarkable discursive freedom that he gained from these impersonations he also applied to the masked displacement of Jacobitism in *An Account of the Great and Generous Actions of James Butler*. This pamphlet praises Oxford University by saying that it could not be more disloyal to George than it had been to Anne! To Defoe's equally ingenuous and subtle persona, it is inconceivable that the university sponsored Jacobite riots during celebrations for George's accession. The persona's counter-factual supposition assumes with knowing falsity that the institution is a rational foundation whose aristocratic and church-oriented students could never be involved in "*Street-Madness*." Since most students "have the Temple and the Altar in their View, and are learning the divine Stile of the Pulpit," they could not be "Disturbers of the Civil Peace." The more the persona cannot credit student misbehaviour, the keener his irony: to believe supporters of passive obedience would riot against the king is to suppose that the pro-Jacobite university had turned "*Presbyterian*" and adopted the anti-monarchical principles of 1641. Treating Jacobitism and Civil War radicalism as contraries, the persona ventures further into ironic absurdity: he asks the university to prove its non-involvement in the riots. Since it was involved, his request proposes that it abide by its Jacobite principles of non-resistance! That his request aims to appease severer critics than himself threatens the university: if it does not disclaim the riots, it will admit its Jacobitism. Defoe attributes self-effacement and menace to his persona, who, in provoking impossible acts, mediates contradictions to pressure Oxford University into recognizing the secular and religious values harmonized in the nation's constitution.[35]

No matter the explicit ideological position of personas who attack Jacobitism, Defoe endows them with chatty informality and discursive amplitude. *A Trumpet Blown in the North* addresses John Erskine, Earl of Mar, who raised James's standard at Braemar on 6 September 1715 to begin the Jacobite Rebellion, through a Quaker. This insultingly familiar persona who ignores Erskine's title embodies one of Defoe's major contrarian tenets: "Truth loseth nothing of its Efficacy and Force by the Meanness of the Person, or the Plainness of the Language, by which it is held forth." Declaring that rebellion is not of the Lord, the Quaker urges John to repent and obey the people's rulers. He refutes the Pretender's hereditary right as having no authority in God's eyes, since David and Solomon ruled although both were younger sons. By regarding monarchy as subject to popular and divine choice, the Quaker integrates political and religious values amusingly and ironically.[36] A year later, the Anglican persona of *The Layman's Vindication of the Church of England* defends the Revolution Settlement and argues that close relations between church and state require the inclusion of Dissenters and the exclusion of Jacobites. To this layman, differences in "Worship, Discipline, and Government Ecclesiastick" do not preclude Anglicans and Dissenters from sharing political identity. The layman insists that Dissenters have been friends to the Church for forty years, citing Paul's words in Romans 13:1, "every soul [must] be subject to the higher Powers," to support the case that Dissenters are politically and socially constructive. This Low-Church Anglican's attack on the Bill for Occasional Conformity at the same time displaces Jacobite ideology.[37]

As George I's reign unfolded, Defoe saw that the constitutional principles of 1688 needed a systematic defence that required him to transfer the discursive inventiveness he had developed through his impersonations into his own voice. To uphold the Georgian administration, he knew he had to call directly for political and economic reform since theocratic powers linked to Jacobitism were undermining Parliament. His discussion of tax policy in *Fair Payment No Spunge* is exemplary, given his defence of William's military policies that led to private financing of the national debt.[38] This text holds that the national debt associates politicians and financiers too closely; financiers of the debt unduly influence taxation and military policies. Stockjobbers thrive on the debt and keep the nation "in Slavery to Creditors" so that the "Means of resisting the Power of Enemies is out of our Hands." Since Parliament submits military plans to the approval of financiers, window and candle taxes overburden the "Oppress'd labouring and Trading People." Excessive tax on consumer goods falls heavily on the "Trading, Manufacturing, Industrious middle sort of People." Arguing that more "Publick Faith" is owed to this class than to a "few Stock-Jobbers, and enrich'd Money-Lenders," Defoe also objects to tax on "the common Necessaries of Life, because the Poor use as much of them as the Rich, or suffer dismal Extremities for want of them." Hence, he urges legislative reform on the grounds that "*Parliamentary Credit*" is a social good; the basis of public welfare and national equity, it is instrumental to the "Common Rights and Liberties of the People." Tax reform is necessary because the national debt keeps interest rates high, while lower rates would lead to investment in commerce and manufacturing. The underlying principle for equitable reform is "that every Member of the Body Politick should be burthen'd with the common Weights of the Government, in Proportion to their Strength of bearing them; that they may draw equally in the same Yoke, and that the united Strength may thereby be increas'd and made stronger." While the rich who produce their own bread and ale avoid the excise, the poor who equally need such goods cannot. Parliament must imitate the Revolution's councils and give tax laws more "Concern for the People." National must trump financial interests; social policies must be reformulated given the increasing sophistication of capitalist instruments.[39]

If his sense of casuistry is one reason why Defoe rarely spoke about political and economic reform in his own voice, the evolution of the Whig party is another. Having long regarded that party as the agent of progress and the bastion of Protestantism, he realized that it needed to renew itself by incorporating the contrarian rule that the good always tends to become the bad. Thus, in *The Old Whig And Modern Whig Revived*, he recalls that until the accession of George I Whig politicians had withstood tyranny on principle.[40] But, once elected to power, they embraced factionalism through their "wicked and absurd Temper." Power was concentrated in ministers because of a "scandalous Engrossment of many great Places and Employments into *one* and *the same hand*." No longer disinterested patriots, they "depreciated the very Party, and brought Contempt upon themselves":

> all of them pursue their private Gain as their ultimate End, and in Default of it, are as ready to act to Day against, what they acted Yesterday for, and join to Day with those who they opposed Yesterday, without Respect to Whig or Tory.

Gross scrambling for power even infects courtiers and businessmen associated with Whigs. Defoe scorns the politicians themselves for being "all Things, and every Thing" as occasion serves. Since the "Nature of State Policy" is to be immune to self-interest, he stresses Christ's dictate in Matthew 12:25 that a kingdom divided against itself cannot stand. As long as they disavow principle, the Whigs will neither produce sound policy nor enjoy solidarity.[41] Although he had written against Tories and Whigs, he does not want to admit that parties can self-destruct. While he had often tried to divide Tories from Jacobites, he hopes Whigs will not form two parties. He does not anticipate one faction becoming a parliamentary opposition since he cannot foresee the collapse of the Tory party which was soon to come about. He will not believe that Townshend, Walpole, and other leading Whigs have joined the Tories and invited Dr Snape the high-flyer to preach before the House of Commons. Changing stance, he warns the Tories against trusting the factious Whigs; on regaining power, they will abandon the Tories. Defoe's persona is tonally desperate since the public good is being made a common "Whore": "every Party will to Day condemn, to Morrow acquit; to Day reproach, to Morrow embrace the same Person." The persona's wish for patriotic Whig solidarity is not upheld by his desperate tones.[42]

Indeed, the conflicted tones in *The Old Whig and Modern Whig Revived* confirm that Defoe fomented political strife even as he sought to remedy it. This contrarian impulse clarifies why his impersonations gnaw at institutions from within. The persona of *The Anatomy of Exchange-Alley*, a stockjobber, calls his occupation a "compleat System of Knavery."[43] To him, jobbers are a "Confederation of Usurers" whose heightening of fear and greed controls the value of money and manipulates stock prices. They will exploit a "Plot" about the Pretender's capture, a "meer Original System of Cheat and Delusion," to keep the market volatile. Their influence is political since government lets them buy up and inflate the price of lottery tickets, this "Confederacy" of jobbers and statesmen aiming "to bite the People." In the recent lottery, £500,000 of tickets sold for £600,000. The difference between face value and selling price, far from reducing the national debt or lowering taxes, ended up in jobbers' pockets. Understandably, this lottery scheme aroused the populace to anger about government corruption and mismanagement of the national debt. To the persona, Whig jobbers who aided the Jacobite rebellion are traitors; they caused the slump in stock prices and the run on the Bank of England during the 1715 uprising. Jacobite stock traders aimed at "disabling the Government, discouraging the King's Friends," and encouraging his enemies. Still "States-men turn Dealers" and Whig brokers job the state. Seats in the House of Commons are jobbed, since the repeal of the Triennial Act has increased the cost of running for Parliament. Brokers, exclaims the disgusted persona, would job the Crown and nation to receive a commission. By distorting news and exciting fear about stock prices, they subject national policy to their greed:

> These Men take upon them to put a Standard upon our Fears; and we are to ask them, when Intelligence comes from Abroad, whether any thing be to be slighted or apprehended; every publick Piece of News, every menace of the Nations Enemies is to receive its Weight from them; and the Price of Stocks is the Rule by which we are to guide our Judgment in publick Affairs, by which we are either to hope or fear when any thing amiss presents it self to our view.

Unless jobbing is suppressed, the government might appropriate jobbers' methods, the money market passing into the control of ministers and proving "many Ways fatal to the Peoples Interest." Should a "degenerated Government" control the rise and fall of stocks, ministers could lower and raise the value of money for wicked "Designs" that would reduce their dependence on Parliament. Arguing for professional self-destruction, the persona declares that the rooting out of stockjobbers would obviate a dangerously new ministerial absolutism. With transparent irony, he hastens to disclaim the possibility of such an eventuality in the current reign. Not many months were to pass before the South-Sea Bubble validated Defoe's criticism of the regressive ties between capitalists and politicians. Not only did he analyse lucidly the systematic problems in stock speculation through his self-critical persona, but also his ideas about the money supply confronted the dangers posed to society by political practices that treated money as a commodity, a thematic consideration explored in *Robinson Crusoe*, which appeared in the same year as *The Anatomy of Exchange-Alley*.[44]

*****

Forced by necessity to serve ministerial factions, Defoe adopted plural voices that he actuated contrarily to satisfy his independent-mindedness. Vulnerability to judicial circumstance by inhibiting him from expressing a systematic political ideology encouraged him to produce diverse texts the contrarian strategies of which permitted him to argue with himself and with stances he had once taken. In this he followed Locke's ideas on identity more than the philosopher's other tenets.[45] Locke's speculations about plural identity that advanced legal definitions of criminal responsibility partly account for Defoe's sense that impersonation might afford him freedom from bipartisan dogma. His deployment of direct and oblique viewpoints and of aggressive and defensive tones deepened his appreciation of the dialectical functionality of literary techniques. While he saw in the early Georgian years that constitutional ideals were in a parlous state and realized that political reform could not be effected by abstract theory and while he subjected theocracy to satire, he continued to invent forms of impersonation that exploited textual experiments through which he explored the cultural implications of a refined political system.

In *The Candidate*, published on 27 January 1715 in the election campaign, his persona satirizes electoral bribery, his target the gentry.[46] In running for Parliament, the gentry demeans itself, its members so bent on winning votes they carouse with the rabble to the extent of getting lice on their clothes. Since they visit playhouses for the same purpose, their bribery would be appropriately exposed by putting them on the stage as butts. After describing how others debase elections, such as innkeepers who, as political agents, overcharge candidates for drink served to voters, the persona advises the gentry not to waste money on bribes that yield only an inaccurate profile of electors but to spend it on public works. He also insists, in an insultingly homely manner, that gentlefolk's bribery renders them corruptible: "Can it be suppos'd, but he that steals a Horse to travel a Journey on the Road, will, if it offers, take a Purse when he is out." Those who bribe are bribable; their public conduct leads to personal vice. Despite being no admirer of the theatre, the persona announces the discovery of an act from a play "written many Years ago." In this playlet, a gentleman bribes his way to a borough seat. Once elected, he sells himself to the first minister to buy his support. He inquires neither into the minister's aims nor into how best to serve the constitution. Seats in parliament are bought and sold like shares by brokers in an organized market. *The Candidate*, then, joins fiction to non-fiction, textuality more than genre conveying how bribery corrupts government and undermines the authenticity of social hierarchy. Defoe's belief in how social mores should underlie political life requires him to spell out the codes in speculative wealth by which politicians corrupt themselves and the nation, thereby anticipating arguments in *The Anatomy of Exchange-Alley*.[47]

By upholding the principles of 1688, Defoe gained experience in textual criticism as well as in many impersonations. One of his remarkable polemical texts is *A Reply to a Traiterous Libel*, which was published on 29 January 1715.[48] This text attacks Francis Atterbury's *English Advice to the Freeholders of England* that appeared in the first week of January. It accuses Atterbury, without naming him, of turning the populace against the election and insulting the royal family by claiming that the High Church should be rewarded for supporting the king's accession. To this persona, the author of *English Advice* is a traitor for being annoyed by the prospect of Whigs controlling "the Publick Interest and Treasure." Calling the author "very rhetorical" and "traytorously Abusive," the persona claims that Atterbury's "Degree of Rebellion" denies his "Doctrine of Passive Obedience" and that his complaints are neither "Legal" nor "the true Church of *England* Method of Complaining under Grievances": his view that George I's Lutheranism endangers the Church ignores the harmfulness of Roman Catholicism; and, since the Act of Settlement requires Protestant princes to commune with the Church, his discontent is sour grapes about the Pretender's displacement. The persona upholds the official view that the Hanoverians "are as much Members of the *Church of England*, as any that were born in her Communion," rejects Atterbury's view that High-Churchmen are more pious than Whigs, and denies that the latter will repeal the Triennial Act and vote for a larger standing army. That they brought these things about in Parliament, disappointing Defoe, matters less here than his point-by-point rebuttal of the leading Jacobite apologist.[49]

Subsequently, his texts retaliate against Jacobite ideology and Whig tergiversations more fancifully and subtly. *The Protestant Jubilee* institutes radical, anti-Catholic codes.[50] With day fatalities in mind, his persona displaces High-Church with Low-Church anniversaries: decrying the dates of Charles I's execution, 30 January, and Charles II's restoration, 29 May, he substitutes George I's accession, 20 January, as the day of liberation from Catholicism, and he celebrates the date of Queen Anne's death, 1 August, for ending the Schism Act and offsetting the dismissal of dissenting clergy on St Bartholomew's Day in 1662. By contrast, the persona of *An Humble Address to our Sovereign Lord the People* addresses the riotous nation as a broad-minded high-flyer who opposes rebellion and holds that loyalty to king and constitution is a divine command. He suggests that, were the people to look up to God, they would respect the king since spiritual renewal leads to civil obedience. He will not preach religious duty since he has no wish to exacerbate popular rage. Unwilling to be accused of Jacobitism, he apprizes high-flying readers he will not support a civil war on behalf of the Pretender.[51] A champion of parliament, this humble high-flyer affirms that reform must be effected by a new ministry rather than by a new king and that High- and Low-Church would unite in the face of rebellion. Promoting the religious rights of Dissenters, he thinks the destruction of "Meeting Houses to Day" would lead to the destruction of "Dwelling Houses to Morrow." Despite his High-Church affiliation, he defends toleration, attacks Jacobites, and upholds the constitution. The contrary codes in this impersonation reveal the playful licence that Defoe took when facing the challenge of scotching rumours of a Jacobite uprising.

The discursive freedom impersonation gives to Defoe's texts renders them palimpsests: offered as singular genres, they reveal extra-literary identities. Take *The Conduct of Robert Walpole.* Besides repairing Walpole's reputation, this biography turns the problems of detecting a person's character into a mode of political reform. Since a man cannot be judged by how parties treat him, praise of Walpole is converted into praise of the Revolution Settlement. Seeing this politician's "Capacity for Business" as cause for his rise to power in Anne's reign, Defoe details the irony by which his enemies, charging him with corruption in 1710 and having him expelled from the Commons and sent to the Tower, increased his power. Walpole is praised for resisting the ratification of the Treaty of Utrecht and the foundation of the South-Sea Company, for attacking the jobbing of the national debt, and for exposing the "*Arcana* of all the Court Intrigues" and the "Secret of the Management of those Times." His chairmanship of the parliamentary committee that examined the careers of Queen Anne's ministers is laudable because it boosted resistance to the Jacobite rebellion. His current fall from office is lamentable since he would have lowered the national debt and improved public credit. This apology for Walpole ends by reaffirming the Protestant constitution and substantiating Defoe's concern for economic reform.[52]

That impersonation led him to master generic ambivalence is evident in *A History of the Clemency of Our English Monarchs*.[53] This work opens by putting George I in the tradition of monarchs who have found mercy problematic. Arguing for the correlation of mercy and judgment, it states that this balance is lost in the amnesty offered to Jacobite rebels. Its informing principle is that the more a prince is committed to the reformed church, the more merciful he will be. Hence, it claims that the English is a *"merciful Constitution"* since it embodies the Reformation. Mercy is equally a political and religious matter: it is

> a Maxim in Government, that Clemency in Princes is not a Stop of the Execution of the Law, for that would be to destroy Government, not uphold it; but it is a compassionate Mitigation of the Extremities of Justice, when Men by exorbitant Offences subject themselves in an extraordinary Number to the Sword of Justice, and when the Prince being more than usually provok'd, yet acting with the truly noble and God-like Principles of Pity and Compassion, lays aside his Anger, justly stirr'd up to destroy, and with a Paternal Pity spares his offending Subjects, as a Father spares the Son that serves him.

After establishing these authoritarian analogies between divinity, monarchy, and patriarchy, Defoe recalls that Queen Elizabeth and James I were blamed for their merciful dispositions and that Charles I lost his head for "mistaken Clemency and Easiness of Disposition." He then views George I in the context of opposing allegations that Jacobites were pardoned before they asked for mercy and that their pardons were too long delayed and too exclusive. He imagines they will abuse their pardons since King George's mercy exceeds that of earlier monarchs in embodying the "Divine Clemency" expressed in the biblical text, *"Not desiring the Death of a Sinner, but rather that he should return, etc."* (Ezekiel 18:32).[54] After asserting that the king followed parliamentary rules in discriminating friend from foe when he acceded to the throne, Defoe concedes that those pardoned may not deserve "Grace" or be "proper Objects of the Prince's Clemency." Becoming more strident about Jacobite intransigence, he states that, had the king imitated God more strictly, he would have issued fewer pardons so that fewer rebels would be alive. His mercy exceeded the "Pattern of his Ancestors." While the gospels make "not one Promise of Pardon to any but the penitent, returning Sinner," the king excluded no "Gentlemen concerned in the late Rebellion." Like several fictional characters, the rebels regret the consequences of crime more than the crime itself: regretful only that they have ruined their families, they are like "the Thief, who when ask'd, if he was not sorry that he had committed so great a Piece of Villany? answer'd sullenly, *That he was sorry to be Hanged*." Their regrets are not true responses to royal clemency. Pardoned rebels sought the king's mercy only to abuse it, for more "are Pardoned than are Reform'd." This pamphlet's ambivalent praise of George I's clemency becomes a critique of lax monarchical authority.[55]

Defoe's generic approaches to monarchy became more ambivalent and ironic on account of odd political alliances, as *Some Reasons Why It Could Not Be Expected* attests.[56] This work defends government censorship given the potential subversion of life writing. The suppression of James Shepheard's biography is the issue. Unrepentant, he had been hanged for plotting to assassinate the king, the Tory press demanding mercy for the would-be assassin.[57] In opposing this call, the text argues that suppression rightly impeded Jacobite ideology that would have been advanced had the biography been read from the gallows. For Shepheard was a "poor enraged Youth" whom madness made the tool of Jacobites who filled his story with treason and slander. To have allowed its publication would have been to

> License the whole *Jacobite Party* upon every Occasion that they can either find or make, to get some harden'd Criminal on their Side, to hand their Poison and Insolence into the World, under the pretence of a *Dying Speech*.

The biography aimed to stir "other Desperate Principl'd Wretches to the same heinous Crime" by "insinuating first the Lawfulness of the Fact, extenuating the Guilt of it, and pretending to reconcile it to Duty, to Principles of Loyalty and Religion." Since its authors realized that "Religion, as it is the best Principle, is the worst Disguise," their theology justified murder and treason, their hypocrisy filling Shepheard's dying speech with "stupid Zeal" for "his dear Redeemer." Incredulous that Shepheard's persona says he opposes "King-Killing and Deposing Doctrines," Defoe contends that most Jacobites accept King George as de facto king. Disgusted by the hermeneutics of Jesuits, by their "reserv'd Meanings and mental Explications of their own Terms," he is more disgusted with Shepheard's Protestant supporters, whose interpretive insincerity eschews Jesuitical "Dispensations or Explications." As authors of his life, they voice the worst contradictions: they "confess a Crime, and yet insist upon it; commit the worst of Villainy, and claim Heaven, not only without Repentance for it, but even upon the Account of the very Crime they ask Pardon for." Defoe does more than expose the self-destructive zeal of Jacobites, for, by dissociating their propaganda from Catholicism, he presents them as crazy Protestants. His defence of censorship leads to an extremely polemical attack on Protestantism's religious and political integrity. His satire on improper notions of liberty returns us to where this chapter began, his displacement of biography illustrating once again an effective rhetorical licence and narrative creativity that are subtly polar.[58]

*****

The rhetorical polarities of his political satire in George I's reign – the generic liberties that create flexible texts which move between self-effacing and authoritarian stances – are evidenced by allusions to Islam through which his non-fiction and fiction achieve cultural reflexivity. As we saw earlier in this chapter, in *Mere Nature Delineated* when proposing that kings should visit the same "wholsome Severity" on "Christian *Viziers*" as the "Grand Seigneur" imposes on officers, Defoe cheekily applies Islamic theocracy to ministerial power and cabinet government in England. Yet, many of his texts gain conceptual power from allusions to Islam and sharia law.[59] Far from agreeing, Rodney Baine says that Defoe disliked Mohammedans more than Roman Catholics, citing *A Supplement to the Advice from the Scandal Club* for November 1704, which holds that Papists can be saved but Mohammedans cannot.[60] He also cites a passage in *A System of Magick* about the Devil wondering how to govern Asia and Africa and discovering

> a Tool fit for his Purpose; a fierce ignorant *Arabian*, bold, subtle, cruel, and merciless; to Men insolent, and audacious to Heaven; who by this meer Magick of Enthusiasm, back'd by the Sword and Spear, set up the boldest, the grossest, and the most senseless of all Impostures that ever was in the World; and which yet at this Time, and for above a thousand Years past, has strangely triumph'd over the Christian World, has spread itself over *Asia* and *Africa*, from the utmost Islands of *India* East, to the utmost Corner of *Africa* to the West; and it was, 'till within a few Years past, Master of a fourth Part of *Europe* besides.

But typical of Defoe's polar thinking, the next paragraphs link "the Force of Ecclesiastick Magick" that disturbs "the Ecclesiastic Affairs of the Christian World" to the conduct of "the Romish Clergy, and … the whole Papal Hierarchy." Defoe insists that "Popery itself" is "one entire System of Antechristian Magick; its Constitutions are all Sorcery and Witchcraft; they prevail upon Sense by Nonsense, upon the Head by the Tail, upon Zeal by Enthusiasm; and upon the Christian Doctrine by the Doctrine of the *Devil*." Catholic liturgy makes the faithful "sink their Reason to erect Notion," uphold "Fraud and Cheat, against Christian Sincerity and Plainness," worship "Priests in the Name of God, and set up Darkness in the room of Light." Like Dryden, Defoe mocks sacramentalism: Catholic priests "make eating their God be a Part of their most solemn Idolatry."[61] Like Dryden, too, he is virulently anti-clerical and cannot tolerate

> That Men should sin against God, and then ask the Priest Pardon for it; as if a Man should commit Treason in *England* against the King, and then go to a Chimney-sweeper, or a Black-guard-boy, to be pardon'd for it: That a Man shall go to a Shopkeeper in *Cheapside* to buy a License to commit Whoredom, or to rob upon the Highway, and stock-job Heaven in *Exchange-Alley* by *Puts* and *Refusal*.

These bathetic analogies degrade Catholic clericalism far more than they do Islam.[62]

That Defoe faults Mohammedanism is indisputable, but he usually does so in a limited way or for cultural reasons that extend beyond Islam. *Serious Reflections*, for example, considers only Barbary corsairs.[63] It calls the "*Moors* of *Barbary* … *Mahometans* of the most degenerate and unpolished Sort." They are as "cruel as Beasts" and as "vicious, insolent, and inhuman as degenerated Nature can make them." Since "Rapine and Injury is the Custom of the Place," its great men are rich "in Slaves," "merciless" in governing them, and "imperiously haughty" in their "whole Houshold." Their religion is "confin'd to the *Biram* and the *Ramadan*, the Feast and the Fast, to the Mosque and the Bath; reading the Alcoran on one Hand, and performing the Washings and Purifications on the other." Their "Conversation is eaten up with Barbarisms and Brutish Customs; so that there's neither Society, Humanity, Confidence in one another, or Conversation with one another." In conquering Christian peoples, they are "the worst of all the Nations of the World" (128).

In deriding their religious formalism and the violence inherent in their cultural hierarchy, Defoe manifests more than a simple curiosity in Islam. This was not unusual for the times, for, as Linda Colley says, "some acquaintance with Islam was a constituent part of polite British culture" and, since views of Islam were "mixed and mutating rather than monolithic," it is best to develop "a more nuanced and variegated view of relations between the British empire and Islam."[64] When James Boswell discussed with Johnson his wish to visit Turkey since its religion and society were "totally different" from those he knew, Johnson declared that the Christian and Mohammedan worlds were "two objects of curiosity" while "the rest may be considered as barbarous."[65] Boswell's desire to explore cultural difference and Johnson's belief that Islam is a civilizing power suggest why Defoe voiced a persistent interest in Turkish affairs. Conflicted about Mohammedanism though he was, being repelled by and attracted to the Ottoman empire, his Islamic allusions show that his support of British imperialism was replete with cultural paradoxes.[66]

The polar ways in which he blames and praises Islamic militarism show that he was willing to distance himself from political and religious allies because of ecumenical concerns and because of his wish to boost Britain's status in Europe as a rival of French economic imperialism. In 1683, he spurned Whig hopes that the Turks' siege of Vienna would succeed. Pointing to the "Cruelty and perfidious Dealings of the Turks in their wars," he hated that they had "rooted out the Name of the Christian Religion in above Threescore and Ten Kingdoms."[67] He had rather strife continue among Christians than see deeper Turkish incursions into Europe: he preferred that "the Popish House of *Austria* should ruin the Protestants in *Hungaria,* than the Infidel House of *Ottoman* should ruin both Protestant and Papist, by over-running *Germany.*"[68] Uppermost in his mind is resistance to Islam. In a letter to Robert Harley twenty years later, he prides himself on having defied those who wanted the Turks to capture Vienna so that Protestantism might flourish there. Only politicians lacking foresight could have believed it "were Bettre for all the Rest of Europe That the Protestants of Hungaria [be] Entyrely Roted Out and Destroyd, Than That the Turks Should Take the Citty of Vienna."[69] This anti-Islamic stance, which takes priority over proselytism for Protestantism, reveals that Defoe's goading of political friends was motivated by an ideological flexibility that defies monolithic accounts of his Whig imperialism.[70]

When he does praise the Ottomans' military imperialism, he assails Christian laxity, as when in *The Complete English Tradesman* he likens Turkish warfare to that of ancient Europe. He grants that their "martial warlike Princes" have "enlarg'd their Empire" so that "their Soldiery might not lose their Vigour, that their swords might not rust, and that they might not want experienc'd Officers." The Turks do well in maintaining a powerful standing army. Making it their "Business to over-run the World," they train up a "furious bloody Generation."[71] They successfully dismiss failed generals, justifying the dismissals by the myth that such generals anger the gods. This form of military efficiency sustained the ruthlessness of Grecian, Roman, and Carthaginian armies.[72] That he sees no difference between the warfare of ancient Europe and the Ottoman empire allows him to derive domestic satirical comparisons from the latter. So, the indulgences of people who bring diseases on their bodies is graphically likened to the action when "*Algerines* assault a Ship with Carcases and Stinking Pots."[73] Similarly, partners who bring "complicated Mischiefs" on themselves by marrying without love are likened to victims of Moorish piracy who "look on their Life as a Slave at *Algier* looks upon his Chains, they fancy themselves as Persons only bought and sold, as Persons committed by Warrant, and made Prisoners for Life."[74]

The Islamic empire is a cultural and economic touchstone to Defoe because he recognized the importance of the Turkey trade, its economic and demographic impact on his native land, and its implications for rivalry with France. Evidence for these claims appears in the topographical survey that *A Tour through the Whole Island of Great Britain* constitutes. When he boasts that the terrace at Windsor Castle built by Elizabeth I is superior to the grandeur of France's royal palaces, he adds that the "grand seignior's terrace in the outer court of the Seraglio, next the sea" comes close yet remains inferior.[75] This allusion to Ottoman architecture disparages France, the immediate imperial rival. As regards the Turkey trade, Defoe shows that rivalry and imitation have complex economic results. His protectionist account of horse breeding in the face of equine imports concedes the negative effect of trade with the Ottoman empire: consumer demand for Persian horses inflates their cost and devalues horses that are being bred better in Yorkshire. Breeders there may not have preserved "the pedigree of their horses for a succession of ages" as in Arabia and Barbary, but they now "christen their stallions," concern with bloodlines instilling strength and speed into stallions so that English horses "will beat all the world."[76] This apology for Yorkshire horses claims that British militarism has improved breeding: having produced faster charging horses for soldiers, breeders' animals now make excellent hunters.[77] The high cost of Arabian horses means that patriots should buy Yorkshire horses because of their improved bloodlines and comparative cheapness.

Defoe was not a single-minded mercantilist about trade with the Levant. Far from simply wanting to increase exports and import bullion, he understood the internal structural changes that competition for Turkish markets was creating. To increase Ottoman demand for English cloth was forcing towns to specialize and transforming regional industries: competition in the Turkey trade was causing towns to seek niche markets. Burstall in Yorkshire now specialized in dyeing broad cloths since the market for kersey and shalloon had been captured by large towns like Halifax, Huddersfield, and Bradford. In turn, these towns could no longer compete with Wiltshire, Gloucestershire, Somerset, and Devon in producing kersies and druggets for the Turkey trade.[78] Such structural change alerted Defoe to "internal colonialism" and the need to measure economic activity accurately in order to replace propaganda with policies that would boost the circulation of trade.[79] His belief that London was the trading hub of Great Britain around which Scotland, Ireland, and Wales should revolve is clear when he rejects claims about Scottish trade to the Orient as "scandalous partiality." If the Scots export to China and the East Indies, to Turkey and the Levant, they do so in "the service of English merchants."[80] Trade with the Islamic world entailed protectionism against rivals domestically in Scotland and Ireland and externally in France. Thus, Defoe exploited commercial propaganda in defence of English imperialism.[81] When he celebrates The Royal Exchange founded by Sir Thomas Gresham, he reads the founder's statue with its bale of silk facing the Turkey Walk as a symbol of Gresham's work for the Levant Company and of the mythical continuity of the English throne.[82]

However, the demographic changes brought about by the Turkey trade by altering family life in the suburbs of London for good and ill meant that Defoe's view of the Levant could not but be contrary. Thus, he records that Eltham near Greenwich, long populated by rich citizens, had sent so many young men to be Turkey merchants that young women there, with reduced marital prospects, were considering leaving the town. By contrast, society had been stabilized at nearby Lusum, where Sir John Lethulier, a distinguished Turkey merchant, in living to a great age helped his sons establish noble seats and estates in the district. A more mixed effect is seen in the case of Sir John Morden, a Turkey merchant who lived at Black-Heath. Despite the "misfortunes of the times" – trading losses caused by Islamic depredations that curtailed his philanthropy – Morden built a hospital to shelter "forty decay'd merchants," affording them a dignified death. This hospital represents the noblest "single piece of charity" offered to London in many years.[83]

The more one studies Defoe's arguments for the Turkey trade, the more one encounters his contrary view that Islamic culture is to be resisted and imitated. In his mind, trade to the Levant should be advanced in the face of the economic regressiveness of Islamic militarism and the complacency of English merchants. First, he wants to counteract Islamic maritime power and restore trade to North Africa by displacing the Moors from Tunis, Tripoli, Algier, and Sallee since they, like the Vandals, plunder trading cities.[84] He insists that "the Followers of Mahomet are, wherever they come, like the Romans, the Destroyers both of Commerce and Cultivation." Being "a rapacious, cruel, violent, and tyrannical People, void of all Industry or Application, neglecting all Culture and Improvement," the Turks of North Africa are "Thieves and Robbers." Once displaced from Valencia, Granada, and Andalusia, they turned pirates, stealing ships from "the Christian Nations of Europe" and raiding Mediterranean settlements for slaves. Secondarily, he would outflank the Ottoman empire in East Africa by building fortified settlements in southern Ethiopia beyond Turkish forces in the northern Red Sea. At this point in *A Plan of the English Commerce,* he turns on the East India Company for not expanding trade: the company had enjoyed exclusive charter rights without pioneering routes. Islam is not the only bar to the Turkey trade. English merchants have failed to assess market potential; they have ignored their scope to outperform France. English cloth, according to ambassadors' reports, is appreciated in oriental courts: "the Grand Seignior, Lord of the whole Turkish Empire, has his Robe of English Cloth, and the Sophy of Persia, amidst all his Persian and Indian Silks, wears his long Gown of Crimson Broad Cloth, and esteems it, as it really is, the noblest Dress in the World." Claiming familiarity with Ottoman consumers, Defoe declares that lightweight, cheap, and highly coloured French cloth wears worse than English cloth. The latter, heavier by the bale, is readily bought, though at a dearer price, by Turkish and Armenian merchants, the chief dealers in woollen goods. Persian gentlemen, the Aga or Bassa, know that English wool is firm, smooth, and solid whereas French wool, which wears rough, light, and spongy, soon turns to rags. Nor have English merchants imported good raw materials. If the Turkey trade is declining, this is not because of a lack of markets for English cloth. Rather, silk from Turkey has so declined in quality that British weavers have turned instead to Piedmont and Bengal silks: Turkey merchants do not import silk of a high enough quality to be turned into an easily worked producer good.[85]

Defoe similarly criticizes English attitudes to the Turkey trade in *The Complete English Tradesman*.[86] Appalled that French was underselling English cloth at Aleppo and Smyrna, he urges merchants to market their superior products energetically: they should not hold back until the French leave Constantinople.[87] They should realize the differences between the advanced manufacture of linen and the primitive one of silk. When merchants from Georgia and the Caspian Sea take silk to Aleppo and Scanderoon to exchange it for British merchandise, "our Turkey merchants" import the silk as a producer good without employing credit or refined accounting methods.[88] By contrast to the linen trade, this silk trade is "a mean remote thing" since merchants accompany their cargoes, vesting their returns in goods of local markets. This contrast does not simply disparage Islamic commodities, for Defoe praises Barbary wool and Turkey's Caramania wool, regretting that small amounts are imported. His comparative point in favour of the wool trade is clear in comments on success in exporting cloth to Spain: this country imports English wool because the Moorish occupation slowed its industrial progress so that British manufacturers produce superior "Spanish-Cloths."[89]

If Turkish military culture is economically regressive, strikingly, when Defoe compares consumerism in London and Constantinople, he finds a model of reform in the latter city. London's growth, it seems, depends on goods from around the globe that cater to gluttony: "our Navigation is chiefly employ'd upon the exorbitances of Life." Whereas London's commerce propagates vice, the Turks exchange only the "more necessary things of Life." Their "treats are Coffee, Sherbet, and messes of Rice, dress'd their own way, a little Flesh and but very little." Their clothes are not ornate except those of the Bassas, Sultans, and persons of rank. Since their fashions are unchanging, their clothes are not costly. Their "Buildings and Furniture, Gardens, Equipages" lack ostentation, giving jobs to few of the artificers abounding in London. Were its trades to imitate Turkish ones, its population would be smaller than Constantinople's. That city lacks the malt, distilling, and wine trades, the drinking establishments that employ thousands in city and countryside, and the trades in personal and domestic fashion, such as wig and coach makers. The Turks neither wear wigs nor keep coaches. Defoe shares the view of Lady Mary Wortley Montagu that the Turks are less subject to luxury and elitism than the English.[90] He claims that their mosques do not separate the high and low; the Bassa kneels with the Janizary, their prayers exclusive of status. Without a colonial empire, a huge mercantile marine, and fashion industries, Constantinople is a city of one million people. Were London to model itself on that city, two-thirds of its population would have to take up a healthy and productive rural subsistence. By contrasting the economies of the two cities, Defoe urges the merchant community to regulate itself morally, for he fears that a threatened re-establishment of sumptuary laws, far from reforming consumer vice, would harm commerce and employment.[91]

While *A Plan of the English Commerce,* against Defoe's usual stance, deploys Mandevillean views of commercial amorality to extract satire from Islamic resistance to capitalism, *Conjugal Lewdness* upholds sharia laws to show that, by treating marriage as a contract rather than a sacrament, Islam offers a model of sexual reform to England.[92] This work holds that Turkish justice respects wives by punishing husbands who sexually abuse them. British women, so abused, receive no justice since modesty prevents them speaking out in court. But a Turkish woman, injured by "the Liberties of the Marriage-Bed," is redressed by having her husband summoned before the Grand Vizier. To validate her complaint, she need say nothing, nor even unveil her face, until she takes her oath: then, after unveiling, she removes a slipper and holds it up to the Grand Vizier "the wrong Side upward." By this symbolic action, she "swears upon the Alchoran that her Husband offers unnatural Violences to her, and that she cannot live with him upon that Account." She gains a divorce unless he clears himself or binds himself not to repeat the offence. Islamic justice, following the law of nature, also shields pregnant women against intercourse: "in the Language of Mahometan Modesty," a wife suffers "an unnatural Violence" if so injured. Should this happen, she similarly performs a symbolic action in court: holding up sticks to signal the number of her husband's wives.[93] Defoe praises "the Modesty of Mahometan Nations" in forbidding intercourse with pregnant wives since polygamy, while an Islamic tenet, is based not on sexual necessity but on patriarchal custom. Were polygamy forbidden, Muslims would abstain from such "Pollution and Impurity" since they regard sexual licence as bestiality. Urging Christian husbands not to commit rape under cover of marriage, Defoe hopes wives may "*turn the Slipper up against them.*" His hope is that "our fruitful Inventions" might add "some Signals, some Figures" in the Turkish mode to expose nauseous crimes modestly.[94]

If symbolism in Islamic jurisprudence might inspire codes in Britain that would spare the sensibilities of abused women and protect authors and readers from charges of obscenity, Defoe does not assume that modes of decency are simply transferable from one culture to another. His sense that mores are culture-specific leads him to satirize orientalism: the eastern method of punishing adulterous women by making them go naked in public is "a Breach of the very Modesty which it was intended to punish." In this vein, he promotes what Roxana ignores: sexual modesty may not be based on "the practice of other Nations." Going naked, or next-to-naked, may be customary in hot countries but is scandalous in England, where Christians "are to cleave so far to the Custom of the Place, as to do all Things that are of good Report."[95]

The satire of Georgian life in *Roxana* rests on the protagonist's self-destructive adoption of Islamic clothes. Betraying English customs and Christian values, Roxana dons Turkish dress to objectify herself for libertine reasons that are intended to appal and even alienate readers.[96] That she gains her name when posturing in a luxurious Turkish costume that contrarily hides and exposes her lust for aristocratic French modes compounds ironies that arise from her abuse of Christianity, Islam, and cross-cultural references.[97] In appropriating and rationalizing culture-specific values, her luxury reflects her self-victimization.[98] Defoe's construction of Roxana as a negative exemplum matches his wish, voiced pointedly in *Conjugal Lewdness*, to treat shocking subject matter inoffensively.[99] By the time she goes on the Grand Tour with the prince whom she idolizes, the inverse relation of her material wealth and spiritual degradation is set. When at Naples he buys her "a little Female *Turkish* Slave" captured by a Maltese man-of-war, this relation is deepened by cross-cultural signs. The slave teaches Roxana "*Turkish*, or rather *Moorish* Songs" and dances as well as "the *Turkish* Language" (102–3). Since the vessel seized between Constantinople and Alexandria had noble ladies on board, Roxana acquires clothes that her slave teaches her to wear. Hence, she displays herself in "the Habit of a Turkish Princess" at a masquerade held for the Court in her grand London apartment. Wearing this exotic Mohammedan costume, she disparages English dancing. Upon agreeing to dance, she calls for music "*a la Moresque*," provoking a masked, French-speaking courtier to say that she has a Christian face and "that so much Beauty cou'd not be Mahometan." After three French dances with this courtier, she performs the figure of a Parisian master with which she had entertained her prince. The company, mistakenly thinking it a Turkish figure, christens her Roxana, her foreign name arising from a concurrence of her vanity and courtly prejudice. While she enjoys being the talk of the town, she is sickened by the decadent masquerade. Another contradiction poses her pride in being close to the grand courtier over against her not knowing "any-body else," including herself (173–7). The second masquerade that leads to a three-year retreat with the king further exposes her Mohammedan impersonations. When dressing, she is visited by ladies of a noble Persian family. Fearing to be outdone by their Georgian and Armenian dresses, she derides their Persian modes because, if their dancing is pleasingly novel, "there was something wild and *Bizarre* in it, because they really acted to the Life the barbarous Country whence they came." Her scorn of the Persian virgins accentuates her cultural duplicity: she thinks herself more pleasing because she has "the *French* Behaviour under the Mahometan Dress" (179).[100] Yet, she is clearly indecent when she dances seductively for the king because she only incipiently feels her dress is "somewhat too thin" since "unlac'd and open-breasted, as if I had been in my Shift" (181).[101]

The ironies challenging Roxana's appropriation of Turkish modes gather force because she displays and conceals herself while evading personal intimacy and cultural identity. Once financial independence prompts her to amend her past life by providing for her children, events she sets in motion frustrate her maternal instincts and make that past painfully inescapable. Through Amy, her servant-confidante, Roxana educates her son to have him "put to a Turkey-merchant" (192). Financing his apprenticeship with an Italian merchant at Messina, she places him in an English house that trades to the East Indies, hoping he will make a fortune. Yet, because he will not marry a woman she sends him, she cuts him off from a "thousand Pound Cargo" and from his legacy on the implausible grounds that he abuses his mother (264).

When she would provide for Susan, who yearns for her biological mother, Roxana's efforts to cover up her past are futile, given her habitual self-display, which incites her daughter to uncover that past. The nearer Susan approaches Roxana's identity, the more the mother must distance herself, until, after this becomes impossible, Amy, goaded by Roxana's unselfconscious hints, probably murders the displaced, identity-seeking girl.[102] Having served two years as cook-maid in Roxana's house in the period of the masquerades, Susan recalls her lady's Turkish costume when Roxana wears form-fitting apparel. Despite lodging with a Quaker to present a modest body to the world, Roxana's ongoing lust for titles and fame makes her entertain her husband, the Dutch merchant, with French songs and the Turkish costume that she knows is not "a decent Dress in this Country" since it is "one Degree off, from appearing in one's Shift" (247). By adorning the dress with her husband's picture in the eastern mode, she goads him to ask her often to don it. She also tempts the Quaker to change her habit for such a dress. On making a surprise visit when Roxana is wearing an Italian morning gown that exposes her figure, Susan pictures the Turkish costume, her reactions to her mother's body transparent on this and later occasions to her husband and Quaker confidante. Trapped by her compulsive indulgence in Turkish modes, Roxana must listen in anguish to Susan as the latter slowly recovers the masquerades and reveres her former lady as an angel. Ironically, Susan's narrative recovery is so exact that it gratifies Roxana's desire for fame, at the same time causing her to view her daughter as "this young Slut," a pejoration that forces her maternal non-entity on Roxana (288). Her attempts to divert and discredit Susan's narrative recovery heighten the negative symbolic power of the Turkish dress. All Roxana can finally do is to remain silent so as not to provoke a fuller narrative, her autobiographical repression signalling her alienation. When the Quaker, in misplaced friendship, decries Susan's narrative by asserting that Roxana has a dress like the one Susan describes, the Quaker exquisitely but unknowingly extends Roxana's "Mortifications," moving Roxana closer to thwarting Susan's quest in the most sinful of ways (290).

*****

Unlike Roxana, Defoe tried through his impersonations of Quakers, his diverse political voices, and his explorations of the cultural interface between Christianity and Islam to stand outside his political and cultural systems, knowing well that, if such efforts were imaginatively healthy and satirically effective, they were inevitably limited.[103] Still, his attitudes to economic progress, consumerism, and marital conduct were affected by appreciation of Islam. As cross-cultural references in *Roxana* attest, Turkish modes helped him address decadence in the early Georgian period. That his contrarian thinking was enlivened by imaginative sympathy for Islam is evident in his other fictions. When

Crusoe is captured at sea by Barbary corsairs and enslaved in Morocco, he is treated well.[104] In *A Journal of the Plague Year*, H.F.'s brother warns him against imitating the "profess'd predestinating Notions" of Muslims who die by the thousands because they go "unconcern'd into infected Places." This warning at first alters the Saddler's mind about remaining in London. But he ultimately resists the warning, his resistance justified by his becoming an accurate reporter of the plague and a solid projector of public policy. By contrast, Londoners display "a kind of a Turkish Predestinarianism"; as the plague's end nears, many are "more obstinate" than Mohammedans, behaving with "audacious Boldness" before death and heeding no admonition about the ongoing "Contagion."[105] Here Defoe again spurns notions of cultural superiority; Londoners in crisis behave according to their worst projections of Mohammedans. While he never stopped condemning Islamic barbarity, he open-mindedly used Islam to develop critical perspectives on English complacency. While the Earl of Shaftesbury condemned the "Moorish fancy" of English readers for favouring barbaric over classic tales and ignoring the Mohammedan clergy's discouragement of "all true learning, science, and the polite arts" on behalf of their perfect scriptures, Defoe preferred to invent satirical procedures that would make this fancy recoil upon itself in the service of broad-minded reform and cultural integrity.[106] His representations of Islam confirm that he could resist his own and his society's prejudices and test received cultural standards with contrarian viewpoints. For him, imagining Islam was socially constructive. Scrutinizing sectarian, political, mercantile, and sexual complacencies in Georgian Britain, he implicated Christian Europe and the Ottoman empire in ways that enhanced his rhetorical and narrative energy.

Chapter Six

Political Imaginings: Sacred and Profane

> The lord and proprietor, who is indeed a true patriarchal monarch, reigns here with an authority agreeable to all his subjects (family); and his reign is made agreeable, by his first practising the most exquisite government of himself, and then guiding all under him by the rules of honour and vertue; being also himself perfectly master of all the needful arts of family government.[1]

The regal imagery in this eulogy of the Earl of Pembroke's rule at Wilton House illustrates Defoe's eagerness to broaden the intellectual and imaginative contexts of monarchy and to look past secular and literal-minded notions of government. His figurative exposition of patriarchal monarchy here and in his fictions has in common with his deployment of biblical allusions an authorial decision not to be constrained by political partisanship or denominational orthodoxies. Given his sympathies with the trading classes and religious dissent, his promotion of courtly values in this epigraph confirms his polarity thinking. The order exemplified by the Earl's "great family" is a political, moral, and aesthetic achievement: the hierarchy his family embodies – its members are "noble and proper inhabitants" of a "princely palace" – symbolically extends government. As patriarch, the Earl himself performs several roles: he is "instructor," "guide," "governour and law-giver" so that his family as a company of subjects flourishes like a "well govern'd city." The "blessing of this noble resident" touches "all the country round." His family government is widely influential because, based on the Earl's self-discipline, it diffuses social order. Like the extended family on the estate, the nation responds positively to the Earl's intelligent leadership and respect for cultural tradition, not the least because it appreciates that his outstanding art galleries are a European cynosure.[2]

While the previous chapter linked Defoe's ongoing commitment to the Revolution of 1688 to the impersonations through which he defended monarchy and upheld the necessary authority of a national figurehead and while it explained the mounting yet oblique methods by which he urged George I to perform his kingly functions, the present chapter analyses the fictional energy he gained by treating monarchical power figuratively and dialectically. The Earl is a good politician because he consciously discharges plural roles and because – in the words of *Serious Reflections* – he has a "stated Composure of Mind" that comes from "nothing but a Fund of Vertue." His effectiveness stems from a mental poise which, unlike the happy delusions of a "Lunatick in *Bedlam*," is cognitively and imaginatively healthy. By contrast, Defoe's fictions depict characters who, lacking this poise, are afflicted by political fantasies. While *Serious Reflections* interrogates the type of person who fancies "himself a Prince, a Monarch, a Statesman, or just what he pleases to be" (78), the fictions elaborate, in ways that will have appealed to Johnson – a great admirer of his writings – why such fancies are forms of madness like those afflicting inmates of Bedlam. In the eighteenth century's most moral and philosophical of fictions, Johnson's Imlac may reflect Defoe's influence when he declares that cognitive disorders commonly visit humans:

> Perhaps, if we speak with rigorous exactness, no human mind is in its right state. There is no man whose imagination does not sometimes predominate over his reason, who can regulate his attention wholly by his will, and whose ideas will come and go at his command. No man will be found in whose mind airy notions do not sometime tyrannise, and force him to hope or fear beyond the limits of sober probability. All power of fancy over reason is a degree of insanity.[3]

These moral reflections are germane to Defoe's fictional depictions of political fantasy. Although Sill helpfully states that the degree to which his unique political ideology informs his fiction has been underestimated, his view that our author made narrative subserve this ideology is not my argument.[4] Defoe's characters and narrators are lonely, alienated creatures who may be absorbed by issues of power, authority, and the constitution, but they neither comprehend nor embody political theory. Their confused political conduct is governed by Defoe's sense of narrative contraries. His characters and narrators no more fully embody political than religious ideas: they suffer as much from political fantasy as from religious inconstancy. Their cognitive and imaginative inadequacies serve moral dialectic because they appropriate religious and political ideas for selfish reasons. Yet, by abusing governmental notions, they paradoxically uphold the ideal integration of personal and political values. By analysing how Defoe sets political misapprehension in reciprocal relations with religious dullness, we gain insight into the imagination with which he integrated sacred and profane concepts. That he so correlates politics and religion clarifies how history and theology inform his fiction.

As we saw in the previous chapter, his criticism of governmental and domestic institutions challenged British mores from inside and outside mainstream society: Quaker personas exposed how political hypocrisy debased biblical theology, and Islamic cultural practices unmasked hedonism. Interestingly from an ironically reflexive viewpoint, in *Serious Reflections* Defoe assails the deluded egotism of Barbary Moors, whom he chides for justifying their degeneracy with absolutist notions. Every Moor, he claims, "is a King within himself, and regards neither Justice or Mercy, Humanity or Civility, either to them above him or them below him, but just as his arbitrary Passions guide him" (128). Political arbitrariness and religious decadence fuse in their self-centredness. By contrast, a Christian theology of divine power leads to responsible collective attitudes to property and political process. Thus, he holds that "the whole Creation" has been "entail'd" upon man

> as an Inheritance, and given to him for a Possession, subjected to his Authority, and governed by him, as Viceroy to the King of all the Earth; the Management of it is given to him as Tenant to the great Proprietor, who is the Lord of the Mannor, or Landlord of the Soil. (208)

This passage assigns an intricate set of terrestrial metaphors to God's relations to mankind: the King of the world entails it upon humans as a legal inheritance. If the ultimate proprietor and landlord requires tenants to view themselves as vice-regents, they must consciously adopt plural roles; they must see themselves as His legatees, managers, and stewards. Since this set of roles indicates that the reciprocity of spiritual and political values is individually and collectively imperative, it clarifies why Defoe speaking as Crusoe in *Serious Reflections* admits that on the island, far from developing faithful political metaphors that would have helped him better recognize God's authority, he was ruled by "Hypochondriack Whimsies" which led him to pray for delivery from evil spirits. Convinced he was dwelling on an "enchanted Island" and that "the Devil was Lord of the Manor," he degraded political and religious ideas with superstitious imagery. Retrospectively, his lack of trust that God rules the world is a reciprocal failure of political and religious imagination (*Vision* 8 and 11).

In *Robinson Crusoe,* his political imagination remains uncertain, his mental images closer to Moorish individualism than to the Earl of Pembroke's self-consciousness. Crusoe suffers political fancies because of unwarranted possessiveness. On recovering from his illness, he tours the island's far side, proud in ownership. If his recovery signals moral potential, this is countered by proprietorial self-assertiveness. His possessive individualism cramps his spiritual growth: casually setting aside "afflicting Thoughts," he surveys *his* property with "a secret Kind of Pleasure" (100). He considers himself "King and Lord" of the "Country indefeasibly," claiming a "Right of Possession" that cannot be annulled: if he could "convey it," he might have it "in Inheritance, as compleatly as any Lord of a Mannor in *England*." Why, readers might ask, does he see himself as a member of the landed gentry while ignoring the theological implications of his metaphors?[5] Far from indicating political shrewdness, his fantasy of power is ungrounded, partly because his isolation from European civilization is undercut by the questionable way in which he associates himself with English constitutional and property law. His equivocal commitment to the island compounds his legal fantasy: he calls himself king when he has no regal duties, and he speaks as if he can impose constitutional values on a state of nature.[6] His self-aggrandizing fascination with monarchy, by evading notions of a social contract or a mixed constitution, simply displaces God. While he claims that God's "Presence" makes up for "the Deficiencies of my Solitary State" (112), Crusoe, unlike Defoe in *Jure Divino,* will not put political ideas into a religious context. He will not acknowledge God's presence by relating secular and spiritual values. Even when he reads the Bible to appreciate his freedom from worldly temptation, he calls himself "Lord of the whole Mannor." Since he is gratified to call himself "King, or Emperor over the whole Country" and relishes having no rivals to dispute his sovereignty, political fantasy continues to stunt his faith (128).

As narrator, Crusoe grants the dubiety of his possessiveness when describing a "Tour" of his "little Kingdom" in the sixth year of his

"Reign, or ... Captivity" (137). This equivocation, inviting readers to entertain contrary standpoints, accentuates his political fantasy, because, despite learning that God spreads a table in the wilderness for him, in his own eyes he remains his "Majesty the Prince and Lord of the whole Island" (148). Penitence does not modify this fanciful absolutism because social isolation stops him contemplating the integration of sacred and profane ideas. Nor does he imaginatively substantiate his role as God's vice-regent. For he dreams of wielding "absolute Command" over subjects by controlling their liberty. That his subjects are cats, a parrot, and a dog, which he views as servants and a "little Family," reveals the comically pathetic aspects of patriarchal fantasy. Remote from the Earl of Pembroke's ethical leadership, Crusoe's inadequate ideas of power cannot instil moral and spiritual health in one isolated from society.

The inadequacy of Crusoe's political imagination is underlined when his fantasy dissolves at the sight of the footprint. Having imagined that to meet one of his species would have been "a Raising me from Death to Life" – a blessing next to salvation – he is terrified at the prospect of "seeing a Man" in the state of nature (156).[7] Still, this fear of confronting the Other is beneficial in alerting him to the idea that divine absolutism is the only legitimate kind: he accepts God's "Sovereignty," His "undoubted Right by Creation to govern and dispose" men absolutely, and His "judicial Right" to punish as He sees fit (157). But, while admitting his subjection to God's absolute kingship, he does not sustain reciprocal images of politics and religion. When Friday, Friday's father, and the Spaniard arrive on the island, he reverts to the "merry Reflection" that he is "like a King" in having "an undoubted Right of Dominion" and being the "absolute Lord and Law-giver" over his subjects (241). His fantasy is mitigated by his endorsement of "Liberty of Conscience," but it still displays an unwillingness to envision plural political roles in the face of divine power.

As the island becomes peopled, his fantasy moderates but he continues to manifest political contradictions. Avid for the "Society of my Fellow-Creatures" (188), he becomes engrossed in aggressive plans to murder cannibals. His attitudes to Friday are no more stable. In Friday, he seeks a "Servant, and perhaps a Companion, or Assistant" (202). Although Friday is of sound mental capacity and of superior religious conduct, Crusoe addresses him in commanding tones. Indeed, his fantasy becomes militaristic: his three subjects make up his "Army" (243), and he allows the Spaniards onto the island only if they take a "solemn

Oath" to obey him as "their Commander and Captain." Only defensively does he relate politics and religion. Fearful of Catholic absolutism, he imposes on the Spaniards the condition that they swear upon "the Holy Sacraments and the Gospel" to accept his authority and to take him to the "Christian Country" of his choice (245). In the end, the Inquisition prevents him from settling in Brasil, where he had once professed himself a Catholic. His island solitude, partly a punishment for conforming to Catholicism, should educate him against that creed. If fear of the cannibals leads him to contemplate behaving in an inquisitorial fashion, he ultimately condemns the Inquisition as "unjustifiable either to God or Man" (172), showing that his incipient political sense arises from opposing Catholicism. While he disclaims "Niceties in Doctrines" and "Schemes of Church Government" from a distaste with priestcraft and theocracy (221), his political imaginings do not, however, attain a constructive spirituality.

For the episode of the mutiny, in exercising his tactics, increases his alienation. He does correct his rescuers' superstitiousness when they call him an angel: demeaning his "*Spectre-like* Figure," he insists "All Help is from Heaven" (254). Yet he behaves deceitfully and pretentiously. Verbal and histrionic tricks hide his powerlessness when he makes his contract with the rescuers. Asserting his Englishness (oddly, given his long separation from his native land), he shows them his "Fortification" and "Castle," claiming to have a "Seat in the Country, as most Princes do" (258). He induces them to participate in his fantasy. When his army goes into action, he is its "*Generalissimo*" (267), the Italian word denying his Englishness. Moreover, he makes the ship's captain call him "Governor" and maintains this illusion by stepping out of that false role: keeping himself "out of Sight, for Reasons of State" (268), he reduces himself to a device for authenticating his fantasy.[8] Ironically, political inflation saps his substantiality. Although he admits his powerlessness when, after the pirates are captured, he embraces the captain as "a Man sent from Heaven to deliver" him (273), he still pretends to an "Authority" by "Commission" upon threatening to punish the pirates (275). His self-destructive fantasy is evident when he entrusts the island to them. No wonder, when reaching home, he is "a perfect Stranger to all the World" (278). An outsider who voices deficiencies in church and state, he makes no social commitment because political fantasy is as limiting to him as it is instructive to readers.

Political fantasy is as salient in *Captain Singleton*, but, whereas Crusoe is vaguely utopian, Singleton knowingly opposes political innovation.

He and William, his mentor, are outsiders whose alienation from orthodoxy lets Defoe implicitly assault the utopianism inherent in pirate narratives.[9] In the first part of this story, Singleton is politically effective yet scorns utopian ideas; in the second part, where he proves to be an ineffective leader, the true critic of piratical conduct is the mischievous, equivocating Quaker.[10] William makes Singleton confront his alienation and the spiritual aspects of political commitment, Defoe employing the protagonist's contradictions to mediate narrative contraries. From the start, Singleton is ethically indifferent yet quick to judge: aloof to government, he displays an innate skill at managing people. A victim of parochial disputes that denied him a home, he is "not much concern'd" (3) when the ship he serves on is taken by the Moors and then the Portuguese. Hardened to crime by the Portuguese, he condemns their immorality: having "no Sense of Virtue or Religion," he assails their hypocrisy; despite spurning political ideas, he blames them for being "so meanly submissive when subjected; so insolent, or barbarous and tyrannical when superior" (7). After being forced to convert by the Inquisition, he entertains the "Hellish Resolution" of murdering his master (9), this malevolence pointing up Catholicism's inhuman absolutism. Declaring as character how corrupt "under Government" the Portuguese are, as narrator he admits he was "unfit to be trusted with Liberty" (11). His erratic perspectives invite readers to observe how the narrative ironically implicates politics and religion.

The mutineers with whom he crosses Africa discover sound political ideas, but he belittles and later appropriates their principles. Forming a "good Troop" on Madagascar, the mutineers pledge to preserve one another, to distribute food equitably, and to be guided by majority opinion (19). Their constitutional impulses include appointing a captain "during Pleasure": while he is to be ruled by the majority, the captaincy is to rotate. Deriding these "Rules" (20–1), Singleton is bent on proving them impracticable. When the "general Council" pools its resources, he withholds his funds (23). He despises the "Counsels of this Assembly." Passively accepting its decisions, he joins debates reluctantly. In the debate about building a canoe, he is both for and against the motion: he wants one in order to capture a larger vessel. In this obstructive spirit, he undermines the skilful gunner, the elected leader, and becomes de facto leader, sapping the pirates' council. Finding their "Debates" about voyaging to Africa tedious, he continues to mock their rules by describing his participation – in Old Testament terms – as taking "State" upon himself "before one of their great Princes" (35).[11] Their political forms, he believes, are a collective fantasy from which he stands apart. He joins "no Side" in the council since he has "no home, and all the World was alike" to him: his alienation impedes political process. Yet he harbours a political fantasy. In proposing to settle in Madagascar since there is no "better place in the World" in which to become "as rich as a King" (36), he couches an acquisitive and absolutist individualism. Although the pirates acquire economic and social solidarity by building a vessel, Singleton, as narrator, insists that they planned the voyage in "Ignorance and Desperation" and executed it without "much Resolution or Judgment" (44). Indifferent to the "hazardous" and "improbable" voyage, he contributes to it in no way. That Singleton did and did not belong to the group of mutinous pirates is a narrative contrary that derides their utopianism even as it exposes Singleton's lack of cognitive and imaginative integrity.

The pirates' failed political experiment is clear when, through default, Singleton becomes leader of the African adventure. Having compromised the planning by submitting to be "governed by the Majority" (50), even as he judged the undertaking to be one of the "rashest, wildest, and most desperate Resolutions" ever taken, he drops his indifference to "the Conduct of our Affairs," because his seniors, "void of Counsel" and "Presence of Mind," cannot fend off natives. He is "forced to command" (54), disgusted that those who proposed the journey are spiritless in the face of adversity: cowardice and inexperience betray their political ideals. That he imposes rules on the mutineers like the ones their consensus had invented reveals his disdain for democratic process. While he preserves "good Company and Friendship" by putting the group's gold into "one common Stock," by preventing "Wagering and Playing for Money" and by inducing them to exploit negroes and enjoy the "Fruit of their Labour" (95), he devalues these rules by taking sole credit for them. Adopting the role of military commander, Singleton, not unlike Crusoe, treats his fellows as an "Army," placing them in "Platoons." If success as leader shows him to be autocratic, it also reveals the mutineers' supine willingness to be directed. Far from amassing gold and ivory, they are content to build "a little Town" and to "keep Councils and Society" in a "publick Tent" (98). Outlaws who admit their need for society, they cannot reconstruct the political order from which they fled. In an alien land, they neither enjoy adventure nor garner wealth. Contrarily, their submission to Singleton reflects anxiety "to get Home" (131); political fantasy in the heart of Africa fades into escapism and conservatism. Back in England, they cannot translate their negative experience into social purposefulness.

The second part of *Captain Singleton* exposes their political and spiritual hollowness, more nearly balancing Singleton's deficiencies with those of the pirate band he leads. Wasting his money in England because of his social alienation, Singleton aims to make a new start in life by joining Captains Avery and Wilmot, the "most famous Pyrates of the Age" (139). In that Defoe refuses to see piracy as a political model, Singleton, as narrator, blasts the "reprobate Schemes" of these historical pirates, while, as character governed by William, the Quaker surgeon, his own piratical enthusiasm is deflated. A "comick Fellow" with a "very good solid Sense" (143), William guides the pirates to success even as he faults their bloodthirsty stupidity. If "fitter to be Captain than any" of them (144), he limits himself to being Singleton's "Privy-Counseller" (168). William's astuteness shames the pirates. He is shrewd partly because he remains unmoved by pirate romances, whereas Singleton has been impressed by "flaming Stories of Captain Avery" (154). William is pragmatic as well as intelligent. When he shows the pirates how to capture an abandoned slave ship and sell its slaves, he insists that "the Law of Nature" justifies the slaves in having turned on their captors and stops the pirates from murdering the killers of white men (157). His amusing contrariness shows up the pirates' lack of acumen and moral sensibility. His duplicity and integrity remind us of Defoe's ongoing exploitation of Quakers' non-conformism.

In using William to deflate the pirates' code, Defoe's subtle yet propagandistic narrative implies that piracy as a model stems from immature imagination and romantic wish-fulfilment. Although William's political inferior, Singleton outperforms the historical pirates. When, under William's tutelage, he blocks Wilmot's futile attempts to seize East Indiamen, Singleton is decisive because informed by a more acute practical understanding than that of the legendary pirates. Despite his unique fame, Avery is shown to be unoriginal. When he declares his intention of building a city on Madagascar (182), Singleton is critical because he can state that such a pirate base would be vulnerable to European forces. When he returns to his "old Acquaintance the Isle of *Madagascar*" (171), readers will recall that the mutineers had lived there for a year and found it no safe haven.[12] By engaging readers' memories of this earlier fictional episode, Defoe's fiction denies historical uniqueness to Avery.[13] When Wilmot and Avery ignore Singleton's experience, they are obtuse. Since they also break "the Agreement of any farther Sharing of Profits" (184), their sense of social compacts is more exploitative than that of the mutineers who crossed Africa. Singleton learns that Avery possessed neither the wealth nor the shrewdness attributed to him by history and legend. Avery's suppositious accumulation of wealth exposes the hollowness of his fame. Since Singleton's band comes to rival Avery's wealth, the latter's riches are not excessive, as his literary reputation suggested.[14] Defoe contrarily upholds and belittles Singleton's leadership to displace piracy as a political model. Still further narrative contraries make Singleton's autobiography invalidate the fictions which led to his becoming a pirate.

In the final pages of *Captain Singleton*, the protagonist and his men react spiritlessly to William, who increasingly expounds the polarities of politics and religion. Although Singleton's group abandons piracy for trade in the South Seas under William's guidance, the ex-pirates do not grow in political intelligence. After relying on William's diplomacy to extricate their ship from the Ceylonese, they try to confirm his claim that thirteen shipwrecked Englishmen are alive in northern Japan, having travelled there from Greenland via the North Pole. But, if the North West Passage has been fictionally traversed, the pirates fail to make amends for their depredations by bringing this discovery to the world; in so failing, they "may have disappointed Mankind of one of the most noble Discoveries that ever was made, or will again be made in the World, for the Good of Mankind in general" (203). Nonetheless, William continues to induce Singleton to appreciate domestic and constitutional life to offset his lazy declaration that he is "at Home everywhere" (256). In the face of Singleton's waverings between alienated listlessness and otherworldliness, William becomes his "Ghostly Father, or Confessor" (268), taking on multiple roles that integrate private and public life, in this not unlike the Earl of Pembroke. As "Steward, Counsellor, Partner," he would instil in Singleton trust in the "merciful Protector" (271). He serves too as his "Guide ... Pilot ... Governour." While Singleton fears his Catholic past will keep him from good works, William urges that his "general Plunder" be returned "to the Community" (276). He incites Singleton to express his need for "a kind of Centre," for a "Residence" that will have "a Magnetick Influence upon his Affections." If Singleton renounces his alienation, he never achieves social integration: he acknowledges the value of harmonizing political and spiritual values, yet he cannot do so. He knows he must reform, but, in secreting his past and opting for a reclusive existence, he grows into an unfulfilled cipher for the desirability of viewing constitutional values in religious terms.[15]

That private life yields political implications, especially when individuals are victimized by society, and that survival in a profane world raises awareness in such individuals about the need to perform plural roles by actively responding to sacred principles are themes as important in *Moll Flanders* as in *Captain Singleton*. Since the young Moll is subjected to sexual power and social intimidation, she early realizes that the private life of women should entail public policy. Yet day-to-day survival involves her in pragmatic strategies rather than in activism, leading her to exculpate herself by rationalizing theories of government, social contract, and colonial propaganda. Like Singleton, she cannot integrate idea and action, Defoe elaborating the relation of politics and religion as he mediates her narrative for the benefit of readers who are invited to ponder why sexual intercourse and marriage have so many public ramifications.[16] When the elder brother at Colchester seduces Moll, the intersection of power and gender is apparent, for she assumes her lover's private words commit him to a public role: she insists, when he wants her to marry his younger brother, that she cannot do so since she views herself as married to the elder as much "as if we had been publically Wedded by the Parson of the Parish" (39).[17] Once aware of her lover's hollow matrimonial promise, she retaliates by turning his argument against ecclesiastical forms upon him. Her impulse to fault men's sexual politics and to rally women is confirmed when she helps a friend avenge herself on a suitor who will not let his assets and character be scrutinized. By what she calls "a just Policy" (73), Moll tricks this man into being "humble in his Applications" and "an obliging Husband." When she urges women not to abase themselves "below the common Station of a Wife" by taking men at their own word and by succumbing to the fear of spinsterhood (74), her appeal to female readers employs the imagery her creator uses in *Religious Courtship* and *Conjugal Lewdness*. Declaring that women who carelessly choose partners "run into Matrimony, as a Horse rushes into Battle" and make "Matrimony like Death, be a *Leap in the Dark*" (75), she heightens the political implications of marriage.[18] That she does not follow her own policy contrarily makes it more important: the necessity forcing her to marry a man who turns out to be her brother emphasizes the importance of her wish to have women examine the background and personality of would-be spouses.

Moll would translate her sense of sexual politics into moral self-government on discovering her incestuous marriage. Despite her legal vulnerability and the threat of being sent to a madhouse, she will not suppress her "riveted Aversion" to her brother-husband, and she resists the "Treaty" of reconciliation her mother designs (100). Insisting on separation, she will not surrender her desire for "Government in the Affair" (103). Her natural scruples would avoid rationalizing political terms. Back in England, she would avoid a common-law relationship that is merely a "*felonious Treaty*" (107). But her extra-legal affair with the man at Bath proves she cannot regulate her conduct by instinctual, untutored sense. She repeatedly undoes "the Government of [their] Virtue," impenitently breaking the "bars of Virtue and Conscience" (116). As narrator, she admits her failure to integrate political and religious ideas by emphasizing that she was all along a "Whore and Adulteress" since her second husband, the linen-draper, had "no power to Discharge [her] from the Marriage Contract" (124). While, as character, she continues to act as if contracts are merely private and have nothing to do with religious convention – as when giving the Bath gentleman "a general Release" on condition he give her sufficient money at their separation – Moll the narrator knows that verbal oaths and pledges are illocutionary deeds which perform social functions and change moral reality.

By abusing the performative discourse that renders contracts effectual, Moll immerses herself in political and legal fantasy. To Defoe, those who abuse contracts believe they may take the law into their own hands and so devalue the political and religious principles upon which it rests. The banker who has Moll "Sign and Seal a Contract with him, Conditioning to Marry him as soon as [his] Divorce" is obtained (140), makes himself vulnerable to her duplicity and incites her anti-social conduct. Abandoning him for Jemy, Moll in turn makes herself vulnerable to the latter's deceitful family: like the banker, she worsens her lot by political naivety and deceit. Greedy for wealth and status and not "Nice in Point of Religion," she is flattered when Jemy's Catholic family treats her as if she had been "of their Opinion" (142). Willing "to speak favourably of the *Romish Church*," she calls religious differences the "prejudice of Education." She deceives the family by conforming to the "Gestures" and "Pattern" of the Mass and by saying she will become a Catholic once properly instructed. If her political folly assumes that the "Romish Clergyman" who conducts her marriage to Jemy performs the ceremony as effectually as a Church of England parson (143), she must face the fact that the marriage is a deceit on both sides and that Catholicism is extra-legal. However, as her wedding to the banker shows, society as well as individuals suffer from political fantasy. For the minister who marries her to Jemy regards church marriages as too "publick," taking as his model the weddings of "our Princes" who marry in their "Chambers, and at Eight or Ten a Clock at Night" (184).[19] This royal model, decried in *Conjugal Lewdness*, spurs clandestine marriages, undermines parochial authority when unlicensed clergymen displace "the Minister of the Parish," and upsets the proper reciprocity of the private and public spheres.[20]

Moll's marital expectations of the banker are disappointed because her political and religious sense is both complacent and incoherent. By replacing "the loose ungovern'd part" of her former life (188) with a "settled State of Living" (128), she hopes to repent. But her trust that domestic and financial stability will improve her shows she wants to forget the past rather than make amends for it. Political vanity and social pretension impede her awareness, as when, despite fearing arrest, she enjoys being treated like a "Princess" at the Dunstable inn (219). Her contrary susceptibility to illusions of rank and marginality exposes her flight from constructively personal and social roles: she displays and disguises herself as a thief. She appears "with some State" to extract compensation from the mercer who arrests her: she makes "a very good Figure" by donning "a new Suit of second Mourning" so that he cannot recognize her (251). When she dresses in the "coarsest and most despicable Rags" on a subsequent thieving venture, the degrading habit, in which she acts and conceals the outcast she is, is "the most uneasie Disguise" (253). Potential victims stand off from her. When she steals a horse, this is "a Robbery and no Robbery," her "Beggar's dress" exposing how "Ominous and Threatning" her kleptomania is becoming to herself and society (254).

Neither imprisonment in Newgate nor transportation to Virginia leads her to read the political signs in her criminality or in institutional penalties. The Newgate Ordinary who secures confessions rather than reform prisoners shows that judicial punishment, including colonial propaganda, may harden individuals. Warned by the conscientious clergyman who moves her towards repentance that colonial life is no panacea, she self-deceivingly equates her experience in Virginia with knowledge of the colony's "Constitution" (157). Forgetting that colonial life did nothing for Jemy, Moll deepens her self-deception by trusting that they can begin "the World upon a new Foundation" (303). That she hides her eagerness for the colonies from the good minister evidences a refusal to sustain her penitential efforts. Political illusion increases her social pride: she sees herself entering the new world "poor and mean, but not ragged or dirty" (312). This self-image is hypocritical since criminal gains detach her from "the wretched Crew" of convicts (313). Besides purchasing an "abundance of good things for [their] Comfort in the Voyage" (316), her money dramatizes her would-be superiority. Far from starting the world anew, she perpetuates her selfish cunning. She conceals her incestuous marriage and wish to secure her mother's bequest from Jemy. When she adopts "another Figure" on meeting her son and pretends to be in "a new World" (335), the newness is illusory: in regretting her marriage to Jemy and giving her son a gold watch stolen from outside a London meeting house, she worsens her dishonesty and manifests no social commitment. Her role playing is merely self-evasive and does nothing to construct her moral identity. On their land grant, Jemy and she depend upon an honest Quaker for the building of their house and ordering of supplies: they neither provide for themselves nor participate in community. Their return to England where Jemy faces capital punishment not only undoes Moll's colonial propaganda but also confirms that she evades the political commitment and social integration that might aid spiritual growth.

By contrast with Moll, H.F., the saddler-narrator of *A Journal of the Plague Year,* is a victim of circumstances assailing a whole society. Hence, he struggles to reconcile history and vision in ways that transcend self-preservation. He knows that political systems involve more than collections of citizens and weighs from oscillating stances how much the public creates its institutions and how much these grow beyond its control. The terrors of the plague that see him defending the regulatory efforts of the authorities in 1665 lead him to the contrary realization that policies better than those enacted then must be implemented in future visitations. He even celebrates the plague of 1665 for exposing deficiencies in public policy. Again contrarily, while writing to mitigate future plagues, he contemplates the benefits of another plague jolting the public into realizing the need for religious reform. So he applies an acutely contrarian perspective to the problems emanating from the formulation, administration, and enforcement of policy: he shows that policy stems from government secrecy as well as openness, that public administrators, besides being considerate, are necessarily repressive, and that the populace reacts to legislation with both complacency and fear.[21] In voicing the need for policies to alleviate epidemics and the equal need to modify existing legislation given the positive values that failures in dealing with the plague delimit, H.F.'s narrative persuasively, if uncomfortably, sharpens and blurs relations between profane description and sacred prescription.

This polar stance lets H.F. sustain a double vision on the conduct of government and populace. He notes that, while the government had sound information about the plague, by delaying counter-measures it inflamed rumours about the restrictions arising from turnpikes and shutting up of infected houses that caused families fearing isolation to conceal the plague. This concealment led the Secretaries of State to ferret out the truth by having houses searched. His double vision realizes that governmental power effects disinformation and harsh regulations along with popular resistance and official corruption. The "Knavery and Collusion" of parish officers with families exercised the Lord Mayor and justices of the peace (6). H.F.'s remarks on demographics and population management are equally provocative because of his double vision, as when he balances comments on the exodus from the "Heart of the City" of the "wealthiest of the People" with ones attributing its large population to "all the ruin'd Families of the royal Party, [that] flock'd hither" (18), and when he offsets praise of governmental refusal to ban books from an unwillingness "to exasperate the People" (25) with dispraise of efforts to suppress "Innumerable Sects" and "shut up" their meeting houses (26). His double vision on the strained relations between government and citizens allows H.F. to propose that politics require a theological framework. Since it thwarted government opposition to Dissenters, the plague, he judges, was beneficial: while it lasted, preachers were heard "without Distinction" and "the Spirit of Charity" abounded. A member of the Church of England sympathetic to Dissenters, he laments that the end of the plague saw sectarianism return. He insists that the plague evinced sound religious rules: the government encouraged public devotion, appointed days of prayer and fasting, and, by furthering the "proper Work of Repentance and Humiliation," enhanced public harmony (29). But he also blames government in order to promote a transcendent perspective. Lauding the civic administration because the Lord Mayor appointed physicians to attend the poor and discouraged them from resorting to magicians by making cheap medicine available, he faults it for having set up only "one Pest-House" (74). The city's failure to shelter thousands of plague victims caused them to run out of their "own Government" from pain, grief, or madness (81). While he applauds the city's charity, he faults it by contrasting the small donations given to plague victims with the huge sums spent on rebuilding after the Great Fire of 1666 (92). Such polar stances on government indicate a wish to move beyond profane analyses to a sacred vision of the future. Thus, he enjoys repeating statements that the plague rendered all political measures useless and "baffled" the "Power of Man" (35).

The policy matter which persistently tests H.F.'s double vision with a sense of contradiction and moves him to adopt a transcendent perspective is the shutting up of houses.[22] Homes in which the plague was detected were blockaded by watchmen, and the sick were shut in with the healthy. He first reports that the measure was carried out "with good Success" (37), despite complaints of its being "very cruel and Unchristian" (47). He insists the healthy were released from their houses or sent to pest houses to perform a quarantine. Yet, in arguing that "publick Good" justifies "private Mischief" (48), he faults the measure because, as the plague spread and the number of infected homes grew, it became impossible to distinguish the sick from the healthy. People, diseased and sound, seeing their homes prisons "without Bars and Bolts" (53), escaped by stratagem. Moreover, far from slowing the plague, the measure sped it by driving desperate people into the world. Sympathetic to those who lost the "Government" of their "Senses" on finding plague tokens on their bodies (56), H.F. concludes that shutting up houses was a destructive policy: of "little or no Service," it did more harm than good (73).

His compassion for the populace is highlighted in the story of three men who flee the city, a story mixing history and theology.[23] Despite his criticism of the urban poor, the men in his story, who lack property, settlement, and the franchise, are idealized by typology, as we have seen.[24] Their manner of escaping the plague is ennobled by diction: they live like "Hermits in a Cell" and like "wandring Pilgrims in the Desarts." Paradox underscores their political dignity: "Exiles" in their native land, they enjoy a surprising "Liberty" (57). In preserving themselves, they respect private property and constitute a "Pattern" to the poor (122). Claiming the right of free movement since "the whole Kingdom" is their "Native Country" (124), they outflank officialdom by holding "a great many Consultations" and creating "one publick Stock" of funds (126). Their deception of suspicious town officers is justified by their religious politics. Others who flee the city live "like Hermits in Holes and Caves" but lack political sense (150), starving or returning and contracting the plague.[25]

The story of the three men who, lacking political rights, gain them through religious sense renews H.F.'s plural roles as apologist, critic, and projector when he returns to the policy of shutting up houses. First, he presents London as a "Pattern to all Cities in the World for good Government and ... excellent Order" for preventing the poor fleeing to the countryside (155). In idealizing the city because its moderately enacted policy had the "publick Good" in mind, he asserts that "private Injuries" were justified by real "publick Benefit" (158). Yet he repeats that, when houses were searched at the height of the plague, infected people roamed the streets so that the policy yielded "no manner of publick Good" (168). He reiterates, too, that containment of the plague was beyond the "Power of the Magistrates, [and] of any human Method or Policy" (166). His critique is no less contrary when he reports that as an examiner he learned that the policy was "incapable of answering the End" and adds that he and fellow examiners practised a "Scheme" to separate the sick from the sound (170). Since apparently what he earlier spoke of as proposals seem to have been put into practice, the distinction between public and private schemes is blurred, as is the boundary between prescription and description. H.F. apologizes for and criticizes public authority, does and does not subordinate private to public interests, and presents competing political models because of the real but difficult need to bring social existence into alignment with a transcendent perspective.

Having found the plague both appalling and stimulating, H.F. keeps dwelling on its positive and negative effects and voicing oscillating stances. The crisis induced people to forget the Act of Uniformity, sectarian differences were minimized, and the prospect of death reconciled "Men of good Principles one to another" (175). Yet, another "Plague Year" would remove the disputes of churchmen and dissenters. As a member of the established church, he voices inclusive hopes even as he regrets the widening splits between the denominations. In the self-effacing mode adopted often by his creator, H.F. disclaims rhetorical efficacy: "who am I that I should think myself able to influence either one Side or other?" But in the next breath in words recalling *Serious Reflections,* he asserts that "In Heaven, whither I hope we may come from all Parties and Perswasions, we shall find neither Prejudice or Scruple; there we shall be of one Principle and of one Opinion" (176).[26] If a future plague would benefit communal faith, he continues proposing ways of avoiding another. For one, he rejects his own conduct as a model. Despite his survival and concession that London's policies re-established the "Minds of the People" (184), he does not promote remaining in the city since most of those who did so "went into the great Pits by Cart Loads." His "many Schemes" for evacuating the city set aside his own conduct. Plans for future visitations must include "quite different Measures for managing the People": the populace must be separated into "smaller Bodies" to increase resistance to the plague (198). Neither

H.F.'s experience nor the city's former policies are recommended to posterity in and for themselves.

The gaps between the political past and present as imagined by H.F. yield prescriptions for policy only contrarily. *Colonel Jack* presents political implications arising from the philosophies of self-interest and benevolence with similar obliqueness, this fiction probing the degree to which political sense is both innate and socially constructed. An illegitimate beggar boy who desires social integration and gentility, Jack is competitive, ambitious, and deceitful, his temperament impelling him to be a social conformist. As a young thief, he makes it a "point of Honour" to perform errands punctually because he aspires to the reputation of "a mighty civil honest Boy" (8). Affecting "the better Sort" (10), he learns military history from common seamen and soldiers: reading no books, he rates himself a "kind of an Historian" of the Civil War (11).[27] Such narrative ironies reveal his genteel aspirations to be both naive and unfounded. Each time he thinks he fulfils his aspirations, gentility eludes him. When he first buys clothes with proceeds from his thieving, he regards himself as a gentleman. But, if as happy in his "own Imagination" as "my Lord Mayor of *London*" or "the greatest Man on Earth," he displays "an utter Ignorance of greater Felicity" (16). When he buys a hat and breeches, he feels "as pleas'd as a Prince is with his Coach and six Horses" (28). Despite the ignorance exposed by his pretentious analogies, Jack's predisposition for economic utility remains strong. He ruminates on stolen "Bills" which fellow thieves cannot cash since the potential waste lies heavily on his mind, although he does not understand how bills are used (29). Without scrupling to live on the proceeds of stolen bills, he will not hurt tradesmen, given his "strange kind of uninstructed Conscience" (55). Still, he converts the yield of thefts into a "Bill" when anxiety about safeguarding his cash leads him to an investment counsellor, much as Moll seeks her banker and Roxana contacts Sir Robert Clayton. But, even as Jack becomes an investor, he knows nothing about the "Value" or "Use" of money, because he has as yet known "no Good" and "tasted no Evil" (39).

Not having experienced this moral dialectic, Jack can only measure himself erratically against ever-changing notions of gentility, while his repeatedly stultifying political commitments expose the basis of his informal learning in reactionary imitation rather than in awareness of the plural roles adult engagement in society requires. When the "Master of the *Glass-house*" where Jack and fellow thieves live reproves a man for using language common to beggar boys, Jack recoils by quashing "the least Inclination to Swearing, or ill Words," renouncing "strong Beer," and standing off from his fellows (61). Despite this show of independence, he is obsequious to the banker on whom he relies. When he gives this man a second deposit, he disguises himself in a servant's "Green Livery, Lac'd with Pink Colour'd Galloon" and makes "abundance of Bows, and Scrapes" (75–7). His eagerness to act as a modish inferior makes his genteel pretensions risible. His inability to confront his agency without self-deception and self-dramatization is underscored when he makes restitution to a poor woman whom he has robbed, but not in his own person: he pretends to act for the penitent criminal – his "chief Instrument" in returning the money (85). When the woman blesses the thief, Jack still does not reveal himself, nor does he admit his criminality to himself. That he does not converse directly with the woman or himself shows that he has not learned to enact Defoe's tenet about the harmony of Christianity and civility. Far from it. He is a "wary Politick Gentleman" (91) who, if unwilling to commit thefts, remains a "Receiver of stolen Goods" living off the avails of Captain Jack's crimes (102). That Colonel Jack's desire for gentility stems from untutored aspirations to climb the social ladder is clear when he turns soldier in Scotland. Grateful to be free of the necessity of stealing, he thinks this "certain way of Living" is genteel (104).[28] However, after aspiring to be a "Gentleman Officer" rather than "Gentleman Soldier," he deserts the army to avoid being shipped to Flanders as a common conscript, risking capital punishment if captured. Ironically, desertion leads to his being kidnapped to Virginia, where he faces "five Years Servitude" on a plantation (117). Accepting that he has been brought "into this miserable Condition of a Slave by some strange directing Power," Jack has another chance to link politics and religion by imitating the sensibility of his master, who, as a "great Man" and revered "Justice of Peace," properly assumes "a kind of State" when he encourages felons on his estate to see that the "Constitution of the Country" allows them to see themselves as "just beginning the World again" (119–20). His colonialism causes the master to talk "mighty Religiously" to a young felon, and Jack, overhearing this discourse, both identifies with the felon and has his conscience pricked. But, when he himself appears before the master, Jack behaves "like a Malefactor" before a "Lord Judge upon the Bench, or a Petty King upon his Throne" (122): privately self-critical, he is evasive publicly. He avoids the parallel between the felon and himself, this evasiveness impeding his converse. He solicits pity from his master but will not examine his self-pity. Rather he uses his banker's bill – a token of the past from which he pretends to be free – to claim a status that changes his relations with his master, who becomes the "faithful Steward" of this wealth (125). The bill helps get him promoted from "Slave" to "Overseer" (126).

Readers will appreciate that altered circumstances do not lead to Jack developing a critical outlook on the several roles he assumes. A survivor because of his pragmatic adaptability, he becomes an effective overseer of slaves, but, by avoiding self-reflection in the face of political and religious dilemmas, his intellectual, imaginative, and spiritual deficiencies are striking. As overseer, he recognizes his master's "Humanity" and "Tenderness" (129) and the systematic brutalization of slaves by corporal punishments that force them to work. But his oversight is self-dramatizing: he abases himself to his master before the slaves, yet alone with his master he presents himself as rigorous, thus trying to impersonate a kind of a middle way. To offset charges that he is too lenient, he pretends to be hard on the slaves; he misrepresents himself to show that owners and overseers wish to be compassionate. Posturing with power and powerlessness, he plays at being blameworthy. He does "Homage" to his master when the latter comes "like a Judge" to hear the case against his leniency (129). Acting as if on trial, he piously claims that he cannot be an "Executioner" since he has been an "Offender." Making his "Defence" against unseen "Accusers," he argues that, by heightening their fear of punishment, he has made the slaves appreciate being pardoned (134). He makes himself an emblem of mercy by pretending to have displeased his master and deserved death for his charity to the slaves: he claims to have sacrificed himself for them to the "Great Master" (137). Besides making his master an authority figure and himself a victim of power, Jack wishes to show himself to be at one with his master about mercy while implementing policies his master cannot. Given such histrionic and hypocritical role playing, second-time readers cannot miss the dramatic irony that motivates Defoe's plot: Jack is going to be made to submit to fears of punishment that will stop him play-acting and force him to confront his criminal evasion of his several roles with true political and religious appreciation.

A "diligent Servant" turned plantation owner, Jack sees himself a model of how the most despicable felon may begin "the World again" (153). But this trust in colonialism along with the responsibility arising from conscious role playing is exemplified more fully by his Tutor, who, still a servant, appreciates freedom from crime in the new world, the parallels in their lives underscoring Jack's spiritual dullness. The Tutor's retrospection is religious whereas Jack faults his life "as dishonourable, and not like a Gentleman" (162). The Tutor's religious sense is closer to the gratitude of the slaves than to Jack's supposedly genteel critique of his past. While he says he is "sincerely Touch'd" (162) by his Tutor's faith in beginning life anew, Jack will not see that parallels in their lives require him to examine himself more keenly.[29] That he avoids learning from his "Pedagogue" (160) shows up in his restless desire to see what is "doing in the World" and to witness the War of the League of Augsburg (1688–97). This desire "to see more of the World" in Europe while experiencing "the Life of a Gentleman" (172), far from manifesting social and moral commitment, leads to a series of political missteps that end in alienation. Taken by a French privateer and exchanged as a prisoner of war, he joins the English army in the Spanish Netherlands as a volunteer in order to observe the war with France, only to be disappointed when King William's troops are beaten and made prisoners of war. Back in England after a futile "second Essay at the Trade of Soldiering" (184), he lives incognito in the French community, speaking French, and going to "the *French-Church* in *London*" (186). Cultural evasiveness and lack of patriotism make him vulnerable to a fortune-hunting wife. Dull to the public repercussions of private conduct, Jack and his wife enter into a "Friendly Treaty about Parting," which, as narrator, he calls "Criminal" (195). That his false gentility aggravates his political ignorance is underlined when he fights his wife's lover: ignorant of duelling codes, he tastes the coarseness of "Gentleman's Law" (201): he fights brutally, only to be knocked unconscious later in the street, with his nose "slit upwards," an ear "cut almost off," and a sword slash on "the Side of [his] Forehead" (204).[30]

Jack's wounds embody his conceptual failure to relate gentility, the constitution, and the established church, a failure aggravated when he joins an Irish regiment in the French army in the War of Spanish Succession (1701–13). He now voices "a great deal of Zeal" for the Pretender (222). Eager to raise troops and to wear "the *Chevalier*'s Brevet for a Colonel," he is "esteem'd as a Man of Consideration" who has "a considerable Interest in [his] own Country" (223). Cultivating this illusion and receiving "a great deal of Honour" from the Pretender, Jack is committed neither to the cause nor to his prince. The "fruitless Expedition" to Scotland where he cannot raise troops for the "dull Cause" breaks his Jacobite illusions and shows him to be a political non-entity. While he knows that, as a traitor, he has "forfeited" his life and property to "the

English Government" (223), he is far from aware that life and property are to be enjoyed only within a legal constitution. Back in Paris, where a second wife proves unfaithful, Jack displaces a stupid lack of self-control, which further accents his ignorance of the Revolution Settlement. He loses all "Government of himself" (225), being violent towards his wife and fighting a duel with her lover, a Marquis. Jack's political commitment is no more salient when he returns to England: settling in Canterbury he passes himself off as "an *English* Man, among the *French*; and a *French* Man among the *English*." Like Roxana, he depreciates patriotism and national identity yet expects to control how society perceives him. He lives "perfectly *Incog.*" by varying his name and tongue and believing that he can know everybody and that, at different moments, nobody and everybody can know him (233–4). His linguistic role playing is fantastically self-deceived. If by now he embraces duelling, he fails to uphold its genteel code, for he canes his third wife's seducer, who will not "defend himself with his Sword like a Gentleman" (244). Jack cannot abandon his cycles of violence and political illusion. After his fourth marriage is conducted by a "*Romish* Priest in Orders" (248), he discounts his wife and follows the seditious urgings of the Catholic priest, "on Fire" to join the Jacobite Rebellion of 1715 (250). When the Jacobites spurn his advice to make "a select Detachment to defend the Pass between *Preston*, and the River and Bridge," he flees, supposedly convinced once again of their and his folly (265).[31]

The motif of flight ironically and contrarily emphasizes Jack's unrealized political sense in the final sections of his autobiography. Returning to Virginia to escape the past, it recoils on him personally and publicly. When his first wife, a penitent convict, arrives among transported criminals, he condescendingly raises her status, assuming he will enjoy a "private Station" with her (263). But his former disloyalty to the crown revisits him when the arrival of transported Jacobites makes him fear being recognized and having his property confiscated. Fleeing under the direction of his wife, he surrenders his colonial roles: he is reduced from a great man, a magistrate, a governor, and master of three plantations to a "poor self-condemn'd Rebel" (267). His estate being "forfeited" to the crown, he must depend on his wife to secure the "King's Pardon." In praise of George I's clemency, Jack admits his sad prejudice "in favour of a wrong Interest." Included in a "general Pardon," which is "a kind of Life from the Dead," he becomes a "Convert" to George's interest (276).[32] Since his prince gives him life, he knows he will never be able to "pay the Debt fully." For Jack as narrator, "preserving the

Life of [his] Prince" is his "natural Duty." Now holding that true gentility integrates political and theological values, he lays it

> down as a Rule of Honour, that a Man having once forfeited his Life to the Justice of his Prince, and to the Laws of his Country, and receiving it back as a Bounty from the Grace of his Soveraign; such a Man can never lift up his Hand against that Prince, without a forfeiture of his Vertue, and an irreparable Breach of his Honour and Duty, and deserves no Pardon after it, either from God or Man. (277)

At this point, his notion of gentility embraces the reciprocity of constitutional and Christian honour. So, he sets out to confirm his loyalty to the House of Hanover by converting the trading voyages by which he escapes Virginia into a patriotic enterprise that defies the Asiento, Spain's control of Caribbean trade. He finds Spanish colonial power arbitrary and merciless by contrast to Hanoverian rule. Although, when captured, he exploits his past efforts on behalf of Catholic powers to get better terms of imprisonment, he discovers that Spanish officialdom follows the letter of the law so much that it weakens its colonial power. But his observations on the vulnerability of Spanish imperialism do not block his political fantasizing. Addicted to selling clandestinely to Spanish merchants at a profit of 400 per cent, he trades in the Gulf of Mexico to the extent of becoming stranded in an enforced retreat that he claims to find the "most agreeable Retirement in the World" since it affords him the luxury of "a Prince" (301). Regal fantasy degrades his retrospection and the composition of his life story in this retreat. Remote from political norms, he never finally works out the relation between gentility and Christianity. Admitting that not having the "Liberty of going home" embitters the pleasures of his retreat, he invites readers to exercise the "Temper of Penitents" by seeing that "at Home" they may profit from "the merciful Dispositions of Providence in Peace, Plenty, and Ease" and develop an understanding of his story that goes beyond his comprehension (307–8).

Among Defoe's protagonists, Roxana should be the most intent to spurn Catholic and Stuart ideologies since her parents moved to England in 1683 before persecution in France became official with the Revocation of the Edict of Nantes in 1685. Yet she betrays her Protestantism by temporizing with Catholicism and exploiting Quaker modes. Of course, her parents set no example. Besieged by fellow Huguenot exiles, they stand aloof, socially superior rather than charitable. Because they lack scruples in marrying off their daughter, her marriage to a brewer is disastrous. His affected gentility sees wedded life sap her refined upbringing; she hardens her heart against him before he abandons her, against her children whom she abandons to save from starvation, and against herself when, cohabiting with the landlord for survival, she infringes religious law, honest enough not to pretend exemption from it. In her mind, "a Woman ought rather to die, than to prostitute her Virtue and Honour, let the Temptation be what it will" (29). Yet, she deceives herself by adopting the role of helpless victim: being more subservient to her landlord than pride should allow, she tells herself she is weaker than she is. She grants him the "Right" to move into the house she rents (32); she claims that his gifts are "powerful" and that his conduct leaves her no "Power to deny him any thing" (34). As his mistress, she claims her conscience is overcome by his "powerful Attraction" (38). Perversely, she thinks him attractive, even as he oppresses her necessity.

But she will not excuse cohabiting with him by the "Cant" of natural law. Despite the "Contract in Writing" he gives her, she condemns him and herself as adulterers "in the Sence of the Laws, both of God and our Country" (42–3). While violating these laws makes her value them more, the rationalizations into which she falls have increasingly harmful repercussions. When the landlord is murdered in Paris, she starts a train of impolitic deceptions that finally dehumanizes her. The landlord, like her a Protestant, is buried with "all the Ceremonies of the Roman Church" (54). Purchasing a splendid Catholic burial since Protestants cannot be buried in their own cult, she acts as if she had been legally married by starting processes on his estate. At the same time, she becomes mistress to a prince. Affecting the highest rank, she acts so subserviently that the prince is induced to treat her as an equal. Enjoying the illusion of equality, she behaves yet more abjectly. As character, she feels treated like "a Princess" (64), but as narrator she underscores her self-abasement. She again enacts the self-deception of powerlessness. To her, the prince is irresistible: no virtue, except that which can "suffer Martyrdom," is proof against him; his goodness would have conquered a "Saint" (65). Rendering herself susceptible to his flattery lets her believe she is a "fit Mistress for a Prince" (66). As narrator, she tells how this self-deception became ideological rationalization: she taught herself the "Doctrine" that it is "lawful" to have an amour with the prince because it eased her mind to do so (68). As her depravity deepens, she seeks to retain some, if only negative, integrity: intent on being a "Protestant Whore," she refuses to consult Catholic priests who, she knows, would give her "the easiest Pennance" and absolution (69). She seeks mental ease on her own terms even as she knows she deserves condemnation. To Roxana the narrator, her former beliefs that she was as good as married to the prince and that Heaven would not punish her are "Absurdities" (69). She exacerbates her profanity by treating the prince as her "only Deity" and herself as "his Idol" (70). While he makes "Sacrifices" to his idol and dresses her as splendidly as the "Queen of France," she resists seeing that she intensified her sexual vulnerability. Further unbalancing her wavering consciousness, she calls herself a prostitute to deflate the prince's obsession with her and to argue that great men waste themselves on "worthless Creatures" (74). She preaches that a man enslaved by passion "defaces the Image of God in his Soul; dethrones his Reason; causes Conscience to abdicate the Possession, and exalts Sence into the vacant Throne," displacing the human and exalting the bestial (75). The political metaphors in this sermon underscore the fantasies in their relations. Roxana's images of dethronement and abdication are spiritually reflexive. Besides preaching as narrator, she preaches in person to the prince because she cannot help acting the "Confessor"; she promotes a "dangerous Doctrine" that requires "Repentance" and their separation (82). But they sin on against this light, Roxana living "like a Queen" or the "Queen of Whores." While regal similes show that sexual pride undermines her conscience, her tour to Italy confirms her occasional disgust with Catholicism. She half-heartedly sustains her call to the prince to return to his princess and obey the "Laws and Rites of Matrimony." This hypocrisy is exposed by the dying princess, who urges her husband to uphold the "solemnest Part of the Marriage-Covenant" (109).

Roxana grows less religiously sensible. She will not see that the Dutch merchant who rescues her from the Parisian Jew may be an agent of Providence, nor will she acknowledge the "Supreme Power" that allows her to keep her treasure (121). Her motives become more perversely conflicted. Her gratitude to the merchant, inadequate in itself, does not obviate her lust for the prince, whose repentance she only uncertainly accepts. The merchant's conviction that she is a "Saint" ironically emphasizes her political fantasies. The more hardened she becomes, the more her religiosity makes her susceptible to sin. Her stance against marriage is a case in point. Mocking the "Authority" of husbands, she defends her "Liberty" as a free agent. Despite having preached marital duty to the prince, she tells the merchant that matrimonial law reduces a woman to a mere "*Upper-Servant*" and "Slave." To Roxana, a single woman is "Masculine in her politick Capacity" and is "fit to govern and enjoy her own Estate, without a Man, as a Man was, without a Woman." While the merchant argues that the subjection of woman in marriage is nominal since there is no "Bondage" in true love, she derides the fact that a woman must live by "Faith (not in God, but) in her Husband" (148–9).

Undermining her libertinism is Roxana's profane subservience in extra-marital affairs. If, given her first husband, she is justified in satirizing woman's obedience to "the Monarch, her Husband" (150), her claim that the "Laws of Matrimony" give "Power" to men is irrelevant to her sexual experience. While conceding the Dutch merchant spoke well about marriage as a "fix'd State of Life" and about "legal Posterity," she simply inverts the notion that the husband is put on a "Throne" and the wife on a "Footstool" (151). Forgetting the imagery of obeisance that gratified her with the prince, she spurns marriage to the merchant that would have let her live "like a Queen," even to being more happy "than a Queen" (159). Far from reaching for happiness through political imagery, she is obsessed with "being Mistress to the King himself" (161). In this obsession, she is "possess'd of the Devil" (157) and "bewitched" (161). Madly thinking she can be queen of England, she cultivates this extreme illusion of self-determination by slurring a lady who marries a nobleman as no better than a "Prisoner of State" (167). She refuses another tradesman who would have let her live "like a Queen" (170), because she wants to replace political imagery with a profane reality.

Roxana's profane illusions are attributable to her Stuart sympathies and to her willingness to exploit the decadent courts of Charles II and George I. The reflexive irony is great when she tells herself not to expect the courtiers to be "Saints" (172) as she prepares to incite the King's attention. This irony is compounded when she is christened Roxana on performing a Turkish dance before the courtiers.[33] It is again compounded when she takes pleasure in being called "Queen of the Day" (179) after her dancing is judged superior to that of real court ladies. There is further irony in the "Retreat" (181) she takes with the "Great Monarch" (202): it may be a "most glorious Retreat," but it leaves her "*a cast-off Mistress*" (182). No religious retreat, it yields her great wealth but not the pseudo-political display to which she has habituated herself, for its pleasures are necessarily secret. Since the aristocrat who next keeps her is above offering her a contract, her anti-social sensibility is reinforced; she feels superior to other mistresses and to the criminal community. If a little gratified by this relationship, its sordidness makes her retreat to a Quaker family. This retreat introduces another narrative irony since the mother of this family, like Roxana, is politically and religiously inconsistent: a social outsider, the Quaker lives "like a Duchess" (211). In this retreat, Roxana's increasingly hollow religiosity is revealed by how she exploits Quaker clothes and mannerisms to avoid the court, to prepare to marry the merchant, and to plan recovering her children.

Claiming to be comfortable in the Quaker community, Roxana is actually "like a Fish out of Water" (214 and 233). Encompassed by ironies, she marries the merchant to screen herself from society, but marriage sees her pursued more keenly by Susan, who is obsessed with discovering her mother. For a fruitless security, Roxana reverses her political independence – her "Platonicks" about being a "*Free Woman*" (232): she calls the merchant "Master" and promises when wedded to "be but an Upper Servant" and "to act the Servant's Part" (233). Yet, her pathological vanity reasserts itself when there is a chance of marrying the prince that would involve again rejecting the merchant. The prospect of being "call'd Her Highness" and living "in all the Splendor of a Court" makes her "truly craz'd and distracted for about a Fortnight"(234). The idea of the prince takes "Possession" of her, this fantasy being "*Lunatick.*" Only fortuitously does she drop her "fancy'd Greatness" (235), her "fancy'd Sovereignty" (238). When the loving but deceived merchant calls her "*his Princess,*" he may touch her "*to the quick,*" but this sensitivity induces nothing in her but "Satisfaction" with her vanity (239–40). So, she encourages him to purchase "Titles of Honour" that will, in his terms, "elevate the Soul" and "infuse generous Principles into the Mind" (240). Besides being inconsistent with Roxana's need for concealment, the titles her husband-to-be theorizes as spiritually uplifting could not be more at odds with her temperament nor promise her more discomfort.[34] Because she exposes herself by wearing her "old *Turkish Habit*" (247–8) and by prevaricating about her past, she increases her spiritual degradation and the emotional distance between herself and her husband. She suffers from a "Dart struck into the Liver" and a "secret Hell within" (260).[35] At the Hague in "the height of [her] Glory and Prosperity" (261), she is so "*Hag-ridden* with Frights, and terrible things, form'd meerly in the Imagination" that she is "not fit for conversing with [her] Family" (264). She no longer confides in the merchant or in the absent and, by this point, hated Amy. That the innocent Susan tracks her down shows up Roxana's insecurity. Fearful about letting her daughter into her past, she is horrified at the notion of being her daughter's "Vassal" (280). Susan voices torturing ironies, as when she recalls that her mother was "a fine modest Lady fit to be a Princess" and "fit to be a Mistress to none but the King" (289). Roxana's political fantasies dissolve as her daughter unknowingly forces her mother's story to trap its author. Vulnerability to her life story is symbolized by the fact Roxana cannot complete her narrative. As Amy and the Quaker relay the unrelenting progress by which her daughter seeks maternal attachment, Roxana closes in on madness, "haunted" by Susan "like an Evil Spirit" (310).[36] That she cannot finish her autobiography symbolizes the dissolution of her political fantasies and the spiritual destruction she has brought upon herself.

Chapter Seven

Marriage and Matrimony: The Dialectic of Sex and Love

> The great Duty between the Man and his Wife, I take to consist in that of Love, in the Government of Affection, and the Obedience of a complaisant, kind, obliging Temper; the Obligation is reciprocal, 'tis drawing in an equal Yoke; Love knows no superior or inferior, no imperious Command on one hand, no reluctant Subjection on the other; the End of both should be the well-ordering their Family, the good-guiding their Houshold and Children, educating, instructing and managing them with a mutual Endeavour, and giving respectively good Examples to them, directing others in their Duty by doing their own well, guiding themselves in every Relation, in order to the well guiding all that are under them; filling up Life with an equal Regard to those above them, and those below them, so as to be Exemplar to all.
>
> To say Love is not essential to the Form of a Marriage, is true; but to say it is not essential to the Felicity of a married State, and consequently to that which I call Matrimony, is not true; and you may as truly say, that Peace is not essential to the good of a Family; as that the Harmony and Conjunction of Souls are not essential to the Happiness of the Persons joyn'd together.[1]

Since the last two chapters have explicated Defoe's institutional conservatism with regard to regal authority and have unfolded in his fictions the self-destructive obsessions with monarchical imagery, it should be less surprising that the above marital prescriptions from *Conjugal Lewdness* involve political concepts that are traditional and progressive.[2] One reason for exploring this dialectic in the present chapter is to see how Defoe conceives of the plural institutional functions of marriage and to show how his polarity thinking about love and domesticity requires narrative structure in his fiction and non-fiction to traverse the boundary between description and prescription constantly. While both genres decry the social customs upholding male sexual dominance, they similarly focus on dysfunctional families and aspirations for marital harmony in order to challenge and defend tradition. Thus, the first epigraph rejects gender hierarchy but upholds social hierarchy, while the second distinguishes between marriage as institutional form and matrimony as spiritual union. The first enjoins love and duty on husband and wife, who must govern their temperaments in the manner of draft animals that wear a yoke but pull a plough in tandem. Marital partners are neither superior nor inferior, imperiousness and subordination no part of family life. The companionable effort required by education of children and household management obliges marital partners to be exemplars to those under and above them. Discipline and equity teach partners that domestic enhances social order. The second passage, in distinguishing matrimony from "the Form of Marriage," makes love the "Felicity" of the "married State." Earlier *Conjugal Lewdness* stresses that love is "so essential to Matrimony, that the Persons should be Lovers as well as Relatives, that there should be an engaged assured Affection before there be a Political Union between them."[3] "Peace" is as essential to the welfare of families as "the Harmony and Conjunction of Souls" are to the "Happiness" of wedded partners. In co-relating the material and spiritual duties of ideal couples, Defoe joins concern for gender equality to respect for patriarchal society.[4]

His stipulations about love as a prerequisite to marital harmony fit his polar sense of natural and learned loving-kindness, illustrating how prescription and description relate when he challenges matrimonial law and custom. For ideal couples love serves plural functions; it is an attribute, purpose, and substrate: "the constituting Quality of their Matrimony, the Reason of it, the Foundation on which it is built, and the Support of it after it is built." This plurality once met, couples "are happy by the meer natural Consequence of Life": their "Tempers" cannot "form any Discord or Strife," and they themselves "cannot Differ, Contend, Rage, Quarrel, Reflect, Reproach, Provoke." They are

> united in Good, and can never be united in Evil too; these Contraries would not illustrate, but destroy one another; in a word, they are all Love, and because they are all Love, therefore their Behaviour is all Peace; the Calm is in the Soul, and when it is so, there can never be a Storm in the Mind; Love is not in them a Passion but a Quality: 'tis rooted and riveted in their very Beings, they have a Disposition to it in their very Nature.[5]

If love enables couples to cope with the contraries of good and evil, this is because they will have disciplined themselves before choosing their mates. Only by knowing their own "Infirmities" can they study the "Suitabilities" of partners. However, marriage remains a "Venture" because biological and temperamental contraries cannot be transmuted:

> after you have done your utmost, you may be mistaken, may be deceived, and, after the utmost Caution, some unsuitable Things must be expected: You must expect Difficulties, and to have many Things to struggle with, an Exercise for all your Virtue, all your Self-denial, all your temper; as long as Flesh and Blood is a Composition of Contraries, and inconsistent Humours, there will be something always left to try your Patience, to try your Christianity.[6]

Defoe also sets religious over secular imperatives because conflicts between marital ideals and custom are unavoidable. Thus, marriage is a "Civil Establishment" since it is "a sacred Institution." Only when "mutual reciprocal Endearments, and unfeigned sincere Love" are founded on religion, can married love enhance society. He reiterates this by affirming that "Matrimony, though it is not so regarded, is really a religious, sacred and divine Institution; it ought to be taken as such, and never undertaken without Regard to its religious Foundation."[7]

Opposing secular customs, he links abuse of matrimony to abuse of religion. Those who marry to gratify "the sensual Part" debauch marriage "because Sensuality is not the true End and Design of the ordinance of Matrimony, but a Corruption of it." Those who hide their sensuality under the cover of "God's *holy Ordinance*" profane and make a "Jest of Religion"; they turn "sacred Things to debauched Purposes … giving religious Titles to corrupt Undertakings, and sanctifying Crimes by the Mask of Innocence." Since customary laxity entails licentiousness, Defoe justifies the oxymora in the title, *Conjugal Lewdness; or Matrimonial Whoredom*, by broadening similar terms: marriage between partners of unequal ages is "a kind of Matrimonial Rape"; if a man marries one woman while loving another, he commits a "kind of civil, legal *Adultery*"; when a wife does not want children, she enacts "a kind of legal Whoring"; and when she marries without love, she commits "a kind of legal Prostitution," her abuse of the "Glory of a Christian Matrimony" deserving "the Title of a Matrimonial Whoredom, or, at least of a Matrimonial Prostitution."[8]

His attack on sexual permissiveness in marriage does not simply reject gender hierarchy, for when describing society's debasement of marital idealism he concedes his awareness of

> how the Subordination of one Sex is laughed at and bantered, and the Dominion of the other abused and turned into Tyranny and Oppression; how the Women, instead of Submission, reign; and the Men, instead of Government in Love, and a superiority of Affection, in which that Government should chiefly consist, insult and oppress their Wives; how the Obligation of forsaking all other, is ridiculed and made a Jest of, and that of keeping your self only unto her, declared to be a meer Church Imposition, a Piece of Priestcraft, and unreasonable.[9]

This assault on infidelity takes in the displacement and excesses of gender hierarchy, the abeyance and reversal of gender roles. This complex, two-pronged satire is made sharper by his institutional sense of religion with its recognition of inevitable tensions between spiritual and ecclesiastical authority. The ordinance of the Church of England and the liturgy of the Book of Common Prayer frame the discourse of *Conjugal Lewdness* because he considers marriage in terms of the necessary relation between church and state. Refusing in *Religious Courtship* to specify whether his characters have been brought up in the Church or Dissent, he insists that marriage must be based on the interdependence of private and public reformation.[10] Apparently, he found it easier to regard sexual conduct as subject to social regulation by adopting an authoritarian outlook closer to that of the Established Church than to that of Dissent.[11]

Had he wanted to make singular pronouncements on marriage, he could not have, given its confused legal status.[12] During his time, marriage was an object of common, equity, civil, and canon laws, being variously interpreted as a natural, commercial, judicial, and religious matter. Given the diversity of these jurisdictions, what marriage was, when and how it was deemed to come about, how partners were to treat one another, and what the extent of parental authority was were moot. Diverse judgments from these jurisdictions might be aggravated by conflicts within them. Since ecclesiastical courts might annul church marriages for common-law reasons, on such occasions the church would be reckoned as undermining its own authority. Again, since divorce was impossible outside Acts of Parliament, even then constituting annulment rather than licence to remarry, and since clandestine marriages were common because canon law was not regularly enforced or licences uniformly required, all ranks of society resorted to desertion, adultery, and bigamy.[13]

Lawrence Stone's thesis that England's middle classes developed between 1640 and 1800 a more personal, emotional sense of marital love by abandoning commercial, patriarchal, and religious standards of marriage is not evident in Defoe's writings.[14] Stone's key phrase, "affective individualism" – his term for the new secular concern for sexual compatibility, mutual parenting, and the nuclear family – discounts Defoe's opposition to secular standards of reform that exclude theology. While Defoe promoted gender equality and love as prerequisites to marriage, he defended the traditional values of the extended family, the procreative imperative of sexual intercourse, and the importance of legal inheritance, and he continued to apply political and biblical imagery to family life in order to reconcile secular and religious imperatives and present them as matters of conscience.

He views the wedding rite through biblical exegesis: its liturgical status was "instituted immediately from the divine Authority"; God "solemnized" it, having the sole "Right to perform the Ceremony." Marriage is "God's holy Ordinance"; as the "Father of Eve," He exercised "Paternal Authority" in giving her to Adam and settling the "Right of Marriage ever after" in the "Priesthood."

> Hence the Parent giving the Bride is to this Day a remainder of that Authority. The Ceremony being truly Religious, and an Ordinance of God, it goes with God's other Ordinances, away to the Priest, whose Business it is to exercise all religious Offices.[15]

Viewing God as the paradigm of priestly and paternal roles and yoking theology and patriarchy, Defoe fortifies his belief that marriages should be conducted in church. Further, as we have seen, he scorns abuse of the Pauline dictates about "Dominion" and "Subordination" when husbands turn their authority into "Tyranny and Oppression" and wives, deriding subordination, care only to "reign."[16] Since St Paul's hierarchical imagery is not at odds with the sexes' spiritual equality, Defoe charges abusers of Pauline imagery with political and domestic disaffection. The secularization of family hierarchy debasing sexual politics, he spurns the "Government … and Obedience" respectively of husband and wife, refusing to "take the State of Matrimony to be designed as that of Apprentices who are bound to the Family and that the Wife is to be us'd only as the upper Servant in the House."[17] Distinguishing between the subordination of wives and servants, he confirms that the equality of loving husbands and wives transcends gender hierarchy embodied only in secular terms.

To renew the ecclesiastical solemnization of matrimony, Defoe displaces legal contracts and spousal promises by cannily embedding common-law standards into his religious discourse. When urging mutual preparation on prospective partners, he stresses that they should be "united before they [are] joined ... married even before they [are] wedded." Here the common-law mode of betrothal, a mode he often faults for its customary licence of pre-marital intercourse, supports religious love: lovers should be spiritually married before they are ritually wedded and wedded before they consummate their love. Behind this displacement lies his belief that a "corrupt Principle dictates the Propagation of the Kind," that sex is sanctioned only in marriage, and that those who "have no Sense of the matrimonial Obligation can have no Sense of the conjugal Duty," for, after they lie together, their relationship becomes "a Bondage; and they as heartily hate the state of Life as a Slave does his Lot in *Algier* or *Tunis*."[18] Yet, those who subject the ordinance to common-law rationalizations by exposing themselves to mutual and social recriminations paradoxically exemplify domestic happiness and good citizenship. Defoe's appropriation of betrothal develops this dialectical thesis: those who spiritually prepare for marriage internalize betrothal and reinforce society, while those who marry for sex weaken society by ignoring the religious sense necessary for personal integrity.

He amplifies his traditional and progressive ideology by detailing how civil relates to common law in the realm of spousal betrothal:

> It may be true, that Promise of Marriage is Marriage, but it is not marrying; it may be called Marriage, or rather a Species of Marriage; and therefore our Law will oblige such Persons to marry afterwards, as well in cases where they have not consummated the Agreement, as where they have; and will give Damages, and that very considerable, in proportion to the Circumstances of the Parties, where these Promises are broken; especially where the person makes the Breach, by marrying another purely in Contravention of those Promises. And this is all the Remedy the injured Person can obtain.

His differentiation between the liturgical rite and betrothal takes precedence over the civil law that obliges people who have pledged to marry to do so, whether or not they have consummated their love. Only after asserting this precedence does he grant that civil law may award damages to victims of broken promises, justify them in forbidding the banns of unfaithful partners, and permit them to introduce broken promises as a "lawful Obstacle or Impediment" to wedding ceremonies. Solely because he assumes that "Promises of Marriage" cannot replace "fair and formal Espousal" does he grant that civil law may enforce "the sacred Obligation of Marriage" by determining "Obligation of Maintenance," "Legitimacy of Children," and "Claim of Inheritances." His point is that, if it assumes betrothed partners to be joined, thereby upholding common law, civil law should not decide marital disputes until "Promises of Marriage" have been legitimated by the "Form of Marriage." His insistence on the church ordinance would make personal aspects of marriage less confusing and confirms that theological imperatives are necessarily implicated in the proper structure of society.[19]

When Defoe decries marriage partners whose seemingly unassailable reputations cover immoral sexual habits, he focuses less on actual whoredom and "forsaking the Marriage Covenant" than on how the marriage bed defiled by licentiousness disorders society. To assail so-called good persons who will not treat marriage as a spiritual practice, he complicates his prescriptions by rejecting as "coarse" St Paul's justification of marriage in terms of preventing "Fornication." For this justification prompts assumptions that sexual indulgence is unrestricted in marriage and that domestic morality has no higher imperatives than public mores. However, true marital love induces partners to turn the natural "Principles of Reluctance and Aversion" into spiritual mortification.[20] If spouses may not decline sexual intercourse, procreative cycles should instil moderate behaviour.

The traditional and progressive ways in which Defoe criticizes sexual indulgence, reinforces sexual morality by refining biblical imperatives, and reads civil law theologically are confirmed by his arguments against divorce. He rejects divorce by setting marriage as an institution above individual happiness: "the Bond is too sacred to be broken at pleasure." His definitions of true love and sexual kinship maintain that marital incompatibility results from deficient religious preparations. Since matrimony is "an irreversible Decree," loveless husbands and wives cannot legitimately propose lovelessness as a justification for divorce. Since marriage as an institution is essential to social order, Defoe treats divorce simply as a form of unprincipled individualism.[21]

This institutional perspective obtains when he discusses procreation: women, he says, should marry only if they aspire to motherhood and, since marriage civilly regulates propagation by ensuring heirs to husbands and security to wives, females who are past childbearing or do not want children need not marry, this absolute stance on their options precluding sexual desire as a womanly motive. He doubly condemns women who detach procreation from marriage: they are whores because they subordinate the religious rite to desire; they are "Lunatick" because they surrender personal and legal independence to physical appetite. Despite having stressed the moral equality of the sexes in marriages, in contrary fashion he emphasizes gender inequality to argue that sexual desire, financial insecurity, and loneliness are for women self-destructive motives to marriage. By heightening their disadvantages, he adopts the conservative view that these disadvantages, far from being subject to reform, may be offset only when mothers recognize the divine blessing of children. Similarly, he condemns married women who prevent conception or procure abortions. Calling them whores for thwarting husbands' desires to "preserve a Name and a Posterity," he judges them guilty of "wilful Murther."[22] Still, he limits how he inures women to procreation since abortion is justifiable in some instances. It may be necessary when "the Dangers and Pains of a hard Travail," injuries caused by midwives, or "Distempers or Disasters" threaten a pregnant woman's life.[23] Valuing a mother's life over that of an unborn child, he uses tradition to persuade women to be more selective in choosing mates. By holding that, even in loving marriages, they have more to lose than men, he wants them to see the dangers that arise from viewing marriage indulgently and to respect it as a state the happiness of which depends on fulfilling their procreative function religiously.

Tellingly, institutional arguments in *Conjugal Lewdness* address men more than women.[24] The judicial penalties Defoe wants enforced against male sexual violence, as his Islamic speculations discussed in the previous chapter suggest, emphasize the ills of patriarchy. Thus, he condemns the abuse of pregnant wives. Once a wife is pregnant, intercourse should cease. Not to stop is "unnatural Violence." Husbands must curb their appetites and accept that "the Necessary Mortifications of a holy Life" enjoin abstinence. Convinced marriage does not legitimate sexual abuse, he declares that a "Woman may be ravish'd in the Marriage-Bed" and that a husband may "deserve the Gallows for Crimes offer'd to his own Wife."[25] Besides arguing that a husband is justly hanged for raping his wife, he extends the meaning of rape by proposing that families who force a daughter to marry when she is neither in love nor consents to marriage impose on her "the worst kind of Rape." A family that so exercises patriarchal authority commits "a wilful Violence upon the Mind" that is "equal or superior to a Violence upon the Body; it is a formal Ravishment upon Virtue, and that in so much the worse a manner, as it is done under the Form of Justice and Law, and is still made worse, in that it is without a Remedy." A woman whose chastity is violated "has her recourse to the Law, and she will be redress'd as far as redress can be obtained"; she is "protected by the Law from any farther Force upon her for the future." But when a woman is

> put to Bed to the Man by a kind of forced Authority of Friends; 'tis a Rape upon the Mind; her Soul, her brightest Faculties, her Will, her Affections are ravished, and she is left without redress, she is left in the Possession of the Ravisher, or of him, who, by their order, she was delivered up to, and she is bound in the Chains of the same Violence for her whole life.[26]

Here Defoe conceptualizes legalized rape with the same satirical insistence he gives to oxymora in the title of *Conjugal Lewdness: Or, Matrimonial Whoredom*: violence against women is not limited to bodily assault. Suitors who comply with fathers against the free will of daughters abuse female identity with society's sanction. Families and friends who perpetuate institutionalized male violence degrade womanhood. Defoe's opposition to sexual, legal, and psychological violence clarifies the progressive side of his promotion of marriage. Spiritual harm inflicted on women epitomizes the travesty of marriage and justifies his religious criticism of male sexual individualism.

Defoe's metonymical extension of "whoredom" and "rape," in exposing rationalizations arising from the double standard of sexual morality, effectively exploits the contrary that, while men and women are jointly responsible in wedlock, men by custom are more likely to debase marriage. Insincere husbands and wives who live in spiritual whoredom often commit actual whoredom because they commit "Adultery in their Hearts every Day of their lives," their lust eventuating in infidelity. Both men and women are to blame when matrimonial whoredom leads to "Excuses for all the wicked Excursions which are made after Marriage." Such excuses pervert marriage by falsely distinguishing between spouses by "Affection" and spouses by "Law."

To offset this perversity, Defoe refines prescriptions about equality of age, wealth, and rank, his view that marital disharmony is aggravated by lax sexual mores deepening his traditional concern with social hierarchy. His complaint that wives are unfairly blamed when things go wrong in marriage since society imposes on them the burden of sexual modesty and domestic order reveals that, behind his argument that both sexes should accept the "Obligation to Decency," lies a wish to erode the customs by which men allow themselves sexual licence. If women are guilty of licentiousness, this is partly due to their understandable, if inexcusable, imitation of the double standard, as is obviously true of Roxana. By seeking to harmonize religious and civil aspects of marriage, Defoe would replace the double standard by holistic rules which, traditionally reintegrating private and public values, progressively recognize sexual equality. So, if he insists that "All indecent Matrimony is mutual; and the Crime is mutual, the Scandal affects both, the Woman is as guilty as the Man, and the Man as the Woman," he holds that men are more responsible than women for the debasement of marriage.[27]

The dialectic promoting the equality of the sexes and deflating male complacency in *Conjugal Lewdness* seems to have been worked out in the narrative structure of *Religious Courtship*, which appeared five years earlier in the period when Defoe was composing his major fictions. This conduct manual embodies a progressive and traditional ideology in its narrative patterning, dramatic dialogues, and female characterization.[28] Yet, perhaps the most striking fictional aspect of *Religious Courtship* is its narrative reflexivity: its story concerns problems to do with storytelling in courtship and daily life. Defoe founds this reflexivity on the polar attributes of strong female characters. Their hope for equality in marriage derives from personal feeling and social sense: resisting patriarchy that upholds materialistic, legalistic, and secular ideas of marriage, they endorse familial authority based on religious discipline, thereby defending as well as challenging the institutional status of marriage. Claiming the religious right to refuse prospective spouses, they do not wish to change the convention by which fathers propose husbands: they want negative, not positive, choice. They understand that social cohesion, in addition to personal identity and domestic virtues, depends on faithful marriages. In this, they connect practical to spiritual values. In attributing polar awareness of personal strength and social vulnerability to female figures, Defoe exploits fiction in his manual. Its motifs, polarities informing characterization, and embedded dialogues create with manifest fictional energy standards of sexual discourse that harmonize traditional and progressive marital principles.

As we have seen, *Religious Courtship* dramatizes conflicting ideas of marriage held by a widower, his three daughters, their extended family and social circle. The widower, retired from a mercantile career removed from his daughters' education, autocratically decides to provide them with husbands. While his wife had pledged her children to marry religious men, he ignores this pledge as an unnecessary "Nicety."[29] In choosing a suitor for his youngest daughter, he regards only the man's material qualifications and the legal settlement. Although he is opposed by his eldest daughter's argument that professed faith is the prerequisite of a husband and although his conscience tells him that his faithlessness made his wife's existence miserable, he would force his choice on his youngest daughter at the risk of alienating her and destroying family concord. His intemperance indicates how much patriarchy may erode masculine integrity. His sexism is initially shared by the suitor, who is a born gentleman. In the biting words of the youngest daughter, he is

> a true Gentleman, perfectly educated, politely bred, that knows about as much of Religion as a *Parson's Horse*; that is to say, knows the Way to the Church-Door, but scorns to debauch his Breeding with such a clumsey thing as Religion; is more a Gentleman, than to trouble himself with the Meannesses of Religion, and not Hypocrite enough to pretend to the sublimer Parts of it; one that has not been long enough in this World, to *think* of the next, nor is yet come to any resolution about *when he shall*.

Typically, the suitor would choose a wife before matching his creed to hers. He is made to confess this by the eldest daughter's account of her aunt's late husband as "*one of the worst good Husbands, that ever a sober woman had*." The dialogues constantly emphasize this female capacity to voice emotional paradoxes and to grasp polar ideas. The more the youngest daughter falls in love with the suitor, the more she knows she must reject him. What her father regards as "canting Scruples" are essential to her personhood. Sorely conscious of her "strange Kindness" for her suitor, she resists him, convinced that her emotional susceptibility may be turned to good only by mutual spiritual encouragement. Her resistance shows she derives strength from internalizing domestic feelings.[30]

The youngest daughter's resistance to patriarchy is accentuated by novel aspects of the setting and dialogues in which she explains her resistance to her eldest sister and because of which the suitor ultimately drops his cavalier attitudes.[31] The father unconventionally picks a suitor for his youngest before choosing for his older daughters. Rather than immediately presenting the dialogue between suitor and youngest daughter, Defoe heightens the latter's expressive power by having her narrate that conversation to her eldest sister, who, in response, elicits her sibling's subtle sensibility and intelligent interpretations. Not only is the youngest daughter given narrative power over her father, suitor, and eldest sister but her discourse motivates events that overcome patriarchal indifference to religious values and counter her lack of social power. Adhering to her mother's fortifying precepts, she becomes the narrative cynosure. At the same time, the suitor compounds his personal and narrative problems when, after telling his intended that he is not "Hypocrite enough to pretend to the sublimer Parts" of religion, he admits he would act the hypocrite if he could gain her for his bride. He foresees neither that she will reject him in the belief that "a religious Life is the only Heaven upon Earth" nor that his frankness will make his penitence more difficult to credit. Rebuffed and "touch'd ... very sensibly," he suffers events that test his self-reflection and confirm his intended's outlook. At first, he has "only the just and natural Reflections of his own Reason" to fall back on. When he entertains a second mistress, his heart is not in it; talking to her is "like Musick to one that had no Ear." Her inanity makes his "very Blood run cold within him" and fills "him with Horror at his own Picture" which is "set before his Eyes in all its just Deformities." Hearing himself in his second mistress's discourse and discomfited by the sentiments he had addressed to his first mistress, he recognizes "*the true Force of what that dear Creature argued for herself against me.*"[32] His moral guilt and aesthetic sensibility further strike him when he hears an "ancient Nobleman" hold forth on St Paul's gentility and on the reciprocity of Christianity and civility in reaction to two opera-going beaux who spurn religious discourse. To this aristocrat,

> Religion was the Beauty of Conversation, and assisted to make it pleasant and agreeable; that without it Company was empty, Discourse unprofitable, Society unpleasant; and, in short, that Conversation, without a Mixture of something regarding Religion, and a due Connection with it, was

> like a Dance without Musick, a Song without Measure; like Poetry without Quantity, or Speech without Grammar.

The aristocrat's reciprocal theology and aesthetics lend authority to the youngest daughter, partly because the suitor admits "how like one of these Fops" put down by the aristocrat he must have seemed to her. He sees that "he had talk'd after the same senseless Way, which he now look'd upon to be the most empty, scandalous Thing in the World."[33]

His sexual complacency challenged by the youngest daughter and by social encounters, the suitor renews his understanding of patriarchy, prompted to do so by an unenfranchised tenant on his Hampshire estate to which, abashed, he retreats. There, after overhearing the poverty-stricken tenant's prayers, he assumes patriarchal responsibilities, becoming "Father" to the tenant's family, establishing them in a rent-free cottage, and calling William "Father" for the spiritual lessons he receives from him. These parenting metonyms reach their acme when the suitor tells the elder sister that his intended "has been a better Instructor to me than my Father, or Mother, or all the Tutors and Friends I had in my life" and that he will "always think of her as the Mother of all that is or ever will be good in me." As a spiritual father who transcends the rational boundaries of dialogue, William induces the landlord, as we have seen, to discover "a secret kind of Hint like a Voice *in him*."[34] Besides alerting the landlord to true patriarchy, William belongs to a wide social network that, in effecting the suitor's conversion, supports the harmony of secular and religious values that inspirits the youngest daughter. That she is the first to stand up to unrefined patriarchy and has her views about marriage confirmed by characters who range from an ideal aristocrat to an ideal poor man endows her with a narrative authority that substantiates her discourse.

Among other characters who balance progressive and traditional ideas of marriage is the widowed sister of the intransigent father. To her brother she confides that Sir James, her late husband, made life wretched by mocking religion and she laments that patriarchy renders wives powerless to effect religious education. Her brother is unmoved by her marital wretchedness, his sympathy blocked by the assumption that Christianity and gentility are incompatible. Collapsing the distinction between faith and hypocrisy, he asserts that no one, let alone his youngest daughter, can determine who is truly religious. To his sister's retort that this assertion proves the need for parents to help daughters choose religious husbands, he is indifferent, but her clinching reply is that young women are therefore justified in looking after their own religious interests. She further opposes his shallow contradictions, transforming them into moral arguments by defying his "Rage and Fury" and insisting that fathers must correct their children "with Calmness and Affection." The model father "must pity when he punishes, exhort when he corrects; he should have the Rod in his Hand, and Tears in his Eyes." Ultimately, her brother accepts his sister's polar view of patriarchal authority when he calls her "a healing Preacher."[35] However, like the suitor the father cannot by himself repair the damage his irreligion has caused. His refusal to see that his youngest daughter could be suffering from a conflict between love and conscience betrays a selfish perversity that is contrasted with her stoic capacity to endure conflict to the point of illness. By aggravating his daughter's suffering, he forfeits the authority to marry her. Hence, the union with the reformed suitor is mediated by the aunt, an old gentlewoman and an old clergyman who bear witness to his conversion. Because of paternal irresponsibility, the extended family and friends validate the distinction between unbelief and faith, Defoe implying that the father would have done so had he been informed by religious sense.

Defoe further critiques patriarchy in the eldest daughter's refusal to marry since her father will neither guarantee her suitor to be of her religious persuasion nor allow her a negative voice in courtship. Despite broaching the proposal with her, he had already drawn up a settlement with his candidate's parents. His deceitfulness proves how little he has learned from his youngest daughter's resistance. He is thwarted, however, because his eldest daughter persuades her intended's parents to accept her matrimonial creed. They agree that couples unmatched in religious tenets of necessity face insurmountable problems: "In their publick Worship, Sacraments, *&c.* neither one Heart or one Voice goes with their Worship." Even if "they communicate in the same Ordinance, they set up two Altars."[36] Against their material interest, these parents agree that uniform creeds are essential to family life, also encouraging the youngest daughter to trust in women's power to reform men. They obliquely tell her the story of her suitor's conversion to begin overcoming her suspicion of his hypocrisy. With strenuous tact, they displace the father as they foster her.

The middle daughter marries unhappily, inevitably experiencing profanity because she will neither resist her autocratic father nor examine her suitor's creed. Warned by her older sister that the suitor might be a Roman Catholic, she equivocates in the belief his passion should compel him to be a hypocrite in order to secure her. This supine irresponsibility goads her elder sister to insist with the "Fathers of our Reformation" that "Communion be given to the marry'd Couple at every Wedding" since partners should be "of the same Communion with one another." While failing to move her sister, after a visit to the newlyweds' home, the elder daughter's account of the icons in their house touches her father "to the Heart," forcing him to confess that, even as he passionately said it was none of his "Business" to examine the suitor's religion, his heart struck him with "Reproach" because he knew it was his "Duty" to do so. He admits that Providence has punished him for ruining his middle daughter. If not ruined, she is more than uneasy in her marriage since she will not compromise Protestantism while her husband exploits her love to win her to Catholicism. Instead of resisting her father, she had exploited her dependence on him to avoid catechizing her suitor and herself. Her conversation with her suitor was no more than a "dull and empty Discourse" because she trusted to the paternal guarantee of her suitor's creed when she had no reason to do so.[37]

Still, her contrary emotions as wife and widow endorse her mother's imperatives. Despite mutual love and respect, she is relieved by her husband's death, experience teaching her that "no Kindness, no Tenderness, no Affection" compensates for partners' different creeds. Ideal love aggravated their religious differences to the point of rendering them intolerable:

> we could not think of one another with Charity, but as deceived Persons, out of the way of eternal Felicity, out of God's Blessing and Protection; we would not look upon one another but with Sighs and sad Hearts.

Her husband treated her profanely as his "Idol," thinking her "Breast should be his Altar." The crucifix he gives her leads the Venetian ambassador and his retinue to give her "so many Bows and Homages" that she does not know what to do with herself nor how to "distinguish their good Manners from their Religion." She concludes that "the more devout and serious the Person is in his way, the worse Husband." By making the middle daughter extraordinarily happy and unhappy, Defoe maintains that sexual passion only aggravates creedal disharmony:

> all social Religion was lost; mutual Help and Assistance in Religion was wanting; publick worshipping God in the Family as a House could not be set up; Education and Instruction of Children, was all destroy'd; Example

> to Servants and Inferiors all spoil'd; nothing could be of Religion, but what was meerly personal and retir'd.

To an extent, contrary experiences develop the middle daughter's identity. Having equivocated about marrying for better or worse, she gains insight into traditional values through painful love. Yet, since her extraordinary passion could not endure the increasing chaos of domestic life, her unthinking acceptance of her father's authority leads to personal, familial, and social unhappiness.[38]

That narrative problems receive narrative solutions in *Religious Courtship* evidences Defoe's trust in the human need for religious experience. The fictional mediation by which he obliquely reconciles individual choice with social hierarchy confirms that those problems are best confronted by paradox: gender and domestic reform depends on an ethic of religious equality that upholds social hierarchy. Thus, William, the major apologist for spiritual egalitarianism, ardently defends rank. By making characters of all ranks acknowledge that marriage is a difficult undertaking and heaven on earth, Defoe harmonizes progressive and traditional values. Hence, his dialogues dramatically enact the disintegration and reconstruction of society. At the beginning of *Religious Courtship*, the father declines converse with his youngest daughter, patriarchal biases keeping him from direct speech. To validate his satire of male prejudices, Defoe presents the suitor's courtship of the youngest daughter through indirect speech. His patterning of dialogues contrasts the unwillingness of men to speak sincerely with women's exploratory discourse. Intensive speaking and listening, the women realize – after the Defoe of *Serious Reflections* – is constructive if performed with religious sensibility. More than the male characters, they explore dialogue's capacity to endow stories with maximal coherence. Thus, the eldest daughter tells of her aunt's experience with Sir James to reform the marital ideas of her sister's suitor while Sir James's widow similarly confronts her brother. Both alert men to the patterns of domestic living, the men reforming only after they disclaim patriarchal autocracy and learn to talk like sensible women. As we saw, when the suitor sees himself in the inane talk of his second mistress, her conversation being "almost the Pattern of what he had done with his first Mistress," he speaks against himself to correct social disorder and acquire personal integrity.[39] Of course, William also re-motivates male discourse. If humility leads him to talk against himself, he transforms confession into a rhetoric that extends dialogue into spiritual and even wordless communication. William embodies Defoe's implication that, far from making people morose, religion makes them socially constructive by enabling them to see traditional values in progressive ways. But Defoe more than renders storytelling into forms of domestic resistance and social reform; he knows that narrative mediates experience for good as well as ill and that, since we live amid probabilities and uncertainties, stories should be as reflexive for readers as for characters and narrators. Narrative discourse is a theme in *Religious Courtship* so that the compound interrelations of its dialogues may effectively fictionalize his contrarian ideology of marriage.

*****

This ideology of marriage obtains in his fictions, less because they are "case studies" than because he was sensitive to codes.[40] His depiction of patriarchy's oppression of women, sexual power in society, and psychological violence reveal that he analysed codes dividing "the feminine domestic" from "the masculine socio-political." Granting women's desire to be agents in their lives and to enter into historical processes, he grasped the textuality of codes, namely, that they are embedded in language, literature, society, and people, including readers. His appreciation of codes explains why he endowed fictional and non-fictional texts with diverse functions and plural rather than singular viewpoints. Acknowledging the plural codes applied by various jurisdictions to marriage, he idealized matrimony without denying its abuses. If novels appropriate romance to delimit their plots by a trajectory of courtship and marriage that solves all problems, this is hardly true of his narratives. For he defies conventions that limit genres and genders facilely.[41] He does not suppress the systemic contradictions in marriage as later authors are said to do. In this way his fiction may be seen to differ from the fully developed novel which is sometimes viewed as a genre conservative in its reliance on romance and in its commitment to secular norms. Joseph Boone claims that, while it was "radically conceived," the novel expresses the "voice of tradition," the contradiction arising from romantic love. Since "ideological structures of belief" are translated into narratives that "at once encode and perpetuate those beliefs," the novel yields "an *inevitable* collision of systems of belief" and clashing "aesthetic ideologies" that convey the "values of the disenfranchised as well as the status quo."[42] For Boone, because the novel promotes wedlock both as a "natural, rather than socially constructed, phenomenon" and as "a metonymy for proper social order," it disguises asymmetries "within the trope of 'balanced' order," with the result that ideological structures in fiction create the illusion of a coherent world by "eliding the multiple social contradictions." That is to say, novelistic structures embody "a mission analogous to that of society's dominant ideological structures."[43]

Given Defoe's deployment of social and textual asymmetries, Boone's hypothesis may not apply to an author who composed fiction before the full emergence of the novel; his fictions deal not with traditional marriage plots but with dysfunctional marital relations. To an extent his non-fiction idealizes matrimony, but his fiction depicts multiple marriages and abuses of marital standards rather than "glosses over the contradictions, the inequities in the institution of marriage itself." Nor do structures of desire in his fiction convey "a restrictive sexual-marital ideology." Boone's claim that the novel relies on "the implications of [a] constant dichotomization of the sexes" hardly fits Defoe since he does not see "as 'natural' mutually exclusive definitions of 'masculine' and 'feminine' behavior." Nor does he "conceal under the trope of oppositional 'balance' the sexual asymmetries inherent in a hierarchical order based on male dominance and female suppression."[44] He does show that when female characters act like men, or think they do, their pretensions recoil on them. By the same token, male characters who think they can act independently of women or can dominate them without suffering a loss of consequence are as mistaken. However, his tenet that women should be self-determining agents in domestic and economic life is a deep source of his narrative energy.

The digest of progressive and revisionist criticism in William Horne's survey of eighteenth-century marriage poems clarifies theoretical issues relating to Defoe's depiction of marital problems. In questioning Stone's optimism about marital companionship, Horne reports that, far from being "always a liberalizing influence," companionate ideology was "fraught with contradictions"; if "a 'kinder and gentler' patriarchy" idealized women of "taste and sensibility" who controlled men by pleasing them, such wives were their husbands' "dearest possession," and if the idealization of wives increased "respect for marriage and the family as social institutions," it replaced "traditional marriage theology with a secularized worship of woman in her roles as wife and mother." This secularization means to revisionists that husbands learned to be more hypocritical in their infidelities and more subtle in their dominance. Such critics hold that, if children gained "more voice in the choice of a mate," patriarchy was not weakened thereby since female children did not "gain power in the legal and economic sphere." Such critical debates point up how Defoe's texts dialectically balance progressive and revisionist ideas; they promote love and fidelity in marriage as they satirize libertinism and the double standard; they praise and blame St Paul's dictates; they challenge and uphold patriarchal authority. Then again, to Defoe, Anglican liturgy was not "a reactionary force blocking softening of patriarchal attitudes and practices" because he was ambivalent about marriage as a civil contract while usually denying its sacramentality. Further, domesticity does not displace patriarchy in his thinking because his idealization of love attacked the notion of female marital servitude rather than promote womanly delicacy. His non-fictional women suffer exquisitely in their moral awareness of social and domestic problems. But they do not recoil from household management, given their keen sense of extended families.[45]

Defoe's protagonists in *Colonel Jack, Moll Flanders,* and *Roxana* are victims of society's legal confusion about marriage, but they also entrap themselves with false notions about matrimony. Their marriages are not personally happy or constructive, but, as plot elements, they shape action and structure denouements ironically. The protagonists' sexual impulses do not lead to pleasure because they are pretentious when not aimless. However, if his characters and narrators cannot convert their negative marital experiences into sustained positive conduct, they do express positive ideas about marriage from the disjunctions they feel between matrimonial desires and achievements, in this contradictory process offering interpretive roles to readers with regard to social and textual codes.[46]

Colonel Jack's experiences are negative because his uneducated aspirations for gentility and unquestioning patriarchal assumptions evade marriage's institutional forms. Pretensions to middle-class status see his first marriage performed privately "to avoid Ceremony, and the publick Inconveniency of a Wedding" (193). That his third is "so very exact a Concealment" confirms his snobbish concern for privacy (239). His individualism is again realized when his fourth wedding is conducted by a Catholic priest in the latter's "own Study" of an evening, thereby evading the reading of banns and the canonical hours (248). That he remarries his first wife "openly" shows an improved sense of the institutional rite but not of gender equality (263). But his wife's penitential self-abasement that leads her to reject proposals from Jack's Tutor because she is a "married Woman" with a "Husband alive" who would prefer to be Jack's "Slave rather than the best Man's Wife in the World" reveals a superior religious sense (261). While Jack raises her from her status as a transported convict by remarrying her, he still has to acknowledge her agency and their mutual dependence. Thus, she secures a royal pardon for his participation in the Jacobite rebellion of 1715.

The selfish complacency and genteel affectation displayed by Jack in his first four marriages expose the psychological incoherence and violence arising from sexual politics that Defoe thought religious courtship would preclude. In his first courtship, Jack is alternately fascinated by and indifferent to the woman whose lively wit spurs him on by insults. When his apparent coolness maddens her, driving her to appear sober, she traps him, making him court her on her terms. Since deceptive tactics dominate this courtship, tensions within and between the partners are unresolved. Still, the woman easily wins the battle of the sexes: to attach Jack she persuades him that men forfeit the power in courtship which they should retain when she declares that marriages are "Treaties of Peace ... Alliances Offensive or Defensive" best mediated by "Ambassadors, Agents, and Emissaries on both Sides" (188). This "meer Posture Mistress in Love," in her role as sober woman, finally wins him by claiming that a forward female lays herself "under the Foot of the Man she pretends to" (190). Jack is dull to the contradictions in her performance; she gains power over him by being forward. Since her sexual politics are so easily effectual, this first marriage degenerates into whoredom and violence and, although Jack secures a divorce from the "Ecclesiastick Court," he learns nothing but is simply "Sick of Wedlock" (198).

Jack's delusory hope to gain military honour, no matter how illicitly, explains why his second marriage is "perfectly undesign'd." Having "contracted a kind of Familiarity" with the daughter of an Italian burgher with whom he billets, he is "guilty" of a "Peice of Honesty" when he marries his whore (221). His genteel self-deception is accented when we learn that the girl got him to marry her by intoxicating him with wine. While he admits being "insensibly drawn" into the "dull Cause" of the Jacobites, his traitorous hope to win honour from the Old Pretender accentuates his undisciplined violence. Soon jealously certain he is a "Cuckold," he "more than once" commits in "Imagination" his wife's "Murther," his "distemper'd Fancy" obsessed with the "Management" of killing her (225). Only thrusting his Catholic "Whore" to the floor, he duels with and mortally wounds her lover, a marquis (228–30).[47] Subsequently, he admits that, having made his "Italian Wife" a whore, he should not have expected her to be otherwise (231). His point, viewed in *Conjugal Lewdness* as a check on the double standard, shows that Jack tells against himself so that readers may interpret him as an ironical source of matrimonial principles.[48] Because this second marriage rouses him to desire a "settled family life," he briefly has courtship scruples. He will "not steal" a girl whose father prevents their marriage (234). But his scruples do not last. Aware he is "not legally divorc'd" from his second wife when he courts a young widow, he forgets he abandoned his second spouse and regards himself as "divorc'd in Law" despite having avoided the "legal Process" (239). Rushing this widow into marriage, which she would delay for decency's sake, Jack fails to convert scruples into principles. He will not complete his story of this "Courtship" since the couple is so "privately Married, and that with so very exact a Concealment" that his wife's "Maid that was so Instrumental in it, yet had no Knowledge of it for near a Month more" (239). The third wife's descent into alcoholism and whoredom reflects symbolically on Jack's narrative and spiritual inadequacies.

His fourth courtship exemplifies patriarchal misogyny. Declaring that "Matrimony was not appointed to be a State of Felicity" for him, he seeks a nurse for his children and housekeeper for himself (244). Denying his next wife full agency, he limits her role to that of "an upper Servant." He will not examine her sexual history in the "careless, and indeed, rash foolish Humour" that, should she turn out to have been a whore, he will transport her to his Virginia plantations (245). After her death, he discovers that Moggy, whom he took as "an innocent Country Wench," had "made a Slip in her younger Days" (246 and 249). While dramatic irony makes his patriarchalism self-defeating, his evasion of religious courtship renders his narrative detailing contradictory, as when he calls Moggy "a middle aged Woman" and a "Girl" (245–6). Rushing her into marriage and his late wife's clothes, he absurdly pretends he has conducted all his "Matches" with "very mature Consideration" (246). His patriarchal folly is confirmed by another narrative contradiction: dissuaded by Moggy from joining the Jacobites, he is persuaded by the priest who marries them to do so. The agency of his first wife finally shows up his betrayal of the Protestant Settlement: she sustains her own agency by both upholding king and constitution and opposing divorce. What denouement *Colonel Jack* achieves rests on her spiritual consciousness, raised "in the School of Affliction," of political and religious principles that give her "Power" over her husband, whose always unreliable narrative invites readers to criticize his marital conduct (260 and 268).

Readers' responses are similarly shaped by *Moll Flanders*, its protagonist, like Jack, marrying five times and ending up with a former spouse. Yet Moll makes herself more notably vulnerable to the double standard of sexual morality. If her first marriage to her seducer's brother is imposed on her, the relation between her subjugation by necessity and her culpability is complex.[49] A whore since she marries without love, she is doubly a whore since in her husband's arms she lusts for his brother, in imagination committing "Adultery and Incest with him every Day" (59). A victim of male duplicity, she becomes a victimizer: her innocence and guilt are implicated. Hating the prospect of "being a Whore to one Brother, and a Wife to the other," she would resist the younger by discovering "Arguments" against his honourable proposal with which she might have defended herself against seduction by the elder (31). But whether he "intended to Marry, or not to Marry me, seem'd a Matter of no great Consequence to me" (25) since she clothes herself in a narrative of riches and gratified vanity, being "so wrapt up with every part of the Story" (26). Despite claiming not to have heeded her seducer's spousal promises, she throws his words back at him by insisting that he had "Engag'd himself to Marry" and that she is as much his wife "as if the Ceremony has passed" (35). She also rejects his words when she reminds him that he said "I was your Wife intentionally, tho' not in the Eye of the World; and that it was as effectual a Marriage that had pass'd between us, as if we had been publickly Wedded by the Parson of the Parish" (39). But her self-seduction is obvious when she declares she will "ever be true" because she had rather "be your Whore than your Brothers Wife" (40), since readers recall that she earlier asserts her innocence by stating there is "no such thing as any kind of Love, but that which tend[s] to Matrimony" (24). In exploring the contrariety of love and lust, Defoe presents Moll at one moment as unthinking and at the next as adept in rationalization.

Her second and third courtships expose her implausible expectations of a husband. Seeking an "amphibious Creature," one who is "something of a Gentleman too" and who "might become a Sword" and carry her to court, she traps herself in the "Snare" she sets for this erratic individual who is no less than a "Rake, Gentleman, Shop keeper, and Beggar" (60–1).[50] After marrying him because she covets the illusion of imitating aristocrats and after being abandoned by this wastrel, she does scruple about committing bigamy and, like her creator, extends her semantic sense of sexual violence by remarking that criminals in the Mint place "a Rape upon their Temper to drown the Reflections" (65). But, her extended semantic sense does not sustain social criticism or self-reflection; she notes that marriages in London are nothing but "politick Schemes, for forming Interests, and carrying on Business" without seeing that her second marriage stands condemned by her observation (67). She admits her contradictoriness when, after helping a friend examine the character of a suitor – and urging female readers "to be the more Nice" in analysing their suitors – she rushes into a third marriage, her own "Case" allowing her "no little Nicety" (74 and 76). The litotes underscores both her sexual guile and her self-entrapment. Playing "the indifferent part" (80) to bait and hook the man she selects from a crowd of suitors, she claims that circumstances oblige her to disregard her prudential rules. She would forget her pledge to avoid bigamy, but Defoe does not let her. Her new husband may be the "best humour'd Man" (82) and she "the happiest Creature alive" (85), but he turns out to be her brother and their marriage "the worst sort of Whoredom" (90). "Family strife" (92) and the "riveted Aversion" of "unlawful incestuous living" (98) drive her brother to insanity and Moll to nausea, the narrative demonstrating that ignoring kinship rules is personally and socially harmful.[51]

Contradictions incrementally inform Moll's accounts of matrimonial whoredom. If prosperity as mistress to "the compleat Gentleman" of Bath (108) leaves her "nothing but to be a Wife" (118), when the six-year affair ends she is struck by "Reproaches of … Conscience" that make her think her "Offence" would have been less had she stayed with her brother in Virginia. As narrator, she admits the partiality of those reproaches: since her second husband "had no power to Discharge" her from their "Marriage Contract," she "had been no less than a Whore and an Adultress" in her last two relationships, having had "no legal liberty to marry again" (124). Still, having been a whore makes her desire a "settled State of living" with a "sober good Husband" and qualifies her to be "the better Wife" (128–9). Yet, when she might attach the sober banker, who like her previous lover has "*a Wife* and *no Wife*" (133), she abandons him to chase a fortune hunter, Defoe here exercising subtle but powerful narrative irony.[52] That she marries into a Catholic family, willing to convert to Catholicism to secure Jemy, so that their private wedding is officiated by "a Romish Clergyman" (143) not only results in their being mutually deceived by acquisitiveness but also undercuts

Moll's translation of marital contradictions into contraries. Governed by society's laxity, she uses others to exculpate herself, at the same time defying their views. In struggling to believe herself no whore and her marriage to Jemy legal, she tells Mother Midnight, midwife to "Ladies of Pleasure" (169), that Jemy had "absolutely Discharg'd" her from their marriage and given her "free Liberty to Marry again" (172). Mother Midnight supports Moll's self-delusion by concurring that Jemy and she "were parted by mutual Consent" and that their "Contract" and "Obligation" were "mutually discharg'd" (173). Moll's refusal to abort Jemy's child and her criticism of Mother Midnight's "Dextrous ... Management" (171) are attempts to resist social laxity and forget she is a whore which are undone by further contradictions. If Mother Midnight's midwifery services are "a Cordial" (162) because "Measures ... taken to rid the Women's unwelcome Burthen of a Child clandestinely gotten" are "easie," Moll still comes "to nauceate the place" (168–9). When Mother Midnight objects to her confused notion of placing her child – "you would see the Child, and you would not see the Child; you would be Conceal'd and Discover'd both together; these are things impossible" – and advises her to do "as other conscientious Mothers have done before you," all Moll can do is denigrate herself and translate the phrase "conscientious Mothers" self-disparagingly into "conscientious Whores" (175–6).

On marrying the banker, she sees herself only obliquely as a whore in her narrative imagination: "having Divorc'd a Whore, he is throwing himself into the Arms of another" (182). Far from cultivating wifely intimacy, she relishes the banker's doting unawareness. There is no steady tension between her admission of whoredom and remorse or between her guilt and evasiveness.[53] In admitting and evading her whoredom, she conveys her desire for integrity and entrapment by sin and circumstance. But her personal energy, social resilience, and picaresque roguishness only accentuate her contradictoriness and poor sense of identity. It is cause for readers' sympathy that, if Moll glimpses the need for reform, no one she meets, apart from the "Good Minister" (289), exemplifies reform. Even the banker rushes her into marriage "in an Inn, and at Night too." The rite is conducted by a clergyman, a "merry good sort of Gentleman," who belittles the rules promoted in *Conjugal Lewdness* and *Religious Courtship*. This minister discounts canon law by objecting that marriage in church is "as publick as a Country Fair," his model being "our Princes" who marry "in their Chambers, and at Eight or Ten a Clock at Night" (183–4).[54] When ministers institutionalize whoredom, it is less surprising that Moll does not resolve her contradictions and that Defoe through her asks readers to do so.[55] Nor is it surprising – since her insistence on a church wedding is but a "Grimace" (184) – that she charges readers with honest self-examination and "just Reflections":

> I am not capable of reading Lectures of Instruction to any Body, but I relate this in the very manner in which things then appear'd to me, as far as I am able; but infinitely short of the lively impressions which they made on my Soul at that time; indeed those Impressions are not to be explain'd by words, or if they are, I am not Mistress of Words enough to express them; It must be the Work of every sober Reader to make just Reflections on them, as their own Circumstances may direct; and without Question, this is what every one at sometime or other may feel something of; I mean a clearer Sight into things to come, than they had here, and a dark view of their own Concern in them. (287–8)[56]

Despite her didactic inabilities, Moll does glimpse the imperative of double vision by which readers are enjoined to develop a contrary sense of clairvoyance and fallibility.

Unlike Moll, Roxana enters marriage aware of matrimony's civil and religious purposes and able intellectually to refute secular rationalizations. Yet, in rebutting common-law justifications of sexual licence, she explores ideas about gender relations which, if effective satirically, are ethically invalid and personally harmful. Her ideas rightly expose the double standard but also degrade her spiritual outlook. When she surrenders those ideas, she falls back onto customs that sap her identity.

In her first marriage, Roxana is victimized by her patriarchal father's poor choice of a spouse. "At about Fifteen Years of Age," she is given in marriage to "an Eminent Brewer in the City." A "Handsome Man, and a good Sportsman," he subjects his business practice and domestic sense to genteel aspirations. The "Coach" he keeps is "a kind of Mock-Coach," and when the couple drives out on Sundays to "Church, or otherways," they rarely agree where to go (7). He is "a conceited Fool," being "positive and obstinate, and the most positive in the most simple and inconsistent Things." Just before the brewer abandons her, Roxana is further victimized by male incompetence when her "Elder Brother" loses her legacy in a business failure (9). Her vulnerability is worsened by her husband's family, who are prepared to put her five children "into the Parish-keeping" (19). Her brother-in-law promotes the Christian duties of extended families, but his family eschews charity, which, in this fictional world, is in short supply and potentially dangerous. The "Bounty" of the landlord who, having seized her goods, pretends to offer "meer Kindness" Roxana reads naively as "Charity." But Amy, her maid, being alert to the implicatures of patriarchal speech, sees that his charitable words signify face-saving lust (26–7).[57] Resisting the libertinism of Amy and the landlord, Roxana insists she will not prostitute her "Virtue and Honour" (29). But her insistence relies on hollow speech acts, for she groundlessly trusts in the landlord's profession that he will make her "beholden to nobody" and takes his words as "a Cordial" to her soul that are like "Life from the Dead."[58] Since the landlord has a wife and she a husband, Roxana balks at his proposal of a "Wedding Supper" (36) and spurns Amy's views that he is "a single Man again" and that her mistress "ought to be free to marry" whom she will despite "the Laws of the Land," Amy's view of marriage as "the Pleas[u]re as well as Convenience of a Woman" implying misogyny (37–8).

Despite spurning Amy's stance as "Cant" and "all Nonsense" (40), Roxana is vulnerable to her maid's discourse: Amy's "too much Rhetorick" stops her from seeing that "the Devil of Poverty and Distress" should have been "a powerful Motive" for resisting "the Power of the real Devil" (38–9). But, in living with the landlord, she is twice a "Whore," a "double Offender" with "a double Guilt" since she does what her "own Conscience convinc'd me at the very Time … was horribly unlawful, scandalous, and abominable" (39–43). While denigrating herself to assail patriarchy's double standards, Roxana touches on arguments in *Religious Courtship*. Whereas the landlord opposes "the ordinary Ceremony of Delay" and "a reasonable Time of Courtship," she stresses the "vast Difference between our Circumstances" and "an Inequality the most essential that cou'd be imagin'd" (41–2). This rhetoric of self-condemnation lets her retaliate against the landlord and Amy. While he takes her "not as a Mistress, but as his Wife," Roxana comments that "we were to call one another Man and Wife, who, in the Sense of the Laws, both of God and our Country, were no more than two Adulterers, in short, a Whore and a Rogue" (43). Since Amy had applied the story of Rachel putting her maid into Jacob's bed to justify her mistress's sexual relations with the landlord, Roxana turns the story upon Amy, putting her to bed with the landlord. Ironically, in retaliating against Amy, the "Engine of the Devil" (38), Roxana becomes "the Devil's Agent" (48). If she correctly challenges the landlord's wish for a "Wife of his Affection" besides a "Wife of his Aversion" (47), her immoral reversal of biblical typology that provokes disgust in Amy and the landlord contrarily anticipates Defoe's attacks on such abuses in *Conjugal Lewdness*.[59]

From this point forward, Defoe compounds Roxana's inconsistencies and self-contradictions to a far greater degree than he does with Jack and Moll.[60] When Roxana says the landlord and she live "the most agreeable Life, the grand Exception only excepted, that ever Two liv'd together" (45), her contrary superlatives heighten that life's incompleteness, there being "no substantial Satisfaction in a Life of known Wickedness" (49). Her viewpoint is increasingly unstable because, having claimed that she has "effectually stifled Conscience" (46), "Conscience will, and does, often break in" on her (49). Her legal and spiritual equivocations accelerate when she has the landlord "Buried with all the Ceremonies of the *Roman* Church" (54). Presenting herself as a "Widow" and "Wife" (56), she undertakes "a Process in Dower upon [the landlord's] Estate, for making good my new Fortune upon Matrimony" (57). Following this illicit securing of his property which is aggravated by her hypocritical affectation of poverty, her contradictory motivation is again highlighted when narcissism impels her to abase herself to the prince: being "more foolishly in Love with myself" (62), she fancies she is "a fit Mistress for a Prince" (66). She satisfies herself "with the Amour, as a lawful thing" by persuading herself that she is "perfectly single, and uningag'd to any other Man." She will not admit that she exploits the prince by seeing through his face-saving discourse and copying Amy's reading of implicatures in the landlord's first speeches. After she confesses that it was "the easier to persuade myself of the Truth of such a Doctrine as this, when it was so much for my Ease, and for the Repose of my Mind, to have it be so" (68), her self-deception entails a more blatant posturing, for, in resisting the temptation of being absolved "upon the easiest Pennance," she claims she cannot "be a Cheat in anything that was esteem'd Sacred." In her own mind, if she is a "Whore," she claims integrity from being a "Protestant Whore" (69).

Roxana's inconsistencies establish verbal and situational ironies that encourage second-time readers to sympathize with her even as her spiritual degradation spirals to its nadir. Living with the prince in "the most profound Tranquility" and "uninterrupted Peace," she finds herself "in a more palpable State of Adultery than before" (69–70). She omits, she says, much of the prince's flattery. Had she reported it fully, her account would be "a little too much like a Romance" (72). Yet she incites him to objectify her; when he puts a necklace on her, he makes "the Object perfect" (73). Even as she satirizes male objectification of women, she objectifies herself: if "Great Men" viciously "raise the Value of the Object which they pretend to pitch upon," she degrades her body to deflate patriarchy and to distinguish herself. Having been a "Whore for Bread," she is caressed by a prince who owns "the Honour of having the scandalous Use of my Prostituted Body" (74). Self-contempt makes her proud of the "Management of my Tongue" (77) when she becomes "Confessor" to the prince in diverting their "Discourse from the Part attending our Children, to the Reproach those Children would be apt to throw upon us, their Originals" (82). That she leaves off the "dangerous Doctrine" that whoring and adultery disturb children alerts readers to the irony that Roxana unselfconsciously here announces the most important motif to recoil on her subsequent narrative. The same irony informs her account of her first husband turning up as a trooper in Paris when she tells readers to decide whether this was for her "particular Satisfaction, or Dissatisfaction" (85). Since readers will recall that she earlier reported that "I never saw my Husband more" (12), her mounting unreliability induces them to seek textual clues outside her narrative control. One such clue is when the ex-brewer turns as "pale as Death" on seeing Amy, who immediately suspects him of wanting to murder her (87). Readers' sense that Amy and Roxana share paranoia about death and murder is confirmed. While deluding the husband with a story intended to make Roxana untraceable, Amy reports his wish that "there had been a Law made, to empower a Woman to marry, if her Husband was not heard of" for four years (90). Ironies are intricate here, for Roxana has enacted her husband's wish. Hence, when she dismisses him as "a meer Sharper" and as "a meer motionless Animal, of no Consequence in the World" (95), she is totally unreflexive. The irony is compounded when she hires a spy to haunt him "*as a Ghost*" (94), thinking mistakenly that her husband is "the only thing that was capable of doing me Hurt in the World." She judges the "Journal of his Life" provided to her each week by the spy to be "the least significant of any-thing of its Kind that was ever seen," implying her autobiographical superiority. That she shuns him "as we wou'd shun a Spectre, or even the Devil" disproves his insignificance (95). She excuses herself from attempting to reconcile with him by lamenting that such a well-bred gentleman "could degenerate into such a useless thing" and by pretending to warn "all the Ladies of Europe" against marrying a fool (96). The clues in the motifs of ghostly haunting and moral degeneration constitute a securely grounded warning to readers of what will transpire in Roxana's life story.

Roxana's self-deceptions are more transparent when her appreciation of life with the prince must take into account that their relationship grew from his desire "to gratifie the meanest of humane Frailties" (102). Only half-heartedly does she persuade the prince to obey "the Laws and Rites of Matrimony" and second his princess's advice that he adhere to "the solemnest Part of the Marriage-Covenant" (109). Indeed, the more Roxana preaches, the further she moves away from practising what she preaches and towards telling against herself desperately. Trying to define herself by moral ideas, she realizes that identity depends on integrating principles and conduct and that this integration recedes ever further from her.[61] Moreover, she continues to misrepresent her ideas and behaviour. In scorning marriage by holding that mistresses are free women, she overlooks her dependence on the prince, the Dutch merchant, and Sir Robert Clayton. Maintaining that "a Mistress is a Sovereign," she forgets how she abased herself to the prince and the king. Her misrepresentation of gender matches her abject acceptance of the double standard. Her declaration that a wife is "but an Upper-Servant" shows that, far from reforming patriarchal distinctions between wives and mistresses, she exploits them (132).[62] That she later criticizes herself for accepting such distinctions points up her appropriation of the double standard both to conceal her wealth from the Dutch merchant and to hide this mercenary motive once she learns he will allow her legal control of her wealth in marriage. From the perspective of *Conjugal Lewdness*, she should reject the merchant: she is economically independent, wants no more children, and is unwise to marry the man who whored her. But, when she adopts her "elevated Strain" (147) to propose that women should be as sexually free as men, she has in mind none of these tenets. In objecting to notions of female passivity and to women's loss of individuality in marriage, she does not see that these notions stem from the double standard. In bedding Roxana to oblige her to marry, the Dutch merchant, far from defending the double standard, expresses Defoe's conviction that submission plays no part in ideal marriages and that "Marriage was decreed by Heaven; that it was the fix'd State of Life, which God had appointed for Man's Felicity, and for establishing a legal Posterity; that there cou'd be no legal Claim of Estate by Inheritance, but by Children born in Wedlock" (151). No doubt, Roxana's criticism of women's legal disadvantages is pertinent to Defoe's sense of how traditional arguments for marriage are debased. But, by his standards, her criticism is not advanced. She engenders no ideas of women's political and narrative power like those found in *Religious Courtship* when the women organize to regulate servants and strengthen domestic and social solidarity. Nor does she see that civil and religious laws need to be spiritualized to bring about marital equality.

Roxana's hypocritical criticism of marriage become clearer as her autobiography unravels. After cohabiting with the king, she becomes mistress to an aristocrat with whom she negotiates in a mode pretending to utopian freedom. In her "Aversion to the Bonds" of "settled Allowances," she will not let the aristocrat address her as if he were bargaining for "something like Matrimony." Their relationship is free in the sense that payment to Roxana is so excessive that it surpasses contractual norms and commits her beyond "the common Obligation of a Mistress" to become a sexual slave (184). This self-subjugation instils in her a superiority that nauseates other gallants, who would have bargained with her as if she were "married, and as virtuous as other People" (185). Despite having her scandalous reputation, she assigns libertinism only to men. Her "fluctuating, and unconcluding" thoughts are now more and more contradictory. In denying "all the seeming Advancements which the pretended Felicity of Marriage-Life" is usually promoted by, she claims to have "maintain'd the Dignity of Female Liberty, against all the Attacks, either of Pride or Avarice" (225). But, on surrendering her "Platonicks" (232) when again taking up with the Dutch merchant, she exposes her posturing. Eager to be "an Upper Servant" (233), she betrays her independence and accepts debased marital ideas in order not to reflect on her past. Her abuse of marital and family responsibilities is so severe that it pushes her towards insanity and nihilism. Her lack of communication with her husband, her daughter Susan's probable murder, and her estrangement from Amy, together with her futile reflections, reveal how personally and socially destructive it is not to have traditional ideas of sex, family, and marriage upheld by spiritual growth. These implications are embedded into as complex narrative patterning and as powerful dramatic ironies as in *Religious Courtship*. Since her daughter has so "compleat an Account" of her (288), Roxana is trapped by her bitter sense of Susan's "charming Story," by her daughter's compulsive narrative energies. Susan keeps on running Roxana "a-ground" (289); she hunts her mother "as if, *like a Hound*, she had had a hot Scent" (317). But Roxana deserves to be preyed upon. By her own admission, she is "the most cursed Piece of Hypocrisie" (300) and "a She-Devil" (301). Casting Susan in the role of an "Evil Spirit" (310), she has made herself "*Hag-ridden* with Frights" (264) to the point that, when she is "haunted" by Susan, she behaves like a "Mad-Woman" because she is such a failure as wife and mother (325 and 323).[63]

*****

Defoe's narrative deployment of ideas about sex, family, and marriage is traditional and progressive; on the one hand, it emphasizes religious evaluations of sexual conduct and social hierarchy and, on the other, in its concern for women's psychological integrity, analyses why sexual rationalization is domestically and socially disruptive. This shows that his non-fictional and fictional didacticism is equally complex, inventive, and dynamic and confirms the importance of his rhetorical and moral contraries. The traditional and progressive aspects of his marital ideology give a new configuration to personal, domestic, and civic duties, a shape reached through a technically inventive use of the dialogue form. His dialogues show how women may turn the contradictions of their experience into polar insights. Moreover, his marital ideology offers a model for relating his non-fiction and fiction because his satire of the secularization of sexuality obtains in both genres. Of course, the realm of probabilities that inheres in fiction means that in his so-called novels there are only sporadic attempts to convert contradictions into moral paradoxes. Usually, the contraries glimpsed by protagonists fall back into contradictions in order to stimulate readers' inferential responses. The more characters and narrators fail and convey why they fail, the more they invite readers, obliquely as well as directly, to draw positive inferences. If characters and narrators cannot solve the problems of personal integrity and moral will, they approach such problems so that readers may more nearly perceive and analyse them. The gap between characters' and narrators' conduct and knowledge forms a discursive space that mediates ironies crucial to reader response.

Chapter Eight

Defoe's Imaginary: Narrative Inference, Figurative Expression, and Spiritual Cognition

As the History I have given of a Family preserv'd by retiring from Conversation, is really the History of Several Families, rather than of one, and is a perfect Model for future Practice. I think that Account with several others, which I cou'd give, within the Compass of my own Knowledge, or the Particulars whereof I have had from the Persons of Credit. I say, these are convincing Proofs, to me at least, of what I build upon, namely, That the Distemper is taken by Contagion from the diseas'd Bodies, let those who believe it otherwise act as they see fit.[1]

The dialectic of traditional and progressive ideas unfolded in the previous chapter shows that Defoe's differentiation between marriage and matrimony entails sets of polarities. So that his commentary on public and legal forms of marriage and on private and spiritual responsibilities of wedded partners will more effectively challenge lax social practices, he exhibits the reflexive functions of narrative discourse in his non-fiction and fiction: figures in his conduct manuals not only tell stories to resist or justify their participation in social practices but also are subject to the remediable power of stories; and narrators in his fictions leave the completion of stories to readers, who, in the process, recognize that narrative discourse, as an aspect of daily life, conveys psychological and spiritual conditions that raise questions about the relation between cognition and imagination. This is to say that he embeds fictionalizing as much into his non-fiction as into his fiction, and to reiterate that his narratives are reflexive and recursive. This final chapter brings together the linguistic, semantic, and rhetorical criticism of earlier chapters in order to produce an incremental account of his uses of fiction and to penetrate more deeply into the contrarian philosophy that sustains these uses. After analysing the significance and relevance of the epigraph above, the chapter builds its account of his uses of fiction in the following five ways: first, it examines his prefaces as paratexts that heighten the critical self-consciousness of readers: second, it explicates his theory of rhetoric and his appreciation of the instrumentality of language; third, it shows that behind his pedagogy lies a contrarian sense of the relation between cognitive deficiencies and spiritual learning; fourth, it exemplifies how he argues in images by analysing his figurative and associative discursiveness; and fifth, it links the motif of listening to the voice of oneself and Providence to engaging or not with the polarities inherent in metaphor and aesthetic experience.

We begin, then, with the above epigraph from *Due Preparations for the Plague* because, in linking domestic history and social policy, it substantiates the polarities in Defoe's narrative theory which we detailed in *Serious Reflections*, polarities that from a contemporary viewpoint represent a questionable, if not unfeasible, attempt to reconcile the irreconcilable and to balance the opposing functions of description and prescription.[2] Conflating the singular and the plural, the particular and the general, this exposition compounds the rhetorical topics of kind, division, similarity, and difference.[3] In describing one family, Defoe claims to represent a class. That one family, far from being unique, is equivalent to many, because its singularity, if specific, paradoxically comprehends a plurality, and even the generality, of families: the analytic description of one family is a synthetic prescription for metropolitan, trading households. The one family is more than exemplary; constituting a "perfect Model," it signifies an ideal form. Given this kind of mimesis, readers might well ask how a reclusive family could be fully known so as to represent a socio-economic class. They might question, too, how Defoe exalts his narrative authority when he says that his one story could have been amplified by others that he withholds, the withheld ones based on personal observation and the testimony of other "Persons of Credit." For how may untold stories validate narrative authority? At best they offer negative testimony; being unable to induce positive conviction, they confirm the analytic one only through assertion. Readers are asked to accept the absent stories as redundant to the credibility of the one told but as necessary to the narrator's authority. They are confronted by negative and positive testimony that his theory of the plague is true and that it is spread by contagious bodies. The implication of his assertions is that, if readers think otherwise, they will be wrong in conduct as well as in belief. Defoe's authority here as elsewhere depends as much on how he fictionalizes his voice in his texts as on the validity of his truth claims.[4]

He encourages readers to appreciate the recursive functions of storytelling by endowing his narratives with reciprocal yet opposing functions and by creating narrators who both do and do not uphold the mixed criteria of their prefaces. He discourages single-minded responsiveness so that readers may be open to counter-rational justifications of narrative. His narrators do not perform steadily partly because their prefaces, far from offering unequivocal criteria, proclaim and disclaim description and prescription in order to privilege dialectical tensions between secular and religious values.[5] His introduction to *Due Preparations for the Plague* in preparing readers to enter this apparently nonfictional work evidences the double vision that typically informs his prefaces. This text addresses "*the present particular Occasion of the Terrors we are under about the Plague*" – a threat of the bubonic plague spreading from France to England. In 1721 newspapers carried accounts of an outbreak in Marseille, accounts Defoe knew since he wrote some.[6] Yet, should the plague not reach England, his text will be worthwhile since, beyond its occasional purpose, it will "*encourage*" contemporaries and posterity to undertake the "*great Work*" of spiritual preparation. This text does and does not depend on a visitation of the plague since its transcendent aims may stand alone. Its polar modes are in harmony with Defoe's theory in *Serious Reflections*: the "*Discourse*" is "*Familiar and Agreeable*" as well as moral, and "*Historical*" as well as proleptic. Given these mixed generic categories, narration needs no single provenance: the "*Accounts of Fact*" stem from several authorities – from the testimony of others, from common report, from public records, as well as from the author's experience. The diverse sources enable Defoe to berate the corrupt age as meriting divine punishment and to assert that his book will reform society. Bent on shocking contemporary sinners while addressing righteous posterity, he elaborates his polar outlook. The "*Cases*" he includes represent "*Circumstances past,*" but they "*more especially*" predict events that may be "*reasonably supposed*" to be coming. Taking historical cases "*as Precedents for our present Instructions,*" he describes "*particular People in their Histories*" yet excises personal details, being more concerned with "*Example*" than facts. The strategies for facing the plague that he recommends are less "*Experiments*" than applications proven to be "*rational and just.*" Similarly, he insists his book's "*religious History*" is an indisputable "*Pattern.*"[7]

As the epigraph from *Due Preparations* shows, generic polarities in the paratext are matched by editorial comments in the text. Another example in the section of the text that treats material preparations for the plague occurs when about the family that makes an "absolute Retreat from the World" Defoe says that his representation of it is "partly Historical and partly for Direction."[8] The boundary between fact and value is as unfixed in the narrative and dialogues as in the introduction, Defoe constantly moving from description to prescription or from prescription to description. As much as he depicts past and present actuality, he considers what may sooner or later happen. He addresses the future by summoning and discarding phenomenal actuality, this dialectic letting him pretend that the patterning of his writing and the operation of Providence reciprocate each other.

This is not to say that paratexts and texts are simply harmonious. As Faller says, their relations are provisional and increasingly sophisticated.[9] The preface to *Robinson Crusoe* declares that the story is a "just History of Fact" without "any Appearance of Fiction" and that it is told with a "religious Application of Events" to provide instruction by example (1). But the text's polar views of writing complicate the preface, for Crusoe explores self-expression and communication with readers. When he writes "to deliver my Thoughts from daily poring upon them, and afflicting my Mind" (65), he focuses on spiritual health. Yet, in feeling that deliverance from sin is better than from affliction, he is sure readers, when "they come to a true Sense of things," will agree (97). When he writes that he has been in all his "Circumstances a Memento to those who are touch'd with the general Plague of Mankind," namely, discontent at the station appointed them by God and nature (194), he sees himself as a mirror to readers. If he embodies the prefatory announcement of religious application, he does not merely incorporate readerly instrumentality. Nor does the statement in the preface to *Serious Reflections* that the "Fable is always made for the Moral, not the Moral for the Fable" (A2) explain the polarities in Crusoe's characterization. When, expatiating on the ethical nature of conversation, he says "Perhaps I may be more particularly sensible of the Benefit and of the Pleasure of it, having been so effectually mortify'd with the Want of it" (75), he sees himself partly as an ironic device that helps readers enjoy the fable. Since he is personally deficient, the fable does not merely subserve abstract truth; the moral cannot be simply detached from the fable since they are fused by contrary relations. In *Serious Reflections*, Crusoe holds that the moral conduct of storytellers is a pre-condition to the intrinsic value of stories. While stories must be told plainly, not wilfully, storytellers who cannot vouch for the truth of their tales must say so in order to leave readers "at Liberty to believe their Share of it." If a story told as true when not authenticated by its teller perpetuates social illusions, a parable which depends on its audience's moral response has a distinct status: to Crusoe and Defoe, "Parables, and the Inventions of Men, publish'd Historically" are unobjectionable because, once their moral is drawn, they acquire the status of allusive histories which do no social harm (117). Yet Defoe's parables are not simply allusive histories; they are more subtle because his storytellers are necessarily and interestingly deficient in narrative integrity.

Lacking a paratext, *Captain Singleton* necessarily places reflexive editorial remarks into the text. Singleton is obliged to "leave upon Record" not only that did he not enjoy pirate wealth but also that he "began sincerely to hate my self for a Dog" (267). When he converses with William and refuses to contemplate mortality until death comes, he ironically admits that his discourse shows how "well qualified" he was to belong to a pirate community: he leaves this "upon Record for the Remark of other hardned Rogues" (258). He also expects general readers to judge him even as they enjoy his story. When he interpolates the life of Robert Knox, he claims it is "very profitable to record" since readers will see by contrast that he avoided capture by the Ceylonese (238). But readers see far more: they notice less the dangers he escaped than his lack of self-scrutiny. Spiritual evasion degrades his narrative authority. In the midst of his maritime account, he refuses to describe a storm because readers will respond only to "the Thunder and Lightning" and will think "nothing of the rest," and even "make a Jest of it" (195). This attribution of evasiveness seems intended by Defoe to goad readers. Singleton subordinates his account of the storm to his pretensions to be superior and indifferent, belittling his audience to further avoid analysing his deficiencies. But his evasiveness imposes tasks on readers: his insults provoke them to criticize his contradictory self-image.

Polar ideas in *Moll Flander*'s prefatory apology for fiction are explicit and sustained, since, in presenting Moll as storyteller and himself as editor, Defoe suggests that story and fable are as distinct as they are equivalent and since he trusts that the "Moral ... will keep the Reader serious" if the "Story" inclines him to be "otherwise," because "the best use is made even of the worst Story." If moral application seems paramount because the "worst Story" exercises the keenest moral sense, the reciprocal relations of moral and story do not displace the sympathetic imagination of readers. For Defoe's equivocations reveal inherent tensions between writing and reading, between text and reader-response, the processes affecting moral judgment clearer when he says:

> as this Work is chiefly recommended to those who know how to Read it, and how to make the good Uses of it, which the Story all along recommends to them; so it is to be hop'd that such Readers will be much more pleas'd with the Moral, than the Fable; with the Application than with the Relation, and with the End of the Writer, than with the Life of the Person written of. (2)

In appearing to set the moral above the fable, reader response above narrative expression, and authorial intention above autobiographical subject, this statement aligns the putative editor with his fiction yet presents story as both upholding and opposing fable: story may be interpreted as speaking against itself. The contrary functions allotted to story match the editor's expectations of readers who are addressed as already proficient and as obliged to become proficient: readers' roles are assumed and stipulated. The story's contrary functions match the double identity of the implied author who is at one and the same time Defoe the editor and Moll the writer. The preface next recommends the story's "delightful Incidents" and "happy Turns," which are "usefully apply'd" because it "naturally Instructs the Reader, either one way, or other" (2). Whereas story is first to be transcended, it is second a pedagogic instrument using polarities. That he proposes no singular model of narrative is confirmed when he says that Moll's story which takes place at Colchester "attones for" her lively account of wickedness. Viewing Moll as writer, he places utility in her story. Yet he recommends the story since it lends itself to "just and religious Inference." So, utility inheres in both the text and readers' responses: if the text is didactic, readers are auto-didacts. Even Moll's thefts are doubly useful; offering insight into mundane reality, they heighten self-consciousness by helping us "to be more present to ourselves in sudden Surprizes of every Sort" (4).

The preface's polar utility is mirrored in Moll's representation of herself as author. Since preaching is not her "Talent" (65) and she is a "very indifferent Monitor" (126), she puts the burden of interpretation onto readers: they are to exercise their "Senses and Judgment" and see in the story of "one Creature compleatly Wicked, and compleatly Miserable" a "Storehouse" of warnings (268).[10] In thus admitting narrative unreliability and inadequate judgment, she embodies the preface's key notions: she indicates an ethical sense beyond herself and directs readers towards her editor's ironic consciousness. Like him, she imagines her readership variably, both widely and narrowly. While she feels incapable of "reading Lectures of Instruction to any Body" and limits herself to former impressions of things (287), she does "read a long Lecture" to her governess about living in Virginia (310). Despite the mendacity of this lecture, she reports the compulsive self-revelation of criminals she has known since she has written her life "for the sake of the just Moral of every part of it, and for the Instruction, Caution, Warning and Improvement to every Reader" (326). When she touches on her "vile Returns" to Providence, she leaves the "Reader to improve these Thoughts, as no doubt they will see Cause" (337). Calling herself a "Memento" when she warns young women to avoid the vanity that leads to sexual licence, she asks to be treated by them as an object-lesson (25).[11] Further, she tells the common reader what inferences to draw. The failure of sexual restraint that she has "often observ'd" in others and that enters her relationship with the Bath gentleman she offers as "a caution to the Readers of this Story" (119). Again, more restrictively "for the Direction of my Sex" (123), she concludes that repentance in men causes them to hate their mistresses.

If H.F. in *A Journal of the Plague Year* addresses readers about reading deferentially, his persona is assertive as well as self-effacing, this psychological tension enhanced by the absence of a preface and by generic dialectic. Endowed with the assured tone of one who composed his text long before the publication date of 1722, he also speaks tentatively as an editor. Not subject to editorial framing, he believes his writing "may be of Moment to those who come after" him; he effaces himself because he wants his account valued by posterity as a "Direction" to themselves rather than as "a History of my actings" (8). Yet he imitates his creator when he calls the interpolated story of the three poor men a "History" and a "very good Pattern" for the poor to follow in future plagues (58): their "Story has a Moral in every Part of it" that will promote social and spiritual regulation in another plague (122). H.F. is not just embedded into a series of historical reflections, for he regularly voices contrary perspectives. If about the shutting up of houses he says at one point that he "may be able to make an Observation or two" which "may be of use hereafter to those, into whose Hands" his text may come (73), at another he feels able to "propose many Schemes" (198). He is similarly assertive and tentative in expressing religious sentiments. He tells the

"Story" of how he decides to remain in London less as personal history than as "the best Method" to help citizens decide whether or not they are called by God to face up to extreme trials (10). He increasingly draws "Observations" from religious aspects of the plague, as when he comments on London's spiritual unpreparedness (92). He has his eye on contemporary readers when he suggests that another plague year would cure sectarianism, his claim to make this point "but historically" not concealing his desire to preach (176). He admits leaving his "minutes upon Record" to "prompt due Impressions of the Awe of God on the Minds of Men on such Occasions" (193). Besides imagining resistance from "the Atheistic part of Mankind," he argues that his sense of divine agency is not "Enthusiasm" (246). He is restrained by imagined opposition: he wants not to appear to give "an officious canting of religious things." He would avoid being accused of "preaching a Sermon" since he wishes to be seen as writing a "History" based on his "Observations" (247). Yet he refuses to conceal his spiritual gratitude, despite the indifference of contemporaries. Besides drawing on personal experience and second-hand knowledge, his commentary is history and not history. Narrating an individual's pathetic discovery of plague tokens, he relates it as "a Fact" within his own knowledge. But he does not vouch for the truth of such episodes. Rather he tells them "to confirm the many desperate Things" into which victims of the plague fell (162). In addition to embodying his creator's dialectical prescriptions for narration, H.F. directs different forms of history at different audiences, at faithless ones of former and current times and at a faithful but remote posterity. By writing so variously, H.F. enjoins readers to think much about their future as well as the past and present and to contemplate what it means to be a member of a reading public.

The preface to *Colonel Jack* emphasizes the fallibility of readers as well as of the protagonist. Neither subordinating fable to moral nor insisting upon truth of fact, it states that it is not *"of the least Moment"* whether Jack tells his *"own Story true or not"*; it will be useful whether read as "a History *or a* Parable," since it encourages every *"wicked Reader"* to repent with the prodigal and say that "his latter end" will "be better than his Beginning" (2). While the typology to which readers are guided seems independent of any factual basis, when Jack discusses telling his story, he often reverts to military facts outside his experience. Spending little time addressing readers until the end of his account, he narrates other characters' stories, thus reinforcing the preface's negative criteria. Moved by the plantation owner's religious "Discourse" to a felon, Jack does feel that what is addressed to this other is addressed to him (121). That he evades his initial reaction does not reduce the value of this story, for his inadequate reader response heightens its spiritual implications for his readers. Such is the effect when he overhears his Tutor's monologue of "delightful Sorrow" and reports the latter's "serious affectionate Discourse" about repentance. Jack does begin to talk to himself and to draw religious inferences; he senses that he has as much to repent of gratefully as his Tutor. But, since his "first Impressions are not deep enough," he never steadily applies his insight to conversation or narrative. He does not reciprocate his Tutor's story but knows he should (168–71).

Occasionally he embodies prefatory criteria. Relative to his third wife's descent into drunken immorality, he repeats a "good Story" about the devil tempting a young man with drink to get him to commit patricide and incest. That it does not matter to Jack whether this illustrative story is "real or invented" echoes one of the preface's remarks (241). However, irony wells up in his text because he avoids treating private life in public discourse and evades parallels between his own and others' stories. Musing about the transported women on his plantation, he reflects on "the Misery of human Life," commenting that hearing the "History" of some of them "would perhaps be as moving, and as seasonable a Sermon as any Minister in the Country could Preach" (252). But these untold narratives are submerged under the embarrassment of discovering that his first wife is one among them. Tensions between his story's potentially wide applicability and his guilty attempts to prevent its disclosure confirm Defoe's experimental interest in how stories mediate selfhood to the point of trapping narrators. If transported women's lives might constitute a sermon, Jack's recommendation of criminal biography would be better exemplified by a full account of the crimes he committed with fewer excuses than the unfortunate women.[12] However, he cannot claim to have directed his story properly or to have detected the elements his life has in common with others. He does not improve his story by making it "Useful, and Instructing"; readers must "make the same just Reflections" he "ought to have made" since they may "reap the benefit" of his "Misfortunes." While he claims to have learned that life writing may be useful if authors accent "moral and religious Improvement" (307), that we have little evidence of his reading clarifies the narrative irony. Readers may improve his story by reaching deductions his inadequate writing and self-analysis stopped him from attaining. Yet, claiming to have written his life in penitential awareness, he asks readers to approach it "with the Temper of Penitents." Having had the leisure to repent in his Spanish retreat, he tells readers they have a better chance to draw penitent reflections from his story than he does since they live "under the merciful Dispositions of Providence in Peace, Plenty, and Ease" (308). Despite being untouched by grace, he invites readers to consider that, if they detect "any Similitude of Cases" between their lives and his, they should ask themselves if it is not time to repent (309). Jack is both an ironic model for unrepentant readers and a positive voice calling faithful readers to renew their penitence. His narrative embraces readers whose spiritual states are contrary, and his estranged stance as an exile upholds the constitutional framework within which narrative is most constructive.

If *Colonel Jack "speaks for it self,"* thereby suggesting prefatory redundancy, its preface says that a second volume is needed to explicate the text's "*Improvements*" on the theme of education. Given the implied redundancy, the paratext too simply heralds the text as "*a Garden*" which has "*wholesome and medicinal Plants, none noxious or poisonous.*" Less schematic and abstract than its predecessor, *Roxana* produces a dialectic of story and fact that is bracing and polemical. Its preface speaks of the book as a "*History*" rather than a "*Story,*" its "*Foundation*" laid in "*Truth of* Fact." Yet its facticity suppresses facts: the historic action is so close to the narrating moment that names have been concealed – individuals protected by anonymity. The excision of "*Names of Persons*" does not reduce fiction's power. Were such narrative licence unhonoured, "*many a pleasant and delightful History wou'd be buried in the Dark.*" The ambivalent promotion of history is reflected in the editor's stance and grammar. This "Relator" or "Writer" is detached from and involved in the story; he is an impartial and partial narrator. Since he knew Roxana's brewer husband and the brewer's father, he personally vouches for the truth of the first part of her account. As the transcriber of her words, he accepts the truthfulness of the rest of her story. He also apologizes for her, admitting that, if he has not adapted the entertaining parts of her story to "*the Instruction and Improvement of the Reader,*" this is due to the "*Defect of his Performance.*" But, when he claims that she "*does not insist upon her Justification in any one Part,*" he undermines his authority, certainly to second-time readers. However, his authority is tenuous throughout the preface given his unsteady pronoun reference: he applies first-person singular and plural as well as third-person singular pronouns to himself besides addressing the reader directly as "*you*" and indirectly through the third-person possessive adjective *"his."* The first-person plural places the writer among his audience in the phrase *"our Imitation"* but distances him from it when asserting *"we make no Question"* (1–3). The preface fragments the writer's voice; he is distant from and close to Roxana, the reader, and himself.

Besides echoing the prefatory claim that her *"History ... is to speak for itself"* when she says of her abandonment that "the Thing spoke it self" (17), Roxana embodies the preface's polyvalency, holding herself aloof from, and intruding into, her narrative because of her impersonality and egoism and because of Defoe's wish to exercise readers' dialectical sense of fictional transparency and opaqueness. When Amy speaks to Roxana's friends in "such moving Terms" as are beyond her (18), Roxana is so pleased with Amy's rhetoric that she takes pleasure in "the relating" (25). While she often talks about herself impassively, as if "speaking of another-body" (6), she also discusses herself with great partiality, this wide-ranging self-presentation offering huge scope for readers' inferences. In detailing the circumstances that drive her into the landlord's arms and upholding what the preface says, she does not "plead" her situation "as a Justification of my Conduct" but to "move the Pity, even of those that abhor my Crime" (39). Yet, when she warns female readers not to marry fools, she seizes the "Liberty" of disregarding whatever she has to reproach herself with in her "after-Conduct" (7). In such instances when she discusses her point of view, she heightens readers' sense of literary perspective to warn them and correct herself, yet, by failing to hold these functions together, she inevitably falls victim to narrative irony. Still, she adopts authorial gestures typical of Defoe and other protagonists. Thus, she reminds herself she is "not to preach, but to relate" (49). Like Moll, she sees herself as "a standing Mark of the Weakness of Great Men" (74). She presents herself as a "Memorial" and "standing Monument" of the madness to which pride leads when she discards her first chance to marry the Dutch merchant so as to be a royal mistress (161). Yet, when she speculates about "how profitable" to readers "the Report" of the self-reproaches of sexual sinners like the prince might be, she will not see that her speculation applies chiefly to herself (75). Sometimes she hopes a scene she describes "may be of Use to those who read my Story," as when she recounts the prince's love for their illegitimate child (80), and sometimes she trusts that an episode serves her moral, as when she claims the story of her relations with him "wou'd not be worth relating" could she not sermonize about his wasting time on her worthless self (101).

In exploring the ironies of narrative reflexivity, Defoe prompts readers to ponder the dynamic relations between egoism and self-contempt, between material ambition and spiritual estrangement, and between appropriating the identity of others and fleeing from selfhood.[13] By also making editorial discourse and embedded stories recoil on his narratives, Defoe raises questions in our minds about why fiction is framed by coincidence and irony. For example, when, after a storm at sea, Amy fears going on shipboard again since she would avoid spontaneously confessing her sins aloud as she did in that storm, her fears are taunted by people who jest conventionally about bad conscience arising from sexual misconduct. Their suppositious jokes cause Roxana to record "*the Reproach of my own Vice*" in order to "expose the Excesses of such Wickedness, as they deserve to be expos'd" (130). Here the contingent motivation of her commentary shows that she is as much controlled by narrative as in control of it. Her topical comments are often thought-provoking because they are fortuitous and incomplete. After differentiating between a wife and a whore, she says that, while she "cou'd dwell upon the Subject a great-while," since her present "Business is History" she will not. She then adds: "perhaps the Moral of all my Story may bring me back again to this Part, and if it does, I shall speak of it fully" (133). On arriving at sections of her story that argue against marriage and wifehood, readers will recognize similar textual evasiveness. Their alertness to her loss of narrative authority after she marries the merchant is sharpened by images of distraction and by her loss of humour. When the merchant jokes about her entering the bondage of marriage, reminding her playfully of the images of slavery she had introduced into her arguments about sexual liberty, she must admit that his jests and allegories are all true in "the Moral of the Fable" (244).

By the end of her text, she presents her life and autobiography as moral fables, often implying that readers should scrutinize her speech acts and probe her identity because of its subjection to superstition. The closing pages of her account invite readers to imagine the metaphysical as well as psychological collapse of her character, Defoe inducing them to contemplate the reciprocity of poor storytelling and degraded consciousness. In this *Roxana* is not exceptional since he assigns unstable awareness to most narrators, unsteady faith seeing them overtaken by spiritual dread and superstition, their diminished verbal and vocal awareness testifying to this susceptibility. As we saw in chapter 2, Crusoe loses consciousness at the utterance of the word "Pump," some time passing before he comes to himself (12), and when his ship sinks, he is carried aboard the boat, his heart being "dead" within him (13). When sick on the island, his inability to know what he says when he attempts to pray "for the first Time since the Storm of *Hull*" stems as much from spiritual fear as from his ague (86). Speaking with "the Voice of meer Fright and Distress," he does not know what his tongue expresses since his words are "extorted" from him (90). Verbal ignorance and linguistic self-deception render Singleton and crew vulnerable to superstition. The "deformed Look and Voice" of a snake on the shore of an African lake make them think the serpent is the devil (105). Singleton thinks their surgeon-artist must use "Witchcraft" when he makes a filter that sweetens salt water (111). Later he commits himself to piratical mutiny with the "most solemn Imprecations and Curses" the devil and he can invent (138). Like his crew, he believes that the fortified tree they encounter is the work of the devil, whereas William spurns "Witchcraft and Dealing with the Devil" (211). Moll rationalizes her disorientation by thievery when claiming she has "an evil Counsellor within" (193). She excuses her victimization by circumstance by alleging that, once in the "Devil's Clutches," she is trapped by a "Charm" that robs her of the "Power to go without the Circle" (203). On entering Newgate she wants to remain aloof from other prisoners, but she surrenders her social superiority, becoming "no more the same thing that I had been, than if I had never been otherwise than what I was now" and admitting she had "perfectly chang'd, and become another Body" (279, 281). Her identity and verbal sense remain unfulfilled: in her mind she appears courageously before her judges addressing them in "a moving Tone," but her rhetoric is ineffectual. When they sentence her to death, the sentence itself is like death, Moll having no "more Spirit left" and "no Tongue to speak" (286).

Jack's trauma when he loses money in a tree and retrieves it with surprising ease limits his verbal consciousness as character and narrator, which he underlines when he says:

> in short, I knew not what, much less do I know now what I did, tho' I shall never forget the Thing, either what a sinking Grief it was to my Heart when I thought I had lost it, or what a Flood of Joy o'er whelm'd me when I had got it again. (26)

This loss of self-control recurs in his first courtship to which he applies images of magic. Taken in by the "Witch-Craft" of the woman and "ensnared," he is confused because "like a Charm she had me always in her Circle." Although his resistance obliges her to change tactics, he is still "drawn in by the Magick of a Genius" (187). Fear of being cuckolded by his second wife gives him a "distemper'd Fancy" that makes him look at everyone who approaches her "with an evil Eye" (225–6). That he never tolerates unsettling contingencies evidences his fragile identity. When his first wife reappears, he is "Speechless ... as a Stone" and so perplexed that he "hardly knew what I did, or said all that Night," reaching no settled decision by morning (255–6). When she begs forgiveness, he is so moved that he loses awareness of what he says or does "for sometime" (261).

At the start of her autobiography, Roxana is so personally and socially secure that she cannot imagine circumstances eroding her moral sense. She takes responsibility for cohabiting with the landlord, strong in critical self-consciousness. Early trauma confirms this selfhood; "Second-Sight" warns her of the landlord's death. Her mental "Terror" is not yet a precursor of a disintegrating identity (52). But, once she persuades herself that her liaison with the prince is lawful to get "Ease" and "Repose" of mind, she speeds to self-destruction by means of verbal dullness and superstition. On recalling the prince to the religious nature of marriage and suggesting they should separate, she admits that her lack of serious intention dulls her to words and speech acts: "All this while I said I knew not what, and said what I was no more able to do" (108). She claims to be magically possessed by him, for, after he leaves her, she admits to a "strange Elevation" when there is a chance of getting back together (234). As her text nears its anticlimactic end, she suffers increasingly from an inability to converse with others and herself. She is overwhelmed by thoughts and images of which she cannot unburden herself: as she says, "I had no Vent, no-body to open myself to" (284). Marriage to the Dutch merchant sees her "Hagridden" and her imaginings are filled with "Apparitions of Devils and Monsters" (264). Superstition aggravates her contradictoriness: if guilt makes her "scarce myself" on hearing Amy threaten to murder Susan, terror at being associated with the crime when Amy proposes it a second time "help'd to bring me to myself again" (273). Prevented from "counterfeiting my Voice," she can no longer invent rationalizations or evade loss of self: there is "no shifting any-thing off" (278). She is so trapped by her own story as it is recovered by Susan that she is forced to attack its representation of herself to try to preserve that self. While she cannot "help being pleas'd and tickl'd with" Susan's story because of her "Reserve of Pride," that story has a "devilish Sting in the Tail"

(287). Forced to sap her own fictional image, Roxana abuses the subject of Susan's story – herself – "as some scandalous Woman" (290). Her "utmost Extremity" intensifies since the daughter she wants to protect in order to avoid the crime of murder haunts her like an "Evil Spirit" (310). Ultimately, the imagined destruction of others involves a complete loss of self; when she surrenders to thoughts of murdering Amy for having murdered Susan, her daughter still haunts her imagination in "a hundred Shapes and Postures" (325).

****

The imaginative achievement that enabled Defoe to offer readers an intensive, even intimate, engagement in textual detail was his realization that fallibility and delusion are narrative resources. In his non-fictional and fictional works, he persistently explores why people tell stories in daily life and why storytelling is subject to rationalization and superstition. With elaborate sympathy, he creates characters who cannot construct themselves satisfactorily in the stories they tell, and he deploys narrators whose unreliability stops them responding properly to their fictions. Besides showing that narrative illusion is potentially an instrument of secular learning and religious truth, he invites readers to imagine his characters and narrators as figures who do not bring themselves to full humanity through storytelling. Textual gaps and inconsistencies make plain the work of readers. As Iser says, "If the reader were given the whole story, and there were nothing left for him to do, then his imagination would never enter the field, the result would be the boredom which inevitably arises when everything is laid out cut and dried before us."[14] Defoe's invitation consists of inducing readers to read past the inconsistencies of his characters and narrators and to recognize textual aporias with a compassion and reflexive awareness that entails sharing self-consciousness about speech acts and figurative thinking with the implied author. That his paratextual explanations of narrative and justifications of its moral nature are subtle and exploratory conveys to readers that their roles involve more than straightforward psychological identification with characters and narrators. No doubt, the unconventional and subversive conduct of the latter is absorbing. But, since the polarity thinking in Defoe's paratextual materials emphasizes that narrative entails concealing as well as revealing, delaying as well as foretelling, the very identity of characters and narrators is problematic and so is conveyed recursively by its instabilities and contrarieties.

On the other hand, what Defoe steadily makes accessible to readers are the speech acts of characters and narrators as well as their cognitive and spiritual aptitudes. That their imaginary worlds are ultimately given integrity by readers' verbal self-consciousness means that readers must probe the Lockean assumptions about language and rhetoric which afflict the characters and narrators.

If Locke created the first semantic theory since Plato, as Stephen Land says, it is problematic. For Locke, words function as names or signs of ideas: they operate as private mental acts, not as social and systematic linguistic phenomena, because he holds that expository clarity is the sole criterion for language.[15] His unwillingness to conceive of meaning in terms other than single rational denotations is clear when he dismisses rhetoric in *An Essay concerning Humane Understanding*: "all the art of rhetoric, besides order and clearness, all the artificial and figurative application of words eloquence hath invented, are for nothing else but to insinuate wrong *ideas*, move the passions, and thereby mislead the judgment; and so indeed are perfect cheat." His refusal to consider that narrative illusion may lead to truth causes him to assert further that rhetoric is "that powerful instrument of error and deceit" that shows how men "love to deceive and be deceived."[16] One problem with Locke's semantic theory is that prose does not only serve reason and clarity. As Richard Lanham says, prose employs semantic vagueness and opaqueness to advance pleasure in words and self-consciousness about style. It is as much a way of seeing as an object seen, a matter of aesthetic form more than of conceptual clarity. Distinctions between the literary and non-literary and between fiction and non-fiction find no place in Lanham's definitions of prose rhetoric. His holistic argument concludes that "Stylistic awareness ... makes possible dialogue with ourselves" and that "By a sense of style we socialize ourselves," these last two points crucial to Defoe's rhetorical deployment of prose style, as we are about to demonstrate.[17]

Defoe's long-term commitment to rhetorical education and his belief that language is a divine gift partly motivate his habitual impersonations and his deployment of unstable identities. His attitudes to linguistic performance, speech acts, and the significance of voice clarify the cognitive and spiritual foundations of his narrative conduct.[18] His experience at Newington Green Academy of Charles Morton's pedagogy that obliged pupils to declaim "in the English tongue" orations and epistles on prescribed and self-selected subjects taught Defoe that language is a social institution and that meaning derives from public usage. In *The Compleat English Gentleman,* he tells how role playing engaged Morton's pupils: "Sometimes they were ambassadors and agents abroad at forreign Courts, and wrote accounts of their negotiacions and recepcion in forreign Courts directed to the Secretary of State and some times to the Soveraign himself." At other times, "they were Ministers of State, Secretaries and Commissioners at home, and wrote orders and instruccions to the ministers abroad, as by order of the King in Council and the like." Rhetorical exercises teaching them "to write a masculine and manly stile" and "the most polite English," they learned "how to suit their manner as well to the subject they were to write upon as to the persons or degrees of persons they were to write to; and all equally free and plain, without foolish flourishes and ridiculous flights of jingling bombast in stile, or dull meanesses of expression below the dignity of the subject or the character of the writer." As a consequence, they were "finish'd orators, fitted to speak in the highest presence, to the greatest assemlies, and even in Parliament, Courts of Justice, or any where; and severall of them came afterward to speak in all those places and capascityes with great applause."[19]

Thirty years earlier, *An Essay upon Projects* reflected Morton's rhetorical pedagogy when Defoe discussed raising standards of public discourse, encouraging pride in the English language, and promoting verbal self-consciousness. These aims, which he thought instrumental to educational reform and social development, led him to explore the relations between the acoustic properties of language and constructive social mores. The language academy he proposes would "polish and refine the *English* Tongue" to "encourage Polite Learning." It would advance "the so much neglected Faculty of Correct Language" and "establish Purity and Propriety of Stile," while removing "all those Innovations in Speech" that "some Dogmatic Writers have the confidence to foster upon their Native Language." "Persons Eminent for Learning" would be academicians, but few scholars would belong since "meer Learned men" are unfamiliar with polite English, their speech and writing "full of Stiffness and Affectation, hard Words, and long unusual Coupling of *Syllables* and Sentences, which sound harsh and untuneable to the Ear, and shock the Reader both in Expression and Understanding." To improve linguistic usage, the academy would study etymology, semantics, and spoken and written style, producing

> Lectures on the *English* Tongue, Essays on the Nature, Original, Usage, Authorities and Differences of Words, on the Propriety, Purity, and *Cadence*

> *of Stile*, and of the Politeness and *Manner* in Writing; Reflections upon Irregular Usages, and Corrections of Erroneous Customs in Words; and in short, every thing that wou'd appear necessary to the bringing our *English* Tongue to a due Perfection, and our Gentlemen to a Capacity of Writing like themselves; to banish Pride and Pedantry, and silence the Impudence and Impertinence of Young Authors, whose Ambition is to be known, tho' it be by their Folly.

Beyond its criticism of jargon, slang, and verbal redundancy, this passage is notable for the phrase "*Cadence of Stile*," which indicates that Defoe probes why words considered merely as signs of ideas do not convey meaning. For him, sound and sense, phonetics and syntax, are reciprocal: without music diction cannot signify nor semantics operate. Sense depends on how words collocate, their cadence bringing inflection, intonation, modulation, and harmony into action. Cadence is a syntactic universal that works like the transformations and substitutions which modern grammarians posit between surface and deep structures:

> there is a direct Signification of Words, or a *Cadence in Expression*, which we call speaking *Sense*; this, like Truth, is sullen and the same, ever was and will be so, in what manner, and in what Language soever 'tis express'd. *Words* without it, are only Noise, which any Brute can make as well as we, and Birds much better; for *Words* without *Sense* make but dull Musick. Thus a man may speak in *Words*, but perfectly unintelligible as to *Meaning*; he may *talk* a great deal, but *say* nothing. But 'tis proper Position of *Words*, adapted to their Significations, which makes them intelligible, and conveys the Meaning of the Speaker to the Understanding of the Hearer; the contrary to which we call *Nonsense*; and there is a superfluous crowding in of insignificant Words, more than are needful to express the thing intended, and this is *Impertinence*; and that again carry'd to an extreme, is *ridiculous*.[20]

In Defoe's mind, verbal self-consciousness attuned to aesthetic experience, stylistic awareness informed by syntactic symbols, and semantic rules based on historical usage are vital to the development of human faculties. Hence, his disgust with upper-class resistance to formal education, linguistic theory, and civic humanism in *The Compleat English Gentleman*, which argues that, because the gentry lack national and linguistic pride, the typically illiterate gentleman is rude and anti-social. The problem is that gentlemen are "drag'd up," not "bred up": they are "left utterly untaught and so far from understanding the ordinary school languages of Greek and Latin, that they are not able to write or spell true English." If "in all languages there is a beauty of stile, a cadence and harmony in the expression," English has "much more than any other vulgar speech in the world." Since "our language" is more "beautifull, strong, expressiv, and polite" than other "vulgar tongues,"

> what shall we say to the gross ignorance of our gentlemen, who slight not the language, for that is abov the contempt not of them onely but of all the world, but slight themselves so as not to be able to either speak, write, read, or spell the beautifullest and best improv'd language in the world, and that with this miserable addition that at the same time they can speak no other neither, no, nor write or read any other?

Here Defoe charges the gentry with verbal and cultural illiteracy in his zeal for the national as well as personal benefits of language learning and stylistic sensibility.[21]

His zeal for linguistic self-consciousness is as keen when he criticizes dissenting academies and congregations in *The Present State of the Parties in Great Britain*. This text, which maintains a critical interest in pulpit oratory and the ministerial calling, examines "the wretched Change among the Lay-part of the *Dissenters*" with regard to "the management of their Ministers."[22] About congregations tolerating low standards of pulpit oratory, he exclaims:

> How is the Energy of the Spirit of God, which accompany'd the last Age, succeeded by Formality, Gaeity, empty Un-meaning Sound and Jingle of Words, without the Power and Force, either of Religion or of true Eloquence, and how are the People pleas'd with it? Metaphors without Meaning; Stile without Cadence; Letters without Learning; and which is worst of all, Divinity without Gospel?

Dissenting congregations mistake the "Excellency" of new ministers to "consist in *Pulpit Gesture*, Powder'd *Hair*, Clean *Gloves*, and a Levity of Behaviour." Such ministers are improper "Instruments for the Great Work of *Converting of Souls*," since unprepared "for the Laborious Self-denying Work of the *Ministry*." They display none of "the Fruits of a *Holy Devoted Soul*, Eaten up with the Zeal of God's House." Congregational illiteracy prevents the deity from rejoicing "at the Appearance and Goings of the Spirit of God in his Sanctuary," because it incites those training for the ministry to leave the academies too early with the result that, despite possessing "a good Stock of Modesty, *some* Well-meaning, *a few* Letters, *and much room for more,*" they are "*Ruin'd* by Flattery, *made Vain* by the Foolish Caresses of the Town," and seduced from study "by Feasting and Treating." The "very People that Caress" a conceited new minister

> do him the greatest Injury in the World, since, as they first run after him in the Lunacy of their Judgement, for the Out-side of his Appearance, and the Surface of his Preaching: So, for want of a serious Taste, a Sence of the Fundamental of the Pulpit Gift; or which is yet worse, upon the appearing of some new *Blazing-Star* above their Horizon, they all run away after the Novelty, and, forsaking the former Idol of their Fancy, they leave him as naked of Admirers, as he was at first of Merit. Thus, having made him waste the pretious Moments in which he should have Improv'd, they leave him to grow more and more Despicable, as he comes to add Age to Emptiness, and Years to want of Judgment: How is this apparent in many Places of this Town, where you find those Meetings Empty and Void, where the same Workmen exert their Parts to the Bare-Walls, who were once the Celebrated Orators of the Town.

After capping his satire of congregations by claiming that "the *Dissenting* Interest is divided against itself" since the city of London is "set up to Starve the Country of their Provision of Ministers," he relates the fragmentation of the community and its failure to constitute a solid national interest to the domination of philology over rhetorical pedagogy in its academies.[23]

Training in them has "ill-Effects" because tutors emphasize "Knowledge of the Tongues." Being "Fond of *Phylology,*" they restrict pupils to "Readings in *Latin* or in *Greek*" so that they leave school "unacquainted with *English,* tho' that is the Tongue in which all their Gifts are to shine." But, while the academies imitate the philological learning of universities, they suffer from a "want of Conversation" that "the Publick Universities enjoy." The academies tend to make a man "a Pedant, a meer Scholar, rough and unfit for any thing out of the Walls of his Colledge," whereas extracurricular university experience endows ministers-to-be with rhetorical accomplishments:

> Conversation polishes the Gentlemen in Discourse, acquaints 'em with Men, and with Words; lets them into the Polite part of Language; gives them Stile, Accent, Delicacy, and Taste in Expression; and when they come

> to appear in English, they Preach as they Discourse, Easie, Free, Plain, Unaffected, and Untainted with Force, Stiffness, Formality, affected hard Words, and all the Ridiculous Parts of a Learned Pedant, which is being interpreted a *School Fop*; while, on the other Hand, from our Schools we have abundance of Instances of Men that come away Masters of Science, Criticks in the *Greek* and *Hebrew*, perfect in Languages; and perfectly Ignorant (if that Term may be allow'd) of their Mother Tongue, especially as to the Beauties of Stile, Cadence, and Politeness of Language.

Defoe regrets that our "greatest Schollars" who "have the whole Mistery of the Gospel in their Hearts, and a Body of Divinity in their Heads, that have a vast Stock of Learning, a whole Ages Reading" drive away "all their Hearers" for "want of the *English* Tongue" while "a Jingling, Noisie Boy, that has a good Stock in his Face, and a Dysentery of the Tongue, tho' he has little or nothing in his Head," draws "the whole Town" to his pulpit. If "the Corruption of our taste in hearing is to be accounted for in this," dissenting academies must realize that "the Tongue must be Tuned" if the preacher is to make "Musick with the Voice." The analogy is to playing "the Viol"; its "Musick will be very harsh" unless its strings are tuned. Hence, the "most taking and valuable Thing in a Minister" is his joining of "Acceptable Words, a good Diction, a Grave yet Polite, and Easie Stile in the *English*." This juncture cannot be "generally Neglected, and left wholly to Nature." If it is, the result is the "Foppish *Gaiety*, Rambling *Distraction*, Stiff *Formality*, and Surfeiting Affectation in *Stile*" of fashionable preachers who soon lose favour since their oratory is "Unpolite, without Cadence, without Energy, or without the easie, Free Plainness which is the Glory and Excellency of the *English* Tongue."[24] If the verbal awkwardness of scholars repels congregations and the jingoism of modish ministers attracts but corrupts hearers, this divide will be overcome only when learning and expression are viewed by society as reciprocal. Since most scholarly ministers are handicapped by rhetorical clumsiness and the showiest preachers win congregations only momentarily, pedagogy in academies must renew its theory of language by appreciating the musicality of English.

As *Augusta Triumphans*, which he published in 1728, shows and as our preface has indicated, Defoe was personally and aesthetically as well as theoretically and morally committed to music. A "Lover of the Science," he played the viol and lute, finding music to be "the most innocent Amusement in Life" because "it gently relaxes, after too great a hurry of Spirits, and composes the Mind into a Sedateness, prone to every thing that's generous and good." It is "a most genteel and commendable Accomplishment," since "it saves a great deal of Drinking and Debauchery in our Sex." Pleased by the compositions of Corelli, Handel, Bononcini, and Geminiani, he celebrated Purcell as the model for English musicians. His proposal for an academy of music funded by the foundation of Christ's Hospital anticipates the English oratorio in calling for "some Performance in Musick" on Sundays "after Divine Service" to which "Sacred Poesy and Rhetorick ... suitable to a Christian and Polite Audience" might be added. Defoe's concern for the music of the human voice and language is clarified by Julian Jaynes's tenet that music and poetry begin "in the bicameral mind," to which we return later in this chapter.[25]

******

Although Defoe's pedagogical theory seems firmly based on relations between rhetoric and cognition and between verbal self-consciousness and innate mental capacities, in his normal dialectical concern with probabilities he qualifies his theory by raising psychological and spiritual questions that modify the presentation of human nature and identity in his non-fiction and fiction. He was partly motivated to raise such questions by observing his son-in-law's efforts to devise a pedagogy for deaf children.[26] In *The Compleat English Gentleman,* he describes the cognitive deficits of deaf children to urge the gentry to change its attitude to education: deaf children may have "all the wit and vivacity of soul" that goes along with a capacity for speech and be more intelligent than siblings who can hear, but their innate capacities are redundant because unactualized. Since learning is unattainable "without hearing and imitacion," a deaf child "can take in no ideas, knows nothing by its name, much less their end, can form no consequences, knows no sound, and, in a word, half the world is, as it were, of no use to him, and half his naturall powers are useless, because unimprov'd." In the context of the gentry's wilful ignorance, deafness indicates that speech is the sine qua non of learning.[27]

The earlier *Mere Nature Delineated* treats the cognitive deficits of Peter the Wild Boy from a general interest in what the experience of marginal individuals reveals about linguistic signification before taking up the topic of deafness. Peter's case confirms that language normally limits as well as enables speech, for it mediates the operation of mental faculties as well as individual and social identity. While words are instrumental to ideas and thoughts, their reflexivity and systemic referents impose themselves on consciousness. When a normal person thinks, he acknowledges that words work for him only if he activates their intrinsic rules, and he grants that semantic processes govern the interior life of thinking, feeling, and imagination. Thus Defoe asserts that

> Words are to us, the Medium of Thought; we cannot conceive of Things, but by their Names, and in the very Use of their Names; we cannot conceive of God, or of the Attributes of God, of Heaven, and of the Inhabitants there, but by agitating the Word God, and the Words Infinite, Eternal, Holiness, Wisdom, Knowledge, Goodness, &c. as Attributes; and even the Word Attribute; we cannot conceive of Heaven, but in the very Use and Practice of the Word that signifies the Place, be it in what Language you will; we cannot muse, contrive, imagine, design, resolve, or reject; nay, we cannot love or hate, but in acting upon those Passions in the very Form of Words; nay, if we dream 'tis in Words, we speak every thing to ourselves, and we know not how to think, or act, or intend to act, but in the Form of Words; all our Passions and Affections are acted in Words, and we have no other Way for it.

Since, in constituting illocutionary and mental acts, discourse imposes formal conditions on normally gifted people, Defoe feels obliged to ask concerning deaf mutes whether linguistic deprivation might induce extraordinary capacities in them. After all, "these silent People" operate "their Senses and Passions upon Things" that are present, future, and past, if inexplicably to "the most refined, or refining Naturalist." Their functional performance with material objects signifies a competence that defies conventional assumptions about the dependence of thinking upon speaking:

> It is absurd to think, that all Mutes are Fools; that because they cannot hear, therefore they cannot think, and that the contracted Soul, under the Fetters of misplac'd Organs, or oppress'd with a Defect of the Organ, must not act at all; for at the same Time, we see that imprison'd fetter'd Soul exerting itself in, and acting on a Thousand other Objects, which demonstrate not its Being only, but the full Exercise of its proper Faculties, both Understanding and Will: This is evident, where we have seen those who have been both Deaf and Dumb, fence, fight, dance, learn to carve, paint, sew, embroider, weave, knit, and almost any kind of handy Works, which do not depend upon the Ear or Voice to perform or to learn.

That the ears and tongues of the deaf do not work is no sign that their souls are inactive; their energy and skills signify comprehension and deliberation. That they also manage immaterial processes suggests not only that they learn differently from normal people but also that they learn in a "superior Way." Since "they must think without the Agency or Interposition of Language" and "cannot call Light or Darkness, Heaven or Earth, God, the Devil, themselves, or any other Thing, by any Name, or conceive of them under any Title or Hieroglyphick Representation," how they learn is "all a Mystery inconceivable to us, as entirely as our Way of conceiving Things must be to them."[28] Defoe emphasizes the mysterious foundation of their learning because he believes that humans have a spiritual access to knowledge. He imagines plural modes of human conceiving that lead him to ask if there may be no universal standard of intellection and identity. He contemplates, too, whether there may be no singular human nature since there seems to be no one mode of learning. He thinks that differences in mental capacity and intuition may be more significant than is assumed: the spirituality of the cognitively impaired may be superior to that of so-called ordinary people; the marginalized and disadvantaged may exceptionally possess unique gifts.[29]

******

As his fiction and non-fiction confirm, Defoe promoted learning in and through figurative thinking. Skilfully compounding metaphors and embedding analogies one within another, he very much enjoys arguing in images. His openness to polysemy – detailed in chapter 1 – allowed him to exploit the multiple meaning of word forms and to privilege semantic vagueness over literal-minded denotation. His deployment of analogies often bypasses logical and rational illustration in order to confront psychological problems and to approach spiritual ineffability. His favourite metaphors clarify his rhetorical dialectic and aesthetic sensibility.[30] He well knew that images may be polyvalent and operate plurally as signifiers and that, because they set up sets of associations, they may involve contrary aspects of a given semantic field.[31] If we consider abstractly his favourite metaphor of the sea, we realize that its features –salt, tides, waves crashing on shore, mid-ocean storms, agency in exploration, and mediation of discovery's risks – may equally be drawn on. The ocean also conjures up images of ships that serve as vessels for kinds of seafaring and emblematic seafarers.

The metaphor of the sea is deployed throughout *Conjugal Lewdness* to oppose conventional ideas of sexual crime and to offer extensive prescriptions for marital harmony. The first instance occurs in the introduction when, in defending himself against charges of indecency that may arise from satirizing sexual vice, he resorts to the indirectness called for by St Mark in one of this study's opening epigraphs.[32] Unable to "speak the Language" and "Dialect" of sexual criminals since their "talk is a great part of the Crime," Defoe, as previously noted, concedes that they triumph over him because he must "talk in the dark, and reprove by Allegory and Metaphor" so "that People may know, or not know what I mean, just as it may happen."[33] He excuses himself by charging hostile interpreters with indecency: depraved readers who accuse him of obscenity ignore the modesty of his reproofs, their fantasizing imaginations realizing things he neither specifies nor details. His first image of the sea stands for the polluted minds of readers:

> The healing fructifying Dews, and the gentle sweet refreshing Showers, which are God's Blessing upon the Earth, when they fall into the Sea are all turned Salt as the Ocean, ting'd with the gross Particles of Salt which the Sea-Water is so full of. The same warm cherishing Beams of the Sun which raise those sweet Dews from the Earth, shining upon the stagnate Waters of an unwholsome Lake or Marsh, or upon a corrupted Jakes or Dunghill exhale noxious Vapours and Poisons, which infect the Air, breeding Contagion and Diseases in those that breathe in it. But the Fault is not in the Showers of refreshing Rain, or in the wholesome Beams of the Sun, but in the Salt, and in the Filth and Corruption of the Places where they fall. And thus it shall be here; Words modestly expressed can give no immodest Ideas, where the Minds of those that read are chaste and uncorrupted. But if a vicious Mind hears the Vice reproved and forms pleasing Ideas of the Crime, without taking notice of the just Reproof, the fault is in the Depravity of the Mind, not in the needful and just Reprover.

Here the salt sea spoils the distilled dews and rains that refresh, heal, and fructify the earth. The meteorological cycle by which stagnant, unhealthy, and fetid waters evaporate to be purified by the sun represents divine benevolence to humanity and Defoe's authorial desire to reform readers. His words are dews and rains that heal stale, corrupt minds.

The next major sea image in *Conjugal Lewdness* exposes the hypocritical mores of pious but loveless spouses who adopt a merely formalistic approach to marriage:

> How miserably do the Pious and the Devout, the Religious and the Conscientious live together! The Husbands here, the Wives there, by jarring Tempers, discording Affections, and, in short, meer want of Love and Friendship, grow scandals to the marry'd Life, and set themselves up for Beacons and Light-houses, to warn the wandering World, and to bid them beware how they marry without Love, how they join Hands and not hearts, unite Interests, unite Sexes, unite Families and Relatives, and yet never unite Hearts?

Pious, loveless couples turn themselves into beacons and lighthouses: they warn the wandering world – a ship on the ocean – about the dangers in marriages undertaken indulgently or acquisitively. Such couples, far from being settled comfortably on land, reside on weather-beaten coasts that threaten ships with rugged rocks and mountainous waves. As beacons and lighthouses, they are warning devices, not exemplary models. In this imagery, the sea is the element on which all the world must travel – the medium of emotional life across which all must voyage who would live safely on shore. As Defoe later explains, marriage is a ship that comes safely to harbour only when love informs marital union with the comforts of settlement:

> the Pleasure of a married State consists wholly in the Beauty of the Union, the sharing Comforts, the doubling all Enjoyments; 'tis the Settlement of Life; the Ship is always in a Storm till it finds this safe Road; and here it comes to an Anchor: 'Tis the want of a taste of Life makes men despise that Part of it which Heaven at first constituted to compleat the Happiness of his Creatures.[34]

A loveless marriage is a ship always at sea and exposed to storms arising from emotional and sexual strife. Since loveless couples have been established as unable to move inland beyond the margins of the sea, at this stage of *Conjugal Lewdness* the sea has become a composite set of allegorical references. In the next image, the sea is the medium of a lifelong, perpetual voyage: it represents the permanently challenging aspects of human nature:

> How foolish then, as well as wicked and unlawful, is it to marry before you love? To rush into a State of irrecoverable Life without the only Article that can make it tolerable? They that marry without Affection go to Sea without a Rudder; launch into the most dangerous Ocean without a

> Pilot, and without a Compass: Love is the only Pilot of a married State; without it there is nothing but Danger in the Attempt, nothing but Ruin in the Consequence.

The association of loveless partners with ocean-going sailors who fail to equip themselves with rudder and compass and who do not employ a pilot to guide them safely in and out of harbours makes marriage an outward-bound voyage as well as a berthing in port. The sea here is the chief element of marriage, an unpredictable medium in which couples face danger and ruination if not navigated by love. However, when equipped by love, their ship will voyage safely. This also means that sexual impulses must be forced to be "Galley-Slaves" chained to oars below decks. The ship will be propelled by sexual energy only if the latter are contained by discipline and fasting.[35]

Defoe's sea images rest on fields of metonymic associations which reveal that his imaginary follows dynamic and contrary rather than stable and logical rules. The figurative polyvalency so far analysed conveys the mixed nature of human life along with its possibilities for emotional and spiritual integrity. Since the images operate negatively and positively at a level of cognition deeper than rationality, they confirm Defoe's polarity thinking. A striking example appears in *Mere Nature Delineated* when the image of a ship differentiates between apparent bodily normalcy and mental underdevelopment: Peter the Wild Boy seems to manifest "the Powers and Motions of sensitive Life, and of rational Life." But "he is a Ship without a Rudder, not steer'd or managed, or directed by any Pilot; no, hardly by that faithful Pilot called Sense, the Guide of Beasts."[36] If humans are ships, not all persons have pilots – the faculties that enable them to navigate their voyages.

Sea images in *The Complete English Tradesman* fuse institutional and autobiographical topics after they promote Defoe's code of business ethics, which contrasts enterprises that operate in charted and uncharted oceans. While sound tradesmen move over established sea lanes, those distracted "by the specious Pretences of Gain" and quick profits "embark" on out-of-the-way voyages without navigational charts. A sound trader searches into "all the Arcana, the Creeks and Corners of the Affair" before taking up an enterprise. He does "not embark first, and then find by the Loss that the Thing would not do." This imagery signals that richer are as likely as poorer tradesmen to take excessive risks. Some pages later, Defoe extends the notion that highly capitalized businesses are no less immune to danger than poorer ones. Not only may big and small ships venture into uncharted waters but big ships encumbered by military equipment or heavy cargoes are more likely to capsize in storms, especially if commanded by pilots who do not know their charts:

> An ill Pilot as soon loses a great Ship as a small, and a rich Cargo is as easily shipwreck'd as a poor: The Rocks and Sands which lie under the Water hid and conceal'd, are as dangerous to a Man of War as to a Merchant Ship; and the Number of its Guns, which makes it terrible to other Enemies, are rather Instruments to forward its Ruin, in case of Tempests and Storms, than helps to deliver it.

Defoe compounds the analogy of poor navigation with gambling references before he applies the seafaring imagery autobiographically. The rich tradesman, he says, who loses on one venture will likely risk more on further ventures so that his capital losses will quickly mount, and, like the gambler, he is undone before he knows it. Should "ill-natur'd" readers think that he speaks "too feelingly" about business failure and criticize the "poor Author," that would "not be the worse for the Argument" because an "old Sailor, that has split upon a sunk Rock, and has lost his Ship, is not the worst Man to make a Pilot of for that Coast." For he can better "guide those that come after him to shun the Dangers of the unhappy Place." He continues:

> Trade is a safe Channel to those that keep in the *fair Way*, (so the Sailors call the ordinary Entrance into an Harbour;) but if in Contempt of Dangers, and of fair Warnings, any Man will run out of the Course, neglect the Buoys and Marks which are set up by the Publick for the Direction of Sailors, and, at all Hazards, venture among the Rocks, he is to blame no body but himself if he loses his Ship.

That Defoe offers himself as a failed sailor whose experience may be constructive implies that he sees his trading manual allegorically as a navigational aid and maritime chart.[37]

Extended metaphors of mining in *Of Royall Educacion* and forestry in *The Compleat English Gentleman* further illustrate the rhetorical basis of Defoe's contrarian ideas, these manuscripts presenting his mature thoughts on education and subtly defying opponents of innatism and religious identity. *Of Royall Educacion* denies that the soul is a blank slate or tabula rasa since it is placed in man "by the author of Nature like a rough diamond in the mine," its "lustre and its most perfect beauties" hidden beneath the "cloudy surface" of the rock in which it is embedded.[38] The soul's properties are inherent if latent, and, like the diamond's, invisible except to the jeweller. Defoe elaborates these properties to create an extended analogy to the soul:

> The jewell has in it all the shining glories of its refin'd composition, its inimitable brightness, its perfect water, its unperishable duracion, its unmallable hardness, by which it cuts every thing and is its self wounded onely by it self. It has, in a word, an instrinsick, unvaluable worth, known as well as unknown; yet all this, in its primitiv state, lyes conceal'd from common view, and is onely discern'd by the penetrating judgement of an experienc'd lapidary or jeweller; and he bringing it to his engine or mill, by which he pares off the gloomy surface, modells and rightly forms the whole fully, at once dissplays the glories which were before eclyps'd and conceal'd, and makes it shine with its full lustre.

Just unearthed diamonds possess the highest qualities despite being invisible since unrealized. The condition of a diamond taken from a mine yet unprocessed by a jeweller is analogous to the unenlightened soul whose insights, impaired by the body, remain to be elicited by teachers:

> Thus the brightest soul, while ecclypst and veil'd in its infant clothing of corrupted or at least corruptible flesh and blood, tho' it may have in it all the brightest capascityes, those beauties of the mind which when clear'd up and interrupted shine out in such an inimitable brightness, yet can not show it self, can not emit the rayes of its nativ lustre and perfeccion, till polish'd by the skilfull applicacion of experienc'd instructors: then it breaks out from those clouds, and recovering the proper space of accion, has room to expand it self and dart out the rays of its divine original glory.

Only when a soul is polished by experienced teachers will it emit its transcendent rays. The soul's divine provenance leads Defoe to compound this mining analogy by further polarities. As diamonds from one mine need not be of equal quality, so souls, while of divine origin, need not have equal capacities. Imperfect organs and natural accidents may explain spiritual inequality. So may biblical history. Kings and military men, such as Joshua, Saul, David, Solomon, and Elisha – leaders celebrated for spiritual superiority – show that Providence equips men for "stations" requiring specific heroic abilities. Hence, Defoe rejects "that gross and inconsistent notion which some have entertain'd of a parity of souls," his "allegory of an unpolish'd jewell" holding that just as some diamonds have a "clearer and more perfect water than others, tho' out of the same mine," so there are souls "of differing glory and ... infinitely greater capascityes" than others, despite all reflecting the one deity. In his "divine wisdome," the Creator did not "confine Himself so in the structure, that He could not furnish" particular men for "eminent stations, exalted glory, and inimitable accions, with souls apt to, and capable of, the reall and intrinsick gallantry and greatness, which should quallifye them to accquire that glory and perform those accions in a manner infinitely beyond the inferiour world, who are onely left to admire, not imitate, them."[39]

Defoe amplifies his belief that heavenly prescience endows kings and nobles with superior souls by celestial imagery: the planets not only move in distinct orbits but also differ in size, density, and volume, reflecting the various degrees of light and heat they "reciev from the sun which is the center of all their reflex glory." Applying cosmology to diversity of souls highlights a spiritual contrary: the more loftily endowed a soul, the more spiritual education it requires. The compounding of imagery returns Defoe to mineralogy with greater pointedness. Just as the finest diamonds require the most skilful cutting and polishing, so superior souls act with the utmost vigour and resolution only if finished by education. The topic of the diversity of souls supports, and is supported by, the claim that the finest diamonds must be polished with "the more and greater care," since those "of the first magnitude may be more beautifull and perfect in themselves, and more capable of shining with a surprising lustre in the world, when they are thus carefully polish'd, than others are!" This "whole allegory" leads Defoe to aver that

> how much the greater the nativ lustre, the reall intrinsick beauty and excellence ... in the souls of men nobly born and of men destin'd for glory, than is found in others of inferior rank: by so much the greater should the skill and care be which ought to be used in the educacion of such persons and cultivating, polishing, and improving those naturall powers in their souls, for the furthering the designs of Heaven and Nature and for enabling them to exert those powers with the utmost vigour and resolution.[40]

His contrarian tenet that the greater the soul and its predestined purposes the more it needs education could not be more emphatic: "The finer the jewell, the more carefully should it be set, the more nicely should it be cut, and all the help of art given it to illustrate nature, and set it off with advantage."[41] Far from promoting one level of education, he recommends hierarchy: the "educacion of princes and the children of noble families ought to differ from that of other people," since the former "are likely to mov in the highest spheres of life" where they will "signalize themselves and ... shine in a more particular manner and from a higher stacion than other people." The education of leaders "ought not to be of the same kind or mannag'd in the same manner as the ordinary school teaching of other people." Governors, tutors, and inspectors must form their minds, temper their geniuses, instil generous principles into them, and divide their studies "between the Muses and the Graces" to prepare them to become Christian heroes who yet are exemplars of "modesty and humility."[42]

Defoe's compounding of metaphors is complex because, as in the apology for the education of kings and leaders, he balances individual equality with social hierarchy to defy false imaginings. The way he joins mining to agricultural and arboreal images in *The Compleat English Gentleman* testifies further to his subtle polarity thinking. That the "brightest genius" must be "polish'd and smooth'd" is all the more reason for an ordinary youth to be sent to school rather than excused on account of so-called gentility. For "the quick parts, the naturall wit, the strong memory, the great capascityes" are given "for some uses"; they are not "wholly fitted for but by the applicacion of other suitable helps." While such a youth easily absorbs "all the glorious things which science, learning, and acquir'd knowledge can furnish," he is "perfectly unquallify'd to act alone." The assumptions that natural capacities are equivalent to learning and that "time and conversation" together with "good estates" will allow "men of parts" to flourish without education are false because they ignore "the true design of Nature, and even of the Author of Nature." The "treasure of wit and parts is given from Heaven to be cultivated and improv'd." Compared here are humanity's need for education and God's command to Adam to till the ground after the Fall, for "without tillage and cultivation" his land would "bring forth nothing but briars and thorns." Adam's land is analogous to disciplined "brains and understanding." Hence, "what ever brightness of parts, what ever genius, wit, and capacity the man is naturally furnish'd with, it is requir'd that those jewells should be polished, that learning be apply'd to them, that rules and instruccions be layd before them, and that historys and examples of times and persons be recommended to them, and that all this be enforc'd by the authority of instructors, parents, schoolmasters, etc." Nature may be "the best fund" of ideas but "dictates of nature are not the best guides." When the learned talk about "the rectitude of Nature and of natural religion" and claim that "meer undirected inclination" guides "mankind to make the best choice of things," they are deluded by simple-minded figments of the imagination.[43]

In discussing imperfectibility and relations between learning, cognition, and genetic inheritance, Defoe turns to timber and arboreal images. Granting that good physique may come from "birth and blood" and that it is an advantage to be born into a vigorous family, he insists that intellect cannot be said to be inherited since the principles of procreation are unknown and unknowable. "Nature seems to have very little concern in the intellectuall part"; "the wise man begets the fool, and the fool gives a wise man to the world." Parentage cannot explain why some men are natural fools and others are "bright, have a sprightly wit, a great genius, a capacious soul, deep reach and clear thoughts even from their birth." He then points up his contrarian appreciation of innate capacities and the need for education with the following compelling timber analogy:

> In a great wood if a fine well grown oak presents it self to the eye, we say there is a fine tree; that's true, and Nature obtains the praise so farr. But when it comes to use, it must be cut down, the bark stript off, the knotty limbs taken away, the sawyers cut it into plank, the carpenter squares it with his rule, and then 'tis smooth'd with the plain, groov'd with one tool, carv'd with another, and then 'tis fitt to be set up against the wall, and wainscott the Hall of Audience or the Presence Chamber of a prince, or the State Room of a pallace. But till all these pains are bestow'd upon it, it is onely potentially good and usefull; 'tis not naturally finish'd and perfect: it must be shap'd and squar'd as art requires. It is also to my purpose to observ, carrying on the metaphor, that even the most crooked, out of shape tree in the whole wood is capable by the help of the same art to be brought to the same perfection in its degree, and onely with this difference, that the crooked stick requires more workmanship, more hewing and cutting, makes more chips, and suffers more wast, before 'tis brought to take place among the ornaments of the pallace, whereas the strait, well shap'd tree is finish'd with less trouble, less difficulty, less workmanship and art. In a word, the strait tree is wrought with less pains than the crooked, but both require some. Thus the bright genius, the naturall beauty of the mind, the

> parts, the witt, the capascities given by Nature to one youth, cause him to be polish'd and cultivated with more ease, and he is finish'd with fewer hands in less time and with much less difficulty than another crooked, knotty, stubborn disposition, which being naturally dul and awkward requires much more hewing and shapeing and dressing.[44]

This comparison of humans to trees employs what philosophers call *habitus* ideas. In the forest, trees vary in straightness and crookedness. To become building materials they are all milled, the crooked ones needing more processing. That specimens suited to palaces must still be processed by "art" confirms that innate capacities must be realized by education. This analogy also holds that, while an ugly specimen may require more labour to be "perfected in its degree," it may still adorn a palace.

Behind this timber imagery lies the tree of the knowledge of good and evil in Genesis 2:9, cited when *Serious Reflections* symbolically invites readers to listen to the voice of Providence. This arboreal image, legitimating spiritual mystery, distinguishes it from both primal disobedience and enthusiastic superstition. Granting "that secret Things belong to God," Defoe vows "to keep my due Distance" from them. But this is no problem since the things "we are forbidden to enquire into" are so deeply "preserv'd in Secrecy" that "by all our Enquiries we cannot arrive at the Knowledge of them." Indeed, "it is a most merciful, as well as wise Dispensation, that we are only forbid enquiring after those Things which we cannot know; and that all those Things which we cannot know are effectually lock'd up from our Knowledge, which we are forbidden to enquire into." However, there are several trees of sacred knowledge that lie within the reach of human capacity, and to this extent we are more fortunate than Adam before the Fall:

> We have not the Tree of Knowledge first planted in our View, as it were tempting us with its Beauty, and within our Reach, and then a Prohibition upon Pain of Death: but blessed be God, we may eat of all the Trees in the Garden; and all those of which we are not allow'd to take, are plac'd both out of our Sight, and out of our Reach.

The tree of "sacred Knowledge" to which Defoe is making his way here is listening to the voice of Providence. Although this tree "may grow in the thickest of the Wood, and be surrounded with some Briars and Thorns, so as to place it a little out of Sight," he believes that "it is our Duty to taste of it: and that the Way to come at it, is both practicable and plain." As there are inaccessible and accessible trees, so there are hidden and revealed secrets. Defoe well knew that arguing in images is an essential form of polarity thinking since we live among probabilities not certainties and since spiritual experience necessitates stepping up to the borders of knowledge and venturing towards the ineffable. His compound metaphors and analogies reveal his wish to render compatible the learning that springs from disciplining the understanding through formal education and the imaginative apprehension that touches the bounds of human cognition. While he honours biblical words, he trusts that sacred imagery will continue to evolve from contemporary engagement with the scriptures.[45]

******

If listening to the voice of Providence is like searching for one tree in a forest, listening to one's own voice is also a discipline in spiritual analogy and typology. Searching for the elusive self in one's own story is the purposeful action towards which characters and narrators haltingly move and in which they invite readers to participate. The ultimate dialectic in Defoe's fictions that tempers the motif that characters and narrators falter and perhaps disintegrate through deficient self-reflection is the counter-motif that sees them struggling to discover their inner voices. Defoe's most profound sense of narrative action is reflexive; it involves internal tensions between losing and finding voice. His most important tenet is that humans possess an interior language that potentially harmonizes secular and religious conversation and integrates sociable and meditative discourse.

When Crusoe leaves home and family, he does not foresee the limits abandoning his speech community will inflict on him. He is rightly proud that his "Conversation" is "not at all disagreeable" to the ship's master who takes him as "Mess-mate" (17). But, when he becomes "a miserable Slave" among the Moors with nobody "to communicate to" (19), he experiences the problems arising from linguistic and psychological autism. In Brasil he misses his speech community when he "used often to say to" himself that he could have had a similar lifestyle had he remained at home (35). Rather than analysing how social displacement degrades his expressive identity and unsettles relations between his exterior and interior voices, he repines: with nobody "to converse with," he "used to say" he lived like a solitary castaway on an island, these words later coming into being. Yet, he does learn Portuguese and contract "Acquaintance and Friendship among my Fellow-Planters" (38). His verbal isolation and sociability indicate a contradictory sense of speech and performance. On the island, this contradictoriness becomes acute when he apostrophizes his gold as a useless "Drug," only "upon Second Thoughts" preserving it for future use (57). In his deepening isolation, however, he begins to respond to his inner voice, to recognize why he talks aloud, and to trace significance in his monologues. When he blames Providence and reason expostulates with him "t'other Way" (62), his discontent is partly offset by self-questioning that imagines material lacks that might have befallen him. On speaking "aloud" about the "Necessaries of Life" which he has, he can more constructively "enter into a melancholy Relation of a Scene of silent Life, such as perhaps was never heard of in the World before" (63). Vocal and silent language slowly become meaningful to Crusoe.

This process continues when in his illness he first attempts to pray without knowing "what to say." Crying out "*Lord look upon me, Lord pity me, Lord have Mercy upon me*," he unknowingly voices phrases from the Psalms and Book of Common Prayer. But, if he is the medium of divine language, he is disturbed by the ineffable. In his "terrible Dream" of the "inexpressibly dreadful" man who descends from "a great black Cloud" being "all over as bright as a Flame," he hears "a Voice so terrible, that it is impossible to express the Terror of it" (87). Verbal lethargy stops his narrative discourse containing this dream. As noted before, far from invoking God with conscious hope, his words are "extorted" from him; not prayers, they are only "like praying" (90). They come from "the Voice of meer Fright and Distress," being merely an "Exclamation" of unworthiness rather than precisely articulated rites. His linguistic passivity is clear when, as narrator, he cannot recall "what my Tongue might express" yet, as character, remembers his "Father's Words," saying "aloud" they had come to pass and confessing that he had "rejected the Voice of Providence." In his confusion, he cries out for God's help, a cry he hesitantly feels to have been his "first Prayer" (91).

The spiritual growth that Crusoe achieves is not reached by way of established devotional forms but accords with William's principles in *Religious Courtship*, namely, that the preparation of the heart and the answer of the tongue come from the Lord, who hears sincere desires in souls, whether or not registered in words, since these desires are formed by Him and are the "Voice of his own Spirit and Grace." For William, as we have seen, such responsiveness constitutes praying since "mental petition is Prayer as well as Words; and is, perhaps, the best mov'd Prayer, and the best exprest in the World."[46] From William's perspective, Crusoe may be said to pray. When he defies God's treatment of him, his conscience, speaking "like a Voice," checks his blasphemy, striking him dumb so that he has "not a Word to say, no not to answer to my self" (92–3). Upon casually reading Psalms 50:15 – Crusoe the narrator telling us he found the verse "very apt" to his case – he slowly undergoes a transformation. The words make "some Impression" on him though "not as much as they did afterwards" (94). At first, the verb "*deliver*" in the verse has "no Sound" for him since he apprehends its sense as an impossibility. Paradoxically, he expresses this negative sense by imitating the recalcitrant children of Israel. But the words make such a "great Impression" on him that he prays to God to fulfil His promise in them. The result of this "broken and imperfect Prayer" emanating from the psalm is that he is "made to ask" himself questions about the meanings of deliverance until his heart is "touch'd" and he thanks God "aloud" for his new "Sense" (96). From this point, he develops a firmer interpretation of the verse and words spoken to him in his frightening dream.

While Crusoe now converses "mutually with my own Thoughts" and "with even God himself by Ejaculations" (136), his life is not "better than sociable," as he pretends (135). Like a "Prisoner" he suffers the "Anguish of my Soul" which, in "the midst of the greatest Composures of my Mind," breaks out "like a Storm" (113). Since lack of social converse unsettles the calm yielded by his new verbal sense, he must "vent my self by Words" (113): if faith re-motivates interior discourse, absence of social intercourse inhibits spiritual integrity, as *Serious Reflections* explains. The anguish caused by isolation and symbolized by interior storms is heightened comically by how Crusoe relates to his parrot. He teaches it to talk and speak its name because he regards it as having a "Mouth" (119). When in the "Bower" Poll wakes Crusoe from a dream about human speech with its "Voice calling me by my Name several times, *Robin, Robin,* poor *Robin Crusoe,* where are you *Robin Crusoe*? Where are you? Where have you been?" (142), then asking "*How come you here*?" (143), the parrot's expansive syntactical intelligence appears in the expletives and interrogatives that fit the specific context. But, of course, Crusoe could not have taught Poll those questions. If he is "at first dreadfully frightened" by Poll's voice when not fully awake, he soon claims to recognize the "bemoaning Language" that he had taught "the sociable Creature" (142). This wish fulfilment upholds linguistic illusions, his anguished desire for the voice of others giving rise at this point in the narrative to no more than the delusory, if echoic, image of his voice.

After discovering the footprint, he weighs mental more heavily than physical discomposure because of the sense of voice and prayer he shares with the William of *Religious Courtship*: to Crusoe, mental discomposure is the heavier because "Praying to God" is "properly an Act of the Mind, not of the Body" (164). Having found his voice in prayer, he learns that his pre-social state on the island is not "the proper Frame for Prayer" (163). Despite enjoying the "Converse of Spirits" (176), he is reduced to mechanical reflexes by a shipwreck which aggravates his frustrated wish for the "Society of my Fellow-Creatures," the "Conversation" of "my Fellow-Christians." On "realizing the Comfort" that discourse with that ship's crew would have offered, his hands "clinch together" and his teeth "strike together" (188). But when companions arrive, he does not win self-possession since he is habituated to using his voice only defensively. The island's lack of constitutional structure means that, despite his invention of political roles for himself, he cannot balance his needs for social organization and spiritual meditation. When he regains "some Use" for his tongue and enjoys speaking to others, he forgets what he has profoundly learned about voice (213). He may explicate the Bible for Friday, may attend to the hints of Providence, and may encourage the captain to lure the mutineers into captivity, but he never steadily listens to his own voice. This reflexivity is left to readers. When they reflect on such declarations as the following, "My Life was a Life of Sorrow, one way, so it was a Life of Mercy, another" (132), they will see that Crusoe never achieves a voice that harmonizes external and internal discourse.[47]

As the variable first-person singular and plural pronouns in *Captain Singleton* indicate, its narrative explores the internal and external pressures on a speech community made up of lawless individuals whose erratic linguistic performance renders personal and group identity precarious. Given Singleton's deprivations, readers cannot expect him to heed his own voice sustainedly. From the beginning of his account, his naming of things and people is disrupted: he does not know the name of the town where he was born; the woman he calls mother is "not my Mother"; the man he "would have called" father will not let him do so (2–3).[48] If the mutineers command maritime diction when they build "a *Periagua*, or Canoe" rather than "a Bark or Sloop, or Shalloup" (24), they cannot identify a ship through their telescopes; it is "neither Ship,

Ketch, Gally, Galliot, or like anything we had seen before" (39). Their verbal unsteadiness is confirmed when the "Frigate" they build ends up being a "kind of a Sloop" (42). When Singleton and the mutineers cross Africa, their boldness turns to irresolution since they are unprepared for the barriers to communication they face. Their linguistic inadequacy is conveyed by Singleton's account of conversing with one friendly tribe:

> What Tongue they spoke, I do not yet pretend to know. We talked as far as we could make them understand us, not only about our Provisions, but also about our Undertaking; and ask'd them what Country lay that Way, pointing West with our Hands. They told us but little to our Purpose, only we thought by all their Discourse, that there were People to be found of one Sort or other every where; that there were many great Rivers, many Lions and Tygers. (48)

Since communication with tribes on Madagascar and in Africa involves "Signs," "Signals," and "Tokens" of various kinds (22, 57–8, 68, etc.), the adventurers' poor semiotic interpretation yields only uncertainty. They are frustrated by linguistic pluralism in Africa: "Every several Nation had a different Speech, or else their Speech had differing Dialects, so that they did not understand one another" (71). When adventurers meet natives, narrative contraries usually highlight discursive limits. One tribe invites the adventurers to sit by friendly signs, Singleton summarizing as follows: "we could not understand them, nor could we find any way to make them understand us; much less whither we were going, or what we wanted, only that we easily made them understand we wanted Victuals" (117). With a restricted ability to express local analogies, the adventurers cannot locate themselves geographically. That analogies derive from beyond the narrated experience implicitly devalues their supposed discoveries. Singleton's narrative cannot operate without alluding to England: the band's carpenter installs into a canoe a "Well" like that the "small Fisher-Boats in *England* have to preserve their Fish alive in" (30); an African river may be "as broad as the *Thames* below *Gravesend*" (64) or "as broad as the *Thames* is at *Windsor*" (65); and the adventurers travel up a river to the point where "there was not Water enough to swim a *London* Wherry" (73).

There is little rhetorical self-consciousness in Singleton and his mates. He does apply litotes to the fearful night-time sounds of animals: the "Musick of their Voices was very far from being pleasant to us" (100).

But the adventurers too easily succumb to the white man who urges them to collect gold: unable to resist the "Charm" of his voice, they surrender to its magic (131). Verbally flat-footed on being mocked by William for turning Quaker and *"flying from the Enemy"* (147), all Singleton can do is swear at his mentor. When William voices the provocative contrary that "it is because Men live as if they were never to dye, that so many dye before they know how to live," Singleton evades the pangs of conscience by talking like a hardened pirate (258). Although under William's guidance, Singleton develops "other Thoughts" of himself and the world (265), he lacks an interior life, as shown when he agrees to return to England only if William and he disguise themselves as "*Grecians* and Foreigners" and "never speak *English* in publick" (277), readers hereby invited to view the protagonist as a spiritual exile because of his betrayal of the language.

The focus on voice in *Moll Flanders* confirms Defoe's commitment to narratives that explore why individuals fail to reconcile personal and spiritual values. As character and narrator, Moll is preoccupied with voice. She prides herself on having a "better Voice" than the daughters of the Colchester family when it comes to singing (18). Her innocence is conveyed when her "Heart spoke as plain as a Voice" that she liked the elder brother's flattering attentions (22). But she is vulnerable to seduction because he "put Words in my Mouth" (24). Seduced by his "fine Words" as much as by his "Gold" (25), she suffers a split between narrative absorption and verbal mistrust, "wrapt up with every part of the Story" yet penetrating his redundant "Circumlocution" (26). Despite her illness she spurns his talk about deceiving his younger brother and the family as "rambling Stuff" (47). As regards the younger's courtship of her, Moll tells his mother that she took his words as "a wild airy Way of Discourse that had no Signification in it" (45). Yet, in relaying Robin's retort to his second sister, Moll happily confirms his view of her beauty by saying "So there was her Mouth stopp'd" (43). The opening episode at Colchester displaces Moll's linguistic innocence with a sense of voice as a duplicitous and aggressive agent that habituates her to defensive and strategic discourse.

Her narrative conduct is increasingly unthinking because her discourse aggravates her self-destructive contradictions and because she both judges others more harshly than herself and retaliates upon them. Her mother's revelations trap Moll in the details of incest and in linguistic confusion; since "every word" of that story "wounded me to the Soul" (96), she treats her husband-brother cruelly, her tongue giving him a "mortal Wound" (93). After forcing narrative consistency on her mother and making her realize the implications of her autobiography, Moll will not measure herself by the same standards. Having whored herself with the Bath gentleman and committed "other Follies which I cannot name," she merely states the fact "*with shame and horror of Soul*" (116). She is yet more evasive and defensive about Jemy. While his "Language" of "Joynture ... Deed of Settlement, or Contract" sees her "beaten out of all my Measures" (143), she deceives "my Deceiver" (144) by not discovering "so much as my Name" (149 and 159). Moll's growing avoidance of self and voice is emphasized when, after he leaves, she calls after him: "*James*, O *Jemy*! Said I, come back, come back, I'll give you all I have" (153). He returns because, "if ever I heard your Voice in my Life, I heard you call me aloud." Moll is "amaz'd and surpriz'd, and indeed frighted" (154) by this telepathy. But, rather than examining her voice, she pretends to be subject to the verbal power of others. After condemning Mother Midnight's lying-in house, she finds this woman's account of it a "Cordial" to her spirit (162). Again, she says she will marry the banker because of his "irresistable Words" (180). That Mother Midnight becomes her "good old Governess" whom she treats as "a Woman of a rare Tongue" (213) heightens Moll's self-exculpating rationalizations.

When she begins to steal, her voice, she says, is controlled by the devil: passing an apothecary's shop in Leaden Hall Street "with no manner of Design in my Head," she is prompted by a "Voice spoken to me over my Shoulder" to rob a maid-servant (191). This "evil Counsellor within" renders her "all Fear without, and Dark within" (193). She excuses her theft of jewels from a child by saying she is reproving the parents: "I only said to my self, I had given the Parents a just Reproof for their Negligence" (194). Such evasiveness transforms her active to a passive voice: "these things I did not steal, but they were stolen to my Hand" (196). About life in prison, she understates her fragile identity, claiming that she hardly retains "the Habit and Custom of good Breeding, and Manners, which all along till now run thro' my Conversation." Aggravating this false claim about her former life is her admission of "Degeneracy." This is the nadir of selfhood and verbal awareness: a "certain strange Lethargy of Soul" induces an apathy that displaces all "Apprehensions" and "Sorrow" (279). While love of Jemy recovers her horror at her "way of Living" in Newgate so that she is "perfectly chang'd, and become another Body," her voice does not substantiate this reversion, for her ejaculations – "Lord! What will become of me, I shall certainly die! ... Lord, have Mercy upon me, what will become of me?" (281) – contain, by her admission, "not a Word of sincere Repentance" (282). When she prays, she "may well call it, saying my Prayers," for she repeatedly voices "the Ordinary Expression" of the liturgy without coming "to any Sense of my being a miserable Sinner" (283). Her failed speech acts are further evident when the sentence of death is pronounced on her: "I had no more Spirit left in me, I had no Tongue to speak, or Eyes to look up either to God or Man" (286). If she gains some verbal self-consciousness from the word "Eternity," as narrator all she can say is that it takes on "incomprehensible Additions" that give her "extended Notions": the word rouses "severe Reproaches of my own Mind" and lively "Impressions" that are "not to be explain'd by words" since she is not "Mistress of Words enough to express them" (287–8). Defoe's verbal play on "word" prepares readers to probe why Moll fails to develop her capacity to dialogue with herself and God. While the minister sustains "the same moving Eloquence" (289), she distances herself from him. She may hang on his "Voice" when he delivers the "Reprieve," but she loses all "Composure of Mind" and is "Dumb and Silent" because unable "to give vent" to penitential joy "by Words" (290–2). Instead of addressing her interior life, she gives herself over to histrionic performances. She "Counterfeited [her] Voice" to dramatize the revelation of herself to Jemy in his Newgate cell so that she can reduce him to "one struck Dumb" (296–7). Her account is anti-climactic given her obfuscating prevarications with Jemy and Humphry, her son; the secrets of incest cloud her narrative discourse until the very end.

By contrast, H.F. is an exemplary narrator whose authority derives largely from episodes that feature distressed voices and present the whole speech community as under duress. He specializes in the symbolic meaning of vocal sounds, his acoustic memories and aural imagination informed by factors that scientists today explore in the realm of synaesthesia.[49] In his mind, the plague visits London with extremes of silence and noise. His attention to the "Voice of Mourning" recognizes the emotional and spiritual pain afflicting the city's streets on account of unattended deaths and the abeyance of public ritual (16). Recalling the "most horrible Cries and Noise the poor People" made when "bringing the Dead Bodies of their Children and Friends out to the Cart" and on to burial pits (178), he senses that the "Silence and Emptiness of the Streets," a "Signal of the Calamity," heightened the "passionate Outcries and Lamentations of the People, out at their Windows"

(186). In noting "the dying Groans of many a despairing Creature" (34), he draws on the testimony of watchmen who guarded infected households. As regards the "Noise and Crying" from the upper storey of one house, he describes a person calling from a window "with an angry quick Tone, and yet a Kind of crying Voice, or a Voice of one that was crying" (49). As in this instance, H.F. deploys rhetorical amplification and semantic vagueness to represent pained voices. He notes the "terrible Shrieks and Skreekings of Women" and the "most inimitable Tone" of their "Frightful Skreetches" (80–1).[50] Acute auditory memories inform his narrative: recalling "the most dismal Shrieks and Out-cries" of people locked up in their homes, he hears "the very Sound" as he is "writing this Story" (55). While citizens had "no Curiosity" about neighbours because unable to offer help (81), he insists that it "would pierce the Hearts of all that came by to hear the piteous Cries of those infected People" driven "out of their Understandings by the Violence of their Pain" (163). His persistent onomatopoeia invokes readers' aural imaginations.

His auditory acuity making him an aural critic, H.F. spurns those who ran through the streets shouting out "their Oral Predictions" and liturgical formulas (21). Solomon Eagles, a Quaker convert, was one who enthusiastically "repeated that Part of the *Liturgy* of the Church continually; *Spare us good Lord, spare they People whom thou hast redeemed with they most precious Blood*" (103). With little or no intention to communicate, Eagles uttered "dismal Cries" with "a Voice and Countenance full of Horror," typifying those who heard "Voices that never spake" (21–2). H.F.'s aural criticism partly arises from a synaesthetic lecture by a sexton, who, to discourage mere curiosity, instructs him on the affect of the burial pits. To the sexton, the view of a pit is the best "Sermon" anyone could hear: it is a "speaking Sight" and has a "Voice" and "a loud one, to call us all to Repentance" (61). Inspired by this synaesthesia, H.F. reproves blasphemers who mock with "Atheistical profane Mirth" a mourner who buries his dead (67). With the "Words" of Jeremiah 5:9 ("*Shall I not visit for these Things, saith the Lord, and shall not my Soul be avenged of such a Nation as this?*") in his "Thought," he chastises their "blaspheming Tongues" while quelling all resentment their insults might rouse (68–9). While the biblical words suggest he is an instrument of Providence, self-examination shows that his voice integrates narrative and spiritual purposes. So he repeats his wish that the sounds of suffering might move readers despite his inadequate reportage:

> I wish I could repeat the very Sound of those Groans, and of those Exclamations that I heard from some poor dying Creatures, when in the Hight of their Agonies and Distress; and that I could make him that read this hear, as I imagine I now hear them, for the Sound seems still to Ring in my Ears ... If I could but tell this Part, in such moving Accents as should alarm the very Soul of the Reader, I should rejoice that I recorded those Things, however short and imperfect. (104)

The priority he attempts to give to mediating and translating vocal sounds carries through to the end of his account in his "Saying" that the plague is controlled by the "secret invisible Hand" of God (246). While he expresses personal gratitude to God, he conveys the plague's contrary effects on the populace: "Abundance of People ... were very thankful at that time; for their Mouths were stop'd, even the Mouths of those whose Hearts were not extraordinary long affected"; the "Impression was so strong at that time, that it could not be resisted, no not by the worst of the People." But to his regret, "Salutations" in the street "giving God Thanks for their Deliverance" lasted but a short while (247). Despite his elegiac tone, he celebrates the fact that faith briefly governed public discourse since he wants his readers to perpetuate his synaesthetic sensibility.

Readers of *Colonel Jack* cannot avoid the protagonist's vocal contradictions. He is repeatedly unclear about when and how he becomes literate. He tells us he had been "taught ... to read, and write" before the age of 10 (7). Later, he reiterates that, since he "could not read" (77) and "could not Write or Read" (103), he is intent on learning "to Read and Write" (80), later reporting that, having "learn'd to Read, and Write" in Scotland, he developed a love for history books in Virginia (157). At the start, Defoe sympathetically suggests that Jack, despite his deprivations, participates in oral culture: his "natural Talent of Talking" lets him speak as purposefully as most educated people; always "upon the Inquiry" with "Seamen and Soldiers," he claims not to have "forgot any thing" they told him and sees himself as a "kind of an Historian" (10–11). Still, when Captain Jack abuses a child, Colonel Jack cannot "remember the whole Story" since it took place "too long ago" and he was "too young" (11). While the businessmen with whom he invests his criminal gains are impressed by the "Innocence of his Talk," he is "too much a Child to speak" for himself and to secure employment from them (40). Suffering "from the gross Ignorance of ... untaught Childhood," Jack is the victim of arrested development: his good instincts lead only to frustration. If a "secret Influence" impedes his "least Inclination to Swearing," he has "no Sense of Conscience" about "ill Words." His "strange original Notion" of "being a Gentleman" escapes his descriptive powers; he cannot define that "Word" (60–2). Despite his experience with business instruments, the word "Duplicate" means nothing to him (125). His nominal ignorance is aggravated by vague identity; he and his so-called brothers share a name: "we were all *Johns*, we were all *Jacks*." Left to call himself "Mr. Any-thing" (4), the Colonel does not know whether he was "ever Christen'd." Since he cannot distinguish between his "Christian-Name" and "Sir-Name," he claims to know "nothing of myself" (123). His poor sense of self and lack of religious education prevent him having interior conversations with himself. When he would give up the "curs'd Trade" of crime, he has a "kind of Wish" which he cannot call "Prayer" since he does not know "what that meant" (83).

Readers will notice that Jack's linguistic dullness relates to the defensiveness impeding him from entering fully into his story and reading himself in his narrative. As we have seen, in making restitution to the poor widow, he does not confess his guilt although his tearful face implicates him. Pretending to be only "the chief Instrument" for securing the money from the thief and conducting himself in the third person, he refuses to acknowledge his agency. When the widow blesses the thief, he merely says "*Amen*" in his heart (85–6).[51] His resistance to narrative parallels is emphasized repeatedly so that his misreading of himself serves as an ironic model for readers. It is not that he totally lacks narrative sensibility. On the plantation in Virginia, he tells his story to the headman in a "moving Tone" (118) and is "exceedingly mov'd at [the] Discourse of our Masters" to a young felon who is an "old Offender" (120–1). But he will not imagine himself into the felon's place despite acknowledging the applicability of that discourse to himself. His limited reflexivity is most evident in his relations with his "Pedagogue" and "Tutor" (160 and 169). He begins to dialogue with himself under this man's influence yet does not advance in self-examination since he will not admit the narrative parallels between them. He does not enter "any farther upon the Discourse" of the Tutor despite recognizing it "*by my own Case*" (161–2). He does not, "as is usual in such Cases, enter into any Confidence with him on my *own* Story" (167). While it is "impossible for [him] to conceal the Disorder" caused by the Tutor's confession, he keeps his own "Part close" (168). He is unresponsive to the Tutor's spiritual discourse largely because of his immaturity. Jack, "now above 30 Year old," regards himself as a "meer Youth" (157). This point is repeated: in response to the Tutor's story, Jack entertains only "some Young Infant Thoughts" although "now more than Thirty Year old" (169). Whereas the Tutor's self-exploration enables him to enjoy "a bless'd Calm of Soul, an Emblem and fore-runner of Heaven" (167), Jack finds it "a strange Relation" that leaves him with a "kind of Dead Lump behind it upon my Heart," a "heaviness on my Soul" that he cannot describe (165). Jack's narrative sensibility regresses rather than progresses because the Tutor's story makes "no Impression" on him (167), its "first Impressions" being "not deep enough" (171).

From the start of her account, Roxana is made sensitive to words and voice by oppressive marital and immoral sexual relations, the sad result being that her speech acts are negative, if not self-destructive. Abusing speech acts, she denigrates herself to preclude others doing so. Tragically, interior monologues weaken her moral identity. She rightly despises her husband because he is "so far from understanding good *English*, that he could not spell good *English*" (14). Since he speaks "Words of Course" with "no Meaning" (11), she talks to herself about his leaving when he mentions doing so: "I us'd to wish secretly, and even say in my Thoughts, *I wish you wou'd, for if you go on thus, you will starve us all*" (11–12). Such guardedness means that her discourse is rarely frank and open. When the landlord speaks to her "chearfully" and "such chearful things" are a "Cordial" to her soul, his practical help compensates for her being a widow "in the worst Sence of that desolate Word" (30). Although she internally rejects the applicability of the word "Wedding" to their relations (36), she tolerates the landlord's rationalizing "Circumlocutions" (41) which include scorn for the "usual Courtship of Words" that for him have "very little Meaning" (43). While his "Discourse" fires her "Blood" (36), she treats his persuasion to cohabit cooly because she determines to live with him by making a "Hole in my Heart" and ignoring "the Light of my own Conscience" (44). The only integrity left to her comes from refusing to commit a speech act: she will not "frame my Mouth to call him Husband," or to refer to him as "my Husband, when I was speaking of him" (45). Yet this trust in illocutionary meaning she surrenders to the prince: he sets himself above the "Language" of courtship (63), but she offers him rehearsed words of respect, abasing herself in the speech act: "I fell down at his Feet, before he could come to salute me, and with Words that I had prepar'd, full of Duty and Respect, thank'd him for his Bounty and Goodness to a poor desolate Woman" (61). Here and later, rationalization and self-seduction govern her interior monologues. The opposing vocal conduct of Amy and herself during the storm at sea strikingly evidences this. Looking "out at the Door of the Steerage," Roxana is stricken with "Horrour" at the "darkness, the fierceness of the Wind, the dreadful height of the Waves" (123). While she runs about "the Cabbin like a mad thing," being "perfectly out of her Senses" (124), Amy is distressed to think that if she drowns she will be damned and, feeling responsible for Roxana's sins as well as her own, admits to having been "the Devil's Instrument." Her cries ring in Roxana's ears as "so many Stabs into the very Soul of one in my own Case" (125–6). Yet, while Amy cries aloud "like one in an Agony," Roxana guards her feelings, uttering "but very little": "I said all these things within myself, and sigh'd, and mourn'd inwardly." This vocal reticence undermines her claim to be "very Penitent": that she "cry'd out, *tho' softly*, two or three times, *Lord have Mercy upon me*" manifests self-avoidance (126). Amy's thoughts get vent, but Roxana's do not because she is consumed with self-pity and spiritual laziness. Safe on land, Roxana finds herself "in a kind of Stupidity, I know not well what to call it," this condition imposing a distressing taciturnity on her: "I had a silent sullen kind of Grief, which cou'd not break out either in Words or Tears, and which was, therefore, much the worse to bear" (129). By this point in the narrative she has lost the ability to measure her words and listen to her own voice.

Paradoxically, however, volubility as much as taciturnity contrarily accentuates her spiritual evasiveness, as when she refuses to marry the Dutch merchant. After he removes her "Objections" to marriage, she is "oblig'd to give a new Turn" to their conversation and to "talk upon a kind of an elevated Strain" that had not been in her "Thoughts at first, at-all" (147). Her energetic proposal for extending the double standard to women recoils on her, as is revealed by the way she at first mocks and then adopts his maritime imagery. In their marriage debate, he says that, in embarking and launching out together in one "Bottom," she may "steer." She retorts that, while she may "hold the Helm" like a boy at sea, he will still "conn the Ship" and issue "orders" as the "Pilot." Accepting her "Simile," he cedes the role of pilot to her, whereat she retorts that "the Laws of Matrimony" put "Power" into husbands' hands so that he may retake the helm at any time (150–1). Roxana gives a sombre cast to the imagery in this banter after the merchant leaves and she turns again to vice:

> I call'd myself a thousand Fools, for casting myself upon a Life of Scandal and Hazard; when after the Shipwreck of Virtue, Honour, and Principle, and sailing at the utmost Risque in the stormy Seas of Crime and abominable Levity, I had a safe Harbour presented, and no Heart to cast-Anchor in it. (161–2)

Here one of Defoe's favourite allegorical metaphors emphasizes Roxana's failure to listen to her inner voice and develop a reflexive sensibility.

One morning while she is lying in bed after having taken up with a lord, a question forms itself in her mind as to why she remains a whore. This question is not framed by her own voice: it is as if "somebody had ask'd me the Question." Instead of searching her conscience, she accepts that the "Evil Spirit" has fortified her "Mind against all Reflection" with "Arguments" for whoredom (201). Since the "Devil" does not answer this question, which sounds "continually in my Head," she tries to ruminate self-critically (203). But, lacking a religious register that might address the question, she evades herself by dressing as a Quaker and mouthing Quaker dialect: "I talk'd like a Quaker too, as readily and naturally as if I had been born among them" since "my particular Plot" was "to be the more compleatly conceal'd" (213). Far from conversing with herself, she isolates herself from her speech community, compounding the difficulty of acquiring confidantes who might comfort her. When her husband is an auditor of Susan's account, Roxana must stop "counterfeiting my Voice." Again, when those close to her believe that Susan's story will divert her, not knowing it to be reflexively hers, all the evasive mother can do is say to herself that their belief is "a damn'd Lye" (286).

Complex ironies increasingly force Roxana to speak to herself in settings that dramatize her frustration and reveal her subject position to be moving inexorably towards oblivion. If a primary irony is that she cannot escape her past through narrative mediation, a secondary one is that those closest to her unknowingly rob her of verbal agency, which, with further irony, she has already stolen from herself. It is no blessing that, since her husband knows nothing of her past, he is heedless of her story and "does not enter into the thing at-all" (299). Moreover, Susan's surprise visit to the Quaker's house deepens her mother's voicelessness, as Roxana admits: "I had neither Life or Soul left in me; I was so confounded, I knew not what to do, or to say" (318). Crying to God on guessing that Amy has murdered Susan, Roxana begs for mercy even as her "Rage" at her maid is great (324). The pain Providence inflicts on her completes readers' awareness that she has betrayed her best instincts and wilfully extinguished the spark of divinity in her. That her voice disappears invites readers to commune with Defoe's text and to recognize that a reciprocally secular and religious interpretation may "improve" her life. For Roxana's narrative shows that the fable is the moral: unfinished, it signifies her social and spiritual inadequacies; embodied in murdered Susan, it wields a paradoxically reflexive mediation. Roxana wants her story closed to the world in which she exists even as she wants it broadcast to the world outside her own storytelling. She hides in her own story to avoid knowing herself but in so doing exposes herself. That she incapacitates her own voice gives the narrative a transcendent dialectic with which readers may sympathetically and morally converse.

******

This study privileges textual explication and rhetorical analysis to show that Defoe was a more powerfully expressive writer and more original fabulist than has been acknowledged. A thoughtful practitioner with the illocutionary and aesthetic aspects of the English language, he was also an accomplished stylist. Grounding itself in his appreciation of how words work, this study analyses motifs, allusions, and images along with verbal and conceptual ironies that are to be found throughout his non-fictional and fictional corpus. Furthermore, by taking his fictions at several reprises and putting them in several literary, historical, and philosophical contexts, it demonstrates that, since he never limited himself to singular viewpoints, he affords readers a pleasingly complex responsiveness. Concentration on his semantic sensibility helps to elicit and accentuate his trust that language entails personal, cognitive, and spiritual conduct in and beyond social contexts. His approach to narrative was informed by the functionality of rhetorical and conceptual contraries, by an emphasis on reflexivity and imagination more than on rationalism and empiricism, and by aesthetic explorations of voice, sound, and music. These topical areas give scope to speculations on the relative contributions that the conscious and unconscious mind makes to Defoe's sense of the narrative polarities integrating secular learning and spiritual awareness.

In addition to standing up to the interdisciplinary insights of discourse analysis, semiotics, the new rhetoric, and twentieth-century theology, Defoe's texts are the richer when viewed through the lenses of cultural anthropology and cognitive psychology, as my text and notes have earlier suggested. Those disciplines were advanced by Jaynes's groundbreaking work on the pre-conscious operations of the bicameral mind and on the evolution of consciousness.[52] One premise of Jaynes's theory is that consciousness evolved after civilization and its institutions displaced the gods and divine absolutism. Another premise is that the bicameral mind still exercises residual functions verifiable by experiments in brain structure and unusual forms of introspection and that its interior dialogues exist in dialectical tension with modern consciousness. Jaynes's theory approaches the nature of consciousness in terms of recursiveness and reflexivity, probing what the consciousness of consciousness is as opposed to what common sense assumes it to be. Jaynes denies that consciousness is a mental space inhabited by sensations and ideas. Nor can it, according to him, be an epiphenomenon given the differences between it and reactivity to the world: "we are continually reacting to things in ways that have no phenomenal component in consciousness" since consciousness plays a smaller part in our lives than we are conscious of. To Jaynes, the continuity of consciousness is an illusion. Moreover, the conscious memory does not store up sensory images. Defoe's contrarian intuitions and understandings of discourse, narrative, and selfhood are more comprehensible in the light of Jaynes's claim that conscious retrospection, often taken to be the basis of autobiography, involves less the retrieval of images of sensation than of previous objects of consciousness. Looking back into memory involves imagining how others view one's person. Jaynes opposes the notion that consciousness has a cranial location where concepts reside. Showing that there is no necessary relation between concepts and consciousness, he argues that the former usually do not cooperate with the latter.

Denying that conscious experience is the substrate of learning and arguing that thinking neither functions in, nor depends on, consciousness, Jaynes concludes that "in reality, consciousness has no location whatever except as we imagine it." Consequently, metaphor is "the very constitutive ground of language" and, since there is nothing in immediate experience that can be likened to immediate experience, we cannot understand consciousness in the same way that we understand things of which we are conscious. Rather, "consciousness is the work of lexical metaphor."[53] Being conscious entails the imaginative placing of the self at the centre of one's story, a placing which Jaynes labels "narrativization." Sound, "a very special modality," because "the least controllable of all sense modalities," is instrumental to this process. Listening to one's own voice in narrativization obliges acceptance of plural voices and openness to the bicameral mind that are both evident in ancient myth as well as being accessible to normal contemporary people. Auditory hallucinations, he adds, "must have some innate structure in the nervous system underlying them," for people "who have been profoundly deaf since birth or very early childhood ... can – somehow – experience auditory hallucinations."[54] He sums up the ongoing evolution of cognition and imagination thus:

> The most obvious and important carry-over from the previous mentality is thus our religious heritage in all its labyrinthine beauty and variety of forms. The overwhelming importance of religion both in general world history and in the history of the average world individual is of course very clear from any objective standpoint, even though a scientific view of man often seems embarrassed at acknowledging this most obvious fact. For in spite of all that rationalist materialist science has implied since the Scientific Revolution, mankind as a whole has not, does not, and perhaps cannot relinquish his fascination with some human type of relationship to a greater and wholly other, some *mysterium tremendum* with powers and intelligences beyond all left hemispheric categories, something necessarily indefinite and unclear, to be approached and felt in awe and wonder and almost speechless worship, rather than in clear conception, something that for modern religious people communicates in truths of feeling, rather than in what can be verbalized by the left hemisphere, and so what in our time can be more truly felt when least named, a patterning of self and numinous other from which, in times of our darkest distress, *none* of us can escape – even as the infinitely milder distress of decision-making brought out that relationship three millenia ago.[55]

Defoe intuited much of what Jaynes and other cultural anthropologists and cognitive psychologists have been exploring in the last forty years. He sensed that writing, fictional and non-fictional, must draw on dialectical insights since he was fundamentally moved by the realization that, were there no problems in relating secular and religious experience, there would be little point to authorship. He also realized that how we classify the material world and human conduct involves deconstructing perceptual categories and moral platitudes if we want to be open to the plenitude of creation and human nature. A major aspect of this plenitude is the plurality of selfhood. That is why his first-person autobiographical texts exploit rather than close the gaps between characters and narrators, why his works do not harmonize the external and internal voices of individuals. His people are usually solitary. Despite acknowledging their need for sociability, they are often anti-social. They try, without much success, to imagine the consciousness of others and to put themselves into the mental spaces of others. They do not readily see others in themselves or take others to be models for themselves. Often they observe, and sometimes acknowledge, the pluralities of selfhood. Their voices attest to bicameral mentality. Paradoxically, they are most fully themselves when they admit to the circumstantial, cognitive, and spiritual stresses on selfhood. They are aware that consciousness involves the abeyance of consciousness. Locke to the contrary, their waking minds are not always conscious and do not always contain memorable perceptual images and cognitive reflections. Embodying the principle that the rational mind, far from being absolute, is subject to contingency, Defoe's characters and narrators show how the imagination is the substrate of consciousness and how the faculties of reason and imagination may be conceived of dialectically, given their creator's trust that the briefest, most evanescent visions may enable individuals to sense the presence of the divine together with their own spiritual vitality.

A summary illustration of the relevance of the bicameral mind to Defoe is afforded by Crusoe in the final pages of *Farther Adventures*. As his travels end, his consciousness of others is limited. In narrativizing himself, his discourse is unsteady. He does not test his imagination nor care how others imagine him. Take his account of the pained voices of "the *Cochinesses*" who utter

> such a Howling and Crying, that I never heard a worse Noise, and indeed nothing like it; for it is worth observing, That tho' Pain naturally makes all People cry out, yet every Nation has a particular Way of Exclamation, and make Noises as different from one another, as their Speech; I cannot give the Noise, these Creatures made, a better Name than Howling, nor a Name more proper to the Tone of it. (270)

Despite connecting phonetic and phonemic systems and accepting that sound is an evolutionary precursor to articulation, he recoils from the natives' acoustic modes. Earlier he admits that his poor management of his island was due to restless pretensions and slack linguistic performance:

> I was possest with a wandring Spirit, scorn'd all Advantages, I pleased my self with being the Patron of those People I placed there, and doing for them in a kind of haughty majestick Way, like an old Patriarchal Monarch; providing for them, as if I had been Father of the whole Family, as well as of the Plantation: But I never so much as pretended to plant in the Name of any Government or Nation, or to acknowledge any Prince, or to call my People Subjects to any one nation more than another; nay, I never so much as gave the Place a Name. (217–18)

If resistance to his crew's viciousness towards aboriginal people leads to his being abandoned in Bengal, he refuses to deliberate over his unwarranted iconoclasm, when in disgust with the idolatry of pagans in the "*Muscovite* Dominions," with "their Stupidity and brutish Worship of a Hobgoblin," he does not hesitate to interrupt their sacrificial ceremony and smash their idol, causing "a most hideous Outcry and Howling": in their village his pretension to uphold the "reasonable Soul" against the prostration of degenerate humans to "a frightful Nothing" is motivated by racist repulsion, not principle (328–31). His interview with the prince, an exile from "the Czar of *Muscovy*," shows how little he listens to himself and others. To the otherworldly prince, "the true Greatness of Life" is "to be Master of ourselves"; "the Height of human Wisdom" is "to bring our Tempers down to our Circumstances; and to make a Calm within, under the Weight of the greatest Scorns without" (351). Crusoe regards the prince as a "truly great Man" for being "not a Monarch only, but a great Conqueror" of himself since "a little Time and Consideration had made him look into himself, as well as round him to things without" (352–3). Yet Crusoe unthinkingly offers to be "an Instrument to procure the Escape of this excellent Person." With a great "Struggle of his Soul" and true gentility, the prince rebuffs the offer to be taken to England, contrarian responsiveness making him a surrogate for readers and perhaps for Defoe:

> Dear Sir, let me remain in this blessed Confinement, banish'd from the Crimes of Life, rather than purchase a Shew of Freedom, at the Expence of the Liberty of my Reason, and at the Expence of the future Happiness which now I have in my View, but shall then, I fear, quickly lose Sight of; for I am but Flesh, a Man, a meer Man, have Passions and Affections as likely to possess and overthrow me as any Man: O be not my Friend and my Tempter both together! (360)[56]

That the prince's sensibility relishes oxymoron and paradox, resists social and political illusion, practises a self-abnegating awareness of human fallibility, and maturely commits itself to spiritual preparation seems simply yet provocatively to be beyond Crusoe for the benefit of readers.

******

This study has endeavoured to demonstrate that Defoe was a genuine artist in words and that his literary achievements arise out of a dialectical awareness that fosters consciously and conscientiously the reciprocity of traditional and progressive authorial modes. Discarding the long-standing view that his voluminous output was the work of a mercenary hack whose success was fortuitous, its argument contends that his linguistic, metaphysical, and literary practices challenged empirical, materialist, and rationalist ideologies in order that both his non-fiction and his fiction might fully engage the hearts, minds, and imaginations of readers. Sharing Joseph Addison's and Richard Steele's wish to remedy the social fragmentation effected by the Civil War and its aftermath in the late seventeenth century, Defoe voiced contrary viewpoints on the world, society, and human nature which, in provoking the deepest personal responses in readers, might renew the reading public's sense of itself. Since his "imaginary" seems opaque to standard formal notions of literary realism, *Daniel Defoe: Contrarian* applies the methods of discourse analysis to unfold the experimental pluralism of his expository and narrative stances, defining and illustrating his "polarity thinking" so as to explicate his protean and many-sided commitment to reader response. Ranging over scores of his works, my chapters respect his lexical and semantic habits, acknowledge his rhetorical and aesthetic sensibility, trace in detail his theological and philosophical subtlety, and explain how the challenging tensions between his explicit and covert allusiveness immerses personas and narrators into biblical hermeneutics. The chapters' trajectory also takes in Defoe's satirical ventriloquism along with the verbal, situational, and dramatic ironies of his pamphlets (especially those exposing developments in political administration that threatened to renounce the principles of the Glorious Revolution and the Act of Settlement). It also takes in both his fictional preoccupation with illusions of power and his conceptual attempts to reconcile gender equality with social hierarchy. The final chapter, in synthesizing the first seven, probes deeply into his experimental arguments through images, showing that they promote a mental outlook that involves moral compassion with spiritual vision. More theoretically, this chapter also shows that Defoe's contrarian outlook upholds a view of consciousness that acknowledges the brain's bicameral structure and that offers insights into synaesthesia and the music of language which suggests how cognitive science might be applied to future explorations into narrative art.

While Joyce and Woolf, as we recalled, admired Defoe's mythic vision, the status of his works as cultural and global icons may be further clarified by authors who have both appropriated and displaced narrative motifs in *Robinson Crusoe*. Their ideological reasons for doing so not only confirm that literary tradition has found Defoe well worth arguing with but also heighten his texts' experimental functions, which have too often been subjected to economic, sociological, and philosophical systematization. The following coda concerning appropriations of *Robinson Crusoe* suggests ways in which the critical tenets employed in this study may be extended to reach more widely into Defoe's contributions to the development of narrative fiction.

In 1725 at Boston, the Reverend John Barnard published *Ashton's Memorial: An History of the Strange Adventures, and Signal Deliverances, of Mr. Philip Ashton*. This spiritual biography tells of a fisherman who avoids serving as a pirate under Edward Low by fleeing to Roatan, an uninhabited island in the Bay of Honduras, where he survives for nine months. Barnard heightens Providence's agency by denying Ashton the marginal comforts enjoyed by Crusoe: Ashton has scanty clothes and no shoes; he has no iron from which to make weapons or tools; he has no shovel for digging animal traps; he learns to light a fire only when he is so weak that he spends most of his time in prayer; he has no fishing equipment but lives on raw turtle eggs. He lacks the consolations of discourse since "the Parrots here had not been taught to Speak." Further unlike Crusoe, while he has his parents' consent to become a sailor, he has no Bible on the island. Clearly, Barnard works over against Defoe's spiritual autobiography in order single-mindedly to promote Providence as the agent which saves Ashton from pirates, Spaniards, beasts of the field, and monsters of the sea.[57]

Three modern novelists similarly appropriate Crusoe's story for doctrinaire reasons. In Muriel Spark's *Robinson*, the third-person narrator, January Marlow, is a chatty Roman Catholic who both admires and dislikes Robinson. Having bought his island in the mid-Atlantic where he cultivates pomegranates, he is a would-be recluse. Educated in a Catholic seminary yet having refused ordination, he writes tracts against Marian theology. No gardener, no planter of food crops, and no builder of his environment, he guards his detachment from the victims of a plane crash by staging his own death, leading his temporary guests to suspect one another of his murder. That he drinks fine brandy, smokes cigarettes, and owns an art collection and excellent library of classics makes him both a modern consumer and an isolationist connoisseur. Michel Tournier's *Vendredi ou les limbes du Pacifique* also appropriates Defoe's narrative to defy his myth making with regard to Crusoe. Not allowing Crusoe to leave the island, Tournier elaborates the confusions with which Defoe confronts his protagonist through the island's intractable natural environment. Consequently, Tournier's Crusoe is so oppressed by psychological and metaphysical observations of his densely textured surroundings that he loses himself in them. In isolating him from people, Tournier makes Crusoe's surroundings dehumanize him. He gradually loses all sense of history and personal origins because nature is omnipotent. If he relies closely on the Bible in order to build a boat, his constructive asceticism turns out to be futile, Tournier emphasizing Crusoe's pointless efforts and miscalculations far more single-mindedly than Defoe. For Tournier, Crusoe's island fantasy requires the exposition of the corrosive and destructive effects of solitude, the dismantling of the scaffold of habits and manners that Crusoe has imported to the island. J.M. Coetzee's *Foe* also deconstructs *Robinson Crusoe* by incorporating characters from *Moll Flanders, Colonel Jack,* and *Roxana,* as well as appropriating episodes from Defoe's life. *Foe* denies the narrative uniqueness of Defoe's fictions and defies generic boundaries between fiction and non-fiction in order to emphasize metafictional recursiveness. As in Spark and Tournier, Coetzee gives far more details about the island's natural history than Defoe. Coetzee's Cruso, seen from the viewpoint of Susan Barton (in *Roxana* the daughter tracking her mother), who is castaway on the island, not only does not want to build a boat to escape but is indifferent to salvation. There are no cedars on his island. Nor does he write a journal or keep a calendar. Like Defoe's Crusoe, Cruso listens to his own voice but distractedly surrenders his agency to Susan, who seeks tools from the wreck. Once Crusoe is killed off, Susan becomes the narrative cynosure as she badgers Foe to write the island story. But he is elusive as well as mercenary, for, as readers will know, the information she supposedly passes to him about daily life in Brazil never finds its way into Defoe's *Robinson Crusoe.*

Interestingly, given the topics of my final chapter, Coetzee presents Foe as one who thinks about conversation as a species of music and about words existing apart from speech. Still, Coetzee's *Foe* probably reflects this author's view that readers do not experience *Robinson Crusoe* as "the literary performance of an author."[58]

However, nineteenth-century novelists thought otherwise about *Robinson Crusoe* as a source of literary and cultural power. In *Vanity Fair*, when William Makepeace Thackeray criticizes male heroism and the moral self-effacement inspired by fantasy, he has William Dobbin, his chief force for domestic and social good, mistakenly abase himself to George Osborne as his "valet, his dog, his man Friday." In George Meredith's *The Egoist*, perhaps the century's most aesthetically refined novel, *Robinson Crusoe* features in a scene the intimacy of which prefigures the coming together of the most sympathetic characters. The mischievous young Crossjay judges Vernon Whitford's eyes in terms of "Robinson Crusoe's old goat in the cavern," and Clara Middleton, in the same scene, fends off for the moment her susceptibility to Whitford by "fixing her mind on Robinson Crusoe's old goat in the recess of the cavern." However, Charles Dickens would perhaps most have admired the Russian prince's appeal to Crusoe, judging from the fact that when the industrial workers in *Hard Times* visit the Coketown library, they take "De Foe to their bosoms, instead of Euclid." Dickens saw Defoe as an antidote to the statistical facts and scientific positivism which stifle the imagination and contort the human psyche. From an early age, he admired Defoe, approving of his non-fiction as well as his fiction. When composing *Oliver Twist* and absorbed in the process of depicting the terrible Fagin with charity, he rejoiced at having purchased *The Political History of the Devil*. To him, this was a "capital work" because of its witty presentation of the contrary relations of good and evil.[59]

Notes

1. Contraries: Linguistic, Narrative, and Theological

1 *The Life and Strange Surprizing Adventures of Robinson Crusoe of York, Mariner*, ed. J. Donald Crowley (London: Oxford University Press, 1976), 139. Subsequent references are to this edition, unless otherwise specified. Henceforth its title is abbreviated to *Robinson Crusoe*. Page references to Defoe's major fictions are given parenthetically in the text while citations of secondary works appear in notes.

2 For Scott's views on Defoe and belief that Defoe's vulgar language possesses an "an air of truth or probability" that gives his writing "an appearance of REALITY" and "an air of perfect veracity," see Rogers 1972: 67, 70–2, and 75. To Watt, "particularity of description has always been considered typical of the narrative manner of *Robinson Crusoe*" (1963: 17). In "Defoe's Theory of Fiction," Novak, claiming that Defoe was eager to "describe 'things' and events with detailed accuracy," traces Defoe's realism to the influence of Locke, calling him a "disciple of Locke" (1964: 659, 662). Granted that Novak has since modified this claim (see note 4), I contend throughout this study that Defoe resisted Lockean epistemology.

3 On the linguistic, semantic, and stylistic resources of Defoe's narrative dialectic, see Merrett 1980: 67–87, Merrett 1989, and Merrett 2004b: 28–34. Furbank and Owens call Defoe's sentences and paragraphs "improvisatory," claiming that his "many" styles are governed by "a common project." His "sentence-construction," marked by "interpolations" and "endless extension," is "expressive of his attitude to narration and to writing generally" (1988: 129–33). For a summary of how Defoe applies his "protean" voices

when writing in his own person, ironically imitating other persons, and creating personas in his fiction, see James 1972: 255–9.

4 Johns compellingly justifies a historical approach to reading: "Reading is a deceptively simple practice. It can seem so obvious and self-evident an activity that the idea of its having a history appears bizarre. But it is becoming increasingly clear that people in the past and of other cultures do not read in anything that might unproblematically be called the same way as us. Reading shares this characteristic with other, more manual skills the historical dimensions of which have also been recently been identified. The historicizing of reading has particularly important implications, however, for the simple reason that it is through reading that documents of all kinds are put to use and thereby produce historical effects. The history of reading is devoted to exploring this theme. It is now a flourishing field. A wealth of work exists showing that if reading is considered as a practice that, like such other practices, changes across time and space, then useful insights may follow about the character of personal, political, and social knowledge" (1998: 384). Blewett's stress on ironic and artistic uses of realism opposes the conventional view that Defoe was preoccupied with "straightforward and unrelieved verisimilitude" (1979: 18); Richetti sees Defoe as embodying in his narratives an intelligent sense of "complex reality" that fuses "observed fact" and "extravagant fantasy" (1975: 6 and 18); Novak claims that, far from inventing "circumstantial realism," Defoe makes it serve "abstract ideas, myth, and fantasy" (1983: 8–9).

5 Brown (1971) emphasizes Defoe's exploration of narrative through narrators' opposing impulses to conceal and reveal; Alkon (1979), working with concepts of reader-response criticism, shows how Defoe's fictions alter readers' textual perceptions and memories; Boardman argues that, since Defoe's narratives "lack single principles of being" and "fit no prescriptive categories," he creates the "possibilities for narrative as he goes along" (1983: 2 and 12).

6 Austin 1965: 6 and 13; Iser 1978a: 55–6; Pratt 1977: 23, 69, 81, 87, and 90–1. For the view that "fictional narrative is unique in its potential for creating a self-enclosed universe ruled by formal patterns that are ruled out in all other orders of discourse," see Cohn 1999: vi. The subtlety of Cohn's perspective appears in the following statement: "When we speak of the nonreferentiality of fiction, we do not mean that it *can* not refer to the real world outside the text, but that it *need* not refer to it. But beyond this, the adjective of my definitional phrase also signifies that fiction is subject to two closely interrelated distinguishing features: (1) its references to the world outside

the text are not bound to accuracy; and (2) it does not refer *exclusively* to the real world outside the text" (1999: 15).

7 Pratt's views are upheld by Jones 1993: 641.

8 Fowler 1981: 55–6; Eagleton 1983: 125.

9 Stout 1993: 189.

10 Scholes 1982: 14, 76; Brown 1984: 11.

11 For a basic account of polysemy, see McArthur 1992: 795. For a comprehensive account, see Ullman 1964: 159–82.

12 Describing Defoe's style as subjective, Starr says that he renders "things and events ... *as* perceived, as in some sense transformed and recreated in the image of the narrator" (1974: 281).

13 On the concept of "speech community," see Black 1968: 24–5.

14 On the structure of vocabulary, see Ullmann 1964: 236–58. On structural aspects of etymology, see Waldron 1967: 115–28.

15 Exodus 15:2 contains the first reference in the OT to "habitation." See Cruden ([1738, 1832] n.d.), for the many other references to this word.

16 Seidel links Crusoe's fluctuating terms for the island and his abodes to "the double-entry accounting that transvalues experience" (Seidel 1986: 21).

17 This ambivalence makes it hard to accept, without qualification, Schonhorn's view that *Robinson Crusoe* expounds the political theory of the warrior-king: "For Defoe it is not the mild law of nature but the violent law of arms that is the foundation of kingship and rule" (1991: 154).

18 On the broadening and narrowing of sense and on melioration and pejoration, see Waldron 1967: 141–61.

19 On Crusoe's political roles, see chapter 6, page 175–7, in this volume.

20 Defoe's characters and narrators try to be myth-makers who hold together cyclical and linear senses of time. Constantly searching for origins, they would remake their worlds. On anthropological views of cosmogony, see Eliade 1965 and 1968.

21 *The Life, Adventures, and Pyracies, of the Famous Captain Singleton*, ed. Shiv K. Kumar (London: Oxford, 1969). Subsequent references are to this edition.

22 Waldron brilliantly accounts for how "semantic vagueness" creates discourse by adapting "traditional categories to changes in circumstances or changes in thought" (1967: 145–56).

23 To keep a journal entails scrutinizing the self and soul. To avoid keeping a journal or to keep one sporadically signifies moral laxity. Defoe heightens this signification by making "journal" a metonym for existence. On his exploitation of spiritual autobiography and emblematic imagination, see Starr (1965) and Hunter (1966). Crusoe will not return home after his first

voyage like "a true repenting Prodigal." He compounds his evasiveness by declining, after the second voyage, to prove his father an exemplary biblical type, an "Emblem of our Blessed Saviour's Parable," who would have killed "the fatted Calf" for him (Luke 15:23; *Robinson Crusoe* 8 and 14).

24 In his first chapter, "Realism and the Novel Form," Watt argues that fictional realism rejects traditional literary principles (1963: 9–35). The dialectic which shapes Defoe's relation of words to things and his depiction of identity questions Watt's positivism. Curtis stresses the "contradictory drives" in Defoe's consciousness to qualify reductive attitudes like Watt's (1984: 7–15).

25 *A Journal of the Plague Year*, ed. Louis Landa (London: Oxford, 1969). All references are to this edition, unless otherwise specified.

26 *Roxana*, ed. Jane Jack (London: Oxford, 1964). All references are to this edition, unless otherwise specified. Blewett provides an excellent account of the double-time scheme in *Roxana* (1979: 121–7). See also Blewett's edition of *Roxana* (1982: 13–14).

27 Hume argues convincingly that the abrupt ending of the novel is structurally controlled to the extent that it is symbolically incomplete (1970: 489–90).

28 In *The King of Pirates* (London: A. Bettesworth, C. King, J. Brotherton, W. Meadows, and W. Chetwood, 1719), Defoe cuts away accretions to Avery's exploits, stripping out all the "*romantick, improbable, and impossible Parts*" (vi). All references are to this edition. Novak accepts Defoe's authorship of this work (2001: 580–3), but Furbank and Owens doubt it (1994: 122). On Defoe's further disparagement of Avery's vain aspirations for "the Dignity of a King" and to be the Founder of a new Monarchy, see *A General History of the Pyrates*, ed. Manuel Schonhorn (Mineola, NY: Dover, 1999), 49. All references are to this edition. On Defoe's tendency to turn pirates' mythical success back on society, see *Review* 4, no. 107 (Saturday, 18 October 1707): 425: "it would make a sad Chasm on the *Exchange* of *London*, if all the Pyrates should be taken away from among the Merchants there." This and subsequent references to Defoe's major newspaper are to: *Review*, 9 vols, 19 Feb. 1704–11 June 1713, ed. Arthur Wellesley Secord, 22 vols. (New York: Columbia University Press, 1938. Reprint. New York: AMS Press, 1965).

29 *The Fortunes and Misfortunes of the Famous Moll Flanders*, ed. G.A. Starr (London: Oxford, 1976). All references are to this edition, unless otherwise specified.

30 *Roxana* 247, 206, and 291.

31 *The History and Remarkable Life of the Truly Honourable Col. Jacque Commonly Call'd Col. Jack*, ed. Samuel Holt Monk (London: Oxford, 1965), 250 and

264. All references to this work, abbreviated to *Colonel Jack*, are to this edition. That the rebels do not follow Jack's advice exposes their strategic ignorance and justifies Jack's abandonment of them. Although Furbank and Owens (1994: 92–3) believe that Defoe was likely not the author of *The Annals of King George, Year the Second* (London: A. Bell, W. Taylor, and J. Baker, 1716), as has been supposed, Defoe heightens the propagandistic value of Colonel Jack's time with the rebels by following very closely pages 135 to 142 of this work. On Jack's self-destructive marital attitudes, see Merrett 1986: 13–15.

32 On Defoe's approval of the Quarantine Act of 12 February 1722, see Lee 1969: II, 407–10. In *Applebee's Journal*, Defoe inimitably assails the self-interest of merchants opposed to the act. See also Landa, *A Journal of the Plague Year* xiv.

33 To Brown, "the gift of self is as 'symbolic' as the sacrificial death. Self will continue to reassert itself and be lost consequently in distraction. For it is Defoe's insight that the essential characteristic of a symbolic death is that it is only symbolic and must be repeated *endlessly*" (1971: 579).

34 On the various distances between the "fallible or unreliable narrator and the implied author who carries the reader with him in judging the narrator," see Booth: 1961 158–9. In Booth's terms a narrator is more or less reliable as he or she "speaks for or acts in accordance with the norms" of a work. Hence, the moral stances of narrators and implied authors are important critically.

35 Faller 1993: 103–4.

36 Defoe will have noticed that Dampier's travel writing used polysemy for narrative amplification. Here are a few examples from *Memoirs of a Buccaneer: Dampier's New Voyage Round the World, 1697* (Mineola, NY: Dover [1968] 2007): "Bumkins, or Vessels" (11); "Barbecu's or Frames of Sticks" (23); "*La Sounds* Key or Island" (25); "Staff, Pole, or Shandle"and "Tholes or Pegs" (33); "Plantation or Cacao-Walk" (51); "house or Hut … Couch or Barbecu of Sticks" (67). Like Defoe's personas, Dampier cannot avoid indeterminacy, e.g., "At length it was concluded to go to a Town, the Name of which I have forgot" (29). Defoe clearly relied on Dampier for ethnographic scenes: that Robin the Moskito Indian throws himself on his face at the feet of his brother Moskito man in an "Interview" that is "exceedingly affectionate" on both sides (67) will remind us of the scene when Friday discovers his father among potential victims of the cannibals (*Robinson Crusoe* 238).

37 These phrases denote a ship's "rigging" and maritime corporal punishment or "whipping." For an extended analysis of Defoe's maritime imagery, see chapter 8, page 254–8, in this volume.

38 Often mixing pronouns in his fiction, he justifies this solecism in the *Review* as an instrument of satire when the Scandalous Club, addressing him as "this Dogmatick Gentleman," resolves

> That whereas he speaks in the First Person Singular, with an *I BELIEVE,* in the very first Articles of his Paper, and jumps into Plurality of Persons, with a *WE MAY ENDEAVOUR* in the very same Page, the Society desires to know what kind of *Singular-Plural-Ungrammatical Monster* we are to understand him to be, and hopes he will unmask himself in his next?

The Club advises him not to keep his promise to write without respect for "Persons or Powers" unless he is prepared for "Martyrdom." It tells him "to ask the Worlds Pardon" for making such a rash promise "or else as my Lord *Rochester* said of *Bedlam, Newgate hath many Mansions*" (1, no. 46 [Saturday, 12 August 1704]: 200). For a fine account of oscillating first-person and third-person singular pronouns that convey Colonel Jack's "duplicity" and dissociated self as he tries to make reparation to a poor widow whom he has robbed yet to whom he cannot admit his criminality, see Faller 1993: 213–14, and chapter 8, note 51, in this volume.

39 *Robinson Crusoe* 24–32 and *Colonel Jack* 96–101.

40 *Robinson Crusoe* 221 and *Colonel Jack* 171.

41 *Robinson Crusoe* 70–2. For a compelling account of how Crusoe's journal heightens readers' awareness, see Alkon 1979: 160–6. Defoe exploits grammatical ambivalence in *A Journal of the Plague Year*: when the Saddler-narrator uses singular and plural first-person pronouns, Defoe dissolves distinctions between the private and public origins of story.

42 *Roxana* 12 and 94.

43 *Colonel Jack* 207 and 263.

44 For Defoe's motif of the failure to keep a journal or to write travel accounts, see *Captain Singleton* 3, 4, and 39; *Moll Flanders* 85; and *Roxana* 103.

45 "One of the common objections to much of Defoe's fiction is that it is apparently disorganized or accords with no established structure or genre. And yet its structure surely reflects the inchoate nature of the experience being recounted: mapped and unmapped, known and unfamiliar, wondrous and horrific" (Chambers 1996: 61).

46 As Faller so nicely puts it, "Defoe's texts work at heightening and shaping their readers' sense of themselves and where they themselves stand" (1993: 46).

47 On Heraclitus's "doctrine of mingling opposites," see Russell 1961: 62. Russell finds "the germ of Hegel's philosophy" in Heraclitus's statement that "it is the opposite which is good for us." I am indebted to Thorslev's account of "polarity thinking" (1989: 103–6). Explaining how dialectical logic allows one to transcend the law of contradiction, Thorslev gives a fine account of the tradition of "'reasoning' from polar opposites toward a new and higher synthesis" (1984: 67–78). In a manner hostile to dialectical and religious criticism, Stamm maintains that Defoe's creative impulses and Puritanism were at odds, that he was a deist without knowing it, that he compromised orthodox dogmas by secularizing them, that he was incapable of true religious experience, and that he imposed moralistic schemes upon his fiction that are unrelated to the action (1936: 225, 228–9, 231, 243). Watt finds Stamm's "account of Defoe's religious position" to be "the most complete" (1963: 88). To Watt, the "heritage of Puritanism is demonstrably too weak to supply" continuous and controlling patterns in Defoe's fiction. The "relative impotence of religion" in his novels "suggests not insincerity but the profound secularization of his outlook." Defoe, Watt continues, is reluctant "to consider the extent to which spiritual and material values may be opposed" (1963: 83–6). The most ungrounded antagonism to Defoe's religion is found in Bastian's claim that he was not a "truly religious man at all" and that the "ostensibly religious themes" of his late works strike moderns as "little more than unctuous and sanctimonious religiosity" (1981: 87). Following Watt, Boardman finds religion an "explanatorily inadequate paradigm" for Defoe's narrative practices (1983: 13). This study, by contrast, follows in the footsteps of Starr and Hunter. Starr's account of spiritual autobiography argues that "the leading religious ideas in Defoe's fiction were in fact commonplaces of the English Protestant tradition, not merely crotchets of his much-discussed Dissenting milieu" (1965: xi). Hunter, after considering that Defoe's library probably contained "many theological and devotional books," provides brilliant accounts of the Puritan "commitment to metaphor" and to typology that apply to Defoe (1966: 98–100 and 122). As indicated in my Preface, I seek to respond to Hunter's call for "students of Defoe" to work out how he sought audiences and matched them up "with particular thematic and cultural concerns" and to explicate his "liberally complex Dissent" (2000: 233 and 237).

48 Faller 1993: 122.

49 *Due Preparations for the Plague, As Well for Soul as Body* (London: E. Matthews and J. Batley, 1722), 245. All references to this work are to this edition unless otherwise stated.

50 *The Free-Holders Plea against Stock-Jobbing Elections of Parliament Men,* 2nd ed. (London, 1701). All references are to this edition.
51 *The Secret History of State Intrigues in the Management of the Scepter, In the Late Reign* (London: S. Keimer, 1715), 30–1. Claiming this work to be Defoe's, Schonhorn calls it "the most complete and most exhaustive diagnosis of the failure of monarchy in his time" (1991: 137). Novak sees the work as evidence of Defoe's protean and strategic viewpoints (2001: 465 and 467–8)
52 *The Conduct of Christians Made the Sport of Infidels* (London: S. Baker, 1717), 36. All references are to this edition. Cf. Novak 2001: 522–3.
53 *The Lay-Man's Sermon upon the Late Storm* ([London], 1704), 21. All references are to this edition. In applying "dialectic" to Defoe's unsuccessful attempt to persuade fellow Presbyterians to desist from occasional conformity, Trent limits the term to irreconcilable ideas in his concern to be judgmental: he finds Defoe's moral nature "warped" and stresses that political duplicity ruined a "remarkable character" (1971: 29 and 43–4).
54 Whateley 1963: 48–50 and 102–3; Aristotle 1926: 265–73. Corbett gives a modern differentiation between "contraries" and "contradictions": contradiction involves things that differ in kind, whereas contraries "involve opposite or incompatible things of the same kind" (1971: 129–32).
55 On the logic of ordinary conversation, see Pinker on Paul Grice's philosophy (2007: 376–9).
56 *Advice to All Parties. By the Author of* The True-born English-man (London: Benj. Bragg, 1705), 3. All citations are to this edition.
57 Cf. "Contraries Illustrate, said the Author of this, when he saw how Exactly the Inverted Sense of the *Memorial,* suits the Circumstances of the Party, in whose Name it was wrote": *Review* 2, no. 65 (Thursday, 2 August 1705): 261.
58 *Review* 2, no. 117 (Tuesday, 4 December 1705): 468.
59 *Review* 2, no. 67 (Tuesday, 7 August 1705): 269.
60 *Review* 3, no. 39 (Saturday, 30 March 1706): 154.
61 In *The True-Born Englishman,* Defoe more than idealizes King William as a Christian hero; he elevates him to a figurative apotheosis (Merrett 2004b: 35).
62 In reporting to Robert Harley his observations of debates in Scotland about the Union, Defoe was less positive in his contraries: members of the Church of Scotland "are the Wisest weak men, The Falsest honest men, and the steadyest Unsettled people" he has ever met, since "There is an Entire Harmony in This Country Consisting in Universall Discords": *The Letters of Daniel Defoe,* ed. George Harris Healey (Oxford: Clarendon, 1953. Reprint. Oxford: Oxford University Press, 1969), 133 and 137.

63 *Review* 4, no. 16 (Tuesday, 18 March 1707): 62; and 4, no. 14 (Thursday, 13 March 1707): 54.

64 *Review* 4, no. 15 (Saturday, 15 March 1707): 58.

65 *Of Dramatic Poesy: An Essay* (1668) in Dryden 1962: I, 59. Earlier in the essay, Neander defends mixing genres and mingling mirth and seriousness since the "old rule of logic" is convincing on the topic "that contraries, when placed near, set off each other" (I, 58). Defoe's example is taken from *The Complete English Tradesman in Familiar Letters*, 2 vols., reprint of 2nd ed. of 1727 (New York: Augustus M. Kelley, 1969), II, i, 74. All references to this work are to this edition. In his dictionary Johnson illustrates the meaning of contraries by referring to Thomas Southerne's dramatic version of *Oronooko* (1696): "Honour should be concern'd in honour's cause; / That is not to be cur'd by *contraries*, / As bodies are, whose health is often drawn / From rankest poisons." See also Harcourt in *The Country Wife* (1675): "Most Men are the contraries to that they wou'd seem; your bully you see, is a Coward with a long Sword; the little humbly fawning Physician with his Ebony can, is he that destroys Men" (Wycherley 1966: 266).

66 *Review* 4, no. 28 (Tuesday, 15April 1707): 110.

67 *Review* 1, no. 19 (Tuesday, 9 May 1704): 89.

68 *Review*, 4, no. 135 (Tuesday, 23 December 1707): 538.

69 *Review* 4, no. 50 (Thursday, 5 June 1707): 199.

70 *The Complete English Tradesman* I, i, 29.

71 For example, after recounting outbreaks of the plague in Europe, Defoe says "I shall make no Theological Inferences, from this Discourse of the Plague, I leave that to your Ministers, whose province it is, and from whom, no question, you will better accept it – In me, you will call it Canting, and Preaching, and perhaps mock, rather than improve it to your own Advantage": *Review* 1, no. 7 (Saturday, 23 August 1712): 14.

72 *Review* 7, no. 8 (Tuesday, 13 April 1710): 30.

73 *Review* 1, no. 38 (Saturday, 20 December 1712): 75.

74 *Review* 7, no. 114 (Saturday, 16 December 1710): 455.

75 *Review* 7, no. 148 (Tuesday, 6 March 1711): 589.

76 *Review* 2, no. 15 (Saturday, 7 April 1705): 59.

77 *The Complete English Tradesman* I, i, 31–2.

78 *An Essay upon Projects* (London: Tho. Cockerill, 1697), 243–4. All references are to this edition. For a fuller account of Defoe's sense of linguistic reform, see Merrett 2004: 27–34 and chapter 8, page 246–52 in this volume.

79 Martin 1975: 86–90; Lodge 1966: 18, 30, and 35; Kermode 1979: 47, 27, and 14; Defoe, *Conjugal Lewdness; or, Matrimonial Whoredom. A Treatise Concerning the Use and Abuse of the Marriage Bed*, ed. Maximillian E. Novak

(Gainesville, FL: Scholars' Facsimiles and Reprints, 1967), 386. All references are to this edition. For an important defence of Kermode's critical pluralism and non-doctrinaire openness to texts, see Ellis 1997: 57-59. On the four kinds of opposites and the syntactic and psychological ambiguities that contraries permitted in Renaissance rhetoric, see McCutcheon 1971: 224–30. In a provocative article, Bechler reads Richardson's *Clarissa* as "a profound fundamentalist reaction against the rational and pragmatic tendencies of the age" and an embodiment of Jacob Boehme's "notion of a first principle which becomes creative by generating its own contrary, which it then proceeds to reconcile to itself." But she excludes Defoe and Isaac Watts from Richardson's "dialectical emphasis on God's inclusivity" (1986: 94–5, 98).

80 In that he viewed the bonds of society and culture to be fundamentally religious, Defoe may be seen to anticipate modern theologians. To Tillich "culture itself is religious"; in *Systematic Theology*, he insists that "religion is the substance of culture, culture is the form of religion" (Cary 1975: 27). Defoe would have agreed with Tillich that "Everything secular is implicitly related to the holy. It can become the bearer of the holy. The divine can become manifest in it. Nothing is essentially and inescapably secular" (Cary 1975: 39). Relevant to Defoe's outlook on material and spiritual relations is Heidegger's deliberations as to how humans may reconcile technology and meditative thinking. For Heidegger, the way lies so near at hand that it is easily overlooked. "For the way to what is near is always the longest and thus the hardest for humans. This way is the way of meditative thinking. Meditative thinking demands of us not to cling one-sidedly to a single idea, nor to run down a one-track course of ideas. Meditative thinking demands of us that we engage ourselves with what at first sight does not go together at all." Heidegger continues: "We can use technical devices as they ought to be used, and also let them alone as something which does not affect our inner and real core. We can affirm the unavoidable use of technical devices, and also deny them the right to dominate us, and so to warp, confuse, and lay waste our nature ... I would call this comportment toward technology which expresses 'yes' and at the same time 'no,' by an old word, *releasement toward things*" (1966: 53–4). This translation of an old German term that denotes letting the world go and giving oneself to God is applicable to *Serious Reflections*, as we shall see.

81 Macquarrie 1977: 65.

82 Bonhoeffer 1971: 104.

83 My Shakespearean epigraph is taken from *The Complete Works of Shakespeare*, ed. Irving Ribner and George Lyman Kittredge (New York: John

Wiley, 1971), 980, and the one from Blake comes from *The Marriage of Heaven and Hell*, ed. Geoffrey Keynes (London: Oxford University Press, 1975), xvi and plate 3. Defoe shares with Shakespeare and Blake a desire to turn dualities into dialectic and to think in and through contraries. Smith emphasizes that "One of the most attractive aspects of Renaissance humanism is this optimistic eclecticism, this conviction that it is possible to have the flesh, the world, and heaven too. It maintains, of course, a scale of values, but to recognize one aspect of experience as contrary or as inferior to another is not to condemn it out of hand." In commenting on Friar Laurence's words, Smith says that the only pattern of order is what he derives from his "diversities and contradictions" (1966: 10 and 31). Frye's explanation of why Blake found it more important to attack Locke than Hobbes clarifies Defoe's dialectic: "Blake saw in Deism, not atheism, the really pernicious foe of Christianity" because "truth in a false context is worse than outspoken falsehood." This notion led Blake to distinguish between a contrary and a negation and to realize that the "clash of contraries is thus an essential part of the 'redemption' of mankind." Blake's visionary thinking thus posited that the "deader a thing is, the more obedient it is to circumstances, and the more alive it is the less predictable it becomes" and that the "source of all tyranny is the mental passivity induced by abstract reasoning in the victim's mind, and until that is got rid of all rulers will be compelled to be tyrants" (Frye 1969: 188–90). Defoe voices his metaphysical interest in educational contraries and spiritual insight when, in *Mere Nature Delineated,* he laments ironically: "Unhappy Man, that his Soul cannot receive the Good without the Evil! Tell us, ye Right Reverend and Reverend, the Guides of the World, whence is it that 'tis impossible to communicate to a human Creature, the Virtues of a Christian Life, untainted with the Knowledge and Gust of Crime; or to bring the Man to the Knowledge of the brightest Part, but the Vice comes in at the very same Door?" He then turns to the Bible: "Even the Tree of Knowledge has this Part discover'd in its Title, and no doubt they came together; it was the Tree of Knowledge of Good and of Evil, they were taken in together, and are still inseparable" *Due Preparations for the Plague* (1722) and *Mere Nature Delineated* (1726), ed. Andrew Wear, vol. 5 of *Writings on Travel, Discovery and History: The Works of Daniel Defoe* (London: Pickering and Chatto, 2002), 181. All citations of *Mere Nature Delineated* are to this edition.

84 Defoe's dialectical sense of individual experience and public reality warrants claims about his protean aspects. The stance of Furbank and Owens in minimizing these aspects is understandable given their wish to determine a biographical consistency of style for bibliographical reasons (1988:

8–14). Defoe's protean nature may be viewed through the eyes of Colley, who says, when arguing that growing Britishness did not "supplant and obliterate other loyalties," that "Identities are not like hats. Human beings can and do put on several at a time" (1992: 6). Backscheider, with regard to Defoe's stratagems for exploiting "different markets for books and pamphlets," describes the variety of voices he applied to the same subjects. She reminds us that his later works adopt the points of view of "an Anglican, a Dissenter, a Quaker, a Scot, a leader of the mob, a Whig, a Jacobite, and others" (1989: 143–4). See also Curtis 1979: 8 and 16. To Macaree, Defoe is a "multi-personed correspondent" because of his imitation of Quaker archaisms, Dissenting allusiveness, Anglican classicism, and Jesuitical bureaucracy (1991: 70).

85 Relevant here is Mitchell's recognition of Job's need to put a "cloud of unknowing ... between himself and God," to remove himself from "the human-centred world of final causes" in the rest of the Bible, and to see that his confrontation with the divine leads him to a "criticism of conventional, dualistic theology" (1987: xix, xxiii, xxiv). Greenberg claims that with "its ironies and surprises, its claims and arguments in unresolved tension, the Book of Job remains the classic expression in world literature of the irrepressible yearning for divine order, baffled but never stifled by the disarray of reality" ("Job" in Alter and Kermode 1987: 301).

86 On the contrary impulses towards concealment and self-exposure in Defoe's characters, see Brown 1971: 569. Richetti remarks well about Defoe's attempt to reconcile the "central myth of consciousness that the self is free and prior to experience" with "the facts of existence which decree that the self is the mere result of experience" (1975: 162).

87 With reference to Crusoe, Brown has expressed this superbly: "Conversion is a recurrent need, a revelation followed each time by another lapse, a forgetting that is like an absence, requiring a new dialectical struggle. Not a completely new conversion, actually – Crusoe must be brought back to the self discovered in the initial conversion and by that movement freed from self-deception, freed in a sense from self. And this must happen again and again" (1971: 576).

88 Henry Fielding, *Tom Jones*, ed. Sheridan Baker (New York: Norton, 1973), 399–400. *The Vicar of Wakefield*, besides relating Crusoe's failure to float his long-boat to the Primrose family's miscalculation of the size of its tasteless family portrait, aligns religious controversies in *Robinson Crusoe*, *Religious Courtship*, and *Tom Jones* (Rogers 1972: 13–14).

89 *Conjugal Lewdness* 218.

90 One of Defoe's strongest statements about original sin appears in *The Family Instructor in Three Parts*, 2nd ed. (London: Eman. Matthews, 1715): "*Fath.* It is very plain, that the Effect of that first Man's [Adam's] Sin is a corrupt Taint which we all bring into the World with us, and which we find upon our Nature, by which we find a Natural Propensity in us to do Evil, and no Natural Inclination to do Good; and this we are to mourn over, and lament, as the Fountain of Sin, from whence all our wicked Actions do proceed; and this is call'd *Indwelling Sin*" (22). All references are to this edition.

91 *A Collection of Miscellany Letters, Selected out of Mist's Weekly Journal: The First Volume* (London: N. Mist, 1722), 230. All references are to this edition. Furbank and Owens say "It is not impossible that Defoe wrote certain of the articles reprinted in the collection" (1994: 129). The section of this work to which I refer typifies Defoe's style and moral ideas.

92 I follow Frank's account of how philosophical ironies extend religious understanding: "Nothing in this world lasts forever. In fact, it is a strange irony that the higher and more valuable an existence, the more perishable it seems to be" (1966: 64).

93 *The Family Instructor. In Two Parts. Vol. II.* (London: Eman. Matthews, 1718), 162. All references are to this edition.

94 On the *via negativa*, see the following passages in *The Cloud of Unknowing*: "Our soul has some affinity with [God], of course, because we have been created in his image and likeness. Only he himself is completely and utterly sufficient to fulfil the will and longing of our souls. Nothing else can. The soul, when it is restored by grace, is made wholly sufficient to comprehend him fully by love. He cannot be comprehended by our intellect or any man's – or any angel's for that matter. For both we and they are created beings. But only to our intellect is he incomprehensible: not to our love"; "If ever you are to come to this cloud and live and work in it, as I suggest, then just as this cloud of unknowing is as it were above you, between you and God, so you must also put a cloud of forgetting beneath you and all creation. We are apt to think that we are very far from God because of this cloud of unknowing between us and him, but surely it would be more correct to say that we are much farther from him if there is no cloud of forgetting between us and the whole created world" (Wolters 1961: 54–5 and 58).

95 *Robinson Crusoe* 139.

96 *Jure Divino: A Satyr. In Twelve Books* (London, 1706), Bk V, 19. All references are to this edition.

97 *Review* 2, no. 50 (Thursday, 28 June 1705): 198.

98 *The Farther Adventures of Robinson Crusoe* (London: W. Taylor, 1719), 247. All references are to this edition.

99 *A Collection of Miscellany Letters … The First Volume* 257.

100 *A System of Magick* (London: J. Roberts, 1727), 117. All references are to this edition. Defoe presents God, "the Perfection of Good," and the Devil, "the Extreme of Corruption," as the "two Contraries" responsible for "all the executive Power of Good and Evil." But these contraries cannot interfuse: "the *Devil* can no more be the Genuine Parent of Good Actions, than an evil Tree can bring forth good Fruit; than Darkness, which is a Privation of the glorious Light, can be a Consequence or Production of it." Moreover, "God can no more be the Author of Evil, than he can Annihilate himself, and Cease to be; and he cannot Cease to be, because, he that Exists from Eternity is Eternal, and Exists necessarily, as well as from himself" (278). NB. this latter statement contradicts my opening epigraph from Isaiah 45:7. Matthew 7:18 is one source for the evil tree. See also *Conjugal Lewdness* 110 and 301.

101 *The Family Instructor. In Two Parts. Vol. II*, 275.

102 On how Locke's dismissal of innate ideas and mathematical trust in God's existence detracted from religious experience, see Cragg 1950: 120. Scruton, in applying the criticism of Leibniz and Spinoza, shows how Locke's hostility to innate ideas, whether actual or virtual, vainly sought to deny a priori concepts and to displace rationalism (1995: 86–9). Locke's rejection of innate ideas and the Calvinistic Fall in which he was raised distinguishes him from Defoe (Parker 2004: 50–66).

103 *A Tour through the Whole Island of Great Britain (1724–26)*, ed. G.D.H. Cole and D.C. Browning (London: J.M. Dent, 1962), II, 176. All references are to this edition.

104 Joyce 1964: 7, 20, and 23–5.

105 Woolf 1953: 94–6.

106 Starr 1971: vii and xi; Furbank and Owens 1988: 146.

107 Boardman emphasizes generic pluralism since our author's fictions "lack single principles of being, fit no prescriptive categories, in part because Defoe is creating the possibilities for narrative as he goes along." Thus, his fiction "stubbornly insists, if one is to make full sense of it, that one forgets it is fiction. At the same time, he experiments with ways of subverting his own illusory structures, of including within an overall illusion of historicity the knowledge that the reader is participating in a basically fictional world." The dialectic in Defoe's fictions, in Boardman's eyes, means that his narratives are "varieties of history, veracious or illusory," which, despite "their obviously dissimilar subjects … share numerous

conventions of technique and narrational stance, the created rhetorical relationship between author and reader that much more powerfully than subject [defining] narrative experience" (1983: 2, 6 and 14). Sill's views on ideology also reject distinctions between fiction and non-fiction. Following J.G.A. Pocock, Sill holds that "civic humanism" for Defoe and his contemporaries was an ideology that "transcended Whig and Tory party questions." One consequence was the "ambivalent rhetoric" by which Defoe constantly tried "to find a middle way" in defining virtue as a balance between "passion and order" (1983: 15).

2. Just Reflections

1 *Colonel Jack* 307.
2 *Moll Flanders* 126.
3 Ong 1982: 109.
4 Wheelwright 1968: 97 and 100.
5 See Ong 1982: 39–40.
6 On Defoe's appreciation of Dryden's poetry, see Moore 1958: 193 and 229–30; and Backscheider 1989: 54–5, 165, and 418. In Merrett 1992b, I analyse the symbolic power generated by incremental verbal repetition in Dryden's *Absalom and Achitophel.*
7 "To a remarkable degree, then, Defoe's criminal novels depend on their readers to give them meaning, which is to say, on what their readers are willing or able to bring to their texts by way of 'reflection'" (Faller 1993:104).
8 Lodge 1966: 82 and 17.
9 After explaining the paradoxical implications in Puritan theology for narrative art, Damrosch says that, while "Defoe is no metaphysician," his fiction, particularly *Robinson Crusoe*, "reflects the progressive desacralizing of the world that was implicit in Protestantism" (1985: 3-12, 192). However, Menippean satire in *The Consolidator* (see below) represents a methodical anti-intellectualism that corresponds to strategies in modern theology. Defoe's writing was dominated by metaphysical topics. On Defoe's religious sensibility, see Merrett 1980: 9–28. Since Watt (1963), scholars tend to overstress Defoe's reliance on Lockean epistemology. McKeon applies a "dialectical theory of genre" to the novel's origins and argues that "questions of truth and questions of virtue" are "analogous versions of each other" in the novel (1987: 1 and 22). He also holds that romance persisted as "an epistemological category" by figuring in a "more comprehensive and decisive dialectic" – "the double reversal of romance

idealism by naive empiricism and of both by extreme skepticism" (1987: 63–4). In this and the next chapters, I explain the theological bases of Defoe's polarity thinking and link his rhetoric to reader-response theory as outlined by Iser (1978a).

10 Pinker argues that the "Blank Slate" distorts human nature and that the denial of human nature arising from empiricism is socially harmful (2002: ix–x). If his "biologically informed humanism" (xi) is irrelevant to Defoe, Pinker's attack on the constructedness of culture and social discourse is. To Pinker, behaviourist psychology has illicitly abandoned innate ideas (2002: 14–29). On circularity in Locke's argument for the blank slate and Leibniz's opposition to it, see Pinker 2002: 34–5: Leibniz was "ahead of his time in recognizing that intelligence is a form of information processing [that] needs complex machinery to carry it out." Chomsky (1980) gives an account of innate, a priori ideas that, by challenging empiricism and rejecting body-mind dualisms, is relevant to Defoe.

11 Novak (1963) remains the most comprehensive account of the philosophical sources of Defoe's fiction. On Defoe's theological explication of natural law, see Merrett 1980: 30–47.

12 *The Consolidator: Or Memoirs of Sundry Transactions from the World in the Moon* (London: B. Bragge, [1705]) 33. All subsequent references are to this edition.

13 *The Consolidator* 99.

14 *The Consolidator* 321.

15 *Serious Reflections* 88–9.

16 *An Enquiry into the Case of Mr. Asgill's General Translation* (London, 1704), 10. Defoe spurns heterodoxy in *An Essay on the Regulation of the Press* (London, 1704): "No nation in the Christian World, but ours, would have suffered such books as *Asgill* upon Death; *Coward* against the Immortality of the Soul; —— on Poligamy; —— against the Trinity; *B——t's* Theory; and abundance more tending to Atheism, Heresie, and Irreligion, without a publick Censure, nor should the Authors have gone without Censure and Punishment, in any place in *Europe*, but here" (4). While the printing press should be regulated, he objects to giving regulatory power to political parties, since lawyers may cunningly twist the words of wary authors as in the case of "*Algernon Sidney's Answer to Sir* Robert Filmer" (15). John Asgill's *An Argument Proving, that … Man May Be Translated* (1700) held that, since Christ had freed Christians from death, true believers would not die but go straight to heaven. Despite rejecting Asgill's theology, Defoe welcomed his land bank (Backscheider 1986: 68–9). William Coward's *Second Thoughts Concerning Human Soul* (1702) denied the soul was an immortal

substance. After Locke, Coward thought human minds consisted of thinking matter. His later works, criticized by Locke, Toland, and Anthony Collins, were burned by the hangman. Gilbert Burnet's An Exposition of the *Thirty-Nine Articles of the Church of England* (1699) applied a latitudinarian critique to the Trinity and all church doctrines. In 1701, the Lower House of Convocation censured Burnet's *Exposition* and Toland's *Christianity Not Mysterious* (1696). Burnet minimized doctrinal differences to prepare for the comprehension of Dissenters. Defoe usually upheld denominational distinctions.

17 *An Enquiry into the Case of Mr. Asgill's General Translation* 8. *A System of Magick* refers to Asgill as "most exquisitely and accomplishtly whimsical" for having "form'd his new System of going the nearest way (Home) to Heaven" (12).

18 Vickers shows that Defoe was impressed by late seventeenth-century followers of Bacon who adapted the latter's scientific program to economic and social life (1996: 15ff.). On the dependence of scientists on civil conversation, see Shapin 1994: 114–25.

19 To Shapin, Boyle is exemplary in consciously embodying Christian gentility in order to harmonize theology and science (1994: 156–70). Defoe urged the gentry to respect "all that Sir Isaac Newton, Mr. Whiston, Mr. Halley had said in English upon the nicest subjects in Astronomy and the secrets of Nature." He promoted Newton's optical experiments and championed "all liberall arts and sciences taught in our mother tongue," criticizing education in Greek and Latin for making learning unnecessarily hard. He is close to Locke in declaring that "The knowledge of things, not words, make a schollar." *The Compleat English Gentleman*, 1728–29, ed. Karl. D. Bülbring (London: David Nutt, 1890), 207, 209–12. All references are to this edition. When Defoe refers to the wise men of Belshazzar's reign, to "the *Flamsteads*, the *Sir Isaacs*, the *Halleys*, the *Whistons*, &c," who cannot decipher the writing on the king's wall, he intends to displace merely intellectual claims to transcendent knowledge (*A System of Magick* 24).

20 *The Compleat English Gentleman* 69.

21 *The Storm* 4 and 9. This work holds that the winds are not susceptible to scientific analysis because they are reserved by God for His purposes. On Defoe's admiration of Boyle's combined theology and science, see Vickers 1996: 26–7. Defoe mentions Boyle's experiments with magnetism eight times on pages 254 and 256–7 of *A General History of Discoveries and Improvements, In Useful Arts* (London: J. Roberts, 1725–6). Subsequent references are to this edition.

22 *The Storm* 6.

23 *A Collection of Miscellany Letters, Selected out of Mist's Journal: The Second Volume* (London: N. Mist, 1722), 242–3. Subsequent references are to this edition.

24 Eliade holds that "To whatever degree he may have desacralized the world, the man who has made his choice in favor of a profane life never succeeds in completely doing away with religious behavior … even the most desacralized existence still preserves traces of a religious valorization of the world" (1959: 23).

25 The preface to *Jure Divino* appropriates John 16:12 when Defoe says *"I have many things to say, but you cannot bear them now"* (iii). This is an epigraph to my next chapter. On contemporary interest in prophetic predictions in almanacs and other works and on Defoe's long-time adoption of prophetic stances, see "Defoe as Prophet" in Baine 1968: 109–28.

26 *The Consolidator* 275.

27 Defoe's family was "centered on the gospel." The ministers he admired were "Bartholomeans," men "ejected by the Act of Uniformity of 1662, and with the exception of Dr. Annesley, a Presbyterian, they were all Congregationalists." Set apart for the ministry, Defoe realized his "temperament and inclination" did not fit him for this calling, but "he never abandoned the pulpit completely; many of his works bear the unmistakable qualities of a sermon" (Shinagel 1968: 8–9, 18 and 21). To Backscheider, because of the persecution of Dissenters, "Defoe learned piety, hard work, economy, long-suffering, self-discipline, and service, but he also learned resistance, distrust for authority, and independence of thought that tended to self-righteousness" (1989: 11).

28 *A Speech without Doors* 6. On a point relating to Defoe's reluctance to specify his indebtedness to Locke, Novak suggests that Defoe's political ideas may be original because they appeared before Locke's two treatises were printed (1963: 14).

29 *Jure Divino*, Book II, the single footnote on page 10. On Sidney's activism in the 1680s, militaristic opposition to tyranny, admiration for medieval life, and religious defence of revolution, see Robbins 1968: 41–7 and Keeble 1987: 99–100.

30 The following points about Sidney appear in notes (b) and (c) on pages 27–8 of *Jure Divino*, Book IV. Clark rejects Trevelyan's "caricature" of Defoe as among the first to see "the old world through a pair of sharp modern eyes"; Trevelyan's account "misses the religious dimension in which all moved … And it misses those traditional, hierarchical, deferential forms which were neither antiquated, tenuous survivals nor mere superstructures … but substantive and prevalent modes of thought and

behaviour in a society dominated still by the common people, by the aristocracy, and by the relations between the two" (1985: 43). However, Trevelyan says that it is "doubly impossible ... for the English historian to ignore religion, if he would explain other phenomena" and that "he must not be tempted to forget that there was more in the religious sense of the nation than the feuds out of which, incidentally, our political liberties in large part arose. The religious life of many quiet parishes and humble families moved on its way, little concerned with partisanship of High and Low Church; English religion was, in the main, a free and healthy function of that old-world life, nicely guiding itself between superstition and fanaticism on the one side and material barbarism on the other" (1944: 329).

31 Schonhorn 1977: 29. Objecting to the myth of Locke's liberalism, Pocock holds that the philosopher stood aside from political debate; while he was not "the received authority or the official apologist on the English Revolution," Defoe was "infinitely more than Locke the ideologist of the emerging Whig order" (1980: 7 and 15).

32 "The point is not that Defoe is Lockeian; it is clear to anyone who inquires superficially into Defoe that he read Locke carefully and favorably; the point is that he rejects so much that is Lockeian" (Schonhorn 1977: 20). To Defoe, Toland was "a Heritick of prostituted Principles" (*Mercurius Politicus* for August 1718: 442 and 447). Toland's rejection of original sin, Christ's divinity, and the Trinity made him, in Defoe's eyes, an archetypal hypocrite who pretended "true Religion" but professed "heresy," who talked like a Protestant but worshipped as a Socinian (*An Argument Proving that the Design of Employing and Enobling Foreigners, Is a Treasonable Conspiracy against the Constitution* [London, 1717: 51]). Furbank and Owens (1998: 168–71) now accept this work as likely by Defoe, having argued for its de-attribution (1988: 160 and 1994: 95–6). On Defoe's hostility to Toland, see Merrett 1980: 23–5. On his opposition to Toland's political journalism, see Sill 1983: 130–37. To Cragg, Toland "ignored the true character of religious experience" (1966a: 154).

33 To Bishop Butler, "Reason alone, whatever any one may wish, is not in reality a sufficient motive of virtue in such a creature as man; but this reason joined with those affections which God has impressed upon his heart" (Downey 1969: 47). On Berkeley's rejection of "the prevailing ethico-rational approach to religion," see Downey 1969: 65. On Butler's brilliant objections to the simplifications of empiricist thought, see Scruton 1995: 118–19.

34 Andrew 1988: 30, 62–3. "It seems likely that Locke's chief impact in eighteenth-century England was not to import contractarianism, but Arianism

into religion; but this in itself raised formidable barriers against the acceptance of his political analysis" (Clark 1985: 47).

35 *Jure Divino* xxii; Andrew 1988: 17.

36 *Jure Divino* xxi.

37 Schonhorn 1977: 22–3.

38 *Jure Divino* xxi.

39 In his introduction, Yolton says that, while Locke divides "the claim for an experiential grounding of all ideas, and those other claims about knowledge and reality which go beyond experiential grounding" to argue that nothing is in the intellect which is not first in the senses, the faculty of reflection is the ambiguous element in his program. If he did not aim to make this division unfalsifiable, he is unclear about the different ways in which ideas derive from experience, turning talk about derivation into "talk about the meaning of our ideas." It is a limitation that he sees innate inscription as the only thesis opposed to his view of the origin of ideas. He ignores the structure of the mind and its faculties, which must pre-exist sensation and reflection (Locke 1961: I, xvi–xviii).

40 On Leibniz's defence of a priori innate ideas against Locke and on Hume's insistence on contingency as a way of challenging Locke's theory of causation, see Scruton 1995: 88 and 124–5.

41 On Defoe's aesthetic awareness, visual thinking, and conformity to his age's practice and theory of representational dialectic, see Merrett 1994: 159–63.

42 For an acute critique of Watt's theory of the realism of presentation, see McKeon's "Dialectical Method in Literary History" (1987: 1–22). Among McKeon's major points are "the persistence of romance and the aristocracy," the lack of contextual evidence for the rise of the middle classes, and the "instability of generic and social categories" (1987: 2–4, 20).

43 For a sympathetic exposition of Lockean epistemology which also criticizes the philosopher's confusions and reliance on "dead ideas," see Scruton 1995: 86–97.

44 Opposing this view, Damrosch says that "Whenever Defoe allows his narrators to try to look within, they do indeed find a chaos of unfocused sensations, but most of the time they simply avoid introspection and assert themselves tenaciously against a series of manageable challenges" (1985: 196).

45 Interestingly Butler claims that "*Robinson Crusoe* is a representation of itself in the process of being created" and that it promotes the "illusion" of being "hopelessly *in*complete" (1983: 77). Yet she does not relate Crusoe's "rhetorical uncertainties" to Defoe's multifarious concrete particulars

which serve to persuade readers of "the actuality of Crusoe and his experience" (1983: 78).

46 "In the writings of Anglicans and Dissenters alike, man is exhorted to observe, interpret, and heed all such phenomena as declarations of the divine will. In any given storm or epidemic, the individual will be either one of the sufferers or one of those spared: in either case he is obliged to scrutinize the event for its significance to him personally" (Starr 1965: 90–1). On reflection as one stage towards repentance in *Robinson Crusoe*, see Starr 1965: 106–8.

47 Hunter attributes Crusoe's vague spiritual terms to his "understanding of events and people solely in terms of things" (1966: 153). Crusoe lacks the emblematic awareness of the sea that was promoted by Providence writers (Hunter 1966: 62–6). On the paradox of imprisonment and deliverance on the island by which Defoe alerts readers to Crusoe's increasing estrangement from God, see Blewett 1979: 31–2.

48 The internalized images of "Current" and "Storm" evidence Defoe's verbal irony and sense of what Jaynes (1976) calls "narrativization." On Jaynes, see chapter 8, page 279–80, of this volume.

49 To Damrosch, "Defoe sets out to dramatize the conversion of the Puritan self, and he ends by celebrating a solitude that exalts autonomy instead of submission" (1985: 187), whereas to Hunter, if "Crusoe's retrospection and introspection produce a good deal of personal discomfort," they "become literally one – and the pattern of his life becomes not only changed but understood in cosmic terms" (1966: 147). I attempt to reconcile these polar stances.

50 The biblical allusion to exile is to Amos 8:11.

51 Singleton's alienation is emphasized when he calls himself a "Roman-Catholick" (276).

52 To Shinagel, Defoe undercuts Jack's gentility: Jack "never gives serious thought to the idea of being a gentleman so long as his primary needs of food, clothing and shelter remain unfulfilled (1968: 163). Extending this insight in a brilliant account of Jack's "association with disguise and deception," Blewett explains Jack's deluded gentility in terms of his name, association with Jacobitism, and superficial notions about clothes and money (1979: 94–100 and 104–14). It is sometimes suggested that Defoe punishes his characters for his own genteel aspirations: "Despite his trenchant attacks on the corruptions of lineage and aristocratic honour, Defoe was obsessed with the illusion of his own gentility" (McKeon 1987: 326).

53 To Faller, Defoe's novels possess "an inordinacy … an incompleteness or overrepletion. They go too far or not far enough … They leave out or put in too much, and none comes to a proper ending" (1993: 50). By employing the paradox that his narrators' texts are incomplete, Defoe not only

foresees reader-response theory but also anticipates semiotic views of the inevitable plurality of codes in texts. Defoe's textual experimentation is elaborated in chapter 8.

54 McKeon recognizes Defoe's experimental narratology when he points to the dynamic relations between character and narrator in *Robinson Crusoe* (1987: 318).

55 Job 42:6.

56 *Religious Courtship* (London: E. Matthews, A. Bettesworth, J. Brotherton, and W. Meadows, 1722), 53 and 78. All references are to this edition.

57 *Religious Courtship* 119, 160, and 178.

58 *Compleat English Tradesman* I, i, 103. On this page, Defoe does not insist that "all pleasure" be "forbidden" the shopkeeper nor denies the tradesman "spare hours," "intervals from hurry and fatigue; that would be to pin him down to the very floor of his shop, as John Sheppard was lock'd down to the floor of his prison."

59 *Complete English Tradesman* I, i, 260, 283; II, ii, 147, 150, 161–9. Mandeville thought "that Virtue is made Friends with Vice, when industrious good people, who maintain their Families and bring up their Children handsomely, pay Taxes, and are several ways useful Members of the Society, get a livelyhood by something that chiefly depends on, or is very much influenc'd by the Vices of others, without being themselves guilty of, or accessary to them any otherwise than by way of Trade" (1970: 117). Defoe treats Mandeville's paradox hypothetically: if "the Nation's Prosperity is built on the ruin of the Nation's Morals" and if tradesmen's "Excesses are the Excess of their welfare," he could not preach "Sobriety, Temperance, and Abatement of Pride or Drunkenness," for that would see tradesmen "undone" (*Complete English Tradesman* II, ii, 105). Later, he cites Mandeville's notion that "our Vices are become Virtues in Commerce" to fortify his satire but denies that his encouragement of trade insinuates that "we must Encourage our Vice for the Encouragement of our Trade." To interpret him thus would be "a Corrupt use of a just reasoning" (II, ii, 169). Defoe upholds a golden mean: "a Reformation might effect Trade in many particular things, but need not overthrow it and destroy it in general." Again, "Trade need not be destroy'd, tho' Vice were mortally wounded, much less need we be oblig'd to encourage Flaming Luxury, for fear of discouraging our Commerce, lessening our Revenue, or starving our Poor" (*Complete English Tradesman* II, ii, 171–4). Novak doubts Defoe's ironical treatment of Mandeville: "He objected to Bernard Mandeville's paradoxical concept of society with its acceptance of private vices as public benefits, but he was obviously so delighted by Mandeville's paradoxes that it is

sometimes difficult to tell whether he is supporting or attacking his theories of luxuries and vice" (1966: 36).

60 *Conjugal Lewdness* 334; *The Shortest-Way with the Dissenters: or Proposals for the Establishment of the Church* (1702) in *Selected Writings of Daniel Defoe*, ed. James T. Boulton (London: B. T. Batsford, 1965. Repr. Cambridge: CUP, 1975), 95. All references to this work are to this edition.

61 Edward and Lillian Bloom provide an excellent account of the hostile reaction on all sides to Defoe's famous satire (1979: 117–18).

62 On the rhetorical proposition that, whereas narration is rooted in orality, logical classification is rooted in literacy, see O'Banion 1992: 12ff. O'Banion cites Ong to the effect that rhetoric is the art by which a literate culture formalizes "the oral communication skills which had helped determine the structures of thought and society before literacy" (1992: 29).

3. *Serious Reflections*: An Apology for Faith and Fiction

1 See chapter 2, note 19. Despite his self-dramatizing habit of narrative withholding, Defoe's closeness to readers is well described by Sutherland: "Defoe's belief in the supernatural must also be related to that strong hold on the popular mind which was one of his greatest assets as a writer. He was one of the people; he understood their thoughts and feelings because to a considerable extent they were his own" (1937: 265).

2 *Serious Reflections* [A7r].

3 Heschel 1962: I, 6–7, 17–18, and 23.

4 "To some extent *Robinson Crusoe* forms part of Defoe's lifelong polemic against secular philosophy. But that religious purpose proved fruitful for Defoe's conception of character" (Richetti 1987: 54).

5 On Defoe's recognition that he cannot "totally control the reading of his work" on account of his ambivalent understanding of Providence, see Hopes 1996: 326. Hopes aligns theological polarities with narrative dialectic.

6 On Defoe and topical repetition, see chapter 1, page 30. To Sutherland, Defoe's "easy natural manner made difficult things appear simple" and his "remarkable gift for finding picturesque illustrations still further helped him reach the popular mind" (1937: 265). Defoe's keen sense of diction clarifies the semiotic functions of lexical redundancy in his narratives, a topic opened up in chapter 1 and elaborated in chapter 8.

7 Although he notes "some kind of demon of contrariness" in "Defoe's soul" that "he often finds a way to let loose in his fictional spaces," Seidel holds that Defoe's "interests in religion are almost always psychological rather than metaphysical' (1991: 89 and 91). By contrast, seeing "revolutionary

nostalgia" in Defoe, Warner says that his contemporaries despised "the appeal to the pre-rational, anti-intellectual modes of being envisioned in his novels." Noting these modes, Joyce saw Defoe's characters "reaching in two directions, backwards toward their animal origins and forward to their roles as historic prototypes." To Warner Defoe "is not a historicist who is hypocritical about his Christian professions, but a Christian-historicist who has a certain nostalgia for mythic remnants." Warner claims that, regardless of "Defoe's religious beliefs, he was too clear-sighted not to recognize, along with Stephen Dedalus, that linear history without a sense of transcendental purpose was a nightmare." To Warner, the difference in the two authors is that, unlike "Joyce, Defoe could not achieve a containing form to structure that insight" (Warner 1993: 10, 24, 36, and 56). Faller says that Defoe precludes "facile inferences" by showing readers that "there is no easy, necessary, or complete fit between the human psyche and the transcendent moral order" and by restoring "the relationship between men and God to a proper disequilibrium" (1993: 104).

8 To Richetti, "preacher and prophet are [Defoe's] recurring modes of self-presentation" (1987: 32). Usually, Defoe upheld the Low Church of England which supported Dissenters and attacked the High Church's Catholic dogma and Jacobite tenets (Novak 2001: 206–7). Yet, as Novak says, "Defoe argued for toleration of all private worship" (2001: 450). He was familiar with the Book of Common Prayer and Anglican liturgy; he married Mary Tuffley on New Year's Day, 1684, in St Botolph's, Aldgate, "according to the Church of England ritual by a proper Anglican minister" (Shinagel 1968: 26–7). For Defoe's poses as an Anglican, see Bastian 1981: 140–1, 147, and 377–9. On his "ambivalent attitude, if not to Roman Catholicism, at least to Roman Catholics," see Bastian 1981: 40. On his rhetorical creation of the seer in his spiritual propaganda, see "Defoe as Prophet" in Baine 1968: 109–28.

9 For Kermode's account of the dialectic in parables, see chapter 1, page 34–5.

10 "The story of Defoe's own life is recast into the destiny of Crusoe … It is remarkable that the symbolism of the story serves as the underpinning of its truthfulness, a truthfulness demanded both by the practical-minded middle-class public and Defoe's Puritan conscience" (Kahler 1973: 92–3). While not taking Defoe's allegorical claim seriously, Sutherland points to Charles Gildon's attack on Defoe that first made the suggestion (1937: 233). Backscheider details the autobiographical claims only to dismiss them. For her, "the autobiographical elements" in *Robinson Crusoe* are "states of mind, not events" (1989: 414). On Gildon's attack on Defoe's self-presentation in the character of Crusoe, see McKeon 1987: 316. To Hunter,

Gildon's attack shows how much contemporaries "viewed the book in religious terms" (1966: 20–1). Seidel suggests that from "Defoe's point of view, adopting Crusoe as a second self makes fiction into a kind of personal history… Crusoe and Defoe are imaginatively and, in many ways, connected" (1991: 72–3).

11 Bastian traces the influence of the "'frantick prophet' Christopher Feake," whom Defoe may have heard in the late 1660s, to the "peroration" of *Serious Reflections* (1981: 40–1). But its final paragraph limits visionary insight. Crusoe asserts that "no such Zeal for the Christian religion will be found in our Days, or perhaps in any Age of the World, till heaven beats the Drums itself, and the glorious Legions from above come down on Purpose to propagate the Work, and to reduce the whole World to the Obedience of King *Jesus*; a Time which some tell us is not far off: But of which I heard nothing in all my Travels and Illuminations, *no not one Word*" (270). Still, Bastian's point that *Serious Reflections* contains text that Defoe produced many years before its publication in 1720 is important (1981: 41 and 210). Defoe's wish to reform conversation goes back to the reign of King William (*Serious Reflections* 91). This work's retrospection also appears in references to Queen Mary (87) and to the coronation of Queen Anne (162–6). Notably, pages 11–14 on the grace of spiritual peace in *A Hymn to Peace* (London, 1706) appear fourteen years later in *Serious Reflections* (79–80). This work is pivotal in deploying voices and themes that Defoe applied to later books. Backscheider says that *Serious Reflections* "largely repeats the theory of 'fable' that Defoe had explained in *The New Family Instructor*" (1989: 414). But the latter work appeared in 1727.

12 Defoe's integration of secular and religious values anticipates modern theology. Cox points out that in "Dietrich Bonhoeffer's term, the early Christians exhibited a kind of 'holy worldliness'" (1965: 24). To Cox, "those whose present orientation to reality is shaped by the biblical faith can hardly in good faith enter the lists as opponents of secularization. Our task should be to nourish the secularization process, to prevent it from hardening into a rigid world view, and to clarify as often as necessary its roots in the Bible. Furthermore, we should be constantly on the lookout for movements which attempt to thwart and reverse the liberating irritant of secularization" (1965: 31). Defoe's hostility to retreats and conventional ideas of the secular seems explicable in Cox's terms: "From the very beginning of its usage, secular denoted something vaguely inferior. It meant 'this world' of change as opposed to the eternal 'religious world.' This usage already signifies an ominous departure from biblical categories. It implies that the true religious world is timeless, changeless, and thus superior to the

'secular' world which is passing and transient. Thus the vocation of a 'secular priest,' one who served in the 'world,' though technically on the same level, was actually thought of as somehow less blessed than that of the 'religious' priest who lived his life in the cloister, contemplating the changeless order of holy truth" (1965: 17).

13 On the need to balance worldly and spiritual matters, Defoe warns tradesmen that "the duties of nature and religion also have their particular seasons, and those seasons so proper to themselves, and so stated, as not to break in or intrench upon one another, that we are really without excuse, if we let any one be pleaded for the neglect of the other" (*Complete English Tradesman* I, i, 52). A little later, he says "our business and trades are not to be neglected, no not for the extraordinary excursions of religion and religious duties" (I, i, 55).

14 "Il est aussi raisonnable de représenter une espèce d'emprisonnment par une autre que de représenter n'importe quelle chose qui existe réellement par quelque chose qui n'existe pas" (Camus 1947: 5). See Cruikshank 1960: 166–7.

15 Cruikshank 1960: 169–74.

16 For an analysis of the relative issues of good works and faith in English literature, see "Grace, Works" by David L. Jeffrey and Peter H. Davids in Jeffrey 1992: 316–20.

17 Defoe alludes to 2 Corinthians 12:2: "I knew a man in Christ above fourteen years ago, (whether in the body, I cannot tell; or whether out of the body, I cannot tell: God knoweth;) such an one caught up to the third heaven." He expatiates on it thus: "When the Soul of a Man is powerfully engag'd in any particular Subject, 'tis like that of St. Paul, wrapt up, whether it be into the third Heaven, or to any Degree of lower Exaltation: Such a Man may well say with the Apostle above, *Whether I was in the Body, or out of the Body, I cannot tell*. It was in such a wrapt up State, that I conceived in what I call my *Vision of the Angelical World*; of which I have subjoined a very little Part" (*Serious Reflections* 12).

18 The full passage reads as follows: "The blessed Apostle St. Paul, seems to have been in this Circumstance, when being assaulted with what is call'd in the text, *a Thorn in the Flesh*; be it what it will that is meant there, is not to my Purpose; but he pray'd to the Lord thrice; that was the first Method the Apostle took, and thereby set a pious Example to all those who are assaulted by any Temptation … But the Answer was, *my Grace is sufficient for thee*, sufficient without the Help of artificial Mortification" (*Serious Reflections* 16). Defoe's comments on 2 Cor. 12:7–9 may have been prompted by the paradox which St Paul applies to himself: "for my strength is

made perfect in weakness ... for when I am weak, then am I strong" (2 Cor. 12:9–10). While Crusoe claims to have been supported by miracles "as great as that of feeding Elijah by Ravens" (1 Kings 17:4–6 and Mark 10:22 [*Robinson Crusoe* 132]), his claim sustains neither his conduct nor his narrative.

19 The title of the final section of *Serious Reflections, A Vision of the Angelick World,* is usually abbreviated to *A Vision* subsequently in this study.

20 *A New Family Instructor; In Familiar Discourses between a Father and His Children, On the Most Essential Points of the Christian Religion* (London: T. Warner, 1727), 51–3. Subsequent references are to this edition. On Defoe's theory of romance, see Novak 1964: 653–4. McKeon claims that Defoe's theory does not involve an absolute dichotomy between romance and history since, while his charge against romance is dissolved "from one direction," it is reconstituted "from another" (1987: 121). Defoe applies the verbal integrity underlined in Zechariah 8:16 and Ephesians 4:25 to storytelling: "the Scripture Command is, *Let every Man speak Truth unto his Neighbour;* if we must tell Stories, tell them as Stories, add nothing willfully to illustrate or set it forth in the Relation; if you doubt the Truth of it, say so, and then every one will be at Liberty to believe their Share of it" (*Serious Reflections* 117). Since his critique of verbal untruth was based on natural as well as divine law, he would have agreed with this statement in *The Wickedness of a Disregard to Oaths* (London, 1723): "it must be insisted on, that a Man's Words and his Thoughts ought always to agree; and, that when they do not, it is, consider'd simply in it self, an Injury done to a natural Right common to all Mankind, and which comes with every Man that is born into this World" (28). Moore's tentative attribution of this work to Defoe (1971: 184–5) is rejected by Furbank and Owens who assert that, while Defoe "would no doubt have given general approval to its sentiments," this is "hardly in itself an argument for his authorship" (1994: 132–3). See note 28 below.

21 See, for example, Philippians 1:27 and Hebrews 13:5.

22 The OED defines hypostasis as: (a) the union of the divine and human nature in the "hypostasis" of Christ; (b) the consubstantial union of the three "hypostases" in the Godhead. The theological sense of the noun is personality, personal existence, person; (a) distinguished from *nature,* as in the one "hypostasis" of Christ as distinguished from his two *natures* (human and divine); (b) distinguished from *substance,* as in the three "hypostases" or "persons" of the Godhead, which are said to be the same in "substance." Johnson thought hypostasis an alien word that occurs only in the field of controversial divinity. In "Trinity: Or, The Divinity of the Son," the

poem closing the *New Family Instructor,* Defoe says that "The Hypostatick Myst'ry" is beyond human reasoning (383).

23 Consider the following disclaimer in *Serious Reflections* and the counter-statements that serve catechetical functions: "I suppose my self talking to Men that have nothing to do with God, and desire he should have nothing to do with them" (95); "I am writing to those who acknowledge the two grand Principles upon which all Religion depends. 1. That there is a God, a first great moving Cause of all things, an eternal Power, *Prior,* and consequently *Superior,* to all Power and Being. 2 That this eternal Power, which I call God, is the Creator and Governour of all things, viz. of Heaven and Earth" (206); "I am supposing myself talking to Men that have a sense of a future State, and of the Oeconomy of an invisible World upon them, and neither to Atheists, Scepticks, or Persons indifferent, who are indeed near of Kin to them both" (232).

24 Scruton's remark that "the truths enshrined in religion are not revealed in, but hidden by, its explicit doctrines, and made available to believers *through* their beliefs, but not *in* their beliefs," like Kermode's view of enlightenment through paradox, clarifies Defoe's intuitive sense of innate spirituality (2006: 126). Among recent books that defend the academic need to apply religion to humanist studies I have found Collins (2006), Eagleton (2009), and Wade (2009) helpful. Collins's narrative of his conversion from atheism and his synthesis of religious and scientific ideas are highly thought-provoking.

25 On Defoe's affinities with the Church of England, see note 8 above. *Serious Reflections* laments "the unhappy Divisions of Episcopal and Presbyterian, Church of *England* and Dissenter" (172).

26 In the preface to *Jure Divino,* Defoe harmonizes denominational differences and political conformity: "Christians of what Denomination soever, being Orthodox in Principle, and Sound in Doctrine, have a Native Right to Liberty of serving God, according to the Dictates of their own Consciences, and ought to be Tolerated, provided they behave themselves peaceably under the Government, and obedient in all other things to the Civil Magistracy" (xxi).

27 Defoe conflates two verses from Job for maximal emphasis: "*These are Iniquities,* as *Job* said, *should be punished by the Judges*" (22:5 and 31:11). He provides the first reference but gives neither a complete nor correct reference for the second (*Serious Reflections* 102).

28 Defoe habitually associates sexual and conversational sins. In *Conjugal Lewdness* he says that "In a word, talking Lewdly … is infamous, but talking lewdly of conjugal Actions is unnatural and odious; 'tis a kind of a

Sodomy of the Tongue; 'tis a Crime that wants a Name, but 'tis great pity it should want a Punishment" (337). He associates sexual violence and mis-education in *The Compleat English Gentleman* when he claims that a child deprived of instruction has a "kind of rape committed" on his "genius" (Owen's edition 117). His deployment of metaphors of violation is taken up further in the final chapter.

29 Defoe's theological approach to natural rights is captured by the claim that trust in conversational truth is "an *Original Natural* Right, not dependent upon any *Humane* Compact or Agreement, but deriv'd from the Nature of Things, Necessary in the Order and Oeconomy of God's Providence, and for which every Man is oblig'd and indebted to *God* alone" (*The Wickedness of a Disregard to Oaths* 28). See note 19 above.

30 The theoretical implications of Defoe's ambivalent narrative terms are more fully treated in chapter 8.

31 Starr 1971: vii and passim.

32 Although Defoe was "imbued with the Presbyterian faith," three of his schoolmasters were Congregationalists who "were reputed to be among the more flexible and loosely structured denominations, offering the individual more interpretative freedom than the Presbyterians" (Shinagel 1968: 8–11). Defoe's religious training took him away from Augustinian theology. Damrosch's claim that Defoe did not see "how deep the gulf was that divided the two poles" of *Robinson Crusoe,* namely, "the Augustinian theme of alienation and the romance theme of gratification" (1985: 187), discounts his broad-minded education. On Defoe's acceptance of St Augustine's criticism of Roman mythology in *De civitate Dei,* see *Serious Reflections* 90. While his attack on religious retreats is not Augustinian, the priority Defoe gives to the soul as the medium for knowing God is. So is his emphasis on the intentionality of sin and on the betrayal of the soul's spiritual essence, the latter leading to his frequent disparagement of the body by applying the word "carcass" to the negative Christian. Elsewhere in *Serious Reflections,* he says that lewd people speak immodestly "till their Carcass stinks as bad as their Discourse" (105). Note that Roxana refers to "this Carcass of mine" when contemplating the prince's caresses of her "prostituted Body" (74) and she demeans Amy's "Carcass" even as the latter is working for her (215). In *Conjugal Lewdness,* a couple who marry without love "come to the Book, two Carcasses without Souls, without assent or consent, but in meer subjection to Circumstances enter into a horrid Slavery" (191–2). Defoe mingles Aristotelean and Augustinian ideas when he insists that it is "absolutely necessary … to reduce the (Carkass) Body into a due Submission to (the Soul) Reason" (*Conjugal Lewdness* 314).

He draws on Aristotelean ideas when distinguishing human and animal natures. Hence, his statement in *Mere Nature Delineated* that fits Crusoe's arrival on the island: "A *Man* is no more fit to be a *Beast*, than a *Beast* is to be a *Man*; the rational Part being taken away from him, his Carcass, left utterly destitute, is unqualified to live; his Skin is tender, not fenc'd against Blows and Disasters, as is that of the Horse or Ox; the very Bushes and Briers, which are the Safety and Retreat of other Creatures, will wound and tear him, and he must not come near those Woods, which are the Shelter and Cover of the Hind, and the Stag" (158–9). For an explication of Augustinian theology, see Tillich 1972: 103–33.

33 "A good name is better than precious ointment; and the day of death than the day of one's birth" (Eccles. 7:1).

34 "Despite the apparent determinism of divine providence it is human understanding of such providential signs that provides the basis for the exercise of free will. To the extent that these providential signs are conveyed by natural means, listening to the voice of providence involves the reading of life" (Hopes 1996: 325).

35 "But the very hairs of your head are all numbered" (Matt. 10:30).

36 For Defoe's reliance on "day fatalities," see Baine 1968: 7–9. Defoe's *Memoirs of a Cavalier* ends with an eleven-page collection of day fatalities.

37 See Matthew 24:14, Mark 13:13, and Luke 24:17.

38 The "present opulence and greatness" of the English nation, says Defoe in *The Complete English Tradesman*, has nothing to do with "martial exploits": "we have no conquests abroad, added no new kingdoms to the British empire, reduced no neighbouring nations, or extended the possession of our monarchs into the properties of others; we have gain'd nothing by war and encroachment" (I, i, 314–15). On this account tradesmen are peaceful agents of colonization. Trade may have displaced but has not tyrannized over native populations. Trade being far more attractive than military life, it is difficult to man the army and navy (I, i, 316–17).

39 The sources not provided in the text are Acts 1:25 and Luke 16:23. Defoe expects readers to be familiar with the provenance of this and the following scriptural allusions.

40 The source is Matthew 15:25–6. The phrase in italics cites 1 Timothy 3:16 tacitly.

41 Luke 24:13–35 and Matthew 20:20–3.

42 1 Samuel 28:17–25.

43 Defoe explicitly provides a textual exegesis of Matthew 2:13 and 19.

44 Here Defoe also explicitly provides exegeses of Acts 9:10–18 and Acts 10:19–34.

45 *Review* 3, no. 104 (Saturday, 31 August 1706): 415.
46 See Wilmot 1968: 100.
47 While Defoe at this point claims he is not "Casuist enough" to rebut atheism but simply observes the "Wickedness of treating these Subjects with Levity and Ignorance in the common Road of Conversation" (100), he answers one of Rochester's lewd verses with one of his own: "*If it should so fall out, as who can tell, / But there may be a GOD, a Heaven, a Hell, / Mankind had best consider well for fear, / T'shou'd be too late when their Mistakes appear.*" He uses this verse to have a servant clinch an argument against his master's professed atheism after a debate about Rochester and oaths in *The Political History of the Devil, As Well Ancient as Modern* (London: T. Warner, 1726), 300–2. All subsequent references are to this edition.
48 Defoe links Rochester and Hobbes as witty critics of religion, God, and eternity in *The Political History Of The Devil* 336. See Novak 1963: 18, 28–9.
49 This adaptation of Rochester is cited in Daniel Defoe, *An Essay on the History and Reality of Apparitions* (London: J. Roberts, 1727), 5. All references are to this edition. For Rochester's original text, see Wilmot 1968: 94.
50 For a wider survey of Defoe's polar stances on Rochester and Milton, see Merrett 1980: 68–76.
51 See *Reformation of Manners: A Satyr* ([London]: 1702), 33 and 59, and *The Compleat English Gentleman* (Owen's edition 2007), 9 and 376.
52 *Jure Divino*, Bk I, 23–4.
53 *Review* [9] 1, no. 58 (Saturday, 14 February 1713): 116.
54 *Review* 5, no. 21 (Saturday, 15 May 1708): 82. On Jowler and Meres, see Wilmot 1968: 98.
55 Defoe repeats these lines to pretend indifference to criticism: "I am so far from being Concern'd at their Reproaches, that, as my Lord *Rochester* said in another case, *I count their censure FAME*" (*Review* 8, no 211 [Tuesday, 29 July 1712]: 846).
56 *Review* 1, no. 100 (Saturday, 17 February 1705): 414.
57 *Review* 8, no. 91 (Tuesday, 23 October 1711): 367. That *Some Account of the Two Nights Court at Greenwich* (London: J. Baker, 1716) cites Rochester from the viewpoint of self-defence and retaliation in a manner typical of Defoe may support the latter's authorship: "My Lord *Rochester* evidently proves there is a necessity to deal with such Men in their own Way, and to fight them at their own Weapons" (62). Furbank and Owens put this attribution to Defoe down to bibliographical inertia (1994: 86–7).
58 Blake's ambivalence towards Milton is not unlike Defoe's. Blake "loved Milton's poems and the true impulses behind them – which he thought he understood more clearly than Milton – but he deplored the

seventeenth-century emphasis on right reason and the Puritan concern with morality" (Schorer 1959: 294).

59 Daniel 1984: 44, 60–2, and 212–13.

60 Robbins 1968: 51.

61 *More Short-Ways with the Dissenters* in *A True Collection of the Writings of the Author of* The True-Born English-man, 2nd ed. 2 vols. (London, 1705), II, 227. See Bastian 1981: 56–7.

62 Bastian 1981: 54.

63 Keeble 1987: 23–4. The lines in *Paradise Regained* to which Keeble refers are: "Yet he who reigns within himself, and rules / Passions, Desires and Fears, is more a King; / Which every wise and vertuous man attains: / And who attains not, ill aspires to rule / Cities of men, or headstrong Multitudes, / Subject himself to Anarchy within / Or lawless passions in him, which he serves" (Milton 1959: 411, ll. 466–72).

64 *The King of Pirates* 55, vi, 73; *A General History of the Pyrates,* 384–8 and 390–1.

65 *Mere Nature Delineated* 171. See *Paradise Lost* Bk 3, l. 48.

66 *Conjugal Lewdness* 2–3. The phrase "*Naked Majesty*" is from line 290 of *Paradise Lost* Bk IV. To Keeble, after 1660 "The rhapsodical inner voice no longer told women to expose themselves" and the Quaker Barclay denied that women "going naked" could be a spiritual sign (1987: 23). On radical sectarians who produced extreme, even fanatical, theologies in the Civil War, see Stuart 2006, chap. 2, "John Robbins: The Shakers' God" (15–25) and chap. 3, "Roger Crab: Levelling the Food Chain" (26–38).

67 *Conjugal Lewdness* 114 and 118.

68 *Jure Divino* Bk VII, 3 and 14.

69 *The Political History of the Devil* 11–12 and 27–34.

70 On "the *je ne sais quoi* 'School of Taste,'" see Bate 1961: 130. Shaftesbury's concept of "inner sense" involved thought and feeling since he equated taste and moral sense (Bate 1961: 50–1). Shaftesbury uses the phrase "a *je ne sçai quoi* of wit" when he argues that erotic love has a "moral part" (Cooper 1964: Treatise II, Part IV, Section II, page 91). On Defoe's dialectically aesthetic and political appreciation of paintings, see Merrett 1994: 160–3.

71 *The Political History of the Devil* 69–70.

72 Defoe's ideological resistance to Milton has affinities to his resistance to Locke. "It seems likely that Locke's chief impact on eighteenth-century England was not to import contractarianism into politics, but Arianism into religion; but this in itself raised formidable barriers against the acceptance of his political analysis" (Clark 1985: 47).

73 *The Political History of the Devil* 70–2 and 74–5. Defoe points out that in Job 1:7 Satan answers God's question about where he has come from by saying that he has been "going to and fro in the earth, and from walking up and down in it."

74 *The Political History of the Devil* 75, 80, 85, 88, and 217. In *A System of Magick,* besides defending the idea that the Devil whispers to men in dreams, as in the case of his taking the shape of a toad to get close to Eve (96 and 113), Defoe leaves open the question of whether the Devil found it "absolutely necessary to settle a Correspondence among Mankind" or whether humans in "their Desires to be wicked" realized their need for "some exotick Helps" from him (81). Here Defoe once more refuses to deal in single narrative postulates.

75 To Shinagel, "the single best-selling category of books in the eighteenth century remained, as in the past, books on religious subjects, of which no less than two hundred were published annually throughout the century" (1968: 120). After reporting that "religious works formed easily the bulk of what every British printing press was producing" in the century, Colley points out that the availability of God's Word in English was fundamental to the formation of national identity as well as to the Protestant world view (1992: 41). Brewer confirms that religion and theology dominated the expansion of publication and that the sermon was the most important literary form (1997: 171–2). Hunter judiciously speculates about Defoe's library of theological books (1966: 8).

76 Defoe's contrary stances on allegory and analogy reflect his desire to uphold sacred awe and to attack Enlightenment views of religion. Scruton is helpful in this regard: "Religion seems to be about the gods; in fact it is about us and our human destiny. But we can understand what it is saying only through analogy and allegory. The allegory transports us to another realm, where the dark secrets of the human soul can be spread out for our contemplation and made comprehensible in the guise of cosmic forces" (2006: 122). Scruton's discussion of Wagner, Nietzsche, and René Girard encourages considerations of why Defoe's double attitudes towards characters and narrators may involve the notion of ritual sacrifice (2006: 122–8).

4. Biblical Allusions as Narrative Resources

1 *A New Family Instructor* 291. This chapter is an expanded version of Merrett 2004a.

2 Sherman 1996: 5–9.

3 Hill 1994: 7. Hill insists that "English men and women had experienced a quarter of a millennium of emphasis on the sovereignty of the Scriptures as the unique source of divine wisdom on all subjects, including politics, and a source which must be open to everybody" (1994: 18).
4 Hill 1994: 6 and 31.
5 See *Serious Reflections* 102. Novak claims that after 1725 Defoe's principal concern was to attack Anti-trinitarians, Socinians, and Deists (2001: 488). On the distinction between metaphor, allegory, and anagoge, see Honig 1966: 151–2.
6 *A New Family Instructor* 289–90, 300, 302, and 260.
7 *An Essay on the History and Reality of Apparitions* 21.
8 *The Family Instructor* 19 and 30. See "Sacred Time and Myths" in Eliade 1959: 68–113 and "The Structure of Myths" in Eliade 1963: 1–20.
9 While recognizing biblical allusions in Defoe's fiction, Novak rejects the proleptic functions of typology. He denies that the reader is "always to be taken back into a total biblical context" and that "the effect of Defoe's texts is entirely typological." Since they "innovate myths of their own, [Defoe's characters] … force us forward rather than backward in time. It is as if his characters have subsumed all prior myths and make references to earlier models superfluous" (1983: 11). However, Defoe's dialectical allusions invite readers to place themselves in a scriptural past so that they may form spiritual futures. Hunter explains how Puritanism advanced typology in the face of science (1966: 98–102). This chapter aims to substantiate Hunter's claims by addressing the contraries of Defoe's biblical hermeneutics.
10 Bruns 1987: 626–35. Hans Frei sees in the "subtlety and breadth of options" of Midrash hope for the repair of Christianity's textual problems. His contention that "Typological or figural interpretation, which was applied not only to the Old Testament but to the meaning of extrabiblical life and events, including one's own, stood in an unstable equilibrium between allegorical and literal interpretations" clarifies the dialectic of Defoe's biblical allusiveness (1986: 73–4 and 40).
11 Earle offers the balanced opinion that Defoe "was certainly worldly, but there seems little reason to doubt that he was at the same time sincerely religious" (1976: 33). After saying Defoe was sustained by a "deeply-held belief" in God's presence in his life and by "Christian imagery and biblical precedent," Richetti says that some of his biblical analogies "feel conventional and at times deeply inappropriate, even comically self-aggrandizing" (2005: 121–2).
12 *A Tour* II, 353; I, 116; I, 173–4. For Defoe's more muted praise of the Reformation, see *An Enquiry into the Occasional Conformity of Dissenters* (1697) in

The True-Born Englishman and Other Writings, ed. P.N. Furbank and W.R. Owens (London: Penguin, 1997), 117–20. Besides indicating the impurity of Henry VIII's motives, he holds that Edward VI's sincerity about reform led shallow conformists at his death to cause the "great fabric" of the Church to be "overthrown." Subsequent references are to this edition unless otherwise stated. In *Of Royall Educacion. A Fragmentary Treatise*, ed. Karl D. Bülbring (London: David Nutt, 1895), I, 1–6, and IV, 56–8, Defoe is even less enthusiastic about Henry VIII, criticizing the gloss the king put on events and arguing that he was motivated less by religious integrity than by self-interest. Conceding that Henry was a leader in education, Defoe praises Edward and Elizabeth more highly. All references are to this edition.

13 *A Tour* II, 41, and I, 368. In *An Enquiry into the Occasional Conformity of Dissenters*, Defoe draws attention to "a most Christian reconciling letter from Bishop Ridley to Bishop Hooper, two of the most glorious triumphant martyrs that ever confessed the truth of Christ at the stake" (119).

14 *A Tour* I, 48; II, 16; and II, 88. While elsewhere Defoe views Oxford, the city and the university, as the seat of courtly and high-church prejudices, especially those opposing the toleration of Dissenters, here he expresses his "preference for Protestant Oxford over the former Catholic university" (Rogers 1998: 30).

15 *A Tour* I, 210 and I, 186. On Defoe's "unusually tolerant position" on Catholics, see Earle 1976: 34 and West 1998: 82 and 366. Rogers holds that Defoe's "treatment of Roman Catholicism" in the *Tour* is "subdued" (1998: 30–1).

16 *A Tour* II, 16. Far from lamenting the disappearance of the Geneva Bible, Defoe happily cites the King James Bible and Book of Common Prayer despite the institutional status given them by Charles II's Act of Uniformity of 1662. On the rise to popularity of the King James Bible, see McGrath 2002: 280–90.

17 *A Tour* I, 219.

18 For perhaps the most sympathetic account of Defoe's "theological studies" and absorption of the Bible, see Freeman 1950: 66–70.

19 *An Essay on the History and Reality of Apparitions* 42–3.

20 *A System of Magick* 147. In "moments of intense feeling" Defoe "turned naturally to the words of the Bible" (Sutherland 1971: 200). To Richetti, he was "steeped in the Scriptures and committed to an uncompromising Christianity. Religious analogies are inevitable for him, even when his situation is thoroughly secular, and preacher and prophet are his recurring modes of self-presentation" (1987: 32). To Backscheider, he modelled his writing on preaching (1989: 144–5). Note her account of his proclivity for associating himself with the prophet Jeremiah (1989: 359–60).

21 For similar disclaimers, see *A System of Magick* 185, *An Essay on the History and Reality of Apparitions* 21, and *Conjugal Lewdness* 267.
22 By ignoring his adaptation of biblical texts, Earle sees Defoe's "defence of the literal truth of the Bible" in conflict with his "very modern faith in the power of reason" (1976: 35).
23 On Defoe's sense of the harmony between preaching and meditation, see *The Storm: Or, A Collection of the Most Remarkable Casualties and Disasters Which Happen'd in the Late Dreadful Tempest Both by Sea and Land* (London: G. Sawbridge, 1704). All references are to this edition. Sermons aid "*present Meditation*"; books address "*Ages to come, to the Eternity of mortal Time.*" An "*ill grounded*" sermon imposes on few; a false book "*upon the whole World*" ([A2v]). Still, concern for "*the Sincerity of the Relator*" and "*the proper Duty of an Historian*" leads Defoe to "*act the Divine*" in drawing "*Necessary practical Inferences*" (A3). He must preach on the storm: "*who can but preach where there is such a Text? when God himself speaks his own Power*" ([A7r]).
24 In the "ancient Israelite Wisdom tradition," Proverbs voices a "sense of order. The world is viewed as an order informed by a principle of retributive justice. As one turns to the world and gives to it, so one receives from it" (Williams, "Proverbs and Ecclesiastes," in Alter and Kermode 1987: 263). Proverbs was not written by Solomon, the putative, non-biblical authors being "the wise men" (Gabel, Wheeler, and York 1996: 137–40).
25 *Complete English Tradesman* I, i, 45; II, i, 32, 45, and 183; I, i, 98 and II, ii, 95.
26 *Complete English Tradesman* I, i, 38–9; I, i, 53–5; II, ii, 95; II, i, 46; I, i, 133 and I, ii, 117; I, i, 13 and II, ii, 120.
27 *Complete English Tradesman* II, i, 41–2; II, i, 66; II, i, 279; II, i, 236.
28 Andrew Wear in his introduction to *Due Preparations* in volume 5 of *Writings on Travel, Discovery and History: The Works of Daniel Defoe* (2002) calls Defoe's book "an *Ars Moriendi* or treatise on the art of dying" (15). Wear annotates many biblical allusions but does not comment on how they are dramatized in the dialogues.
29 *Due Preparations* 134–5, 137, 146–7, 158–9, and 161.
30 *Due Preparations* 161–2, 164. For other instances of ironical disclaimers of preaching, see the mother ("I am no Preacher, take it there, the rest will follow, of Course" [159]), and the daughter ("I do not take upon me to teach you, or say anything but just when you ask me" [169] and "I am no Preacher, *Brother*, I am but a Girl, a Child in these things, but the Story of the Prodigal came into my Head just then" [195]).
31 *Due Preparations* 184, 187, 190, and 194.

32 *Due Preparations* 200 and 203. On pages 201 and 202, the sister quotes Hosea 6:1; Isaiah 55:7; Isaiah 19:22 and 25; Lamentations 5:21; Jeremiah 31:18; Ezekiel 18:30–2 ; Ezekiel 33:11.
33 *Due Preparations* 215–16, 206, 208–10.
34 When it seems awkward to separate references to biblical texts from page references to Defoe's primary fictions, I put the latter in square brackets within the same parentheses.
35 A highly accessible discussion of figural thinking appears in the first two chapters, "The Decline of the Figural Imagination" and "The Sacramental Vision," in Scott 1971.
36 *Religious Courtship* 15 and 25. The allusions are to Isaiah 8:20 and Luke 16:8.
37 *Religious Courtship* 18. The allusion is to Proverbs 22:25.
38 *Religious Courtship* 31.
39 *Religious Courtship* 49, 53, 55, 59–60. The suitor is oppressed by the weight of Matthew 4:16, Luke 1:79, and Isaiah 50:10.
40 *Religious Courtship* 65–6.
41 *Religious Courtship* 70–1 and 73–5. On the relation between reflection and grace, see chapter 2, pages 52–3, 65. On the concept that faith is "endemic" in language, see Ong 1958: 80–105.
42 *Religious Courtship* 98 and 111.
43 *Religious Courtship* 120 and 161.
44 Compare with the use of the allusion in *Roxana*: "my Measure of Wickedness was not yet full; I continued obstinate against Matrimony" (159).
45 Defoe attacks rationalizing abuses of this biblical story in *Conjugal Lewdness* 98 and 123.
46 See *Colonel Jack* 268 and 275 and the previous page. Defoe's repetition of biblical verses in his fictions alerts readers to his consistent appeal to their exegetical reading of key texts.
47 For Defoe's attack on the metaphor of the wife as an underling, see *Conjugal Lewdness* 26: "I don't take the State of Matrimony to be designed as that of Apprentices who are bound to the Family, and that the Wife is to be us'd only as the upper Servant in the House."
48 Roxana's allusions to money as fire in flax and to having a dart stuck in her liver are seen by Starr as images of despair (1965: 179–80). For Defoe's further use of the dart stuck in the liver, see *Conjugal Lewdness* 92 and 393.
49 The motif of a secondary character as a superior interpreter is common in Defoe's fictions, e.g., William in *Captain Singleton*, the ordinary in *Moll Flanders*, the Tutor in *Colonel Jack*, and the Quaker lady in *Roxana*.

50 On the shaping of the English language by the King James Bible, see McGrath 2002: 253–76. He elucidates two paradoxes that help to contextualize Defoe's allusiveness. Firstly, "the king's translators achieved literary distinction precisely because they were not deliberately pursuing it." Secondly, while the translators were instructed to resist linguistic developments, their texts so steadily repeated archaic idioms that the latter became naturalized and rendered highly recognizable in standard speech (254, 259, 263, and 269).

5. Political Impersonations and Cultural Implications

1 *The Great Law of Subordination Consider'd* (London: S. Harding et al., 1724), 20. All references are to this edition.
2 Schonhorn 1991: 161–2.
3 Porter 2001: 192, 185, 193, and 188.
4 I elaborate these points in Merrett 2004b: 34–6.
5 *The Great Law of Subordination* 40–1. Regarding his "uneasy mixture of fascination and panic in the face of what was widely felt to be a sharp and widespread increase in levels of violent crime" in the 1720s, Gladfelder attributes Defoe's "divided response" in *The Great Law of Subordination Consider'd* and other works to "his assumption of distinct and often rhetorically extremist personae" (2008: 65). But more remarkable is Defoe's willingness to argue against himself while adopting strange personas whose ironies support their creator's moral and religious tenets.
6 *Mere Nature Delineated* 153. Ignoring Defoe's facetious impersonations, Wear reads this work as a treatise in which the "sense of the soul is very nearly the same as that of the modern meaning of mind" (2002: 20). To Wear, Defoe rejects Descartes's innate ideas and upholds Locke's sense of the tabula rasa. But Defoe's statement that "Nature's production is a *Charte Blanch,* and the soul is plac'd in [man] like a piece of clean paper, upon which the precepts of life are to be written by his instructors, and he has the charge of keeping it fair lay'd upon himself" (28–9) is less concerned with how ideas arise in the mind than with how individuals should submit to pedagogical authority. Wear's view of Defoe's Lockean stance repeats Boulton's editorial claim (1975: 247), which is restated by Porter 2001: 383. Wear grants that "Defoe's position on the philosophical-political fashions of the early eighteenth century was not a simple one" but reads *Mere Nature Delineated* as "ultimately a pessimistic work" (25).
7 *Mere Nature Delineated* 155 and 159. This paragraph glosses Crusoe's experience on the island: he sleeps the first night in a tree; he burrows into the

earth; and he sets great store on having a doorway to his cavern and an entrance to his enclosure. See chapter 3, note 32.

8 *Mere Nature Delineated* 162, 164, 167–8, 171, and 173–4.

9 *Mere Nature Delineated* 174, 177, 189, 193, 206–7, 211, and 225.

10 *Mere Nature Delineated* 226–7.

11 *Memoirs of a Cavalier*, ed. James T. Boulton (London: Oxford University Press, 1972). All references are to this edition. In his introduction and appendix, Boulton describes Defoe's historiographical sources (x–xi, 281–99).

12 Roxana prefers Naples and Venice on account of the "Swarms of Ecclesiaisticks of all Kinds" at Rome (103).

13 *Strike while the Iron's Hot, Or, Now Is the Time to Be Happy* (London: S. Keimer, 1715), 11. Subsequent references are to this edition. Furbank and Owens call this a "bellicose Whiggish tract," the periodic style of which does not "sound like" Defoe (1994: 68–9). Novak (2001: 476) attributes it to Defoe, as does Schonhorn (1991: 137).

14 Schonhorn 1991: 161. Furbank and Owens reject the application of "protean" to Defoe because, they say, he has none of the "miraculous inventiveness" of Shakespeare or Dickens. They assert that there is "no feat of impersonation in Defoe's novels" that can "compete with Dickens's" (1988: 9–10). Cognitive science regards the "unified self" as an "illusion" that the brain works hard to produce (Pinker 2002: 42–3). On the plurality of brain functions and the physiological implications for identity, see the accounts of "neuroplasticity" and "the plastic paradox" in Doidge (2007: 46–50, 208–11, and 316–18). See also Jaynes's account of the relation of plasticity to the evolution of consciousness out of the bicameral mind that was characterized by hearing admonitory voices (1976: 122ff.) I take up these matters in the final chapter.

15 To Moore, *The Shortest-Way with the Dissenters* "no longer attacked individual Dissenters who had proved too weak to undergo oppression, but the organized power which used oppression as an instrument of national policy" (1958: 109). On the Earl of Nottingham's persecution of Defoe for this textual "banter," see Moore 1958: 113–18. Backscheider's view of this "dramatic impersonation" emphasizes Defoe's careful exploitation of political slogans (1989: 94–6). For her, the aftermath of Defoe's being pilloried left him with severe "mood swings" that affected his depiction of fictional characters and led him to "an uneasy peace with the Dissenters," whom he "never trusted again, never felt himself truly one of them, and they returned the feeling" (1989: 129 and 134).

16 This paragraph draws on "The Establishment of the Hanoverian Dynasty" in Speck 1977: 169–84.

17 On the formation of the Whig schism, the temporizing by which the Whig opposition of Walpole co-opted Tory members of parliament and the Country party, and the Erastian principles of the Whig bishops, among whom Hoadly was only the most famous, see Owen 1974: 12–14 and 152–5.

18 These political events are nicely tied into the disintegration of the Tory party and its control of the patronage system by Plumb (1969: 163–73). He explains how Walpole not only manipulated Tory backbenchers to empower himself in the Whig schism but also turned his back on Old Whig principles, eroded the power of the Court, and belittled Cabinet government in order to establish political stability and the oligarchy of the New Whigs (1969: 174–9). Defoe was no more impressed with this so-called stability than he had been with party strife and Whig factionalism.

19 To Schonhorn, Defoe thought hard about perpetuating monarchism: "As he watched at century's end the disintegration of his ideal of a Heaven-sanctioned warrior-king, Defoe moved unswervingly towards a full articulation of the royal triune. From the standing army debates of 1697–98, he had learned that 'when Kings the sword of Justice first lay down, / They are no Kings, though they possess the Crown'" (1991: 135–6).

20 Novak says that whether Defoe "was still the thoroughgoing Whig ideologue who composed *Jure Divino* is doubtful" (2001: 464). The grounds of Whig ideology shifted too much for him.

21 Hanson explains how Defoe's steadfastness to Harley gave the government cause to suspect his journalistic commissions (1967: 100–5).

22 In proposing how Defoe maintained his monarchist ideals, Schonhorn says that "If, in the *Reflections upon the Late Great Revolution,* he had tended to stress the elective nature of monarchy, or the mutuality of the ceremonial act of the coronation, in *Jure Divino* the voice of God undermines the populist emphasis of that earlier tract and challenges the extravagant tendencies of whiggish thought in his day. In *Jure Divino* the election-coronation-compact sequences seem to carry the same weight as they did sixteen years earlier, yet now consecration by the people merely confirms and ratifies an existing condition" (1991: 130). N.B. Furbank and Owens de-attribute the 1689 pamphlet (1994: 3–4). Relevant is Sill's account of the variability of political writers' allegiances. Elaborating Pocock's claim that Augustan authors were motivated by a "civic humanism" that transcended Whig and Tory perspectives, Sill holds that to achieve this ideological goal, they employed "a highly ambivalent rhetoric, replete with alternatives, conflicts, and confusions, of which they were well aware and in which they were to some extent trapped" (1983: 15).

23 The following comments by Sill are helpful: "Defoe's tendency to balance contradictory ideas by setting them against each other and to discredit the opposition by revealing how their ideas served the interest of a specific faction were legacies from Harley that Defoe carried to the end of his writing career. At the same time, however, Defoe was deeply frustrated by the lack of ideological direction in Harley's ministry"; "his decision to defend Harley as the emblem of civic virtue after the Hanoverian succession had a high degree of psychological, if not historical, validity: the country needed to believe that the transition was not a radical one and that there was room in the new reign for men who had acted a part in the old ... Defoe's readers imposed on themselves the hegemony of the new Whig culture and, at the same time, the restraining virtues of moderation, experience, and tradition, thus contributing to the stability of the new order"; in vindicating Harley and supporting Walpole, the chairman of the Secret Committee charged with Harley's prosecution, Defoe played "each side against the other in order to achieve his own ideological ends" (1983: 23, 26, and 98).

24 Backscheider says brilliantly that "Defoe often quotes the lines from St. Paul's description of his ministry: 'I am made all things to all men, that I might by all means save some,'" explaining his citations of 1 Corinthians 9:22 as signifying a "pleasure in assumed voices" that "comes from what he believes is the skillful performance of his job: to bring the mistaken to truth" (1989: 298–9).

25 For the influence of Samuel Keimer, the Quaker publisher, on Defoe's style of impersonation, see Backscheider 1989: 376–7.

26 Quakers were known as the Society of Friends. On their quietism and pacificism, see Keeble 1987: 28–9 and 193–4. On George Fox's emphasis on the inwardness of spiritual experience and the inner light, see Olney 1972: 168–77. *A Friendly Epistle* was published in London on 19 February 1715 by Keimer. For its bibliographical context, see Furbank and Owens 1998: 153–54. To Novak, disgust with his political situation made him regard the Quaker stance as an "escape from intellectual slavery" (2001: 477). To Furbank and Owens, this tract "throws light on Defoe's political stance at this moment, for he is plainly making no bid for reconciliation with the Government and Court and indeed exploits the 'plain speaking' of Quakers to say some harsh things about them" (2006: 147).

27 *A Friendly Epistle* 10 and 27. While Defoe "knew Restoration drama exceptionally well, and he quoted passages long after the authors had lost their vogue," he objected to "the licentious lives of many actors and actresses, to the profanity and indecency of many spoken lines, to the emptiness of many plays, to the stupidity of audiences, to the waste of time in habitual

attendance at the theater" (Moore 1958: 25). For Sill, his "animus is not against the theater as such, but rather the political advantage" that the "disorders" it provoked gave "to the Church," Defoe seeing "a direct connection between the stability of the state and the condition of its morals." In 1717 and 1718, "the major threat was not the playhouses, but the passions and ambitions of the Whigs" (1983: 101 and 152).

28 See Furbank and Owens 1998: 154. Curiously, Defoe assails the theatre when developing his skills with the dialogue form in conduct books and employing dramatic form for political satire in *The Candidate* (see note 46). Backscheider provides sources for the Quakers' rejection of Keimer's and Defoe's representations of them (1989: 594n66).

29 *A Sharp Rebuke from One of the People Called Quakers* (London: S. Keimer, 1715), 8. On Sacheverell as a rabble-rousing high-flyer, see Cragg 1966b: 62–3 and 118–19. For Defoe's verbal attack on the leader of the high-flying party, Francis Atterbury, see Bennett 1975: 189–93.

30 *A Declaration of Truth to Benjamin Hoadly* (London: E. More, 1717). While he opposed the Jacobite rebellion, Hoadly's extreme Latitudinarianism in defence of the Hanoverians degraded episcopal government, belittled priesthood, and undermined the principles of Dissenters (Sykes 1928: 120, 123, 142–55). See also Novak 2001: 522. To Furbank and Owens, this pamphlet is an elegant example of "teasing" (2006: 159).

31 *A Declaration of Truth to Benjamin Hoadly* 6, 18–20, 22, and 29.

32 *A Friendly Rebuke to One Parson Benjamin* (London: E. More, 1719).

33 Corinthians 13:1. On Defoe's ambivalent view of Hoadly and occasional conformity, see Backscheider 1989: 396–401.

34 *A Friendly Rebuke to One Parson Benjamin* 7, 10–11, and 22. Defoe had recently expressed similar views in *Memoirs of the Life and Eminent Conduct of Daniel Williams, D.D.* (London: E. Curll, 1718), especially pages 25–7.

35 *An Account of the Great and Generous Actions of James Butler* (London: J. Moore, 1715), 11 and 18. Compare his stance to Oxford University in *A Tour* as presented in chapter 4, page 116–17, of this volume.

36 *A Trumpet Blown in the North* (London: S. Keimer, 1715), 3.

37 *The Layman's Vindication of the Church of England* (London: A. and W. Bell, et al., 1716), 3.

38 *Fair Payment No Spunge* (London: J. Brotherton et al., 1717). This pamphlet ostensibly defends Walpole's scheme for a sinking fund to pay off the national debt (Furbank and Owens 1998: 171–2).

39 *Fair Payment No Spunge* 9–10, 23, 61, and 64. Citing the 1701 pamphlet *The Villainy of Stock-Jobbers Detected*, Nicholson points out Defoe's criticism of how little the new financial instruments were understood despite being

eagerly exploited (1994: 15). He then shows that in 1711 Defoe's *Review* cannot determine whether "the interdependence of personal and national credit" is a "'Service'" or "'Prejudice'" (1994: 16). Such ambivalence supports Thompson's claim that "One of the most intriguing aspects of Defoe's writing is that political economy and the novel are not yet separable and distinct discourses" (1996: 90 and 131). To Davis, Defoe's adherence to the "bounds of the news / novel discourse" treated readers to "an inherent doubleness or reflexivity" (1983: 157).

40 *The Old Whig and Modern Whig Revived* (London: S. Baker, 1717). Furbank and Owens find this "tract caustic both towards the Government and the Walpole Opposition," Defoe writing "as a saddened Whig, on the fatal capacity of politicians to ruin their own, and their country's, prosperity by their personal competitiveness, thinly disguised as 'patriotism'" (2006: 156). "Though Defoe welcomed the accession of George I as much as anyone, he knew that it would also bring into power the coalition of Modern Whigs and Hanover Tories that he had charged with failing to help secure the Protestant Succession" (Sill 1983: 96).

41 This view is what Sill has in mind when he sees Defoe as agent of the ideology which eventually brought about the Whig hegemony.

42 *The Old Whig and Modern Whig Revived* 32, 35–7, and 47.

43 *The Anatomy of Exchange-Alley* (London: E. Smith, 1719), 3.

44 *The Anatomy of Exchange-Alley* 3, 6–7, 12, 28, 42, 59–60, and 62–3.

45 The following passage from chapter 27, "Of Identity And Diversity," in *An Essay Concerning Human Understanding* appears to have informed Defoe's presentation of characters and narrators as well as the licence he gave himself in his impersonations: "But if it be possible for the same man to have distinct incommunicable consciousness at different times, it is past doubt the same man would at different times make different persons; which, we see, is the sense of mankind in the solemnest declaration of their opinions, human laws not punishing the *mad man* for the *sober man's* actions, nor the *sober man* for what the *mad man* did, thereby making them two persons: which is somewhat explained by our way of speaking in *English* when we say such an one *is not himself*, or is *beside himself*; in which phrases it is insinuated, as if those who now, or at least first used them, thought that *self* was changed, the *self*-same person was no longer in that man" (Locke 1961: I, 287–8). For Scruton, "Locke argued that to be a human being is one thing, to be a person is another. Human beings can endure where a person ceases, and perhaps vice versa. A human being is an organism, whose identity is determined by the continuity of that organism in accordance with the real essence which it possesses. But the organism is not identical

with the person" (1995: 97). Later in the same chapter, Locke says that "Nothing but consciousness can unite remote existences into the same person: the identity of substance will not do it; for whatever substance there is however framed, without consciousness there is no person; and a carcass may be a person, as well as any sort of substance be so, without consciousness" (Locke 1961: I, 289). On Defoe's use of the word "carcass" to designate a person without identity, see chapter 3, note 32.

46 This section analyzses works that Furbank and Owens (1994) have "de-attributed" with varying degrees of certainty but that appear in Novak's bibliography (2001). The former doubt Defoe's authorship of *The Candidate* (London: S. Keimer, 1715) because the writer's self-presentation as a playwright does not ring true to Defoe's contempt for the theatre (1994: 71–2). Novak calls it "one of Defoe's best pamphlets." Defoe's long-term deployment of dialogue favoured dramaturgical methods. To Novak, publishing with Keimer, a former member of the enthusiastic French Prophets, gave "a special character to some of [Defoe's] publications" (2001: 476). His ties to Keimer suggest that, since the latter printed Susannah Centlivre's *The Gotham Election*, which satirizes electioneering bribery, that play may have influenced the composition of *The Candidate*. See Backscheider 1989: 594n68, Moore 1971: 117–18, and note 28 above.

47 *The Candidate* 21–2 and 41. From 1662 when Robert Howard's *The Committee* was published, the country gentry that had been politicized by the Civil War became stereotypical figures in Restoration and early eighteenth-century comedy. Prominent examples include George Etherege's *She Would If She Could* (1668), William Wycherley's *Love in a Wood* (1671), William Congreve's *The Double Dealer* (1694), and George Farquhar's *The Beaux' Stratagem* (1707). For an analysis of political satire in these and other comedies, see Merrett 2002: 209–11 and 212–16.

48 *A Reply to a Traiterous Libel* (London: J. Baker, 1715). See Moore 1971: 118. Furbank and Owens find the "simple-minded polemical style" of this tract inconsistent with Defoe's earlier support for a standing army (1994: 72). Novak accepts Defoe's authorship (2001: 476).

49 *A Reply to a Traiterous Libel* 8–9 and 23. On this point, see Sill 1983: 107–8.

50 *The Protestant Jubilee* (London: S. Keimer, 1715) was published on 8 February 1715. Furbank and Owens dismiss this work as a "rabid Whiggish mock-sermon" and an "anti-Harleyite farrago" (1994: 72–3). But Novak accepts it as by Defoe (2001: 477). See also Moore 1971: 118–19. Baine places Defoe in the tradition of writers who upheld day-fatalities (1968: 7–9).

51 *An Humble Address to Our Sovereign Lord the People* (London: J. Roberts, 1715), 25. Furbank and Owens de-attribute this work (published in the

early summer of 1715) because it "neither expresses his own views nor can be interpreted as a lampoon" (1994: 81). Without commenting on the impersonation of high-flying ideology, Novak says Defoe wrote this pamphlet from "a more conservative standpoint" (2001: 480 n.39). See also Moore 1971: 126.

52 *The Conduct of Robert Walpole* (London: T. Warner, 1717), 3 and 31. Furbank and Owens once de-attributed this "windy and vacuous piece" because, while it cites *Fair Payment No Spunge*, this alone does not make this work Defoe's (1994: 100). They now accept it as Defoe's while finding it "unrelievedly eulogistic" (2006: 148). Novak sees this work as integral to Defoe's criticism of self-interest in the Whig party (2001: 514). See also Moore 1971: 146. One wonders about the reflexive function of this biography since page 59 enters Defoe's name into journalistic debates about the author of *Fair Payment No Spunge*: "others, who pretended to speak from better Information, said it was done by *Daniel de Foe*." See note 38 above.

53 *A History of the Clemency of Our English Monarchs* (London: N. Mist, 1717). Furbank and Owens de-attribute this work because it eulogizes Charles II in Ciceronian sentences (1994: 103–4). Novak accepts it (2001: 519n16). Moore says that Defoe summarized this tract (and Matthias Earbery's to which he was replying) in *Mercurius Politicus* for September 1717: 561–78 and 578–93 (1971: 151).

54 The text of Ezekiel 18:32 in the King James Bible reads: "I have no pleasure in the death of him that dieth, saith the Lord God: wherefore turn yourselves, and live ye." The fourth definition of "return" in Cruden's *Concordance* is as follows: "*To return, as when a sinner, who has erred from the ways of God's commandments, doth return to God by unfeigned repentance*" (398). See also Isaiah 55:7: "Let the wicked forsake his way, and the unrighteous man his thoughts: and let him return unto the Lord, and he will have mercy upon him; and to our God, for he will abundantly pardon." The verse from Ezekiel is adapted in *The Book of Common Prayer* as the third confessional in The Order for Morning Prayer and Evening Prayer.

55 *A History of the Clemency of Our Englis h Monarchs* 7–9, 18–19, and 23–6.

56 *Some Reasons Why It Could Not Be Expected* (London: W. Boreham, 1718). Furbank and Owens de-attribute this work because its tone "never remotely suggests Defoe" (1994: 111–12). Novak accepts it as by Defoe (2001: 519n17). Also, see Moore 1971: 156.

57 Besides elaborating this point, Novak explains how publication of the biography would have disseminated Jacobite ideology (2001: 519).

58 *Some Reasons Why It Could Not Be Expected* 7, 9, 11, and 28.

59 For earlier Islamic references in this chapter, see pages 142–3 above. This section is a revised version of Merrett 2005.
60 Baine 1968: 58–9.
61 Viz. "The *Jewish Rabbins* thô their Enemies, / In this conclude them honest men and wise: / For 'twas their duty, all the Learned think, / T'espouse his Cause by whom they eat and drink" ("Absalom and Achitophel," ll. 104–7, *The Poems of John Dryden* [Oxford: Clarendon], I, 219).
62 *A System of Magick* 351–3.
63 Barbary corsairs were famous for capturing slaves from Europe, most of whom were taken for ransom: see Lewis 2001: 191.
64 Colley 2002: 106 and 103. On Islam's historical relations with Europe, see Lewis 2002 and 2003.
65 Boswell 1953: 1218. Lewis notes that this conversation typifies "the ignorance and prejudice of the time" yet recognizes the comparability of Christianity and Islam (2001: 5).
66 Loomba's digest of Edward Said's *Orientalism* and its critics challenges generalizations about Augustan writing which claim that individual authors advance rigid ideological positions. Loomba points out that early modern attitudes to orientalism were neither fixed nor certain (1998: 48–54).
67 Backscheider claims that Defoe's first publication evidences "the impetuousness and extremism" that led him to join the Monmouth Rebellion (1989: 44–5). She does not consider that Defoe's polemical stance detaches him from the sectarian thinking he was expected to uphold. If, as Horn says, the religious enthusiasm that greeted the relief of Vienna was "almost unaffected by political calculation" (1967: 360), Defoe was not single-mindedly enthusiastic. Since his satire needs external standards, he equates Ottoman and Roman imperialism to unsettle British ideology.
68 *An Appeal to Honour and Justice* in *Selected Writings of Daniel Defoe* 1975: 191.
69 Letter 14 [July–August 1704?] in *Letters* 46.
70 Laura Brown emphasizes "the self-confident, monolithic truth of the Augustans" that is matched by critics' concern with "political stability, cultural consolidation, canonical authority, and formal complexity." By focusing on the "radical, protofeminist advocacy of female liberty" in *Roxana,* she sees Defoe repudiating his protagonist's feminism in the end (1993: 2, 9, and 17). But he faults as much as celebrates British imperialism, just as he satirizes and sympathizes with Roxana throughout.
71 *Complete English Tradesman* II, i, 275.
72 Letter 11 [June 1704?] in *Letters* 24.
73 *Conjugal Lewdness* 394–5. In "Of Heroic Virtue," Sir William Temple degrades Islamic militarism: the Grand Vizier's lust for gold which he will

not share with his army explains the Ottomans' defeat before Vienna. To Temple, their empire rests on "the practices of a subtle man upon the simplicity of a credulous people" (*Five Miscellaneous Essays*, ed. Samuel Holt Monk [Ann Arbor: U of Michigan Press, 1963], 163–4). Temple's Eurocentrism claims the Ottoman empire had been dormant for a century (162), a claim refuted by Colley (2002: 65).

74 *Conjugal Lewdness* 172. Enslavement by Islamic forces was familiar to Britons. Colley estimates that 20,000 were captured as slaves by the Moors in the hundred years between the middle of the seventeenth and eighteenth centuries (2002: 56). Faller is helpful about Defoe's "ideas of sinfulness" in saying that Defoe "critiqued the belief that society might depend on the 'civility' of its members by subverting the very notion of individual identity on which it was based. Defoe's criminals have no solid sense of self and, it might well be argued, no characterological core." Faller concludes that "Defoe was not in his own time quite the celebrator of individualism he has been made out to be, but then he escapes most such simple categorizations" (1993: 254). His satirical deployment of Islam illustrates Faller's contentions about the portrayal of individualism.

75 *A Tour* I, 303. To Vickers, Defoe models *A Tour* on the Baconian experimentation of the Royal Society. Yet, given his concern to promote useful knowledge and to balance natural improvements with submission to nature's powers, he subtly plagiarizes and adapts the works of scientists and antiquarians (1996: 151–76).

76 *A Tour* II, 221.

77 *A Tour* II, 224. Defoe was familiar with the idiom of horse trading: the market for horses involved a vocabulary of body parts and diseases which, if customers did not know, they risked being fleeced (*Complete English Tradesman* I, i, 31).

78 *A Tour* II, 203.

79 See Sorenson 2002: 53–8.

80 *A Tour* II, 279. While Scotland had less than 10 per cent of Britain's population in 1750, the East India Company was "at the very least half-Scottish" (Ferguson 2003: 45). On Defoe's disgust with Scotland's failure to exercise scientific and commercial energy, see Vickers 1996: 174–5.

81 Nicholson 1994: 46.

82 *A Tour* I, 351. One aspect of Gresham's significance to Defoe was that he was a founder of the Bank of England. On the commercial, imperial, and cultural significance of The Royal Exchange, see Joseph Addison's panegyric of 19 May 1711 in *The Spectator*, vol. I (London: Dent, 1945), 212–15.

83 *A Tour* I, 100 and I, 96. That Roxana sends a wife to her son, a trader to Turkey, shows she is aware of the plight of brides-to-be caused by bachelors engaged in imperial commerce.
84 *A Plan of the English Commerce* 234–9.
85 *A Plan of the English Commerce* 258–9, 136, 132–3, 208–9.
86 While Thompson posits an inverse relation between images of exchange in *A Plan of the English Commerce* and *The Complete English Tradesman* (1996: 126), my focus on the rhetorical use of Islam in these works emphasizes ideological continuity founded in imperial rivalry with France.
87 *Complete English Tradesman* II, i, 123.
88 *Complete English Tradesman* I, Supplement 32–3. Nicholson acutely explicates Defoe's contrary sense of credit: it is omnipresent, godlike, immaterial, and imaginary (1994: 86–7).
89 *Complete English Tradesman* II, ii, 52.
90 See "Letters during Mr. Wortley's Embassy to Constantinople (1716–1718)" in *Letters from the Right Honourable Lady Mary Wortley Montagu 1709–1762* (London: Dent: 1906), 56–202.
91 *Complete English Tradesman* II, ii, 110–20, 129–44. To Defoe, tradesmen are "a growing race of gentlemen," their opulence symbolizing the growth of Britain's economic empire. He felt that the nation's wealth derives not from military conquest and occupation of foreign lands. Peaceable trade explains commercial growth. Discoveries of unknown lands, settlements on uninhabited islands, and colonies on the uncultivated continent of America explain the size of the home economy. Apart from the transplantation of negroes and the displacement of treacherous natives, the colonies have been peopled by transplanted felons. Full domestic employment, population growth, and the fact the poor need not go to be mercenaries in foreign armies bear witness to the dynamism of the English economy (*Complete English Tradesman* I, i, 313–16). See also chapter 3, note 38.
92 For his contrarily sacramental and contractual sense of marriage, see chapter 3, page 102, and chapter 7 passim. Abse sees "outrageous *chutzpah*" in Defoe's imaginary fiction of Turkish court procedures (2006: 205).
93 Birdsall's claim that Defoe equates "pagan Turks with irrationality and lack of government" is unfounded (1985: 159). Novak confirms Defoe's view of Turkish rationality (1983: 116).
94 *Conjugal Lewdness* 297–304 and 337.
95 *Conjugal Lewdness* 386 and 357. The biblical allusion is to Philippians 4:8. See note 101 below.
96 Pointing to Iser's reader-response theory and the emotional tensions in *Roxana*'s final scenes, Faller remarks that "What Roxana truly *is* becomes

a question not of essences or psychology merely, but of the effect (and affect) she has on her reading audience. The basis for this closing effort is the active role the text has allowed (or imposed upon) readers up to this point – a role that involves more than moving back and forth between opposite feelings, and which, even as one's sympathies or antipathies are engaged, promotes a special kind of distance from Roxana and her story" (1993: 231).

97 To Sherman, Roxana evades history since Defoe aims to maintain generic indeterminacy (1996: 157–8). Tracing fictionality in his works, she declines to differentiate between truth and fiction; to classify his fictions as novels, in her view, depreciates his imaginative creativity.

98 Novak calls *Roxana* "a novel of moral decay": Roxana's abuse of primitivism makes the text a "curious combination of mythic synchronic time and the particular serial chronology of history" (1983: 100 and 116).

99 *Conjugal Lewdness* laments that satirists are charged with indecency when exposing sinners: "Shall it be Criminal to reprove the Offence which they think it is not Criminal to commit?" (15); "It must be acknowledged the Age is ripened up in Crime to a dreadful height, and it is not a light, a gentle Touch, that will bring them to blush" (17); "The Dialect these people talk is a great part of the Crime; and as it is not to be made use of for their Reproof, so we are straiten'd exceedingly in Reproving; and they triumph over me in this very Part, that I talk in the dark, and reprove by Allegory and Metaphor, that People may know, or not know what I mean, just as it may happen" (386).

100 See Novak 1963: 118n1. For a full account of the Turkish costume, see Blewett 1979: 141–3. His summation of its narrative significance is important: "It serves within the structure of the novel as a device linking the public immorality of the masquerade party, Defoe's vivid example of the moral and social decay of his age, directly to the destruction of private individuals" (1979: 143).

101 For Defoe's objections to salacious objectification of the body, consider the following passages from *Conjugal Lewdness*: "It were to be wish'd we had nothing to say of the Indecency even of the Clothing, and how we study to go naked in our very Clothes, and that after God himself put them on to cover us too … God having then appointed, and Nature compelled Mankind to seek Covering, all the Pretences for going naked on that account are at an End" (3); "It is the Custom in some Nations to go naked, and in others they cloath so light, that is to say, next Door to going naked, their Cloaths being so thin and light, that all the Parts of the Body are, as it were, described to the Eye, by the Garments setting so close to them; as in *Italy*, in *Turkey* and *Barbary*, and other hot Countries: But such

a Practice, though 'tis thought nothing of there, would be thought immodest here to the last Degree, and indeed scandalous" (357). The biblical allusion in the first passage is to Genesis 3:21; in the second to Philippians 4:8. On Defoe's hostility to naturalists for whom nakedness was a reparation of the Fall, see chapter 3, page 104.

102 The murder of Susan is not narrated but glimpsed through the theology of *Serious Reflections*. Thus, Roxana berates Amy: "why you ought to be hang'd for what you have done already; for having resolv'd on it, is doing it, as to the Guilt of the Fact; you are a Murtherer already, as much as if you had done it already" (273).

103 For further probable evidence of Defoe's topical familiarity with Islam, see Lee (1969): the "Balm of Mecca" from a tree blessed by the "great Prophet Mahomet" (II, 392); in December 1721, English captives released by the King of Fez and Morocco marching in "Moorish Habits" through London to St Paul's (II, 461); the likely Treaty of Partition between Russia and Turkey for the territories of the Sophy of Persia (III, 210–11); and courtly oriental bombast (III, 221–4). In the 1721 ransom, the British government handed over 1,200 barrels of gunpowder and 13,500 gunlocks, thus confirming Colley's view of the interdependence of European and Islamic states (2002: 68).

104 Colley 2002: 1 and 58.

105 *A Journal of the Plague Year* 11–12, 193, and 230.

106 Anthony Ashley Cooper, *Characteristics of Men, Manners, Opinions, Times*, ed. John M. Robertson (Indianapolis, IN: Bobbs-Merrill, 1964), I, 221–3 and II, 301.

6. Political Imaginings: Sacred and Profane

1 *A Tour* I, 193.

2 Relevant to Defoe's presentation of the Earl of Pembroke is McKeon's explanation of how "capitalist or 'middle class' values" transformed seventeenth-century aristocracy. For McKeon, "both merchants and aristocratic landowners are permeated by the values of a class orientation by the early eighteenth century." In his mind, "status values – deference and paternalistic care – that we commonly associate with aristocratic social relations" did not "lose their force" but underwent "the more elaborate sort of 'theatricalization' that is likely to occur whenever social convention is raised to the level of self-conscious practice." McKeon's discussion of "the dialectical antithesis of progressive and conservative ideology" that arises from the fluidity of social change, less to resolve its conflicts than to render that change

intelligible, underlies my study (1987: 167–9 and 171). Far from rejecting aristocracy, Defoe aimed to refashion it by minimizing hereditary rights and breeding and by advancing moral conduct and constructive social actions. His interest in renovating aristocracy also stemmed from concern to raise the rank of national identity and to project a European status on Britain. *A Tour* views the "mansions of the 'British nobility and gentry' newly built on the banks of the Thames" in polar terms (I, 167): they are "visual symbols of the harmony between nature and art created by the new political order" and they "impart a 'character to the island of Great Britain in general,' for, when seen close up, they are 'meer pictures and paintings' and 'all art,' but, from a distance, they so fit into the landscape that they are 'all nature'" (Merrett 1994: 160). The paintings in aristocratic mansions represent the nation's cultural progress begun by the early Stuarts. The family portraits by Van Dyck and Lely at Wilton House are the cynosure of European eyes since the best of them is modelled on a portrait of "King Charles I, with his queen and children" (*A Tour* I, 196). Given his avoidance of partisanship, he also claims that Kneller's "gallery of Beauties" done for Queen Mary contains "as good faces and as good painting" as that done by Lely for Charles II (*A Tour*, 304). On the ideology embedded in aristocratic Whig mansions, see Rogers 1998: 182–4.

3 Samuel Johnson, *The History of Rasselas Prince of Abissinia*, ed. J. P. Hardy (Oxford: Oxford World's Classics, 1988), 104. Besides thinking *Robinson Crusoe* one of the very few books readers wanted longer, Johnson was familiar with most of Defoe's writings (Rogers 1972: 58–9).

4 For Sill, "Defoe turned to fiction as a way of demonstrating the historical necessity of emerging cultural formations and a way of reconciling the contradictions between the various factions competing for hegemony in the wake of the Glorious Revolution of 1688." In his closing remarks about Defoe's fiction, Sill subordinates narrative to political theory: "If Defoe's claim for the validity of his fictions rests on their subordination to an ideological intention, which is itself valid, then the final proof of the worth of his work depends not on the validity of the idea of fiction itself, but on the validity of ideology as a form of knowledge" (1983: 22 and 174). This chapter argues that his fiction critiques political ideology through narrators who uphold and question it, following Richetti's views of how Defoe makes his narrators and characters participants in ideology (1988: 50–4).

5 From French critics, this question provokes interesting responses. Baridon, exploring the cultural relations between horticulture and Calvinism, holds that the purchase and improvement of rural land allowed London's commercial classes to sense "la possibilité de prendre part à la vie politique."

For French Protestant garden theorists, the "travail de la terre doit être rentable, l'homme est ici-bas pour faire fructifier les dons que Dieu lui fait" (1996: 77 and 79). The island experience is a code for domestic values, as Lestringant confirms: "Robinson n'est pas vraiment un aventurier, mais quelqu'un qui transporte ailleurs tout son monde et qui le reconstruit." If Crusoe's voyage to the island represents a dream, it is "un rêve en définitive très conformiste. Il ne s'agit pas du tout d'un rêve de dépaysement, d'étrangeté ou de rencontre avec l'étranger. Au contraire, c'est un retour au même à travers une illusion de déplacement" (1996: 63–4).

6 Furbank and Owens read Crusoe's political fantasies as "humanly triumphant" (2006: 176). This optimistic reading, filtered through Rousseau's *Emile*, ignores the structuring of self-recrimination that pervades Defoe's fiction. Spacks long ago argued for Crusoe's constructive fantasies, holding that through them love overcomes aggression (1976: 35–7). Pro-Enlightenment readings remain common, even from structuralist viewpoints. For example, Green, before commenting on Rousseau's mediation of the Crusoe story, comments that Crusoe is "the island's king or governor, with subjects. All this is said jocularly, but the jokes conceal, or ensure against, hubris, a swelling excitement. The narrative curve of the book is strongly upward; it is a success story, and Crusoe is lucky – not unbelievably, and no more than he deserves to be, but lucky" (1990: 22). Speaking from the antihumanist stance of cultural studies, Brantlinger spurns optimistic readings of the Crusoe story: "No doubt the moral Defoe intended stresses mastery – including self-mastery – as the primary value. But it seems just as possible to see in Crusoe's mastery – of the island, of the cannibals, of Friday, of fate – a kind of madness, the antithesis of self-mastery" (1990: 3). For a balanced account of Crusoe as imperial governor, see Rogers 1979: 44–5. Focusing on the failed colony in *Farther Adventures*, Rogers upholds Novak's critical view of Crusoe's political fantasy.

7 The biblical allusion is to Romans 11:15. See note 32 below for Defoe's application of this allusion in *Colonel Jack*.

8 This deceptive self-presentation recalls Avery's standing outside himself and calling himself "our General" in *The King of Pirates* 73.

9 The most comprehensive account of pirates' economic and egalitarian organization is to be found in Rediker 1989: 261–78. Defoe treated pirates' innovative self-government disparagingly except when satirizing society at large. Novak points out that Defoe first dealt ironically with pirates and Captain Avery in the *Review* of 18 October 1707, which suggests offering Avery a pardon because "pirates were no worse than respectable financiers to be found at the stock exchange" (2001: 580–1). On the collapse of the utopian experiment

on Madagascar of "Defoe's hero, Captain Misson" see Novak 1963: 60–1. The account of Captain Roberts's crew typifies Defoe's attitude to pirates' fantasies and their debasement of monarchical ideas: "Notwithstanding the successful Adventures of this Crew, yet it was with great Difficulty they could be kept together, under any kind of Regulation; for being almost always mad or drunk, their Behaviour produced infinite Disorders, every Man being in his own Imagination a Captain, a Prince, or a King" (*A General History of the Pyrates* 224). While Schonhorn acknowledges that Defoe's authorship of this work is "yet to be convincingly proven," he finds in it the "unique Defovean voice" that is capable of overcoming "the moral scruples of his day, questioning the ethical, even religious, considerations of his readers, and yet catering to their hidden pleasures in the illicit, the immoral, and the profitable that result from industry, energy and courage" (1999: 711).

10 William's equivocal morality owes much to Defoe's exploitation of Quaker tenets and personas described in the previous chapter. Novak sees William as an expanded characterization of the Quaker Captain in *The King of Pirates* (2001: 583). The countenance of this "Commander," an "old Quaking Skipper," reveals his evasion of pacificism: he "would not have been afraid of his Flesh, or have baulk'd using the Carnal Weapon of Offence, *viz*, the Cannon-Ball" (*The King of Pirates* 9–10). Furbank and Owens de-attribute this work, their major reason being that its presentation of Avery seems incompatible with what is presented in *Captain Singleton* and in *The General History of the Pyrates* (1994: 122). Doubtless, Defoe subjects Avery to ironical displacement in the latter works. Yet, that *The King of Pirates* treats Avery's "*being proclaim'd King of* Madagascar" ironically (vi) and that Avery himself scorns the world's romantic views of "my new Kingdom in *Madagascar*" (2) consists with Defoe's strategic deployment of kingship imagery. Moreover, Singleton displays the same contrary features as Avery, being an accomplished political organizer of pirates and a restless, deceptive, unreliable betrayer of them, if to a degree greater than Avery.

11 At this stage, Singleton seems infected by the European myth of Avery as one who had "raised himself to the Dignity of a King, and was likely to be the Founder of a new Monarchy" (*A General History of the Pyrates* 49). Yet Singleton disparages Avery as *The King of Pirates* and *A General History of the Pyrates* do. The latter work's mockery of the pirates on Madagascar includes the following facetious remarks: since they "come out of their Holes, attended like Princes, and since they are actually Kings *de Facto*, which is a Kind of a Right, we ought to speak of them as such." Not only does the dwindling community that Avery abandons involve "the most savage Figures that a Man's Imagination can frame" but also they exist "in

a great deal of dirty State and Royalty." "One of their great Princes" was a murderous waterman from the Thames, and "their Secretaries of State" were no more literate and educated, the result being that any "Account" of "these Kings of *Madagascar*" must be satirical and anti-climactic (*A General History of the Pyrates* 61–2).

12 The challenges of surviving on Madagascar are described between pages 13 and 32, the mutineer adventurers rejecting it as a haven on page 28. Singleton's subsequent denigration of Madagascar and Avery's kingdom represent Defoe's fictional efforts to erode romance and popular history.

13 Alkon elaborates the issues entailed by Defoe's modification of pirate sources and suggests that, beyond avoiding verisimilitude as Schonhorn points out, Defoe may not have intended his novel to resemble pirate sources in his creation of Singleton (1979: 26–8). On his important concept of "retrodiction" and its guidance of readers' textual memories, see Alkon 1979: 85–8.

14 While his structuralist stance presents Defoe as committed to adventure since uncommitted to literary aesthetics, the *Robinson Crusoe* story being one of "masculinism and imperialism," Green admits the dialectic in Defoe's sense of adventure when he says that "few adventures carry anti-imperialist signs that are as convincing as *Robinson Crusoe*'s" (1990: 6 and 23). Novak goes beyond considerations of adventure when he views Singleton and William as imaginative projections of Defoe's own divided ego (2001: 583).

15 The motif of the incomplete return home is comparable in *Captain Singleton* and *The King of Pirates*. In the latter, Avery moves through Persia to Constantinople from where he aims to voyage to Marseilles and to an "inland Town" some distance from the sea (92–3). In the former, Singleton and William travel incognito through Persia learning Persian and Armenian and disguising themselves as Armenian traders. They travel to Venice and Naples in this disguise. When they return to England, they agree to live in seclusion and to "never speak English in publick" (276–7).

16 For Defoe's view that marriage is a "Political Union," see *Conjugal Lewdness* 77. The ramifications of sexual and marital politics are unfolded in the next chapter.

17 To Defoe, if a "Promise of Marriage is Marriage … it is not marrying; it may be called Marriage, or rather a Species of Marriage; and therefore our Law will oblige such Persons to marry afterwards, as well in Cases where they have not consummated the Agreement, as where they have." Hence, he will not grant that promises of marriage render the ritual ceremony of marriage redundant: were they sufficient, "we should have very little open

Marrying among us," the result being "Confusion … in the World" since the "the sacred Obligations of Marriage" could not "be enforced," inheritances legitimated and maintenance obligations upheld (*Conjugal Lewdness* 273–4). This important passage is explored more fully in chapter 7, pages 205–6.

18 For the image of a horse rushing into battle see *Religious Courtship*, preface [4], 130, and 203 and *Conjugal Lewdness*, 33, 118, 217, and 339; for the image of Hobbes's "leap in the dark," see *Religious Courtship*, preface [4], 216 (twice) and *Conjugal Lewdness*, 32 and 179.

19 Defoe upheld the parish system of public admiration and the liturgy of the established church. Thus, "Marriages should not be esteemed fair and legal, if not performed in a fair and open Manner, by a Person legally qualified to perform the Ceremony, and appointed to it by Office; and the Government is always concerned and careful to punish any defect, in the Performance even of those qualified Persons, when they connive at any Breach upon the Institution in the Office of Matrimony; such as marrying People clandestinely, in improper Places, at unseasonable Times, and without the apparent Consent of Parties; and though the Law is very tender with respect to making such Marriages void, yet they are much the more severe in fixing a Punishment upon the Person that officiates" (*Conjugal Lewdness* 274).

20 For Defoe's rejection of state marriages as domestic models, see *Conjugal Lewdness* 97–8 and 369–70.

21 On Defoe's idea of "the plague as a determinant of national policy," see Landa 1969: xii and xiv. While, for Landa, Defoe supported the 1721 Quarantine Act, Backscheider's edition states that his "analytical and independent thinking" must have contributed to the repeal of that act and to the "drastically altered" one of 1722, given his acuity about "the limits of public authority" (1992: x). His polar stances on the Quarantine Act of 1721 are brilliantly detailed by Novak 1992: 310–11.

22 I introduced H.F.'s polar thinking on this topic in chapter 1, page 17.

23 On Defoe's long-term compassion for the working poor, see Novak 1992: 311–12.

24 See chapter 4, page 126.

25 The ideal poor men conduct themselves more purposefully than the pirates of *Captain Singleton*, whereas more typically poor victims of the plague recall how Crusoe lives when threatened by discovery. In his fanciful invulnerability, Crusoe likens himself to "one of the ancient Giants, which are said to live in Caves, and Holes, in the Rocks" (179). See also chapter 4, notes 9 and 10.

26 To Defoe, in Heaven "we shall look upon all we have done and said in Prejudice of the Character of our Brethren with a just Change, and sufficiently repair to one another all the injurious things we have said, or indeed but thought of one another, by rejoicing in the common Felicity, and praising the sovereign Glory, that had receiv'd those we had foolishly rejected, and let those into the same Heaven, whom we had in the Abundance of our Pride, and the Penury of our Charity, shut out" (*Serious Reflections* 176–7).

27 On Defoe's prescriptions for vernacular learning, see *The Compleat English Gentleman* 218–20.

28 To Defoe, the "Excellency of any State of Life consists in its Freedom from Crime" (*Serious Reflections* 11).

29 The ten-line "Prayer in Verse" composed by the Tutor and read to Jack (163) is very close to the consolatory prayer Defoe sent to Samuel Keimer five or six years before he composed *Colonel Jack* (Letter 232 [1717?] in *Letters* 449). The transposition of the prayer into the Tutor's mouth evidences Defoe's sympathy for this character.

30 To Bastian, Defoe's stance on duels suggests a personal involvement of which he was ashamed yet determined to share (1981: 77–9). On Defoe's hostility to duelling, see also Novak 1963: 143. The following critique of the code of honour embodied in duels may be Defoe's: "As there is nothing more Fantastical than to Refine and Sublimate Honour, such an airy Nicety, that the least Puff of inconsiderate Breath can either blow or blast it; so nothing can be more Degenerous in reasonable Man, the visible Image of his Maker and Prince of Sublunary Creatures, than in a Beastly manner to Gore, Kill, and Destroy his Fellow-Creature, for a Thing that hath no Subsistence, but in the vain Imagination of a Whimsical Mind; and no kind of Countenance in those Parts of the World where Civility and Religion have been Cultivated" (*An Account of the Abolishing of Duels in France* [London: John Morphew, 1713] the preface, [A2]). Furbank and Owens de-attribute this work (1994: 60), but Novak accepts it as Defoe's (2001: 420–1).

31 *The Annals of King George, Year the Second* reports that the rebels at Preston ignored the advice of their most competent military leader. Had the bridge been defended, the town could not have been attacked. The failure to defend the bridge signals Jacobite folly. No one witnessing this folly would have stayed with the rebellion unless forced to (135-42). On the de-attribution of *The Annals,* see chapter 1, note 31. Backscheider says Defoe wrote "parts of *The Annals*" (1989: 389).

32 On the biblical phrase, "Life from the Dead," see chapter 4, pages 131–2.

33 See chapter 5, pages 168–9.

34 The Dutch merchant's view of titles is questionable in the premarital context. For he holds that, while "Principles of Honour must come by Birth and Blood," titles may "infuse generous Principles into the Mind" when there is a "good Foundation laid in the Persons" (240). Roxana's character being opaque to him, he groundlessly believes that in marriage they each will wear "a Title without undue Elevation" (241). Aiming to be an English Lady and a Dutch Countess, in sheer vanity Roxana gets both titles. When she becomes a Lady, she enjoys "an unaccountable Pleasure at the Novelty," yet pride in this title soon wears off (246). Still, she reaches the "height of [her] Glory and Prosperity" when she becomes a Countess (261). But then her moral decline sets in fast. Defoe's view that gentlemen who rest content with titles are unhappy, stupid, and unproductive is stressed in *The Compleat English Gentleman* (89–90). By contrast, gentlemen who, when elected to Parliament, refuse to be bought by titles and are above "bribery and corrupcion" are "reckon'd dangerous" by courtiers and party managers (*The Compleat English Gentleman* 178–80). Defoe thought resistance to purchased titles signified political worth. In *The True-Born Englishman*, he praises King William's virtuous actions thus: "He needs no character but his own fame, / Nor any flattering titles, but his name" (ll. 929–30).

35 On the dart struck through the liver, see *Conjugal Lewdness* 393. See also chapter 4, pages 129 and 133, and note 48.

36 About Roxana's "near megalomania," Richetti suggests that her "self asserts its naturalness by its very madness" because she refuses to acknowledge her "elaborate feats of social mastery" as "fantasies" (1975: 227).

7. Marriage and Matrimony: The Dialectic of Sex and Love

1 *Conjugal Lewdness* 26 and 110.

2 I first explored this topic in Merrett 1986.

3 *Conjugal Lewdness* 77. Defoe considered the material functions of marriage since, as Earle says, money was "a vital element in marriage," and love, if "not forgotten," was "felt by most commentators to be something that came after marriage, not before." Defoe, while accepting "this general proposition, was rather more romantic. Love was required even before marriage." To Earle, "Few writers had Defoe's confidence in the power of love to create a happy marriage" (1976: 254).

4 Peterson's remarks on "uncertainty in the prevailing matrimonial law" and on "popular misconstruction" of that law are helpful, but his view that Defoe's "attitude as a journalist was extremely legalistic and conservative in

tendency" whereas his "love for paradox" generated "greater freedom" for marital ideas in his fiction is less so (1955: 173–5). Contrary views of matrimony abound in both his non-fiction and fiction. Earle judges that it was hard for moralists to detach themselves from hierarchical practices upheld by common law: "Law and custom were supported by even liberal conduct books, which emphasized partnership, love and mutual respect as the basis of marriage, but still made it clear that the husband was the senior partner" (1989: 199).

5 *Conjugal Lewdness* 115.

6 *Conjugal Lewdness* 217–18. See also chapter 1, page 37.

7 *Conjugal Lewdness* 38–9 and 342. To Stone, the "growing secularization of elite society" culminated in Lord Hardwicke's Marriage Act of 1753 which, rejecting the marriage ceremony as a sacrament, viewed it as "a contract like any other, subject to statutory controls for the public good." Unsurprisingly, Stone's attitude to Defoe is ambiguous. On one occasion, he denigrates his objection to sexual intercourse during pregnancy by calling him a "Layman most puritanical and long winded." On another, he calls him an "archetypal bourgeois moralist" who could be revolutionary about children choosing marriage partners. *Conjugal Lewdness*, Stone claims, contains an "advanced position about companionate marriage." Stone calls this work a "pamphlet" written in Defoe's "crabbed old age" (1977: 35–6, 501, 275–6, 326, and 497). Richetti questions Stone's charge that Defoe simply upheld patriarchy; the charge made "melodramatically" and "with insufficient sense of Defoe's polemical rhetoric." Still, Richetti finds Defoe's conduct manuals "Heavily and oppressively didactic" (1982: 20).

8 *Conjugal Lewdness* 364, 355, 181, 149, and 105–6.

9 *Conjugal Lewdness* 95–6. To Earle, although Defoe was "remarkable in his generation for the good opinion" he held of women, he "was sufficiently authoritarian to think, like everyone else, that a wife should be subjected to her husband, but he thought that the nature of their subjection should be that of a junior partner, not an upper servant" (1976: 245).

10 Defoe shuns a sectarian appeal to readers: "I shall most carefully avoid giving any room here so much as to guess what Opinion in Religion they were bred up in, or whether the old Gentleman was a Churchman or a Dissenter; and the same Caution I shall use with all the rest of the Persons whom I shall bring upon the Stage in the Course of this Story: My Reason for which every Body will understand by the Nature of the Relation, and of the Times we live in (*Religious Courtship* 2). This recalls the introduction to *The Family Instructor* of 1715: "In the pursuit of this Book care is taken to avoid Distinctions of Opinion, as to Church of *England* or Dissenter, and

no Offence can be taken here either on the one Side or the other; as I hope *both* are Christians, so *both* are treated here as such, and the Advice is impartially directed to *both* without the least Distinction" (3).

11 See chapter 6, note 19. To Curtis, Defoe's conduct manuals embrace "both Anglican and Dissenting positions" and "appealed as much to the squirearchy as to the Non-conformist urban middle-classes." She argues that "a family structure somewhere between patriarchy and affective individualism was what became most acceptable to the predominant squirearchy in eighteenth-century England and that the cultural alliance between the landed elite and the urban bourgeoisie did not rest as solidly upon shared values of affective individualism as Stone has claimed" (1981: 419). On affinities between Defoe and Dr William Fleetwood, the Anglican Whig preacher and progressive moralist of family life who addressed Dissenters as well as his own congregation, see Blewett 1981: 81–4. Defoe's ecumenical thinking is indicated by Novak in his introduction to *Conjugal Lewdness*: "his examples for punishment of the flesh, for fasting, and even for self-flagellation, as methods for controlling sexual desire, are chosen from Anglican and Catholic authors" (ix). On Defoe's Anglican perspectives, see chapter 3, note 8.

12 For Stone, the four kinds of marriage available before 1754 are: (1) the legal contract between parents; (2) spousals or the formal exchange of oral promises; (3) proclamation of banns in church; and (4) the church service that formally blessed the union (1977: 31). Earle classes them as follows: (1) spousals were accepted by canon law but increasingly questioned by common lawyers, who held that succession necessitated the formality of the rites of the Church of England; (2) "Fleet" marriages requiring no publication of banns and no parental consent that took place in inns and taverns; (3) marriage by diocesan licence preferred by middle-class gentry who wished to avoid public rowdiness and the scrutiny that might be directed at their financial arrangements; (4) the open wedding in church after banns according to Anglican liturgy, the most common type. Earle's research finds that private weddings were the trend (1989: 177–80). Defoe's resistance to them indicates his class position. Earle challenges Stone's thesis about the urban bourgeoisie pioneering companionate marriages. Trumbach holds that the aristocratic family fostered domesticity and the nuclear family between 1690 and 1780. He contends that aristocrats were the first to "deal moderately with their children and wives" and to favour "ties of kindred over those of patrilineage" (1978: 287–92).

13 Stone nicely conveys the laity's confusions about conflicting marital jurisdictions (1977: 32–3).

14 Greenberg's article on the legal status of women in the first half of the eighteenth century complicates Stone's views by showing how equity law theoretically modified the inferiority placed on females by common law. But, while equity law recognized women as individuals in their own right, the paternalism inherent in common law imposed "certain social and psychological realities" on females which they could not easily overcome (1975: 171 and 179). On "the improvement of the common law in the decisions of the courts of equity," see Peterson 1955: 187–91.

15 *Conjugal Lewdness* 22–3.

16 See Ephesians 5:22 and note 11 above.

17 *Conjugal Lewdness* 26. See also chapter 4, pages 132–3 and Exodus 21:5–6.

18 *Conjugal Lewdness* 32, 60, and 37.

19 *Conjugal Lewdness* 273–4. Defoe next insists that marriages are lawful only when conducted according to canon law by licensed priests. Those who "connive at any Breach upon the Institution in the Office of Matrimony; such as marrying People clandestinely, in improper Places, at unseasonable Times, and without the apparent Consent of Parties" are justly punished, although the law does not "void" marriages at which they officiate. A church ceremony, continues Defoe, is required by law as "an open and formal coming together, as a just Recognition and Execution of all previous and private Engagements." Private "Engagements, however solemn, and however attested," cannot "pass for a real and legal Marriage … till the open and appointed Form of Marriage, settled by the Legislature, is submitted to, and mutually performed." While a man and woman who exchange vows are husband and wife in the forum of their consciences, "they are not legally Man and Wife, till they are legally and publickly married in due Form." Couples who have not formalized their vows "cannot be lawfully separated, much less joined to any other Person." They are not man and wife "in the Sight of God, till they are so also in the Sight of Man; till the Publick Marriage, *which is a Part of the Ordinance it self*, is performed, whereby the Espousals are recognized, and the Law satisfied" (*Conjugal Lewdness* 274–5 and 279–80).

20 *Conjugal Lewdness* 29, 120, and 60. Defoe does not provide the source of the allusion to St Paul. It comes from I Corinthians 7:9: "it is better to marry than to burn."

21 *Conjugal Lewdness* 119 and 217. On Milton's promotion of divorce, see Peterson 1955: 174–5. Milton's "libertarian argument" about the wife as "a meet help," insistence on "the totality of the husband's private authority," and doctrine of divorce that authorizes "husbands to create the will and consent of their wives by acts of interpretation" treat "domestic privacy as

a form of power that defines the relations among men in the public sphere as those of autonomous individuals" (Haley 1988: 244 and 246). Defoe's rejection of the wife as an upper servant and his dialectic of private and public values help explain why he spurned Milton's defence of divorce. Milton's acceptance of Henry VIII's decision to divorce Anne of Cleves on the basis of his own authority lies behind Defoe's rejection of divorce. See also chapter 3, page 104.

22 *Conjugal Lewdness* 129 and 140. For a recent religious apology for marriage, see Scruton's chapter "Meaningful Marriage," which holds views close to Defoe's (2006: 81–102). To Scruton, that marriage is governed by secular law makes it "possible for commitments to be evaded, and agreements rescinded, by rewriting them as the terms of a contract." He continues: "Rescindable civil unions cannot conceivably have the function of marriage as traditionally conceived. They cannot guarantee security to children, nor can they summon the willing endorsement of society, by showing the partners' preparedness to make a sacrifice on the future's behalf" (2006: 86–7).

23 *Conjugal Lewdness* 164–5.

24 Richetti makes the important point that "Defoe's conservative opinions about sex and his call for a reform of male sexual exploitation become under the pressures of novelistic form and occasion a subversion of the entire institution of male sexuality" (1982: 25).

25 *Conjugal Lewdness* 297, 306, and 337. The OT requires that adulterers be put to death (Lev. 20:10 and Deut. 22:22–7). In *Journal to Stella*, Swift's views on rape are like Defoe's. Rejecting the "old notion that a woman cannot be ravished," Swift urges punishment of a rapist who had lain "a hundred times" with the complainant. He expostulates: "What! Must a woman be ravished because she is a whore?" (Vol. I, Letter XXVII, pages 319–20). On the several theological meanings of adultery, see Merrett 1992a: 22–5.

26 *Conjugal Lewdness* 166 and 198.

27 *Conjugal Lewdness* 181, 199, and 340. For Defoe's morally rigorous treatment of adultery in *Serious Reflections*, see chapter 3, page 79.

28 Starr regards *Religious Courtship* as "a satire on secular modernity" that "portrays a world of *in*creasing irreligion, and of resulting domestic *dis*harmony." His explanation of how Defoe's dialogues gradually establish an "inductive spirit" of discovery is helpful (2006: 1, 3, and 6). Noting the "extraordinary religious dynamism within the work," Abse attributes Defoe's sympathy for its female characters to his "psychic bi-sexuality" (2006: 177 and 180).

29 *Religious Courtship* 13.

30 Religious Courtship 35, 20, 28, and 18. From her feminist stance hostile to Defoe's characterization of women, Mason finds his wives' polar criticism of husbands implausible (1978: 60). In his defence of *Conjugal Lewdness*, Abse calls Defoe "Britain's first feminist" (2006: 200).
31 The suitor's family, like him, are "People of Levity and Gallantry, being rich and gay; a Family that dealt very little in Matters of Religion" (*Religious Courtship* 51).
32 *Religious Courtship* 46, 49, 51, and 53. The youngest daughter "focalizes" the narrative. In his introduction, Starr understates the fusion of religion and narrative when he says that "This young woman's version of heroism has a religious component, yet Defoe emphasizes the strength of character displayed in her words and deeds, rather than their conformity to a philosophically or supernaturally sanctioned ideal" (2006: 2).
33 *Religious Courtship* 54, 56, and 55.
34 *Religious Courtship* 80, 74, 124, and 73–7. On the spiritual relationship between the landlord and William and the foundation of their dialogues on the Bible, see chapter 4, pages 126–7.
35 *Religious Courtship* 111.
36 *Religious Courtship* 143.
37 *Religious Courtship* 202–3, 234, and 239.
38 *Religious Courtship* 257–8, 265, 267, 270, and 278–9. While Roxana is anti-Catholic, she indulges in idolatry: see chapter 6, page 196.
39 *Religious Courtship* 53.
40 Backscheider argues that Defoe put "case studies" in his fiction as well as in his non-fiction (1976: 116).
41 For a fine theoretical account of the textuality of codes, see Rabine 1985: 1–13.
42 Boone 1987: 1–3. Boone's remarks about the polyvalent novel stealing from established genres and violating distinctions between literary and non-literary modes in its emergence as a self-sufficient form seem germane to Defoe (Boone 1987: 3–4).
43 Boone 1987: 6–7.
44 Boone 1987: 8–10 and 33.
45 Horne 1993: 1, 3–5, 7–14, 17–8, 20–1, and 23.
46 For the view that there is little in common between the marital ideas of Defoe's non-fiction and fiction, see Richetti 1982: 22–3. For an opposing view, see Blewett 1979: 66–7. Swaminathan, in maintaining that *Moll Flanders* is an alternative conduct manual because of its presentation of Moll's dependence on other women for survival, neither remarks the "female networking" in *Religious Courtship* nor analyses the dialogic inventiveness of Defoe's conduct manuals (2003: 188–9).

47 His wife makes "a thousand Crosses about herself" and "a great many callings upon the *Blessed Virgin*, and her Country *Saints*" as she laments the death of the marquis (*Colonel Jack* 230).

48 The following sentence in *Conjugal Lewdness* is germane: "It is not unlawful for a Man to make his Whore his Wife, however foolish; but it is unlawful for any Man to make his Wife his Whore, however seemingly and intentionally Honest" (278).

49 Females are "entrapped by circumstances and by social codes hospitable only to married women. Because they are trapped, Defoe can present them sympathetically. Because they are strong women with a developed sense of self, they fight back against the social evils which victimize them. But in doing so, they become predators and for this Defoe judges them guilty" (Backscheider 1976: 103).

50 *The Complete English Tradesman* applies the term "amphibious" to men who "trade by water and by land" (I, xi). While Defoe holds that "trade in *England* makes Gentlemen" and denies it is "so much nonsense" to talk about "a Gentleman-tradesman" (I, i, 310 and 313), he thinks that tradesmen merit gentility at the end of careers, for he "that will be a Tradesman should confine himself within his own sphere." Tradesmen "should either shut up their shops, or hire some body else to look after them," if they intend becoming statesmen. Indeed, "never was the gazette so full of the advertisement of commissions of bankrupt as since our shop-keepers are so much engaged in Parties, form'd into clubs to hear news, read journals, and study politicks" (I, i, 38). A tradesmen with genteel pretensions, like Moll's partner, deserves to be ostracized: "What is an impertinent Purse-proud Shop-Keeper among a Society of Gentlemen, but linking the Inns of Court and the Bear-Garden, and condemning the Well-bred, the Polite, the Wise, and the Sensible, to be baited at a Stake, not by Dogs, but much worse, by the Man-Brute" (II, i, 249). Defoe's remarks about punishing such a man recall the punishment of Malvolio: "Ambition and aspiring Thought are Plagues and Diseases to a Tradesman: When they work in his Mind, his Friends should get his Head shav'd, and put him into a dark House for a little while, administring proper Physick to him, to keep him from the Vapours" (*The Complete English Tradesman* II, i, 62).

51 For an anecdote detailing "Matrimonial Incest" as "a superlative in Wickedness," see *Conjugal Lewdness* 353. On the parallels and reversals in the patterned experiences of Moll's imaginary and actual forms of incest, see Brooks 1973: 42–6.

52 The wife of Moll's Bath lover, being "distemper'd in her Head," lives "under the Conduct of her own Relations." He lives apart from her to

avoid being accused of mismanaging her "Cure" (109). Unlike the Bath gentleman, the banker is a "*Cuckhold*" (135)

53 Katharine Rogers holds that Defoe's feminism creates situations in *Moll Flanders* and *Roxana* that cannot "be adequately dealt with in terms of conventional sexual morality" and sympathetically presents "heroines who must violate the most sacred laws laid on women." Since "Defoe thought more deeply and boldly than his characters," she does not "accept Moll's or Roxana's expressions of guilt at face value" (1976: 10). In her critical survey of *Moll Flanders,* McCoy relegates Defoe's feminism to arguments for Moll's "asexuality," concluding that "Moll's character is a product of a set of vital ideas, lower middle-class dissenting Protestant ideas, which are extra-literary but through which Defoe found an original concept of characterization. The concept still disconcerts, because the modern reader continues to put gender identity first" (1978: 421).

54 On Defoe's rejection of the marital practices of kings and princes in *Conjugal Lewdness,* see chapter 6, pages 183-4 and page 341, note 20.

55 That the landlord of the inn in which the banker marries Moll is unwilling to have "the Minister of the Parish" learn of the marriage signifies its clandestine manner. The ringing of the church bells counteracts the landlord's wish for secrecy (184).

56 Novak's study of Defoe's "complex use of language," his stylistic self-consciousness in *Moll Flanders,* is fundamental to understanding how psychological contraries in his characterization of Moll invite readers to attend to the patterning of narrative implications (1970: 353–7).

57 Readers of *Roxana* will note that the protagonist often will not recognize the alogical sense inherent in conversational language. If, however, she turns a deaf ear to the "conversational implicatures" that she might share with others in her fictional world, she expects readers to respond to her implications. For a succinct and accessible account of how "conversational implicatures" work and of the semantic rules they assume, see Pinker 2007: 376–80, 388–90, and 398–400.

58 This last phrase is taken from Romans 11:15. Here Roxana unconsciously cites the scriptures in terms of psychological, not spiritual, restoration. On the equally ironical implications arising from the non-biblical word "Cordial," see chapter 8, pages 270 and 275.

59 To Kropf, the plot of *Roxana* reverses the story of Hagar and Rachel to help the novel signify "the triumph of earthly bondage over spiritual freedom." Her appropriation of the story shows that Roxana is "gradually moving toward Amy's pragmatic, materially expedient point of view" (1972: 470–1).

For Defoe's explication of the account of "*Jacob* marrying two Sisters, and then lying with both their Maids" and his opposition to arguments that propagation should be "wholly Patriarchal" and not subject to "Constitution-Regularities," see *Conjugal Lewdness* 123–4. On Roxana's imitation of Amy, see Castle's reading of the "paradoxical relation of sameness and otherness" that Amy and Roxana share: "Roxana's deepening inertia and powerlessness" convey "the types of destruction wrought by the heroine's deep-seated transference onto Amy" (1979: 84, 86, and 91).

60 In claiming that the episode with the landlord "probably develops within itself as much depth or complexity as the book ever attains," Starr privileges Roxana's rhetoric over her logic and proposes readers' consequential experience of sympathy for, rather than judgment, of her (1970: 65, 67–70, and 75). However, the return of the brewer-husband complicates Roxana's self-contradiction and introduces narrative motifs that affect the denouement. Hume's focus on the final episode of *Roxana* shows that events in the novel are "tightly integrated into a clear and coherent structure" which helps erode Roxana's self-justifications by presenting a "clear progression in vice and unnecessariness." The "most unusual deviation from the normal linear time-scheme" makes its inconclusive conclusion symbolize Roxana's spiritual ruin (1970: 477, 479–80, 483, and 488–9). Novak (1983) also provides an excellent account of Roxana's moral decline. On Defoe's deliberate chronology in *Roxana*'s plot and its mounting satire of the court of George I, see Baine 1975: 160–1.

61 Backscheider's comments on Roxana's alienation and "conflicting feelings of isolation-centrality and control-helplessness" are germane (1984: 175). She provocatively reduces the incompleteness of Roxana's narrative by the generalization that "Regardless of a preexistent order, the human experience is one of conflict and limits, and to conclude a life is to falsify it" (1984: 177).

62 On the recurring notion of "upper-Servant,' see chapter 4, pages 132–3. In this chapter, see pages 204–5, 220, 228–9 and pages 344, note 9 and 346–7, note 21.

63 Hammond and Regan, speaking of Bakhtin's "novelization" of culture, affirm that Defoe's complex delineation of "whore-protagonists" contributes "to an ongoing debate about how the social problem of prostitution is to be treated." They claim that his "circumstantial and material account of the whore-figure contributed greatly to the perception that women were prostituted by circumstances beyond their control." They hold that fiction through its depiction of social structures offers systemic programs for change (2006: 61).

8. Defoe's Imaginary: Narrative Inference, Figurative Expression, and Spiritual Cognition

1 *Due Preparations for The Plague* 115. Defoe's belief that contagion caused the plague opposed medical theories of miasma: see Landa's introduction to *A Journal of the Plague Year*, xxiv–xxix.
2 Eagleton thinks it "farcically obvious" that Defoe's stories do not exist "for the sake of the moral" (2005: 36).
3 On these topics, see Corbett 1971: 110–24.
4 On the contrarian theory implicit in Defoe's phrase "allusive all[e]gorick History," see chapter 3, page 86. While not granting Defoe ironical sense, Ehrenpreis's approach to impersonation and implication is helpful. Since "sympathetic penetration is a mystery," he claims that eighteenth-century writers "normally respected" a "standard of lucidity" which they "also undermined, covertly, for special purposes." His premise that they were "self-conscious" about "techniques of indirection" and his account of Swift's rhetorical "system of contraries" in *The Examiner* apply to Defoe (1980: 6–7, 10, and 56–60). Attributing "revolutionary nostalgia" to Defoe, Warner claims that his contemporaries despised "the appeal to the pre-rational, anti-intellectual modes of being envisioned in his novels." Defending Joyce's view that Defoe's characters reach "in two directions, backwards toward their animal origins and forward to their roles as historic prototypes," Warner states that Defoe "is not a historicist who is hypocritical about his Christian professions, but a Christian-historicist who has a certain nostalgia for mythic remnants." Ultimately, whatever "Defoe's religious beliefs, he was too clear-sighted not to recognize, along with Stephen Dedalus, that linear history without a sense of transcendental purpose was a nightmare" (Warner 1993: 10, 24, 26, and 56).
5 McKeon approaches this dialectic from a logical and sociological perspective: "in the historically transitional territory of early modern Protestantism, spiritual and secular motives are not only 'compatible'; they are inseparable, if ultimately contradictory, parts of a complex intellectual and behaviour system" (1987: 319).
6 On Defoe's views of the plague in *A Review,* see Landa's introduction to *A Journal* xi–xiv. Lee reprints passages from the newspapers of 1719 to 1721 which describe the plague in Marseille and the administration of the 1665 plague (1969: II, 142, 265, 277, 284–5, 291–2, 294–5, 427–30, 449–51, and 453–550).
7 *Due Preparations for the Plague* ix–xi.
8 *Due Preparations for the Plague* 62.

9 Germane to the anti-categorical, extra-factual nature of Defoe's prefaces are Faller's remarks: "Defoe's prefaces condition his readers in still more sophisticated ways by suggesting that the narratives which follow are highly provisional renderings of realities that lie somewhere behind or beyond them. It is difficult to fix the status or provenance of any of these narratives; they are somehow peculiar and extra-categorical ... By marking out the ambiguous status of his texts, Defoe alerts his readers to move through them with maximal curiosity. Trying to sift the actual out from the invented is not so important as looking for the meaning that stands behind both, and which makes both 'equally useful'" (Faller 1993: 89–90).

10 Disclaiming is a rhetorical motif basic to Defoe's writing. See chapter 3, pages 74 and 84 and note 23 on page 314; chapter 4, pages 117–18, 123, and 131 and notes 21 and 31 on page 322; chapter 5, pages 144, 146, 151, and 154.

11 The term "Memento" in the preface describes the effect of Moll's robbing the innocent child whose vain mother decks her out for dancing school (4).

12 Armstrong observes that narrative reflexivity in *Colonel Jack* makes the protagonist an oral historian who represents his society and a political criminal who spurns it: "Making history and being made by it are impossible to distinguish here. Paradoxically, the personal ambition which makes Jack careless of his fellow human beings is what binds him to them and to his historical moment, for it proves that he is the offspring of that careless and divided society in the first place, even as he perpetuates its history of conflict and betrayal" (1996: 111–12).

13 Kahn helpfully describes Defoe's oblique relations with readers: "We read Roxana's story as her own, yet we share the authorial perspective that allows us to make of that story the coherent history that she never experiences. And it becomes increasingly difficult to separate the reader from the author in ourselves" (1991: 102).

14 Iser 1978b: 275.

15 Land 1974: 10, 13, 17, and 20.

16 Locke 1961: III, x, 105–6.

17 Lanham 1974: 10, 13, 33–4, 64, and 132. The following account of Defoe's rhetoric and cognition is also indebted to Tufte's final chapter on syntactic symbolism (1971). For Tufte, style embodies and performs meaning for responsive minds.

18 On Defoe's rejection of traditional philology and belief that discourse, far from setting up generic borders between non-fiction and fiction, needs oratorical flexibility and idiomatic metaphors, see chapter 1, pages 4–5 and 32–4.

19 *The Compleat English Gentleman* 218–20.
20 *An Essay upon Projects* 233–4, 237, 244–5. Defoe's resistance to Lockean semantics and his promotion of the universality of syntax is typical of his time: see Cohen 1977: 56–7.
21 *The Compleat English Gentleman* 121–2.
22 *The Present State of the Parties in Great Britain: Particularly an Enquiry into the State of the Dissenters in England* (London: J. Baker, 1712), 313. All references are to this edition.
23 *The Present State of the Parties in Great Britain* 313–15.
24 *The Present State of the Parties in Great Britain* 316–18. Illuminating Defoe's concern for rhetorical education is the section of *An Essay upon Projects* that proposes an academy for women which would teach "all the Graces of Speech, and all the necessary Air of Conversation." Women should be taught to read books, especially histories, so as to be familiar with the world and able to judge things of which they hear. For Defoe, it was a priority that women's intellect be cultivated in order that they might join in all sorts of conversation profitably as well as pleasantly (292–3).
25 See *Augusta Triumphans: Or, The Way to Make London the Most Flourishing City in the Universe* (London: J. Roberts, 1728), 16 and 22. Jaynes also holds that "poetry begins as the divine speech of the bicameral mind" and that the "continuance of poetry, its change from a divine given to a human craft is a part of ... nostalgia for the absolute" (1976: 369 and 374–5).
26 Henry Baker was secretive and proprietorial about his methods for curing the deaf and dumb: see Freeman 1950: 275–6 and Moore 1958: 327.
27 *The Compleat English Gentleman* 110. Davis, referring to *The History of the Life and Adventures of Mr. Duncan Campbell* (London: E. Curll, 1720), approves of Defoe's acceptance of the deaf's ability to translate sign language into writing (1995: 57–8). However, the latter title was de-attributed by Baine (1968: 137–80).
28 *Mere Nature Delineated* 178–80.
29 Defoe's appreciation of mystery and the limits of human knowledge anticipates current ideas of human nature. Ehrlich's view of evolution as "an ongoing force that not only has shaped the attributes and behaviors shared by all human beings but also has given every single individual a different nature" offers an important perspective on Defoe, as do his following claims: "Human nature is not the same from society to society or from individual to individual, nor is it a permanent attribute of *Homo sapiens*. Human natures are the behaviors, beliefs, and attitudes of *Homo sapiens* and the changing physical structures that govern, support, and participate in our unique mental functioning"; if the "Use of art, in one form or

another, is a universal human characteristic and a major feature of all societies," it is also "a place where the plurality of our natures is most readily seen" (Ehrlich 2002: 3, 12, and 221). Doidge's survey of neuroplasticity reporting how biological brain structures may evolve in individuals and how perceptual capacities interact and compensate for one another challenges the "theory of the unchanging brain" which "decreed that people who were born with brain or mental limitations, or who sustained brain damage, would be limited or damaged for life." For Doidge, the "idea that the brain can change its own structure and function through thought and activity is ... the most important alteration in our view of the brain since we first sketched out its basic anatomy and the workings of its basic component, the neuron" (2007: 294–6 and xiv–xvi).

30 On Defoe's literary apprenticeship and ambitions, see Backscheider (1989: 193–4, 363–6, and 468–9). My following paragraphs drawing on *Conjugal Lewdness* seek to extend Defoe's imaginary beyond the traditional emblems discussed by Starr and Hunter. Given the previous discussion of narrative withholding, it is remarkable that Defoe makes the suppression of narrative facts in *Conjugal Lewdness* crucial to his satire on abuses of marriage (34–5). This conduct manual holds that narrative examples "import nothing, but as they confirm the subject" since, while narrative may please, "'tis the improvement of the Story, that fixes the Truth of the Argument, which it is brought to support" (157–8). *Conjugal Lewdness*, like *Serious Reflections*, justifies the recoil of irony on narrators who dramatize themselves while claiming to control their stories: there is no "Novelty" or "Instruction" in the "telling a scandalous Story of a scandalous Person" except when such persons "pretend to understand themselves, to have a Sense of Reputation, of Virtue, Prudence, and, above all, of Religion; this indeed has something wonderful in it, and is worth recording" (352).

31 This section draws on the field of cognitive semantics. In arguing that how we categorize is crucial to thought, perception, action, and speech, Lakoff rejects the Western tradition of treating reason as "disembodied symbol-manipulation." He holds that reason is embodied by pre-conceptual metaphors. Hence, the contrary relations between the prepositions 'in' and 'out' which reveal that we think of our bodies both as containers and as being placed in containers. From this and other examples, Lakoff concludes that "meaning postulates themselves only make sense given schemas that are inherently meaningful because they structure our direct experience" (1990: 8 and 272–3). While sympathetic to Lakoff, Pinker thinks he goes too far in dismissing "truth, objectivity, and disembodied reason." For Pinker, "People not only can ignore metaphors, but can question and discount them,

and analyze which aspects are applicable and which should be ignored" since there is "an underlying medium of thought that is more abstract than the metaphors themselves" (2007: 247–9). Pinker's qualification of Lakoff seems to apply to Defoe's operation of metaphors.

32 Mark 4:11–12.

33 *Conjugal Lewdness* 386. Two pages later, Defoe admits the limits of "Simily, Allegory" and other figurative forms of "Representation." There are other "Matrimonial Whoredoms" which "must be buried in Silence" (388).

34 *Conjugal Lewdness* 8–9, 28–9, and 97. Defoe later extends the metaphor of marriage partners being in the same ship on a long voyage to emphasize the spirituality of their relationship. Since they will be saved or damned together, they should practise the same religious principles: matrimony is not a "Partnership in Trade, 'tis what is ten thousand times more solemn, 'tis a Partnership in Life; a Partnership of Souls, they are embarked in the same Ship, they go the same Voyage, and give me leave to say, they swim, they sink, they are happy, they are miserable, they are poor, they are rich, just as they agree, or not agree; Love or Hate, are united or not united; they go hand in hand, and have but one Fate; they rise and fall, are blest or curs'd, nay, I believe I might add, (with but few Exceptions) they are saved or damned together" (*Conjugal Lewdness* 215). A sexually motivated marriage is a short ferry ride across a river for criminal purposes: the two people "resolving to go over a River to commit a Theft; the passing the River, and the Robbery, is the Intent; the Ferry-Boat is only the lawful Assistant to an unlawful Purpose" (*Conjugal Lewdness* 344).

35 *Conjugal Lewdness* 119. The full passage about suppression of sexual impulses reads as follows: "If it be true, that the Affections, which are the grossest Part of the Man, are up in Arms; if this Mob is rais'd in his Soul, for such it is, the Militia must be rais'd to suppress them; Violence must be suppress'd by Violence; the Torrent must be check'd, and the Man be reduced to the Government of himself, and brought into good Order by proper Powers; for as it is (in short) a Tumult in his Soul, and a Rebellion against the just Dominion of his Reason, so he must use the means Nature has put into his hand to quash and suppress the Rebellion, and chain them down like Galley-Slaves to the Oar, to humble and mortify them" (*Conjugal Lewdness* 315).

36 *Mere Nature Delineated* 169.

37 *The Complete English Tradesman* II, i, 75–6 and 104–6.

38 *Of Royall Educacion* 1. Defoe's habitual correlation of the soul to a diamond is evident in an early analogy in *An Essay upon Projects*: "The Soul is plac'd in the Body like a rough Diamond, and must be polish'd, or the Lustre of

it will never appear: And 'tis manifest, that as the Rational Soul distinguishes us from Brutes, so Education carries on the distinction, and makes some less brutish than others: This is too evident to need any demonstration" (283). This image appears in an argument for the "early Education of Children" in *Mere Nature Delineated*: "The Soul is plac'd in the Body like a rough Diamond, which requires the Wheel and Knife, and all the other Arts of the Cutter, to shape it, and polish it, and bring it to shew the perfect Water of a true *Brilliant*. If Art be deficient, Nature can do no more; it has plac'd the Capacity in the Jewel; but till the Rough be remov'd, the Diamond never shews itself. Thus the Soul, unpolish'd, remains bury'd under the Rubbish and Roughness of its own Powers." This extended metaphor displaces Lockean images of the soul's "organick Powers" that Defoe likens to "a Lump of soft Wax, which is always ready to receive any Impression; but if harden'd, grow callous, and stubborn, and, like what we call Sealing-Wax, obstinately refuse the Impression of the Seal, unless melted, and reduc'd by the Force of Fire" (Wear's edition: 193). His diamond image resists Locke's sense of the mind passively receiving ideas of sensation into its "empty cabinet" (I, ii, 15). Discussing substances, Locke refers four times to a diamond but not metaphorically (e.g., II, xxiii, 246). He usually takes the mind to be "white paper void of all characters" (II, i, 77), impressions "from things without" being "characters" stamped by nature "within" it (I, ii, 22). Presuming that the mind's paper cannot resist printing, he contends that "white paper receives any characters" (I, iii, 40). The mind cannot refuse to have simple ideas, nor alter them "when they are imprinted, nor blot them out and make new ones itself" (II, i, 89). Leinster-Mackay puts the difference between Locke and Defoe thus: "although Defoe adopts the Lockean motif of tabula rasa or wax tablet he differs from Locke in his attitude to young children's education. Locke would advise that reason be applied in the handling of children but Defoe is convinced of the need to stamp out original sin which children display when naughty and Locke's waxen analogy in Defoe's hands becomes a rationale for traditional strict discipline" (1981: 64). Defoe's metaphor of sealing wax refers to correspondence: a letter is written then sealed up; only soft wax is impressionable; wax, far from mediating the letter, only contributes the seal.

39 *Of Royall Educacion* 1–3.

40 *Of Royall Educacion* 4. On the cosmological imagery with which Defoe supports his theory of contraries, see chapter1, page 28, and note 65, page 295.

41 Defoe supports his polar outlook with an analogy: the finer a woman, the more she enhances her charms: "You seldome find that a beautifull woman thinks that, because she is handsome, she has no occasion to set her self off

by dress and decoracion; on the contrary, the handsomer the lady thinks her self to be, the more carefull she generally is to giv her charms all the advantages of fine cloths and of a proper disposition of them, too, which we call dress, to render her self the more agreeable and the more charming to the eyes of her admirers" (*Of Royall Educacion* 5).

42 *Of Royall Educacion* 5–6. This passage throws into relief Defoe's growing defence of monarchy and kingship, as demonstrated in chapters 5 and 6.

43 *The Compleat English Gentleman* 109–11.

44 *The Compleat English Gentleman* 107–9. Defoe treats the imagery of diamonds and trees in polar terms: the finer the diamond the more polishing it needs to elicit its qualities; the straighter the tree the less work is needed before it is installed in a palace. There is a powerful analogy between timber and landowners in *Conjugal Lewdness*. Forest management is a sign of frugality, temperance, and concern for posterity: "Who shall supply in Age what the Spendthrift, the Extravagant has wasted in Youth? A frugal Use of an Estate preserves it for the Heirs; whereas he that cuts the Timber down young, shall have no large high Trees to leave behind him; and he that, without manuring and good Husbandry, leaves the Land to be beggar'd, and plough'd out of Heart, shall be sure not to keep up the Rent; but the Estate will decay, and the Heir be reduc'd. In a Word, Temperance and Moderation keeps Nature in a due state of Health, and lays in an early Provision for Time, a Stock for old Age to live upon, hands on Vigour with the Years, and makes Age triumph in the goodness of the Constitution" (393–4).

45 *Serious Reflections* 205–6. On the evolutionary nature of biblical hermeneutics, see chapter 4 passim.

46 *Religious Courtship* 74–5.

47 On the motif of Crusoe's retreat into silence and his "dwindling humanity," see Carnochan 1977: 38–42. Sill's claim that Defoe wrote *Robinson Crusoe* "to erect a new model of conduct and self-regulation" in a "work of ideology as well as a work of fiction" cuts short the route that Defoe invites readers to follow. If Crusoe experiences a "limited and precarious 'sovereignty'" on the island," it is unclear that he attains "the gradual perfection of his moral knowledge" and learns that "a man's proper business is to venture only where both ease and safety are assured" (Sill 1983: 157–9). Simply put, his restlessness leads to further, aimless travels.

48 Abse views the creation of Singleton as "outrageously provocative." From Abse's psychoanalytic stance, Defoe creates Singleton as a "thoroughly anti-social" orphan to retaliate against his parents' "principled religiosity" (2006: 155).

49 Scientific research into synaesthesia probes the normalcy of "unisensual existence." The Greek roots imply the "experience of two, or more, sensations occurring together." Apparently, infants experience synaesthesia for the first few months of their lives before areas in the brain that "receive and process auditory information" become "insulated" from those that deal with visual information (Harrison 2001: viii, 3, 13–15). That Defoe's characters experience interior voices, whether by memory, telepathy, dream, hallucination, or even grace, is a narrative phenomenon that warrants further study because it questions empirical epistemology. However, the ideological dangers of poets and artists deriving transcendental theories from synaesthesia is high, according to Dann (1998).

50 For a fine account of "the sounds of sickness" in *A Journal*, see Kickel 2007: 49–57. In detailing his concern "to simulate the chaos of oral culture in 1665" (49), Kickel contends that "Defoe explores the consequences of moving from an oral to a print culture and suggests that the soul, rather than the brain or the mouth, is the true source of all speech and that the responsibility that accompanies speaking – whether in speech or in print – should not be taken lightly. Voice is not merely a physical expression that occurs in person or on paper; rather, it is a spiritual function as well" (51).

51 As partly discussed in chapter 1, Faller brilliantly analyses the restitution scene, noting the mysteriousness of pronouns when they function as "shifters," that is, when they switch "referents again and again in the full stream of speech" between first and third person and demonstrate how "Jack's criminality redounds against him, paradoxically, even as he tries to escape it" (1993: 213).

52 Jaynes 1976: 8, 22–5, 28, 30–1, and 33.

53 Jaynes 1976: 36, 46, 48, 53, and 58.

54 Jaynes 1976: 63, 96–7, and 91.

55 Jaynes 1976: 318. The way in which William James takes religious feelings as a scientific subject supports the present study. To James, "Individuality is founded in feeling; and the recesses of feeling, the darker, blinder strata of character, are the only places in the world in which we catch real fact in the making, and directly perceive how events happen, and how work is actually done. Compared with this world of living individualized feelings, the world of generalized objects which the intellect contemplates is without solidity or life." James's insights fit Defoe's fallible characters and narrators: "The individual, so far as he suffers from his wrongness and criticises it, is to that extent consciously beyond it, and in at least possible touch with something higher, if anything higher exist. Along with the

wrong part there is thus a better part of him, even though it may be but a most helpless germ" (1961: 389, and 393).

56 In recognizing Defoe's "pure narrativity," Eagleton stresses the paradox that Defoe's "events seem both vivid and insubstantial" since his "novels are fascinated by process itself, not just by its end-product." Eagleton concludes that "There is no definitive settlement in Defoe, as there is in Fielding. All endings are arbitrary, and all of them are potential beginnings. You settle down only to take off again." Among the polemical challenges that Eagleton brings to capitalism, enlightenment progress, and religion, which would have appealed to Defoe, is the following maxim: "faith is for the most part performative rather than propositional" (2009: 30, and 111).

57 Barnard 1725: 245–8.

58 Coetzee 1987: 96 and 143, and 2001: 18.

59 Thackeray 1963: 51; Meredith 1968: 108; Dickens 2003: 53; Johnson 1952: I, 21 and 214.

Bibliography

Primary Sources: Works by and Attributed to Defoe Including First and Modern Editions

An Account of the Abolishing of Duels in France. London: John Morphew, 1713.

An Account of the Great and Generous Actions of James Butler. London: J. Moore, 1715.

Advice to All Parties. By the Author of The True-born English-man. London: Benj. Bragg, 1705.

The Anatomy of Exchange-Alley. London: E. Smith, 1719.

The Annals of King George, Year the Second. London: A. Bell, W. Taylor, and J. Baker, 1716.

An Argument Proving that the Design of Employing and Enobling Foreigners, Is a Treasonable Conspiracy against the Constitution. London, 1717.

Augusta Triumphans: Or, The Way to Make London the Most Flourishing City in the Universe. London: J. Roberts, 1728.

A Brief Explanation of a Late Pamphlet, Entituled, The Shortest Way with the Dissenters [1703]. In Vol. I of *A True Collection of the Writings of the Author of The True-Born English-man* 1705: 441–4.

The Candidate. London: S. Keimer, 1715.

A Collection of Miscellany Letters, Selected out of Mist's Weekly Journal*: The First Volume*. London: N. Mist, 1722.

A Collection of Miscellany Letters, Selected out of Mist's Weekly Journal*: The Second Volume*. London: N. Mist, 1722.

The Compleat English Gentleman. 1728–9. Ed. Karl. D. Bülbring. London: David Nutt, 1890.

The Compleat English Gentleman and Of Royal Education. Ed. W.R. Owens. Vol. 10 of *Religious and Didactic Writings of Daniel Defoe: The Works of Daniel Defoe*. London: Pickering and Chatto, 2007.

The Complete English Tradesman in Familiar Letters. London: Charles Rivington, 1727. 2 vols. 2nd ed. Reprint. New York: Augustus M. Kelley, 1969.

The Conduct of Christians Made the Sport of Infidels. London: S. Baker, 1717.

The Conduct of Robert Walpole. London: T. Warner, 1717.

Conjugal Lewdness; or, Matrimonial Whoredom. A Treatise Concerning the Use and Abuse of the Marriage Bed. London: T. Warner, 1727. Ed. Maximillian E. Novak. Gainesville, FL: Scholars' Facsimiles and Reprints, 1967.

The Consolidator: Or Memoirs of Sundry Transactions from the World in the Moon. London: B. Bragge, 1705.

A Declaration of Truth to Benjamin Hoadly. London: E. More, 1717.

Due Preparations for the Plague, As well for Soul as Body. London: E. Matthews and J. Batley, 1722.

Due Preparations for the Plague (1722) and *Mere Nature Delineated* (1726). Ed. Andrew Wear. Vol. 5 of *Writings on Travel, Discovery and History: The Works of Daniel Defoe*. London: Pickering and Chatto, 2002.

An Enquiry into the Case of Mr Asgill's General Translation. London, 1704.

An Enquiry into the Occasional Conformity of Dissenters. London, 1697. In *The True-Born Englishman and Other Writings*. Ed. P.N. Furbank and W.R. Owens, 1997.

An Essay on the History and Reality of Apparitions. London: S. Roberts, 1727.

An Essay on the Regulation of the Press. London, 1704.

An Essay upon Projects. London: Tho. Cockerill, 1697.

Fair Payment No Spunge. London: J. Brotherton et al., 1717.

The Family Instructor in Three Parts; ... The Second Edition. Corrected by the Author. London: Eman. Matthews, 1715.

The Family Instructor. In Two Parts. Vol. II. London: Eman. Matthews, 1718.

The Farther Adventures of Robinson Crusoe; Being the Second and Last Part of His Life, and of the Strange Surprizing Accounts of His Travels Round Three Parts of the Globe. London: W. Taylor, 1719.

The Fortunes and Misfortunes of the Famous Moll Flanders. 1722. Ed. G.A. Starr. London: Oxford University Press, 1976.

The Free-Holders Plea against Stock-Jobbing Elections of Parliament Men. 2nd ed. London, 1701.

A Friendly Epistle. London: S. Keimer, 1715.

A Friendly Rebuke to One Parson Benjamin. London: E. More, 1719.

A General History of Discoveries and Improvements, In Useful Arts. London: J. Roberts, 1725–6.

A General History of the Pyrates. 1724–8. Ed. Manuel Schonhorn. Mineola, NY: Dover, [1972] 1999.
The Great Law of Subordination Consider'd. London: S. Harding et al., 1724.
The History and Remarkable Life of the Truly Honourable Col. Jacque Commonly Call'd Col. Jack. 1722. Ed. Samuel Holt Monk. London: Oxford, 1965.
A History of the Clemency of Our English Monarchs. London: N. Mist, 1717.
An Humble Address to Our Sovereign Lord the People. London: J. Roberts, 1715.
A Journal of the Plague Year. 1722. Ed. Louis Landa. London: Oxford University Press, 1969.
A Journal of the Plague Year. 1722. Ed. Paula R. Backscheider. New York: W.W. Norton, 1992.
Jure Divino: A Satyr. In Twelve Books. London, 1706.
The King of Pirates. London: A. Bettesworth, C. King, J. Brotherton, W. Meadows, and W. Chetwood, 1719.
The Lay-Man's Sermon upon the Late Storm. [London,] 1704.
The Layman's Vindication of the Church of England. London: A. and W. Bell, et al., 1716.
The Letters of Daniel Defoe. Ed. George Harris Healey. Oxford: Clarendon, 1953. Reprint. Oxford: Oxford University Press, 1969.
The Life, Adventures, and Pyracies, of the Famous Captain Singleton. 1722. Ed. Shiv K. Kumar. London: Oxford University Press, 1969.
The Life and Strange Surprizing Adventures of Robinson Crusoe of York, Mariner. 1719. Ed. J. Donald Crowley. London: Oxford University Press, 1976.
Memoirs of a Cavalier. 1720. Ed. James T. Boulton. London: Oxford University Press, 1972.
Memoirs of the Life and Eminent Conduct of Daniel Williams, D.D. London: E. Curll, 1718.
Mercurius Politicus. May 1716–October 1720. London: J. Morphew.
More Short-Ways with the Dissenters. In *A True Collection of the Writings of the Author of the True-Born English-man*. Vol. 2, 272–95.
A New Family Instructor; In Familiar Discourses between a Father and His Children, on the Most Essential Points of the Christian Religion. London: T. Warner, 1727.
The Old Whig and Modern Whig Revived. London: S. Baker, 1717.
A Plan of the English Commerce. London: C. Rivington, 1728. Reprint. Oxford: Basil Blackwell, 1927.
The Political History of the Devil, as Well Ancient as Modern. London: T. Warner, 1726.
The Political History of the Devil (1726). Ed. John Mullan. Vol. 6 of *Satire, Fantasy and Writings on the Supernatural by Daniel Defoe*: *The Works of Daniel Defoe*. London: Pickering and Chatto, 2005.

The Present State of the Parties in Great Britain: Particularly an Enquiry into the State of the Dissenters in England. London: J. Baker, 1712.

The Protestant Jubilee. London: S. Keimer, 1715.

Reformation of Manners: A Satyr. [London,] 1702.

Religious Courtship. London: E. Matthews, A. Bettesworth, J. Brotherton, and W. Meadows, 1722.

Religious Courtship (1722). Ed. G. A. Starr. Vol. 4 of *Religious and Didactic Writings of Daniel Defoe: The Works of Daniel Defoe*. London: Pickering and Chatto, 2006.

Review. 9 vols. 19 Feb. 1704–11 June 1713. Ed. Arthur Wellesley Secord. 22 vols. New York: Columbia University Press, 1938. Reprint. New York: AMS Press, 1965.

A Reply to a Traiterous Libel. London: J. Baker, 1715.

Robinson Crusoe. 1719. Ed. John Richetti. London: Penguin, 2002.

Of Royall Educacion. A Fragmentary Treatise. Ed. Karl. D. Bülbring. London: David Nutt, 1895.

Roxana. 1724. Ed. David Blewett. London: Penguin, 1982.

Roxana. 1724. Ed. Jane Jack. London: Oxford, 1964.

The Secret History of State Intrigues in the Management of the Scepter, in the Late Reign. London: S. Keimer, 1715.

Selected Writings of Daniel Defoe. Ed. James T. Boulton. London: B.T. Batsford, 1965. Reprint. Cambridge: Cambridge University Press, 1975.

Serious Reflections during the Life and Surprising Adventures of Robinson Crusoe: With His Vision of the Angelick World. London: W. Taylor, 1720.

Serious Reflections during the Life and Surprising Adventures of Robinson Crusoe (1720). Ed. G.A. Starr. Vol. 3 of *The Novels of Daniel Defoe: The Works of Daniel Defoe*. London: Pickering and Chatto, 2008.

A Sharp Rebuke from One of the People Called Quakers. London: S. Keimer, 1715.

The Shortest-Way with the Dissenters: Or Proposals for the Establishment of the Church (1702). In *Selected Writings of Daniel Defoe*, ed. Boulton 1975.

Some Considerations on the Danger of the Church from Her Own Clergy. London: J. Roberts, 1715.

Some Reasons Why It Could Not Be Expected. London: W. Boreham, 1718.

A Speech without Doors. London: A. Baldwin, 1710.

The Storm: Or, A Collection of the Most Remarkable Casualties and Disasters Which Happen'd in the Late Dreadful Tempest Both by Sea and Land. London: G. Sawbridge, 1704.

The Storm. 1704. Ed. Richard Hamblyn. London: Penguin, 2005.

Strike while the Iron's Hot, Or, Now Is the Time to Be Happy. London: S. Keimer, 1715.

A System of Magick. London: J. Roberts, 1727.

A Tour through the Whole Island of Great Britain (1724–26). Ed. G.D.H. Cole and D.C. Browning. London: J.M. Dent, 1928. Rev. ed. 2 vols. in 1, 1962.

The True-Born Englishman and Other Writings. Ed. P.N. Furbank and W.R. Owens. London: Penguin, 1997.

A True Collection of the Writings of the Author of the True-Born English-man. 2nd. ed. 2 vols. London, 1705.

A Trumpet Blown in the North. London: S. Keimer, 1715.

The Wickedness of a Disregard to Oaths. London, 1723.

The Works of Daniel Defoe. Ed. W.R. Owens and P.N. Furbank. 44 vols. London: Pickering and Chatto, 2000–8.

Secondary Sources

Abrams, M.H., ed. 1958. *Literature and Belief*. New York: Columbia University Press.

Abse, Leo. 2006. *The Bi-Sexuality of Daniel Defoe: A Psychoanalytic Survey of the Man and His Works*. London: Karnac.

Adams, Robert M. 1975. *Sir Thomas More Utopia*. New York: W.W. Norton.

Addison, Joseph, and Richard Steele, et al. [1711–14] 1945. *The Spectator*. 4 vols. Ed. C. Gregory Smith. London: Dent.

Alkon, Paul K. 1976. "Defoe's Argument in *The Shortest Way with the Dissenters*." *Modern Philology* 73 (S4): S12–23. http://dx.doi.org/10.1086/390689.

Alkon, Paul K. 1979. *Defoe and Fictional Time*. Athens: University of Georgia Press.

Alkon, Paul K. 2002. "The Invisible Man Returns: New Defoe Editions." *Eighteenth-Century Fiction* 14:199–213.

Alter, Robert, and Frank Kermode, eds. 1987. *The Literary Guide to the Bible*. Cambridge: Harvard University Press.

Andrew, Edward. 1988. *Shylock's Rights: A Grammar of Lockian Claims*. Toronto: University of Toronto Press.

Andries, Lise, ed. 1996. *Robinson*. Paris: Éditions Autrement.

Aristotle. 1926. *The "Art" of Rhetoric*. Ed. John Henry Freese. London: William Heinemann.

Armstrong, Katherine A. 1996. *Defoe: Writer as Agent*. Victoria: English Literary Studies, University of Victoria.

Austin, J.L. (Original work published 1962) 1965. *How to Do Things with Words*. Ed. J.O. Urmson. New York: Oxford University Press.

Backscheider, Paula R. 1976. "Defoe's Women: Snares and Prey." Vol. 5 of *Studies in Eighteenth-Century Culture*, ed. Ed. Ronald C. Rosbottom. Madison: University of Wisconsin Press: 103–20.

Backscheider, Paula R. 1984. *A Being More Intense: A Study of the Prose Works of Bunyan, Swift, and Defoe*. New York: AMS Press.

Backscheider, Paula R. 1986. *Daniel Defoe: Ambition and Innovation*. Lexington: University Press of Kentucky.

Backscheider, Paula R. 1989. *Daniel Defoe: His Life*. Baltimore: Johns Hopkins University Press.

Baine, Rodney M. 1968. *Daniel Defoe and the Supernatural*. Athens: University of Georgia Press.

Baine, Rodney M. 1975. "Roxana's Georgian Setting." *Studies in English Literature* 15 (3): 459–71. http://dx.doi.org/10.2307/449991.

Baridon, Michel. 1996. "Robinson, jardinier en l'île." In Andries 1996: 69–85.

Barnard, John. 1725. *Ashton's Memorial: An History of the Strange Adventures, and Signal Deliverances, of Mr. Philip Ashton*. Boston: Samuel Gerrish. In Dow and Edmonds 1996: 224–69.

Bastian, F. 1981. *Defoe's Early Life*. Totowa, NJ: Barnes and Noble.

Bate, Walter Jackson. (Original work published 1946) 1961. *From Classic to Romantic: Premises of Taste in Eighteenth- Century England*. New York: Harper and Row.

Bechler, Rosemary. 1986. "'Triall by what is contrary': Samuel Richardson and Christian Dialectic." In *Myer* 1986: 93–113.

Bender, John. 1987. *Imagining the Penitentiary: Fiction and the Architecture of Mind in Eighteenth-Century England*. Chicago: University of Chicago Press.

Bennett, G.V. 1975. *The Tory Crisis in Church and State 1688–1730: The Career of Francis Atterbury Bishop of Rochester*. Oxford: Clarendon.

Bennett, Gareth Vaughn, and John Dixon Walsh, eds. 1966. *Essays in Modern English Church History in Memory of Norman Sykes*. New York: Oxford University Press.

Birdsall, Virginia Ogden. 1985. *Defoe's Perpetual Seekers: A Study of the Major Fiction*. Lewisburg: Bucknell University Press.

Black, Max. 1968. *The Labyrinth of Language*. New York: New American Library.

Blake, William. [1790?] 1975. *The Marriage of Heaven and Hell*. Ed. Geoffrey Keynes. London: Oxford University Press.

Blewett, David. 1979. *Defoe's Art of Fiction*. Toronto: University of Toronto Press.

Blewett, David. 1981. "Changing Attitudes toward Marriage in the Time of Defoe: The Case of *Moll Flanders*." *Huntington Library Quarterly* 44:11–58.

Blewett, David, ed. 2000. *Reconsidering the Rise of the Novel: Eighteenth-Century Fiction* 15.

Bloom, Edward A., and Lillian D. 1979. *Satire's Persuasive Voice*. Ithaca: Cornell University Press.
Boardman, Michael M. 1983. *Defoe and the Uses of Narrative*. New Brunswick: Rutgers University Press.
Bobrick, Benson. 2001. *Wide as the Waters: The Story of the English Bible and The Revolution It Inspired*. New York: Penguin Books.
Booth, Wayne C. 1961. *The Rhetoric of Fiction*. Chicago: University of Chicago Press.
Bonhoeffer, Dietrich. (Original work published 1960) 1971. *Christology*. New York: Collins.
Boone, Joseph Allen. 1987. *Tradition Counter Tradition: Love and the Form of Fiction*. Chicago: University of Chicago Press.
Boswell, James. (Original work published 1799) 1953. *Life of Johnson*. Ed. R.W. Chapman. London: Oxford University Press.
Brantlinger, Patrick. 1990. *Crusoe's Footprints: Cultural Studies in Britain and America*. New York: Routledge.
Brewer, John. 1997. *The Pleasures of the Imagination: English Culture in the Eighteenth Century*. New York: Farrar Straus Giroux.
Brooks, Douglas. 1973. *Number and Pattern in the Eighteenth-century Novel: Defoe, Fielding, Smollett and Sterne*. London: Routledge and Kegan Paul.
Brown, Homer O. 1971. "The Displaced Self in the Novels of Daniel Defoe." *ELH* 38 (4): 562–90. http://dx.doi.org/10.2307/2872266.
Brown, Homer O. 1997. *Institutions of the English Novel: From Defoe to Scott*. Philadelphia: University of Pennsylvania Press.
Brown, James W. 1984. *Fictional Meals and Their Function in the French Novel, 1789–1848*. Toronto: University of Toronto Press.
Brown, Laura. 1993. *Ends of Empire: Women and Ideology in Early Eighteenth-Century English Literature*. Ithaca: Cornell University Press.
Bruns, Gerald L. 1987. "Midrash and Allegory: The Beginnings of Scriptural Interpretation." In Alter and Kermode 1987: 625–46.
Butler, Mary E. 1983. "The Effect of the Narrator's Rhetorical Uncertainty on the Fiction of *Robinson Crusoe*." *Studies in the Novel* 15: 77–90.
Camus, Albert. 1947. *La Peste*. Paris: Gallimard.
Carnochan, W.B. 1977. *Confinement and Flight: An Essay on English Literature of the Eighteenth Century*. Berkeley: University of California Press.
Cary, Norman R. 1975. *Christian Criticism in the Twentieth Century: Theological Approaches To Literature*. Port Washington, NY: Kennikat Press.
Castle, Terry J. 1979. "'Amy, Who Knew My Disease': A Psychosexual Pattern in Defoe's *Roxana*." *ELH* 46 (1): 81–96. http://dx.doi.org/10.2307/2872604.

Chambers, Douglas. 1996. *The Reinvention of the World: English Writing 1650–1750*. London: Arnold.

Chomsky, Noam. 1980. *Rules and Representations*. New York: Columbia University Press.

Clark, J.C.D. 1985. *English Society 1688–1832: Ideology, Social Structure and Political Practice during the Ancien Regime*. Cambridge: Cambridge University Press.

Cleary, Thomas R., ed. 1994. *Time, Literature and the Arts: Essays in Honor of Samuel L. Macey*. Victoria: English Literary Studies, University of Victoria.

Coetzee, J.M. (Original work published 1986) 1987. *Foe*. New York: Viking.

Coetzee, J.M. 2001. *Stranger Shores: Literary Essays 1986–1999*. New York: Viking.

Cohen, Murray. 1977. *Sensible Words: Linguistic Practice in England 1640–1785*. Baltimore: Johns Hopkins University Press.

Cohn, Dorrit. 1978. *Transparent Minds: Narrative Modes for Presenting Consciousness in Fiction*. Princeton: Princeton University Press.

Cohn, Dorrit. 1999. *The Distinction of Fiction*. Baltimore: The Johns Hopkins University Press.

Colley, Linda. 1992. *Britons: Forging the Nation 1707–1837*. London: Pimlico.

Colley, Linda. 2002. *Captives*. New York: Pantheon.

Collins, Francis S. 2006. *The Language of God: A Scientist Presents Evidence for Belief*. New York: Free Press.

Cooper, Anthony Ashley. Earl of Shaftesbury. [1711] 1964. *Characteristics of Men, Manners, Opinions, Times*. Ed. John M. Robertson. Indianapolis: Bobbs-Merrill.

Corbett, Edward P. J. (Original work published 1965) 1971. *Classical Rhetoric for the Modern Student*. New York: Oxford University Press.

Cox, Harvey. (Original work published 1965) 1966. *The Secular City*. Toronto: Macmillan.

Cragg, G.R. (Original work published 1950) 1966a. *From Puritanism to the Age of Reason: A Study of Changes in Religious Thought within the Church of England 1660 to 1700*. Cambridge: Cambridge University Press.

Cragg, G.R. (Original work published 1960) 1966b. *The Church and the Age of Reason 1648–1789*. Harmondsworth: Penguin.

Cruden, Alexander. (Original work published 1769). n. d. *A Complete Concordance to the Old and New Testament or a Dictionary and Philosophical Index to the Bible*. Ed. William Youngman. London: Frederick Warne.

Cruickshank, John. (Original work published 1959) 1960. *Albert Camus and the Literature of Revolt*. New York: Oxford University Press.

Curtis, Laura Ann, ed. 1979. *The Versatile Defoe: An Anthology of Uncollected Writings by Daniel Defoe*. London: George Prior.

Curtis, Laura Ann. 1981. "A Case Study of Defoe's Domestic Conduct Manuals Suggested by The *Family, Sex and Marriage in England, 1500–1800*." Vol. 10 of *Studies in Eighteenth-Century Culture*. Ed. Harry C. Payne. Madison: University of Wisconsin Press: 409–38.

Curtis, Laura Ann. 1984. *The Elusive Daniel Defoe*. London: Vision.

Dampier, William. (Original Dover edition published 1968) 2007. *Memoirs of a Buccaneer: Dampier's New Voyage Round the World, 1697*. Mineola, NY: Dover.

Damrosch, Leopold, Jr. 1973. "Defoe as Ambiguous Impersonator." *Modern Philology* 71 (2): 153–9. http://dx.doi.org/10.1086/390464.

Damrosch, Leopold. 1985. *God's Plot and Man's Stories: Studies in the Fictional Imagination from Milton to Fielding*. Chicago: University of Chicago Press.

Daniel, Stephen H. 1984. *John Toland: His Methods, Manners, and Mind*. Montreal, Kingston: McGill-Queen's University Press.

Dann, Kevin T. 1998. *Bright Colors Falsely Seen: Synaesthesia and the Search for Transcendental Knowledge*. New Haven: Yale University Press.

Davis, Lennard J. 1983. *Factual Fictions: The Origins of the English Novel*. New York: Columbia University Press.

Davis, Lennard J. 1995. *Enforcing Normalcy: Disability, Deafness, and the Body*. London: Verso.

Dickens, Charles. (Original work published 1854) 2003. *Hard Times*. Ed. Kate Flint. London: Penguin.

Doidge, Norman. 2007. *The Brain That Changes Itself: Stories of Personal Triumph from the Frontiers of Brain Science*. New York: Viking.

Dow, George Francis, and John Henry Edmonds. (Original work published 1923) 1996. *The Pirates of the New England Coast 1630–1730*. New York: Dover.

Downey, James. 1969. *The Eighteenth Century Pulpit: A Study of the Sermons of Butler, Berkeley, Secker, Sterne, Whitefield and Wesley*. Oxford: Clarendon.

Dryden, John. 1958. *The Poems of John Dryden*. 4 vols. Ed. James Kinsley. Oxford: Clarendon.

Dryden, John. 1962. *Of Dramatic Poesy and Other Critical Essays*. Ed. George Watson. London: Dent.

Eagleton, Terry. 1983. *Literary Theory: An Introduction*. Minneapolis: University of Minnesota Press.

Eagleton, Terry. 2005. *The English Novel: An Introduction*. Oxford: Blackwell.

Eagleton, Terry. 2009. *Reason, Faith, and Revolution: Reflections on the God Debate*. New Haven: Yale University Press.

Earle, Peter. 1976. *The World of Defoe*. London: Weidenfeld and Nicolson.

Earle, Peter. 1989. *The Making of the English Middle Class: Business, Society and Family Life in London, 1660–1730*. Berkeley: University of California Press.

Ehrenpreis, Irvin. 1980. *Acts of Implication: Suggestion and Covert Meaning in the Works of Dryden, Swift, Pope, and Austen*. Berkeley: University of California Press.

Ehrlich, Paul. R. (Original work published 2000) 2002. *Human Natures: Genes, Cultures, and the Human Prospect*. New York: Penguin Books.

Eliade, Mircea. (Original work published 1957) 1959. *The Sacred and The Profane: The Nature of Religion*. Trans. Willard R. Trask. New York: Harcourt, Brace and World.

Eliade, Mircea. (Original work published 1962) 1965. *The Two and The One*. Trans. J.M. Cohen. New York: Harper and Row.

Eliade, Mircea. (Original work published 1963) 1968. *Myth and Reality*. Trans. Willard R. Trask. New York: Harper and Row.

Ellis, John. M. 1997. *Literature Lost: Social Agendas and the Corruption of the Humanities*. New Haven: Yale University Press.

Faller, Lincoln B. 1987. *Turned to Account: The Forms and Functions of Criminal Biography*. Cambridge: Cambridge University Press.

Faller, Lincoln B. 1993. *Crime and Defoe: A New Kind of Writing*. Cambridge: Cambridge University Press. http://dx.doi.org/10.1017/CBO9780511553455.

Ferguson, Niall. 2003. *Empire: The Rise and Demise of the British World Order and the Lessons for Global Power*. New York: Basic Books.

Fielding, Henry. (Original work published 1749) 1973. *Tom Jones*. Ed. Sheridan Baker. New York: Norton.

Fowler, Roger. 1981. *Literature as Social Discourse: The Practice of Linguistic Criticism*. Bloomington: Indiana University Press.

Frank, Erich. (Original work published 1945) 1966. *Philosophical Understanding and Religious Truth*. New York: University Press.

Freeman, William. 1950. *The Incredible De Foe*. London: Herbert Jenkins.

Frei, Hans W. 1986. "The 'Literal Reading' of Biblical Narrative in the Christian Tradition: Does It Stretch or Will It Break." In McConnell 1986: 36–77.

Fritz, Paul, and Richard Morton, eds. 1976. *Women in the Eighteenth Century and Other Essays*. Toronto and Sarasota.

Frye, Northrop. (Original work published 1947) 1969. *Fearful Symmetry: A Study of William Blake*. Princeton: Princeton University Press.

Furbank, P.N., and W.R. Owens. 1988. *The Canonisation of Daniel Defoe*. New Haven: Yale University Press.

Furbank, P.N., and W.R. Owens. 1994. *Defoe De-Attributions: A Critique of J.R. Moore's "Checklist."* London: The Hambledon Press.

Furbank, P.N., and W.R. Owens. 1998. *A Critical Bibliography of Daniel Defoe*. London: Pickering and Chatto.

Furbank, P.N., and W.R. Owens. 2006. *A Political Biography of Daniel Defoe*. London: Pickering and Chatto.

Gabel, John B., Charles B. Wheeler, and Anthony D. York. 1996. *The Bible as Literature: An Introduction*. 3rd ed. New York: Oxford University Press.

Gallant, Christine, ed. 1989. *Coleridge's Theory of Imagination Today*. New York: AMS Press.

Girard, René. (Original work published 1972) 1977. *Violence and the Sacred*. Trans. Patrick Gregory. Baltimore: The Johns Hopkins University Press.

Gladfelder, Hal. 2008. "Defoe and Criminal Fiction." In Richetti 2008: 64–83.

Green, Martin. 1990. *The Robinson Crusoe Story*. University Park, PA: The Pennsylvania State University Press.

Greenberg, Janelle. 1975. "The Legal Status of the English Woman in Early Eighteenth-Century Common Law and Equity." Vol. 4 of *Studies in Eighteenth-Century Culture*. Ed. Harold E. Pagliaro. Madison: University of Wisconsin Press: 171–81.

Haley, Janet E. 1988. "Female Autonomy in Milton's Sexual Poetics." In Walker 1988: 230–53.

Hammond, Brean S., and Shaun Regan. 2006. *Making the Novel: Fiction and Society in Britain, 1660–1789*. Basingstoke: Palgrave Macmillan.

Hanson, Laurence. (Original work published 1936) 1967. *Government and the Press 1695–1763*. Oxford: Clarendon.

Harrison, John. 2001. *Synaesthesia: The Strangest Thing*. Oxford: Oxford University Press.

Hawkes, Terence. 1977. *Structuralism and Semiotics*. Berkeley: University of California Press. http://dx.doi.org/10.4324/9780203443934.

Hearnshaw, E.J.C. 1928. *The Social and Political Ideas of Some English Thinkers of the Augustan Age,* A.D. *1650–1750*. London: Harrap.

Heidegger, Martin. 1966. *Discourse on Thinking*. Trans. John M.Anderson and E. Hans Freund. New York: Harper and Row.

Heiss, Robert. (Original work published 1963) 1975. *Hegel Kierkegaard Marx: Three Great Philosophers Whose Ideas Changed the Course of Civilization*. Trans. E.B. Garside. New York: Delacorte Press/ Seymour Lawrence.

Heschel, Abraham J. 1962. *The Prophets: An Introduction*. 2 vols. New York: Harper and Row.

Hill, Christopher. 1994. *The English Bible and the Seventeenth-Century Revolution*. London: Penguin.

Honig, Edwin. 1966. *Dark Conceit: The Making of Allegory*. New York: Oxford University Press.

Hopes, Jeffrey. 1996. "Real and Imaginary Stories: *Robinson Crusoe* and the *Serious Reflections*." *Eighteenth-Century Fiction* 8:313–28.

Horn, David Bayne. 1967. *Great Britain and Europe in the Eighteenth Century*. Oxford: Clarendon.

Horne, William C. 1993. *Making a Heaven of Hell: The Problem of the Companionate Ideal in English Marriage Poetry 1650–1800*. Athens: University of Georgia Press.

Hume, Robert. 1970. "The Conclusion of Defoe's *Roxana*: Fiasco or Tour de Force?" *Eighteenth-Century Studies* 3 (4): 475–90. http://dx.doi.org/10.2307/2737863.

Hunter, J. Paul. 1966. *The Reluctant Pilgrim*. Baltimore: Johns Hopkins University Press.

Hunter, J. Paul. 2000. "Serious Reflections on Daniel Defoe (with an Excursus on the Farther Adventures of Ian Watt and Two Notes on the Present State of Literary Studies." In Blewett 2000: 229–37.

Iser, Wolfgang. 1978a. *The Act of Reading: A Theory of Aesthetic Response*. London: Routledge and Kegan Paul.

Iser, Wolfgang. 1978b. *The Implied Reader: Patterns of Communication in Prose Fiction from Bunyan to Beckett*. Baltimore: Johns Hopkins University Press.

James, Eustace Anthony. 1972. *Daniel Defoe's Many Voices: A Rhetorical Study of Prose Style and Literary Method*. Amsterdam: Rodopi.

James, William. (Original work published 1902) 1961. *The Varieties of Religious Experience: A Study in Human Nature*. Ed. Reinhold Niebuhr. New York: Collier Books.

Jaynes, Julian. 1976. *The Origin of Consciousness in the Breakdown of the Bicameral Mind*. Toronto: University of Toronto Press.

Jeffrey, David Lyle, ed. 1992. *A Dictionary of Biblical Tradition in English Literature*. Grand Rapids, MI: William B. Eerdmans.

Johns, Adrian. 1998. *The Nature of the Book: Print and Knowledge in the Making*. Chicago: University of Chicago Press.

Johnson, Edgar. 1952. *Charles Dickens: His Tragedy and Triumph*. 2 vols. Boston: Little, Brown.

Johnson, Samuel. (Original work published 1759) 1988. *The History of Rasselas Prince of Abissinia*. Ed. J.P. Hardy. Oxford: Oxford World's Classics.

Jones, J.R. 1978. *Country and Court: England, 1658–1714*. Cambridge: Harvard University Press.

Jones, Manina. 1993. "Textuality." In Makaryk 1993: 641–2.

Joyce, James. 1964. *Daniel Defoe*. Ed. Joseph Prescott. Buffalo: State University of New York Press.

Kahn, Madeleine. 1991. *Narrative Transvestism: Rhetoric and Gender in the Eighteenth-Century Novel*. Ithaca: Cornell University Press.

Keeble, N.H. 1987. *The Literary Culture of Nonconformity in Later Seventeenth-Century England*. Athens: University of Georgia Press.

Kermode, Frank. 1979. *The Genesis of Secrecy: On the Interpretation of Narrative*. Cambridge, MA: Harvard University Press.

Kickel, Katherine E. 2007. *Novel Notions: Medical Discourse and the Mapping of the Imagination in Eighteenth-Century English Fiction*. New York: Routledge.

Knabe, P.-E., R. Mortier, and F. Moureau, eds. 2002. *L'Aube de la Modernité*. Vol. 16 of *A Comparative History of Literatures in European Languages*. Amsterdam and Philadelphia: John Benjamins.

Kropf, C.R. 1972. "Theme and Structure in Defoe's *Roxana*." *Studies in English Literature* 12 (3): 467–80. http://dx.doi.org/10.2307/449946.

Laden, Marie-Paule. 1987. *Self-Imitation in the Eighteenth-Century Novel*. Princeton: Princeton University Press.

Lakoff, George. (Original work published 1987) 1990. *Women, Fire, and Dangerous Things: What Categories Reveal about the Mind*. Chicago: University of Chicago Press.

Land, Stephen K. 1974. *From Signs to Propositions: The Concept of Form in Eighteenth-Century Semantic Theory*. London: Longman.

Lanham, Richard A. 1974. *Style: An Anti-Textbook*. New Haven: Yale University Press.

Lee, William. (Original work published 1869) 1969. *Daniel Defoe: His Life and Recently Discovered Writings*. London: Hotten. 3 vols. Reprint. New York: Burt Franklyn.

Leinster-Mackay, D.P. 1981. *The Educational World of Daniel Defoe*. Victoria: English Literary Studies, University of Victoria.

Lestringant, Frank. 1996. "L'île de Jonas ou Robinson, prophète malgré lui." In Andries 1996: 45–65.

Lewis, Bernard. (Original work published 1982) 2001. *The Muslim Discovery of Europe*. New York: W.W. Norton.

Lewis, Bernard. 2002. *What Went Wrong? The Clash between Islam and Modernity in the Middle East*. New York: Harper-Collins.

Lewis, Bernard. 2003. *The Crisis of Islam: Holy War and Unholy Terror*. New York: Modern Library.

Locke, John. (Original work published 1706) 1961. *An Essay Concerning Human Understanding*. 2 vols. Ed. John W. Yolton. London: Dent.

Locke, John. (Original work published 1693) 1964. *John Locke on Education*. [*Some Thoughts Concerning Education*.] Ed. Peter Gay. New York: Teachers College Press, Columbia University.

Locke, John. (Original work published 1706) 1966. *John Locke's "Of the Conduct of the Understanding"*, ed. Francis W. Garforth. New York: Teachers College Press, Columbia University.

Lodge, David. 1966. *Language of Fiction: Essays in Criticism and Verbal Analysis of the English Novel*. London: Routledge and Kegan Paul.

Loomba, Ania. 1998. *Colonialism / Postcolonialism*. London: Routledge.

Lund, Roger D., ed. 1997. *Critical Essays on Daniel Defoe*. New York: G.K. Hall.

Macaree, David. 1991. *Daniel Defoe's Political Writings and Literary Devices*. Lewiston, NY: E. Mellen Press.

Macquarrie, John. (Original work published 1966) 1977. *Principles of Christian Theology*. Rev. ed. London: SCM Press.

Maddox, James H. (Original work published 1984) 1997. "On Defoe's *Roxana*." In Lund 1997: 266–84.

Makaryk, Irena R., ed. 1993. *Encyclopedia of Contemporary Literary Theory: Approaches, Scholars, Terms*. Toronto: University of Toronto Press.

Mandeville, Bernard. (Original work published 1724) 1970. *The Fable of the Bees*. Ed. Phillip Harth. Harmondsworth: Penguin.

Martin, Graham Dunstan. 1975. *Language Truth and Poetry: Notes towards a Philosophy of Literature*. Edinburgh: Edinburgh University Press.

Mason, Shirlene. 1978. *Daniel Defoe and the Status of Women*. St Alban's, VT: Eden Press.

McArthur, Tom, ed. 1992. *The Oxford Companion to the English Language*. Oxford: Oxford University Press.

McConnell, Frank, ed. 1986. *The Bible and the Narrative Tradition*. New York: Oxford University Press.

McCoy, Kathleen. 1978. "The Femininity of *Moll Flanders*." Vol. 7 of *Studies in Eighteenth-Century Culture*. Ed. Roseann Runte. Madison: University of Wisconsin Press: 413–22.

McCutcheon, Elizabeth. 1971. "Denying the Contrary: More's Use of Litotes in the *Utopia*." In Adams 1975: 224–30.

McGrath, Alister. 2002. *In the Beginning: The Story of the King James Bible and How It Changed a Nation, a Language, and a Culture*. New York: Random House.

McKeon, Michael. 1987. *The Origins of the English Novel, 1600–1740*. Baltimore: Johns Hopkins University Press.

Meredith, George. (Original work published 1879) 1968. *The Egoist*. Ed. George Woodcock. Harmondsworth: Penguin.

Milton, John. (Original work published 1956) 1959. *Milton's Poems*. Ed. B.A. Wright. London: J.M. Dent.

Mitchell, Stephen. 1987. *The Book of Job*. San Francisco: North Point Press.

Merrett, Robert James. 1980. *Daniel Defoe's Moral and Rhetorical Ideas*. Victoria: English Literary Studies, University of Victoria.

Merrett, Robert James. 1986. "The Traditional and Progressive Aspects of Daniel Defoe's Ideas about Sex, Family and Marriage." *English Studies in Canada* 12: 1–22.

Merrett, Robert James. 1989. "Narrative Contraries as Signs in Defoe's Fiction." *Eighteenth-Century Fiction* 1: 171–85.

Merrett, Robert James. 1992a. "Adultery" and "Madness." In Jeffrey 1992: 22–5 and 469–72.

Merrett, Robert James. 1992b. "Diction and Verbal Sequence in Dryden's *Absalom and Achitophel*: The Rhetorical Confirmation of Religious Typology." *Études Anglaises* 45 (2): 129–42.

Merrett, Robert James. 1994. "Pictorialism in Eighteenth-Century Fiction: Visual Thinking and Narrative Diversity." In Cleary 1994: 157–91.

Merrett, Robert James. 2002. "Les Formes Théâtrales Anglaises, 1660–1780." In Knabe et al. 2002: 205–24.

Merrett, Robert James. 2004a. "Daniel Defoe's Biblical Allusions and Spiritual Voices." *Khthónios* 2: 27–44.

Merrett, Robert James. 2004b. *Presenting the Past: Philosophical Irony and the Rhetoric of Double Vision from Bishop Butler to T.S. Eliot*. Victoria: English Literary Studies, University of Victoria.

Merrett, Robert James. 2005. "Daniel Defoe and Islam." *Lumen* 24: 19–34.

Metzger, Bruce M., and Michael D. Coogan, eds. 1993. *The Oxford Companion to the Bible*. New York: Oxford University Press.

Miller, Henry Knight, Eric Rothstein, and G.S. Rousseau. 1970. *The Augustan Milieu: Essays Presented to Louis A. Landa*. Oxford: Clarendon.

Montagu, Lady Mary Wortley. 1906. *Letters from the Right Honourable Lady Mary Wortley Montagu 1709–1762*. Ed. R. Brimley Johnson. London: Dent.

Moore, John Robert. 1939. *Defoe in the Pillory and Other Studies*. Bloomington: Indiana University Press.

Moore, John Robert. 1958. *Daniel Defoe: Citizen of the Modern World*. Chicago: University of Chicago Press.

Moore, John Robert. (Original work published 1960) 1971. *A Checklist of the Writings of Daniel Defoe*. Hamden: Archon Books.

Myer, Valerie Grosvenor, ed. 1986. *Samuel Richardson: Passion and Prudence*. London: Vision.

Nicholson, Colin. 1994. *Writing and the Rise of Finance: Capital Satires of the Early Eighteenth Century*. Cambridge: Cambridge University Press.

Novak, Maximillian E. 1963. *Defoe and the Nature of Man*. Oxford: Oxford University Press.

Novak, Maximillian E. 1964. "Defoe's Theory of Fiction." *Studies in Philology* 61: 650–68.

Novak, Maximillian E. 1966. "Defoe's Use of Irony." In *Uses of Irony: Papers on Defoe and Swift Read at a Clark Library Seminar*. Los Angeles: William Andrews Clark Memorial Library.

Novak, Maximillian E. 1970. "Defoe's 'Indifferent Monitor': The Complexity of *Moll Flanders*." *Eighteenth-Century Studies* 3 (3): 351–65. http://dx.doi.org/10.2307/2737876.

Novak, Maximillian E. 1977a. *English Literature in the Age of Disguise*. Berkeley: University of California Press.

Novak, Maximillian E. [1977b] 1992. "Defoe and the Disordered City." *PMLA* 92: 241–52. Rpr. in *A Journal of the Plague Year*. Ed. Backscheider 1992: 301–18.

Novak, Maximillian E. 1983. *Realism, Myth, and History in Defoe's Fiction*. Lincoln: University of Nebraska Press.

Novak, Maximillian E. 2001. *Daniel Defoe Master of Fictions: His Life and Ideas*. Oxford: Oxford University Press.

O'Banion, John D. 1992. *Reorienting Rhetoric: The Dialectic of List and Story*. University Park: The Pennsylvania State University Press.

Olney, James. 1972. *Metaphors of Self: the meaning of autobiography*. Princeton: Princeton University Press.

Ong, Walter J. 1958. "Voice as Summons for Belief." In Abrams 1958: 80–105.

Ong, Walter J. 1982. *Orality and Literacy: The Technologizing of the Word*. London: Routledge. http://dx.doi.org/10.4324/9780203328064.

Owen, John B. 1974. *The Eighteenth Century 1714–1815*. New York: W.W. Norton.

Parker, Kim Ian. 2004. *The Biblical Politics of John Locke*. Waterloo, ON: Wilfrid Laurier University Press.

Peterson, Spiro. 1955. "The Matrimonial Theme of Defoe's *Roxana*." *PMLA* 70 (1): 166–91. http://dx.doi.org/10.2307/459844.

Pinker, Steven. 2002. *The Blank Slate: The Modern Denial of Human Nature*. London: Penguin.

Pinker, Steven. 2007. *The Stuff of Thought: Language as a Window into Human Nature*. New York: Viking.

Plumb, J.H. (Original work published 1967) 1969. *The Growth of Political Stability in England 1675–1725*. Harmondsworth: Penguin.

Pocock, J.G.A. 1980. "The Myth of John Locke and the Obsession with Liberalism." In *John Locke*. Los Angeles: William Andrews Clark Memorial Library, University of California.

Porter, Roy. 2001 *Enlightenment: Britain and the Creation of the Modern World*. London: Penguin.

Pratt, Mary Louise. 1977. *Toward a Speech Act Theory of Literary Discourse*. Bloomington: Indiana University Press.

Rabine, Leslie W. 1985. *Reading the Romantic Heroine: Text, History, Ideology*. Ann Arbor: University of Michigan Press.

Rader, Ralph W. 1973. "Defoe, Richardson, Joyce, and the Concept of Form in the Novel." In *Autobiography, Biography, and the Novel*. Los Angeles: William Andrews Clark Memorial Library, University of California.

Rediker, Marcus. (Original work published 1987) 1989. *Between the Devil and the Deep Blue Sea: Merchant Seamen, Pirates and the Anglo-American Maritime World, 1700–1750*. Cambridge: Cambridge University Press.

Richetti, John J. 1975. *Defoe's Narratives: Situations and Structures*. Oxford: Clarendon.

Richetti, John J. 1982. "The Family, Sex and Marriage in Defoe's Moll Flanders and *Roxana*." In Snow 1982: 19–35.

Richetti, John J. 1987. *Daniel Defoe*. Boston: G.K. Hall.

Richetti, John J. 1988. "The Novel and Society: The Case of Daniel Defoe." In Uphaus 1979: 47–66.

Richetti, John J. 2005. *The Life of Daniel Defoe*. Oxford: Blackwell. http://dx.doi.org/10.1002/9780470754665.

Richetti, John J., ed. 2008. *The Cambridge Companion to Daniel Defoe*. New York: Cambridge University Press.

Robbins, Caroline. (Original work published 1959) 1968. *The Eighteenth-Century Commonwealth Man: Studies in the Transmission, Development and Circumstance of English Liberal Thought from the Restoration of Charles II until the War with the Thirteen Colonies*. New York: Athenaeum.

Rochester, Earl of. 1968. *The Complete Poems of John Wilmot, Earl of Rochester*. Ed. David M. Vieth. New Haven: Yale University Press.

Rogers, Katharine. 1976. "The Feminism of Daniel Defoe." In Fritz and Morton 1976: 3–24.

Rogers, Pat, ed. 1972. *Defoe: The Critical Heritage*. London: Routledge and Kegan Paul.

Rogers, Pat. 1979. *Robinson Crusoe*. London: George Allen and Unwin.

Rogers, Pat. 1998. *The Text of Great Britain: Theme and Design in Defoe's "Tour."*. Newark: University of Delaware Press.

Rothman, Irving N. 1995. "Coleridge on the Semi-Colon in *Robinson Crusoe*: Problems in Editing Defoe." *Studies in the Novel* 27: 320–40.

Russell, Bertrand. (Original work published 1945) 1961. *A History of Western Philosophy*. London: Allen and Unwin.

Scholes, Robert. 1982. *Semiotics and Interpretation*. New Haven: Yale University Press.

Schonhorn, Manuel. 1977. "Defoe: The Literature of Politics and The Politics of Some Fictions." In Novak 1977a: 15–56.

Schonhorn, Manuel. 1991. *Defoe's Politics: Parliament, Power, Kingship, and Robinson Crusoe*. Cambridge: Cambridge University Press. http://dx.doi.org/10.1017/CBO9780511519109.

Schorer, Mark. 1959. *William Blake: The Politics of Vision*. New York: Vintage.

Scott, Nathan A. 1971. *The Wild Prayer of Longing: Poetry and the Sacred*. New Haven: Yale University Press.

Scruton, Roger. (Original work published 1981) 1995. *A Short History of Philosophy: From Descartes to Wittgenstein*. 2nd ed. London: Routledge and Kegan Paul.

Scruton, Roger. 2006. *A Political Philosophy*. London: Continuum.

Seidel, Michael. 1986. *Exile and the Narrative Imagination*. New Haven: Yale University Press.

Seidel, Michael. 1991. *Robinson Crusoe: Island Myths and The Novel*. Boston: Twayne.

Seidel, Michael. 2008. "Robinson Crusoe: Varieties of Fictional Experience." In Richetti 2008: 182–99.

Shakespeare, William. 1971. *The Complete Works of Shakespeare*. Ed. Irving Ribner and George Lyman Kittredge. New York: John Wiley.

Shapin, Steven. 1994. *A Social History of Truth: Civility and Science in Seventeenth-Century England*. Chicago: University of Chicago Press.

Shattuck, Roger. 1996. *Forbidden Knowledge: From Prometheus to Pornography*. New York: St Martin's Press.

Sherman, Sandra. 1996. *Finance and Fictionality in the Early Eighteenth Century: Accounting for Defoe*. Cambridge: Cambridge University Press. http://dx.doi.org/10.1017/CBO9780511582219.

Shinagel, Michael. 1968. *Daniel Defoe and Middle-Class Gentility*. Cambridge: Harvard University Press.

Sill, Geoffrey M. 1983. *Defoe and the Idea of Fiction 1713–1719*. Newark: University of Delaware Press.

Smith, Adam. (Original work published 1963) 1971. *Lectures on Rhetoric and Belles Lettres*. Ed. John M. Lothian. Carbondale: Southern Illinois University Press.

Smith, Marion Bodwell. 1966. *Dualities in Shakespeare*. Toronto: University of Toronto Press.

Snow, Malinda, ed. 1982. "Daniel Defoe: The Making of His Prose Fiction." *Studies in the Literary Imagination* 15: 1–113.

Spacks, Patricia Meyer. 1976. *Imagining a Self: Autobiography and Novel in Eighteenth-Century England*. Cambridge: Harvard University Press.

Spark, Muriel. (Original work published 1958) 1964. *Robinson*. Harmondsworth: Penguin.

Speck, W.A. 1977. *Stability and Strife: England, 1714–1760*. Cambridge: Harvard University Press.

Sorenson, Janet. 2002. "Internal Colonialism and the British Novel." *Eighteenth-Century Fiction* 15: 53–8.

Stamm Rudolf, G. 1936. "Daniel Defoe: An Artist in the Puritan Tradition." *Philological Quarterly* 15: 225–46.

Starr, G.A. 1965. *Defoe and Spiritual Autobiography*. Princeton: Princeton University Press.

Starr, G.A. 1970. "Sympathy v. Judgement in Roxana's First Liaison." In Miller et al. 1970: 59–76.

Starr, G.A. 1971. *Defoe and Casuistry*. Princeton: Princeton University Press.

Starr, G.A. 1974. "Defoe's Prose Style: 1. The Language of Interpretation." *Modern Philology* 71 (3): 277–94. http://dx.doi.org/10.1086/390490.

Stone, Lawrence. 1977. *The Family, Sex and Marriage in England, 1500–1800*. New York: Harper.

Stout, John. 1993. "Semiotics." In Makaryk 1993: 183–9.

Stuart, Tristram. 2006. *The Bloodless Revolution: A Cultural History of Vegetarianism from 1600 to Modern Times*. New York: W.W. Norton.

Sutherland, James. 1937. *Defoe*. London: Methuen.

Sutherland, James. 1971. *Daniel Defoe: A Critical Study*. Boston: Houghton Mifflin.

Swaminathan, Srividhya. 2003. "Defoe's Alternative Conduct Manual: Survival Strategies and Female Networks in *Moll Flanders*." *Eighteenth-Century Fiction* 15: 185–206.

Swift, Jonathan. 1948. *The Journal to Stella*. 2 vols. Ed. Harold Williams. Oxford: Clarendon.

Sykes, Norman. 1928. "Benjamin Hoadly, Bishop of Bangor." In Hearnshaw 1928: 112–56.

Tallis, Raymond. 1988. *In Defence of Realism*. London: Edward Arnold.

Temple, Sir William. (Original works published 1691 and 1701) 1963. *Five Miscellaneous Essays*. Ed. Samuel Holt Monk. Ann Arbor: University of Michigan Press.

Thackeray, William Makepeace. (Original work published 1848) 1963. *Vanity Fair: A Novel without a Hero*. Ed. Geoffrey and Kathleen Tillotson. Boston: Houghton Mifflin.

Thompson, James. 1996. *Models of Value: Eighteenth-Century Political Economy and the Novel*. Durham: Duke University Press.

Thorslev Jr, Peter L. 1984. *Romantic Contraries: Freedom versus Destiny*. New Haven: Yale University Press.

Thorslev Jr, Peter L. 1989. "Dialectic and Its Legacy." In Gallant 1989: 103–12.

Tillich, Paul. (Original work published 1967, 1968) 1972. *A History of Christian Thought from Its Judaic and Hellenistic Origins to Existentialism*. Ed. Carl E. Braaten. New York: Simon and Schuster.

Tournier, Michel. (Original work published 1967) 1972. *Vendredi ou les limbes du Pacifique*. Postface de Gilles Deleuze. Paris: Gallimard.

Trent, William P. (Original work published 1916) 1971. *Daniel Defoe: How to Know Him*. Reprint. New York: Phaeton Press.

Trevelyan, George Macaulay. 1944. *English Social History: A Survey of Six Centuries Chaucer to Queen Victoria*. London: Longmans, Green and Co.

Trumbach, Randolph. 1978. *The Rise of the Egalitarian Family: Aristocratic Kinship and Domestic Relations in Eighteenth-Century England.* New York: Academic Press.

Tufte, Virgina. 1971. *Grammas as Style.* New York: Holt, Rinehart and Winston.

Ullman, Stephen. 1964. *Semantics: An Introduction to the Science of Meaning.* Oxford: Basil Blackwell.

Uphaus, Robert. 1979. *The Impossible Observer: Reason and the Reader in 18th-Century Prose.* Lexington: University Press of Kentucky.

Vickers, Ilse. 1996. *Defoe and the New Sciences.* Cambridge: Cambridge University Press.

Wade, Nicholas. 2009. *The Faith Instinct: How Religion Evolved and Why It Endures.* New York: Penguin.

Waldron, R.A. 1967. *Sense and Sense Development.* London: Andre Deutsch.

Walker, Julia M., ed. 1988. *Milton and the Idea of Woman.* Urbana: University of Illinois Press.

Walton, James. 1971. "The Romance of Gentility: Defoe's Heroes and Heroines" *Literary Monographs.* Madison: University of Wisconsin Press 4: 89–135.

Warner, John M. 1993. *Joyce's Grandfathers: Myth and History in Defoe, Smollett, Sterne, and Joyce.* Athens: The University of Georgia Press.

Watt, Ian. (Original work published 1957) 1963. *The Rise of the Novel.* Harmondsworth: Penguin.

West, Richard. 1998. *Daniel Defoe: The Life and Strange, Surprising Adventures.* New York: Carroll and Graf.

Whateley, Richard. (Work originally published 1846) 1963. *Elements of Rhetoric.* Ed. Douglas Ehninger. Carbondale and Edwardsville: Southern Illinois University Press.

Wheelwright, Philip. 1968. *The Burning Fountain: A Study in the Language of Symbolism.* Bloomington: Indiana University Press.

Williams, James G. 1987. "Proverbs and Ecclesiastes." In Alter and Kermode 1987: 263–82.

Wilmot, John, Earl of Rochester. 1968. *The Complete Poems of John Wilmot, Earl of Rochester.* Ed. David M. Vieth. New Haven: Yale University Press.

Wolters, Clifton. 1961. *The Cloud of Unknowing.* Harmondsworth: Penguin.

Woolf, Virginia. 1953. *The Common Reader.* First Series. New York: Harcourt Brace Jovanovich.

Wycherley, Willliam. 1966. *The Complete Plays of William Wycherley.* Ed. Gerald Weales. Garden City, NY: Doubleday.

Zimmerman, Everett. 1975. *Defoe and the Novel.* Berkeley, Los Angeles: University of California Press.

Index

www.ingramcontent.com/pod-product-compliance
Lightning Source LLC
LaVergne TN
LVHW090146080826
844660LV00013B/689/J

9781442646100